The Feminine Middlebrow N

The Feminine Middlebrow Novel, 1920s to 1950s

Class, Domesticity, and Bohemianism

NICOLA HUMBLE

OXFORD
UNIVERSITY PRESS

OXFORD
UNIVERSITY PRESS

Great Clarendon Street, Oxford ox2 6DP

Oxford University Press is a department of the University of Oxford.
It furthers the University's objective of excellence in research, scholarship,
and education by publishing worldwide in

Oxford New York

Auckland Bangkok Buenos Aires Cape Town Chennai
Dar es Salaam Delhi Hong Kong Istanbul Karachi Kolkata
Kuala Lumpur Madrid Melbourne Mexico City Mumbai Nairobi
São Paulo Shanghai Taipei Tokyo Toronto

Oxford is a registered trade mark of Oxford University Press
in the UK and in certain other countries

Published in the United States
by Oxford University Press Inc., New York

© Nicola Humble 2001

The moral rights of the author have been asserted
Database right Oxford University Press (maker)

First published 2001
First published in paperback 2004

All rights reserved. No part of this publication may be reproduced,
stored in a retrieval system, or transmitted, in any form or by any means,
without the prior permission in writing of Oxford University Press,
or as expressly permitted by law, or under terms agreed with the appropriate
reprographics rights organization. Enquiries concerning reproduction
outside the scope of the above should be sent to the Rights Department,
Oxford University Press, at the address above

You must not circulate this book in any other binding or cover
and you must impose this same condition on any acquirer

British Library Cataloguing in Publication Data
Data available

Library of Congress Cataloging in Publication Data
Data avaliable

ISBN 0-19-818676-2
ISBN 0-19-926933-5 (pbk.)

1 3 5 7 9 10 8 6 4 2

Printed in Great Britain
on acid-free paper by
Biddles Ltd,
King's Lynn, Norfolk

For

MARTIN *and* LUKE

Acknowledgements

MANY people have been generous with their time, expertise, and interest over the years I have been thinking about this topic. Clare Brant, Simon Edwards, Linda Holt, Zachary Leader, Cat Ledger, Kimberley Reynolds, Ann Thompson, Sarah Turvey, and Frances Wilson have all read chapters and outlines at different stages of the book's conception, and offered valuable advice. Terry Eagleton, Jenny Hartley, Ian Haywood, Tom Jeffery, Angela Smith, Elaine Showalter, and Cathy Wells-Cole made extremely helpful suggestions about the direction and scope of the project. The germ of the book was a paper I gave at the 1992 Exeter University Conference, 'Feminist Criticism in the Nineties', and I would like to thank the organizers Jo McDonagh and Sally Ledger for the opportunity. I have delivered papers arising from this work at conferences at the Universities of Leeds, Oxford, Stirling, and Roehampton, and I owe a considerable debt of gratitude to my fellow delegates on those occasions for their comments and suggestions, notably to Nicola Beaumann, Jennifer Holberg, Avril Horner, Maroula Joannou, Kathy Mezei, Nickianne Moody, Suzanne Raitt, Valerie Sanders, Carolyn Steadman, and Sue Zlosnik. Andrew Lockett at Oxford University Press first expressed an interest in the project, and Jason Freeman steered it into something like its present form: I am grateful to both of them for their involvement. Sophie Goldsworthy has been a generous and patient editor, and I am very thankful for her faith in the project. Two semesters of study leave in 1994 and 1998, and two periods of timetable relief enabled me to work on this book, and I am very grateful to the University of Surrey Roehampton for this time, and to my colleagues in the English Department for their support. Some of the book was written during a semester's exchange visit in 1995 to Michigan State University, where I had very helpful discussions with a number of people, including Donna and Victor Paananen, Steve Rackman, and Jo Marsden. My thinking about the women's writing of this period has been considerably developed by seminar discussions with students at Roehampton, Exeter, and Michigan State, and particularly with those on the Roehampton MA in Women, Gender, and Writing. The expertise of the librarians at the Bodleian Library, the British Library, the London Library, the Fawcett Library, Exeter University Library, Sussex University Library, the Learning Resources Centre at the University of Surrey Roehampton, and the library of Michigan State University has enabled me to locate many forgotten texts. I owe a particular debt of thanks to Dorothy Sheridan at the Mass-Observation Archive at Sussex University and the staff of the John Johnson Collection at the Bodleian, who pinpointed some extremely valuable resources, and kindly gave me permission to reproduce material from their archives. My parents Patricia and Brian and my sisters Julia and Rachel have lived with this project for many years, and have retained a generous interest in its progress. My mother-in-law Rosalind Priestman has gently corrected some of my wilder generalizations about the period. My longest-standing debt is to the friends with whom I first discovered and enjoyed so many of these novels: Stephanie Bird, Katrina Chapman, Tara Lamont, Judith Murray, and Frances Wilson. Above all, I want to thank Martin Priestman, whose wisdom, unfailing support, and endless patience have bolstered me throughout. Without him, this book would not have been finished. And I thank him also for our darling Luke, without whom it would have been finished a lot sooner.

Contents

Introduction	1
1. 'Books Do Furnish a Room': Readers and Reading	7
2. 'Not Our Sort': The Re-Formation of Middle-Class Identities	57
3. Imagining the Home	108
4. The Eccentric Family	149
5. A Crisis of Gender?	197
Bibliography	257
Index	267

Introduction

> The middlebrow is the man, or woman, of middlebred intelligence who ambles and saunters now on this side of the hedge, now on that, in pursuit of no single object, neither art itself or life itself, but both mixed indistinguishably, and rather nastily, with money, fame, power, or prestige.
>
> Virginia Woolf, 'Middlebrow'[1]

'Middlebrow' has always been a dirty word. Since its coinage in the late 1920s, it has been applied disparagingly to the sort of cultural products thought to be too easy, too insular, too smug. While the lowbrow has undergone a process of critical reclamation in recent decades, with the development of popular culture studies as a legitimate area of academic interest, the middlebrow has remained firmly out in the cold.[2] My central aim in this book is to rehabilitate both the term and the body of literature to which it was generally applied in the four decades from the 1920s to the 1950s. 'Middlebrow' fiction dominated the publishing market in these years, but has been in the main ignored by literary critics and historians, except those interested in rescuing particular authors from

---

[1] Collected in *The Death of the Moth and Other Essays* (London: The Hogarth Press, 1942), 115.

[2] There are, thankfully, a few notable exceptions. Nicola Beauman's pioneering *A Very Great Profession: The Woman's Novel 1914-39* (London: Virago, 1983) rediscovered a lost tradition in the women's domestic novels of the interwar years, which she describes with sympathetic appreciation. Joseph McAleer's *Popular Reading and Publishing 1914-50* (Oxford: Clarendon Press, 1992) offers a meticulously researched history of popular reading and publishing in the first half of the 20th century, which touches on my concerns, but is in fact more interested in lowbrow magazines, genre fiction, and so on. The most extended and analytical study of the middlebrow is offered by Alison Light's excellent *Forever England: Femininity, Literature and Conservatism Between the Wars* (London: Routledge, 1991), which I have found inspirational in its bold redrawing of the map of English literary culture. Light makes a compelling case for her claim that women's writing between the wars was instrumental in the construction of what she calls a 'conservative modernity', but I would argue that this case rests on an ingeniously restricted choice of writers—Compton-Burnett, Christie, Jan Struther, du Maurier—and does not account for the more radical elements also to be found in the women's middlebrow writing of this date.

I find it significant that despite their emphases none of these writers is comfortable employing the term middlebrow. McAleer does not use it at all, preferring to conflate the various types of literature he discusses with the rather woolly 'popular', while Beauman

what appears to be a slew of mediocrity.[3] One important reason, I contend, for the subsequent critical neglect of the major part of the fiction published in Britain in these years is that it was largely written and consumed by women. In the literary-critical story of the first half of the twentieth century, as it has been told until very recently, women—with the notable exception of Virginia Woolf—remain marginal figures.[4] Convenient literary fictions like 'Modernism', 'the Auden generation', 'the angry young men' leave little space for writers like Rosamund Lehmann, Rose Macaulay, Elizabeth Bowen, and Elizabeth Taylor, and none at all for their more frivolous contemporaries such as Stella Gibbons, Dodie Smith, and Nancy Mitford.[5] Yet these are the writers the majority of people read—

employs it only once, to differentiate the domestic novel from the formula romance. Even Light is inclined to use it with some hesitancy, introducing her project as one which 'takes us further towards understanding the meaning of what used to be called a middlebrow culture in the period' (p. 11).

[3] A case in point is the recent attempt of feminist critics to extend the concept of modernism to embrace certain women writers previously dismissed as middlebrow. See e.g. Suzanne Clark, *Sentimental Modernism: Women Writers and the Revolution of the Word* (Bloomington: Indiana University Press, 1991) and Gillian Hanscombe and Virginia L. Smyers, *Writing for Their Lives: The Modernist Women 1910–1940* (London: Women's Press, 1987). The issue of 'para-modernism' is further discussed in Chapter 1.

[4] When I began work on this book there was very little published on the women's writing of this period, but I am glad to say that the last few years have seen a growing interest in the women's novelists of the inter-war years and the Second World War, with a number of academic conferences on the subject and a trickle of academic studies. Maroula Joannou traces feminist impulses in the women's writing of the inter-war period in her closely researched *'Ladies, Please Don't Smash These Windows': Women's Writing, Feminist Consciousness and Social Change 1918–38* (Oxford: Berg, 1995). She has also collected work by a number of the key writers in this newly emerging field in *Women Writers of the 1930s: Gender, Politics and History* (Edinburgh: Edinburgh University Press, 1999). Jenny Hartley offers an engaging and culturally embedded account of *Millions Like Us: British Women's Fiction of the Second World War* (London: Virago, 1997), while Gill Plain's *Women's Fiction of the Second World War: Gender, Power and Resistance* (Edinburgh: Edinburgh University Press, 1996) examines some of the same writers from a more straightforwardly literary-critical perspective. Heather Ingman's *Women's Fiction Between the Wars: Mothers, Daughters and Writing* (Edinburgh: Edinburgh University Press, 1998) considers the construction of the mother–daughter relationship in the work of six representative writers, drawing on both contemporary and more recent psychoanalytic thought. Although most of these studies focus on writers whom I also consider, none of them overlap with my major concerns.

[5] Some of these writers have begun to be reassessed in the last decade, with a number of critical studies appearing of Bowen and Macaulay in particular. See e.g. Andrew Bennett and Nicholas Royle, *Elizabeth Bowen and the Dissolution of the Novel* (London: Macmillan, 1995) and Phyllis Lassner, *Elizabeth Bowen* (London: Macmillan, 1990). On the whole, though, the approach has been to lift the writer away from the besmirching associations with other middlebrow writers in order to claim them as 'serious'. So

their novels made the Book-of-the-Month lists in the newspapers, sold in their tens of thousands in book club editions, and packed the shelves of the lending libraries.[6] If this is a feminine literature, it is also very much the literature of the middle classes, paying a meticulous attention to their shifting desires and self-images, mapping their swings of fortune at this most volatile stage in their history. As a result, it not only reflected shifts in middle-class opinion and ideology, but also inspired them. I will argue that what I call the 'feminine middlebrow' in this period was a powerful force in establishing and consolidating, but also in resisting, new class and gender identities, and that it is its paradoxical allegiance to both domesticity and a radical sophistication that makes this literary form so ideologically flexible.

My study is divided not by authors but by themes. It begins with an analysis of the feminine middlebrow and its readers, and then considers what seem to me the key concerns of this literature: class, the home, gender, and the family. The same authors, and indeed novels, reappear in several chapters: the intention is to argue for the essential interconnection of these thematic concerns in the middlebrow women's writing of this period, and to demonstrate that this body of writing is united by shared generic features and ideological preoccupations. My approach combines a traditional literary-critical focus on the close reading of texts with an impulse towards cultural history that seeks to relocate those texts in the rich context from which they emerged. I therefore read the women's middlebrow novel alongside a range of other discourses, including cookery books, childcare manuals, the reports of Mass-Observation, women's magazines, cartoons, market research reports, and the debates of contemporary literary critics and social commentators.

My selection of novels is determined by two main contentions. The first is that although the feminine middlebrow as I understand it is clearly a product of the inter-war years, its form, themes, and successes were not immediately disrupted by the Second World War.

Jeanette N. Passty, in her *Eros and Androgyny: The Legacy of Rose Macaulay* (London: Associated University Presses, 1988), finds it necessary to assure the reader that 'the author of the present biocritical analysis takes Rose Macaulay very seriously indeed' (p. 12).

[6] Detective writers such as Margery Allingham, Ngaio Marsh, Dorothy Sayers—and of course Agatha Christie—have been better served by critical fashion, but have tended to be read in terms of the development of the genre rather than in the context of their historical moment.

In defining my period as running from the end of the First World War to the mid-1950s, I challenge the prevailing convention that would see the Second World War as effecting a decisive ideological and cultural break, and offer a revision to the way we currently map the changing politics of femininity and the domestic in the twentieth century.[7] In each chapter I discuss texts drawn from across these four decades, while simultaneously constructing an historical argument that traces the changes in the ways the feminine middlebrow represents its major concerns, and the social and cultural developments that may account for these changes.

My second contention is that the middlebrow is a hybrid form, comprising a number of genres, from the romance and country-house novel, through domestic and family narratives to detective and children's literature and the adolescent *Bildungsroman*. I discuss roughly sixty novels by over thirty authors who include Margery Allingham, Elizabeth Bowen, Ivy Compton-Burnett, E. M. Delafield, Margaret Kennedy, Elizabeth Taylor, and Angela Thirkell.[8] The extremely well-known (Agatha Christie, Stella Gibbons, Nancy Mitford) are considered alongside the largely forgotten (Rachel Ferguson, Diane Tutton, E. Arnot Robertson). Although the main focus is on women writers, some representative male writers (Evelyn Waugh, E. F. Benson, Angus Wilson) are considered in order to establish a distinctive identity for the feminine middlebrow. My intention is to establish the shared concerns of this disparate body of writers, and to suggest that the middlebrow novel in this period acquires a generic identity of its own—one

---

[7] I give no precise end-date for my study, but follow Randall Stevenson, who in *The British Novel Since the Thirties* dates to the mid-1950s 'a general realisation . . . that irrevocable changes in the life of the first half of the twentieth century had been completed by the Second World War, and that a new kind of life had begun to emerge in the years which followed the Suez crisis' (London: Batsford, 1986, 118). There is a valedictory note in the middlebrow women's novels of the 1950s, as many of the fundamental concerns of the fiction are overtaken by changing historical circumstances. The newly fashionable writing that emerged in the mid-1950s was assertively male—that of John Osborne, Kingsley Amis, and John Wain—and explicitly rejected the domestic, feminized, class-conscious world that had spawned the feminine middlebrow. The next generation of women writers—Doris Lessing, Muriel Spark, Margaret Drabble—explored a world of bed-sits and careers, where women's lives were no longer absolutely constrained by the domestic.

[8] Despite the wide-ranging trawl I have made through the literature of the period, there are inevitably some writers who did not make it in. Among those who would certainly repay further study are Richmal Crompton, Antonia White, and Daphne du Maurier (who has, in fact, been fairly well served of late, with a chapter in Alison Light's book, and an excellent full-length study by Sue Zlosnik and Avril Horner, *Daphne du Maurier: Writing, Identity and the Gothic Imagination* (London: Macmillan, 1998)).

established through a complex interplay between texts and the desires and self-images of their readers.

Arguing that we have crucially overlooked the significance of middlebrow writing, I propose that we might begin to understand its cultural, social, and political significance by taking into account the issue of textual pleasure, and by establishing a history of its readership. I suggest that the feminine middlebrow had a significant role in the negotiation of new class and gender identities in the period from the 1920s to the 1950s. In the obsessive attention it paid to class markers and manners it was one of the spaces in which a new middle-class identity was forged, a site where the battle for hegemonic control of social modes and mores was closely fought by different factions of the newly dominant middle class. In its overriding concern with the home, it worked through the middle-class woman's anxieties about her new responsibility for domestic labour, and helped to redefine domesticity as stylish. Its feyness and frivolity and its flexible generic boundaries allowed it to explore new gender and sexual identities which were otherwise perceived as dangerously disruptive of social values. Its construction of the family as an eccentric, essentially anti-social organization allowed it to reflect the still covert dissatisfactions of several generations of women whose new social, physical, and educational freedoms were not matched by their employment prospects: women who were all hyped up with nowhere to go. Finally, I argue that the middlebrow women's fiction of this period indulged in a curious flirtation with bohemianism, a fantasy about the imagined life of the creative artist that allowed new radicalisms concerning sex, gender, and class to creep into a literature that simultaneously prided itself on its ineffable respectability.

To end with a personal statement: my own interest in what I have come to define as the feminine middlebrow began with pleasure. Studying English—and a great deal of literary theory—at Oxford in the mid-1980s, my circle of female friends developed a cultish taste for what we called 'girly books'—those women's novels of the first half of the century discovered in second-hand bookshops, and just beginning to be reissued by Virago. The generic 'girly book' combined an enjoyable feminine 'trivia' of clothes, food, family, manners, romance, and so on, with an element of wry self-consciousness that allowed the reader to drift between ironic and complicit readings. A classic of the type would also reveal a maelstrom of thwarted impulse struggling beneath the surface of the text, even a hint of psychosis beneath its ebullient fripperies. We read these books not in a spirit of analysis but of pure self-indulgence: they were at one with the bright red lipstick we decided offered no contradiction to our radical feminist principles. I think we saw them as a form of camp—revelling in their detailing of a mode of feminine existence that seemed eons away from our own. They certainly had no direct bearing on the model of English literature we constructed for the benefit of our finals examiners. Fifteen years later, I no longer see these novels as camp: their concerns seem both more serious and less safely distant, and the world of the women who wrote them and the women who read them is central to the way I now understand the first half of the twentieth century. Yet the issue of pleasure still seems to me crucial: it is our thinking about the pleasure of the first readers of these books—of their own oscillations between knowing and surrendered readings—that will open up for us a sense of what the middlebrow really meant in this period.

I

'Books Do Furnish a Room': Readers and Reading

> Paul walked over to the small, untidily crowded bookshelves, looking instinctively for Walpole and Galsworthy, Maugham and Mackenzie, and finding them; but finding also *Don Quixote, Anna Karenina, Le Père Goriot, The Wind in the Willows*. It was an odd assortment. *The Diary of a Nobody* stood next to *Voyage au Bout de la Nuit*; *Tom Jones* rubbed shoulders with Virginia Woolf; and into the midst of a uniform edition of Jane Austen had been thrust a paper-covered work by Pierre Louÿs. Tucked away in a corner was a faded and battered copy of *Little Women*....
>
> He was looking at this and smiling when she came back with the coffee. She had taken off her dress and was wearing a black velvet gown that covered her from neck to ankles and wrists. She glanced over his shoulder.
>
> '*Little Women*! Now that's something I bet you've never read!'
>
> 'Never', said Paul.
>
> 'My favourite book, my very favourite! I still read bits of it now and then!'
>
> <div align="right">Norman Denny, <i>Sweet Confusion</i> (1947)[1]</div>

THIS episode of a man scrutinizing a woman's reading habits takes place just before Paul, a small-time publisher, begins an adulterous affair with Judy, his wife's oldest friend. Norman Denny's novel wholeheartedly approves of this affair, as Paul's wife, the coolly competent Cicely, has never loved him. Judy and Paul are among the very few emotionally literate characters in *Sweet Confusion*, which is set in 1938 and depicts a world of middle-class comfort and certainties turned inside out by the pressures of the imminent war. This obscure and long-forgotten novel is almost formulaically middlebrow in its

---

[1] Norman Denny, *Sweet Confusion* (London: John Lane, 1947), 269–70.

range of concerns: calibrating precise degrees of middle-class status, showing an intense interest in domestic details, and combining a fascination with the life of the bohemian artist with a faint suspicion of intellectuality. The anatomizing of Judy's book collection establishes her as the ideal woman reader as imagined by the middlebrow novel. Hugh Walpole, John Galsworthy, Somerset Maugham, and Compton Mackenzie are the established middle-of-the-road writers of the previous generation, standard fixtures on any 1930s' bookcase, but the mixture of English classics like the works of Austen and Fielding with European novels—some, like Louis Ferdinand Céline's *Voyage au bout de la nuit*, notoriously shocking—denotes a taste that can embrace the conventional and the radical. Virginia Woolf is a talisman of highbrow intellectual credibility, while the presence of children's classics, particularly *Little Women*, suggests a woman in touch with her emotions, taking an almost kitsch pleasure in reliving the abandonment in reading enjoyed in childhood.

The list of Judy's books tells us a great deal about the woman reader the middlebrow novel has in mind.[2] An essential feature of her collection is its hybridity—the middlebrow woman reader is not committed to middlebrow novels, but ranges widely in her interests, encompassing many genres of literature, and combining high and lowbrow interests in a daring disregard for conventional judgements. She is voracious in her reading, and responds to literature with a visceral immediacy: Judy's self-mocking passion for *Little Women* is typical of the emphasis on pleasure in the middlebrow depiction of women and their reading. This contrasts with the cool distance of the response of men to books in this fiction. Paul approaches literature from a commercial point of view; his publishing house 'produces a small but steady stream of commendable volumes' (p. 55) along with a growing list of detective stories which bring in large profits. Going through his slush pile of

[2] We find a very similar list in Rosamund Lehmann's 1953 *The Echoing Grove* (Harmondsworth: Penguin, 1983), in which middle-aged Dinah looks over the books her sister (with whose now-dead husband Dinah had conducted a lengthy afffair) has placed for her in the spare room: 'Sleepless in the small hours, Dinah switched on her lamp and looked through the pile of books upon the bedside table. A brand new novel—Book Society Choice; an anthology of modern poetry; two thrillers; a recent collection of delicious Continental recipes; Keats's letters; *Green Mansions*; a worn copy of *The Phoenix and the Carpet* with her name, Dinah Dorothea Burkett, pencilled inside in her own sprawling nine-year-old hand; last, a small volume in a honeycombed Victorian binding, dark blue stamped with gold; *Tuppy the Donkey*. She opened this, and an aroma of sour pages and dead nurseries came out of it' (p. 31).

manuscripts, he actively condemns precisely the sort of novel that *Sweet Confusion* is:

> He had been flicking over the pages of one of the typescripts he had brought with him for his week-end reading. It was a novel, written in correct English and correctly punctuated. The characters were correct members of the middle classes inhabiting that desirable novel-world which the middle-class soul may explore from end to end in search of itself, being happily safeguarded from encountering anything else. A glance at the first line of each paragraph afforded a sufficient indication of the progress of the search. The pages could be flicked over at the rate of ten a minute. (p. 83)

It is notable that Paul reads without enjoyment, never committing himself to the text or giving it his full attention: he remains resolutely outside the world of the novel he reads, resistant to its bourgeois blandishments. In *Sweet Confusion*, as in many other novels, men are the producers of fiction and women its consumers. But the role of consumption is far from passive: it is imagined by the middlebrow novel as a life-enhancing, joyous experience, and one that serves to bind the woman reader into a community of other readers through an almost cultish involvement with favourite books.

Questions about what women read, and why, and in what ways they do so became a major preoccupation in this period. Critics, intellectuals, writers, librarians, publishers, and sociologists interrogated female reading habits as if they held the key to the significant changes in cultural values that were becoming increasingly apparent. Middlebrow novels repeatedly portray scenes in which women discuss books, list their favourite authors, or imagine themselves into the plots of their favourite novels.

In this chapter I want to complicate the notion of the middlebrow and what it stood for in this period. It is by examining the types of books women read, and looking at what was said about women's reading, that we can come closer to an apprehension of the particular characteristics of what I am calling the feminine middlebrow. And by paying attention to the representation of the act of reading in women's middlebrow fiction we can trace the ways in which this mode of writing both established itself as a distinctive literary form, and worked to remake its readers in its own terms.

The term 'middlebrow' is a derivative of 'highbrow', a slang label for intellectuals which seems to have originated in America in 1911, and which, according to Robert Graves, was popularized in England by

H. G. Wells.[3] 'Highbrow' quickly gave birth to its opposite 'lowbrow', with the first recorded example of the latter occurring only two years later. It took nearly two decades for this simple binary opposition to be fractured by the concept of the middlebrow. The need for such a concept begins to become apparent in the review columns of English newspapers in the late 1920s: so a critic in the *Observer* of 10 July 1927 comments of a book that 'this is not a highbrow's book, nor is it a lowbrow's', while the new music critic of the *Daily Express* announced on 7 May 1927 that 'our aim will be ... to steer a course between the "highbrow" and the "lowbrow" in music'. It was the following year that the concepts of 'the person of average or moderate cultural attainments' and the cultural phenomenon 'claiming to be or regarded as only moderately intellectual' (*OED*) were given the label towards which these reviewers were groping. The first recorded example (according to the *OED*) occurs in the *Daily Express* 17 June 1928: 'success is less commonly achieved—perhaps because the standard of "middlebrow" music and plays is always rather low.' The date at which this concept emerged is no accident. It was becoming clear throughout the 1920s that a new sort of reading public had emerged: the expanded suburban middle class, more affluent, newly leisured, and with an increasingly sophisticated taste in narratives encouraged by the cinema. A number of the major best-sellers of the 1920s such as Margaret Kennedy's 1924 *The Constant Nymph* and Michael Arlen's *The Green Hat* of the same year, were notably middlebrow confections, concerned with matters of middle-class identity and taste, daring in their treatment of sexuality, with analytical and meditative elements as well as exciting plot and romance. While the thriller or 'shocker', and romance genres in their most basic form (as typified by Sax Rohmer, author of the Dr Fu Manchu stories, in the one case and prolific romance novelist Berta Ruck in the other) represented the most 'popular' strand of publishing after the First World War, various forms of middlebrow novels took a steady share of the market. As argued in the Introduction, despite the standard assumption of popular culture studies that 'popular' is synonymous with 'working class', it is clear that, at least in the years between the wars, it was

---

[3] Robert Graves and Alan Hodges, *The Long Week-end: A Social History of Great Britain 1918–1939*, 1940 (Harmondsworth: Penguin, 1971), 46. NB: In all citations please note that when the edition used is not the first edition, the date of first publication is also supplied.

the middle class who represented by far the largest portion of the book-reading public.[4] The middle class did not, of course, read only middlebrow fiction, but, as I shall argue, the middlebrow as it emerged in these decades was a form of fiction uniquely designed to appeal to the changing identity and tastes of this expanding and altering class. In a curious symbiosis, it shaped its readers as they shaped it.

A significant shift in literary culture also necessitated the development of a concept of the middlebrow in the 1920s: where poetry had been the main literary vehicle for intellectual debate and stylistic experimentation throughout the nineteenth century, the influence of Henry James and the coming of modernism concentrated the attention of the avant-garde on the novel. The works of James Joyce and—especially—Virginia Woolf became the models of what could be done with the novel, and there was an increasing need to distinguish between such radical remakings of the form, and more conventional fictional narratives. The stylistic and thematic blueprints of the sort of literature that became seen as middlebrow—a particular concentration on feminine aspects of life, a fascination with domestic space, a concern with courtship and marriage, a preoccupation with aspects of class and manners—are little different from the conventions that dominated the mainstream novel throughout the nineteenth century (we need only think of Austen and the Brontës, Trollope and Charlotte M. Yonge). It is not (as many critics would have us assume) that novelists, and particularly female novelists, suddenly started writing meretricious, class-obsessed fripperies in the years after the First World War, but rather that the status of the realist novel was dramatically altered by the coming to public consciousness of the modernist and associated avant-garde movements.

Defining the parameters of the fictional middlebrow is clearly problematic. The broad working definition I employ throughout this book is that the middlebrow novel is one that straddles the divide between the trashy romance or thriller on the one hand, and the philosophically or formally challenging novel on the other: offering narrative excitement without guilt, and intellectual stimulation without undue effort. It is an essentially parasitical form,

[4] Claud Cockburn, *Bestseller: The Books That Everyone Read 1900–1939* (London: Sidgwick & Jackson, 1972), 3: 'During the first decades of our century the middle class made up the bulk of the novel-buying and novel-borrowing public.'

dependent on the existence of both a high and a low brow for its identity, reworking their structures and aping their insights, while at the same time fastidiously holding its skirts away from lowbrow contamination, and gleefully mocking highbrow intellectual pretensions. It is also a predominantly middle-class form. In fact, as I will argue at length, its changing structures and preoccupations offer us a map of the shifting fortunes and identities of the middle classes throughout the period from the 1920s to the 1950s.

Other ways of defining and understanding the middlebrow which will be explored in this chapter have to do with the responses of readers—both private and professional. A study of private lending libraries like the Boots Booklovers' Library, Mudie's, and W. H. Smith's library offers some insight into just what the middle classes were reading throughout the period, because, as George Orwell noted, it is 'in a lending library you see people's real tastes, not their pretended ones': people may buy books for mixed motives of pretension or display, but they borrow the books they really want to read.[5] The opinions of certain critics and writers allow us to define the contemporary conception of the middlebrow with some precision: Queenie Leavis, at least in her 1932 *Fiction and the Reading Public*, is one very good barometer of the heady air currents separating the intellectually serious from the merely frivolous in the minds of a generation of intellectuals (though her usefulness diminishes in the work of her later *Scrutiny* days, where she and her cohorts are so widely condemnatory that very little is allowed to survive their anatomizing gaze). Critics such as George Orwell, Cyril Connolly, and Robert Graves, with their interests in codifying popular taste, and in taking the temperature of the nation's culture, provide some useful accounts of literary consumption.

The middlebrow literature of this period encompassed a wide range of genres, including romances and country-house sagas, detective stories, children's books, comic narratives, domestic novels, and adolescent *Bildungsroman*. It is important to note that few, if any, of the writers of this fiction would have been happy to have the label 'middlebrow' attached to their works. The term was used throughout the period (and has been ever since) as a form of disapprobation,

---

[5] George Orwell, 'Bookshop Memories', 1936, in *The Collected Essays, Journalism and Letters*, ed. Sonia Orwell and Ian Angus, i, *An Age Like This: 1920–1940* (London: Secker & Warburg, 1968), 245.

suggesting a smug 'easy' read, lacking significant intellectual challenges. For many who applied the term, one suspects that the central tenet that allowed a novel to be dismissed as middlebrow was the issue of whom it was read by: once a novel became widely popular, it became suspect, and bestseller status, or adoption as a Book-of-the-Month choice by a major book club was sufficient to demote it beneath serious attention. A novel was therefore middlebrow not because of any intrinsic content, but because it was widely read by the middle-class public—and particularly by the lower middle classes. If anything, such a process of categorization extends the usefulness of the term for the purposes of analysis, allowing us to pinpoint the moment at which certain books 'became' middlebrow, and examine the ways in which their social status shifted as a result. What is significant from our point of view is that although the term middlebrow was used in different ways by different commentators, most novels that fell into the above classes were so dismissed on at least one occasion. One of the things I want to suggest here is that such novels have more in common than being tarred with the same brush of faint disapproval: that the label middlebrow allows us to move outside the boundaries of genre to trace the shared qualities of the leisure reading of a class in the process of being remade.

This category of leisure reading could be surprisingly broad—in fact, as indicated by the quotation with which this chapter opened, a breadth and hybridity of taste was one of the hallmarks of the ideal reader as imagined by the middlebrow novel. The middlebrow could thus range from intellectual, abstruse novels such as those of Ivy Compton-Burnett and Elizabeth Bowen to light *jeux d'esprit* by P. G. Wodehouse and E. F. Benson. Despite their verbal complexity, the former both acquired middlebrow status because their intense interest in class and domestic interiors spoke to the increasing middle-class fascination with status—a quality affectionately parodied by Benson's monstrous Mapp and Lucia. P. G. Wodehouse attained major success with his Jeeves and Wooster stories, which offered the middle-class reader an enjoyable fantasy of a luxurious aristocratic society, reassuringly peopled by endearingly foolish toffs. There is often an implied pecking-order within the middlebrow category: so, 'country-house' novels, because dealing with aristocrats, appear to have ranked rather higher than domestic novels, with their averagely middle-class heroines. Detective fiction ranked high as it was the preferred leisure reading of men, particularly intellectual ones.

Children's fiction, and novels read in childhood, such as those of Jane Austen and the Brontës, score highly for their cultish, quirky associations; while anything with a daring or racy atmosphere—such as Rosamund Lehmann's 1927 *Dusty Answer*, with its lesbian content, and Margaret Kennedy's *The Constant Nymph* (1924), with its titillating account of sexually active adolescent girls—offered the reader the reassurance of being up-to-the-minute. Romance was probably bottom of the pecking order because of its regrettably lowbrow associations (worryingly close to the sort of thing shop-girls read in magazines): to be appropriately middlebrow, romantic fiction needed to be redeemed by the more literary qualities of a du Maurier who could interweave a love story with nostalgia and an intense evocation of landscape.

At the centre of my argument in this book is the notion of a distinctively feminine middlebrow. In one sense, this could be defined as middlebrow novels written by women, but this is not sufficiently accurate, since works by male writers such as E. F. Benson, Angus Wilson, and Evelyn Waugh, also fit into the broad parameters of this fiction. Rather, it is works largely read by and in some sense addressed to women readers that are denoted by this term. A contemporary recognition that the average middlebrow novel appealed mainly to women is afforded by George Orwell:

It is not true that men don't read novels, but it is true that there are whole branches of fiction that they avoid. Roughly speaking, what one might call the *average* novel—the ordinary, good-bad, Galsworthy-and-water stuff which is the norm of the English novel—seems to exist only for women. Men read either the novels it is possible to respect, or detective stories.[6]

Orwell's language here is heavily weighted: women gulp indiscriminately at watered-down, average novels, while men are considered and judicious in their literary tastes. I would suggest that it is largely because particular novels were read by women that they were downgraded at the time and subsequently seen as so insignificant that literary histories of the 1930s as recent as Valentine Cunningham's 1988 *British Writers of the 1930s* can cover women's writing in barely a dozen pages of a more than 500-page book.[7] There is a

[6] 'Bookshop Memories', *Collected Essays, Journalism and Letters*, i, 244.
[7] Though he goes further than most writers on the inter-war period in stating that women writers 'cannot simply be left, as most books about the 1930s leave them, out of the account', and noting that many 'resuscitated names from the Virago Modern Classics

sense in which virtually all women's writing of the period in question (with the standard exception of Virginia Woolf) was treated as middlebrow. This is one of the reasons that, as a number of recent critics have suggested, our understanding of modernism is so limited: because the work of writers such as Katherine Mansfield, Elizabeth Bowen, and Rose Macaulay has been persistently left out of the picture. Part of my project in this chapter will be to explore the relationship between the middlebrow and this newly-recognized 'para-modernist' feminine sphere.

It was clear to many commentators in the 1930s that literary culture had changed dramatically in the recent past, and a number attempted to map and account for these changes. For Cyril Connolly, in *Enemies of Promise* (1938), literature since the First World War had been marked by an alternation of the styles he called 'Mandarin' ('Bloomsbury, Huxley, etc') and 'The New Vernacular' (typified by Lawrence and Hemingway).[8] His is an interesting model, as it bypasses the impeding bulk of modernism to allow a clearer view of the literary scene as it appeared to a contemporary. One of the effects is that to the modern eye his categories often seem rather curiously applied: Evelyn Waugh's *Decline and Fall*, for example, he sees as Vernacular, while Rosamund Lehmann's *Dusty Answer* is declared to be Mandarin. Some novels he sees as fitting neither category—Elizabeth Bowen's *Encounters* (1923) and Ivy Compton-Burnett's *Pastors and Masters* (1925) are the examples he gives: interestingly in our context, since both, as I shall establish later, are texts occupying that curious borderland between modernism and the middlebrow. Connolly's model avoids the highbrow/trivial dichotomy that is adopted by most other literary critics of the period, but he sees the Vernacular style as one very open to degeneration because of the impulses of the market:

This, then, is the penalty of writing for the masses. As the writer goes out to meet them half-way he is joined by other writers going out to meet them half-way and they merge into the same creature—the talkie journalist, the advertising, lecturing, popular novelist.

The process is complicated by the fact that the masses, whom a cultured writer may generously write for, are at the moment overlapped by

List are all most competent novelists, and some of them are much more than that' (Valentine Cunningham, *British Writers of the 1930s* (Oxford: Oxford University Press, 1988), 26).

[8] Cyril Connolly, *Enemies of Promise*, 1938 (Harmondsworth: Penguin, 1979), *passim*.

the middle-class best-seller-making public and so a venal element is introduced. (p. 83)

Like a number of other left-leaning thinkers in the 1930s (and he mentions his friends Orwell and Isherwood as briefly rising above the flotsam of surrounding rubbish), Connolly sees the writing of very popular literature as part of a process of bonding with the common man. The catch is that popularity might inevitably lead to a middle-class, middlebrow audience, and the consequent denigration of the writing in the eyes of all intellectuals. What becomes very clear is that for much of this period, and particularly in the 1930s, the great bugbear for the self-consciously serious writer was not the literature of the masses, but that of the middle classes.

Of all the commentators on reading habits, and denigrators of the new middlebrow, Queenie Leavis was the most far-reaching in the scope of her argument and her influence. Her 1932 *Fiction and the Reading Public* is designed as an analysis of public tastes in reading, and an attempt to account for what she sees as their significant slide down-market in the early decades of the twentieth-century. The book is in essence her Ph.D. thesis, and as such, gave her entry into the exclusive coterie of specialists in the newly institutionalized university study of English literature, whose interests and perspectives her book so energetically defends. As with the other members of the Leavis circle, Queenie's central tenet was the need to define principles of discrimination that would allow for the establishment of a category of 'literature' distinct from more trivial forms of writing. She combines this pedagogic project, however, with a strong sense of the cultural significance of popular literature:

> To be brightly ironical at the expense of bestsellers would no doubt be easy, but to yield to such an unprofitable temptation is not part of the present writer's undertaking. The very popular novelist . . . is now commonly considered a figure of fun by those who cannot read his work with enthusiasm; it has occurred to the writer that it might be more useful to take him for what he is—partner in a relation very important for literature, the relation, of course, that exists between novelist and reader. . . . The popular novelist, dependent upon a public for his living, frequently making it by regular contributions to the magazines . . . is identical with his public in background of taste and intellectual environment.[9]

[9] Q. D. Leavis, *Fiction and the Reading Public*, 1932 (London: Chatto & Windus, 1978), 41–2.

Despite her highbrow distaste for most of the popular literature she discusses, Leavis recognizes that it is a significant guide to the mind and culture of the public who so eagerly consumes it, and that for this reason, if no other, it is worth writing about. Nevertheless, she has little interest in the content of most of the novels she mentions, seeing them as fairly indistinguishable forms of mental pap. She finds the profligacy with which the general public reads pitiable rather than encouraging, arguing that 'the reading habit is now often a form of the drug habit' (p. 7). Orwell also considered that people were reading too much and too indiscriminately, describing with horror the habits of a customer of the lending-library-cum-bookshop in which he once worked who

> read four or five detective stories every week for over a year, besides others which he got from another library. What chiefly surprised me was that he never read the same book twice. Apparently the whole of that frightful torrent of trash (the pages read every year would, I calculated, cover nearly three-quarters of an acre) was stored for ever in his memory. He took no notice of titles or authors' names, but he could tell by merely glancing into a book whether he had 'had it already'.[10]

This reader's consumption of detective stories is seen as a form of undiscriminating gluttony. It is notable that Orwell cannot comprehend that the individual novels are in any way distinguishable one from the other: for him, this is literature by the yard, to be measured as acreage rather than accorded the compliment of critical attention. Where Leavis places the blame for the deluge of mediocre literature on the complicitous relationship she finds between reader and popular writer, Orwell blames the critical industry of newspaper reviewers and book publicists for treating all literary texts as equal, and thereby devaluing serious writing:

> It hardly needs pointing out that at this moment [November 1936] the prestige of the novel is extremely low, so low that the words 'I never read novels', which even a dozen years ago were generally uttered with a hint of apology, are now always uttered in a tone of conscious pride. It is true that there are still a few contemporary or roughly contemporary novelists whom the intelligentsia consider it permissible to read; but the point is that the ordinary good-bad novel is habitually ignored while the ordinary good-bad book of verse or criticism is still taken seriously.[11]

[10] 'Bookshop Memories', *Collected Essays, Journalism and Letters*, i, 245.
[11] George Orwell, 'In Defence of the Novel', *New English Weekly*, 12 and 19 Nov. 1936, in *The Collected Essays, Journalism and Letters*, i, 249–50.

For Orwell as well as for Leavis, new principles of discrimination in reading, reviewing and publishing are required if the intellectual reader is not to give up on the novel altogether. It is significant that both critics insist on the distinction between the ordinary reader—uncritical and voracious—and the intellectual reader, who is imagined as calm and judicious. It is no accident that they both apply exactly the same terms of distinction to men and women as readers: Orwell, as noted above, seeing most men (with the notable exception of his obsessive reader of detective stories) as extremely selective in their reading, and most women as precisely the opposite: '[Ethel M.] Dell's novels, of course, are read solely by women, but by women of all kinds and ages and not, as one might expect, merely by wistful spinsters and the fat wives of tobacconists.'[12] This wonderfully revealing compound of misogyny and snobbery manages to damn all women readers of popular romantic fiction as pathetic and vulgar while apparently saying quite the opposite. We might expect Leavis to be more sympathetic to the woman reader, but she too blames women in particular for the rampant spread of meretricious literature, seeing the fact that 'women rather than men change the books (that is, determine the family reading)' as the main contributing factor behind the lack of critical intelligence she finds in the book-borrowing public.[13] Although she pays some attention to the most genuinely popular forms of reading matter of her day (the magazines and comics and cheaply-produced serial 'shockers' and romances largely consumed by working-class readers), Leavis's main target in her polemic is the reading matter of the middle classes; the writing, that is, that most seriously threatened to encroach on the space that she and her fellow dons were meticulously clearing for the occupation of certifiable literature. Her work demonstrates a palpable fear of fiction run wild, proliferating beyond control, and her need to dismiss the reading matter of the non-academic leads her, paradoxically, to make a closer study of middlebrow writing than any of her contemporaries. Undertaking a survey of the opinions of a range of contemporary novelists, she divides their work into four categories: 'A: "Highbrow"; B: "Middlebrow", read as "literature"; C: "Middlebrow" not read as "literature", but not writing for the lowbrow market; D: Absolute bestsellers' (p. 45). The division of the middlebrow into categories B

[12] 'Bookshop Memories', *Collected Essays, Journalism and Letters*, i, 244.
[13] *Fiction and the Reading Public*, 7.

and C allows Leavis to include under this heading large numbers of books that many of her contemporaries took seriously, so that her list of the middlebrow writers published by the Book Society includes Rebecca West, Ernest Hemingway, and Osbert Sitwell(p. 23). For Leavis, the middlebrow is the dominant element of contemporary culture, the highbrow an embattled enclave of dedicated intellectuals. Her argument is particularly interesting in the emphasis it places on literary institutions such as publishers, review-columns, libraries, and book clubs, which she sees as engaged in a process of establishing and organizing middlebrow taste. She finds an active hostility towards the highbrow in the statements issuing from these institutions, quoting literature from the Book Guild which condemns 'the highbrows' as precious, affected, and pedantic (pp. 24–5). Despite casting middlebrow fiction in opposition to 'real', original literature, however, Leavis also recognizes an interdependency between the two, damning with faint praise the work of 'respected middling novelists of blameless intentions and indubitable skill' (she includes Thornton Wilder, Galsworthy, and J. B. Priestley in this category), because they are consciously 'literary':

> A representative criticism from the high-level reader would be that they bring nothing to the novel but commonplace sentiments and an out-worn technique; echoes of the Best People of the past, their productions would be dismissed by him as 'literary'. 'Literary' novels, the account would continue, are all on the traditional model, and therefore easy to respond to, yet with an appearance of originality; they deal (like the magazine fiction of the age) in soothing and not disturbing sentiments, yet with sufficient surface stimulus to be pleasing; their style, in one case a careful eighteenth-century pastiche, in another a point-to-point imitation of well-known novelists of repute, but in most cases chosen merely to give an impression of restraint and subtlety, is easily recognised by the uncritical as 'literature'. Not so obviously dead (in this view) as such literary works as *The Testament of Beauty* or Landor's *Imaginary Conversations*, but equally sapless. (pp. 36–7)

Such novels are 'sapless' because they are worn out and traditional in technique and sentiment, yet those that resemble works by 'well-known novelists of repute' (that is, original, 'serious' novelists such as Woolf, Joyce, and Lawrence) are dismissed as mere pastiches. The problem for Leavis is that middlebrow novelists were quick to adopt many of the themes and stylistic developments of the avant-garde, making meaningful distinctions very hard to draw. She is forced to construct her argument around notions of originality, authenticity, and pastiche precisely because of the close resemblances between the two varieties of writing she is discussing. Buried in her text is the faint realization that the distinction she is searching for is in fact essentially fluid, with the categorization of particular texts having to do not with stable literary values but with the type of reader they attract. (So E. M. Forster, whom Leavis embraces as one of her select band of highbrow writers, was to appear irredeemably middlebrow to a later generation, once his general popularity was assured.) Class judgements underlie all her other statements: hence she distinguishes the reading matter of 'the superior sort of schoolmaster' from that of 'the other sort' (who reads Kipling and P. G. Wodehouse). In fact, she comes very close to articulating the same insights that were to establish Pierre Bourdieu's reputation for original cultural thought half a century later: that middlebrow culture is a culture of pastiche because the middle class (and particularly the lower middle class) is positioned in an eternally reverential and docile relationship to what Bourdieu calls 'legitimate culture', that the middlebrow is essentially an anxious misreading of high culture and—crucially—that middlebrow cultural objects are illegitimate not because of any intrinsic qualities, but simply *because* they are to the taste of the middle class.[14]

Where Leavis also anticipates later academic responses to literature is in her understanding of middlebrow fiction as a part of a wider cultural movement, produced, in part, by the new suburbia: 'it is now only the suburban or urban dweller who counts, the average man is "the man in the street" ' (p. 209). The purpose of this middlebrow culture as she understands it is to reassure; to affirm middle-class cosiness and complacency as dominant and abiding values: 'the principle endeavour of the popular contemporary novelist at all levels . . . is to persuade the ordinary prosperous citizen that life is fun, he is living it at its fullest, and there are no standards

[14] 'What makes the petit-bourgeois relation to culture and its capacity to make "middle-brow" whatever it touches, just as the legitimate gaze "saves" whatever it lights upon, is not its "nature" but the very position of the petit bourgeois in social space, the social nature of the petit bourgeois, which is constantly impressed on the petit bourgeois himself, determining his relation to legitimate culture and his avid but anxious, naive but serious way of clutching at it. It is, quite simply, the fact that legitimate culture is not made for him (and is often made against him), so that he is not made for it; and that it ceases to be what it is as soon as he appropriates it.' Pierre Bourdieu, *Distinction: A Social Critique of the Judgement of Taste*, 1979; trans. Richard Nice (London: Routledge & Kegan Paul, 1986), 327 and *passim*.

in life or art other than his own' (pp. 79–80). Although Leavis astutely recognizes the significance of the rather hectic gaiety of the middlebrow novel, what she fails to acknowledge is its dynamism— the ways in which it was able continually to remake itself, and consequently the values of its readers. Far from being unaware of the existence of values other than its own, middlebrow fiction works constantly to affirm and renegotiate its own values in the face of cultural challenges from all directions. A good example is Agatha Christie's *The Hollow* (1946), where Christie, who Alison Light has called 'the queen of the "middlebrows" ', depicts a self-consciously middlebrow world which continually measures itself against other values.[15] At the centre of this society is Lady Lucy Angkatell, possessor of a variety of that quirky mental originality that Christie prizes most highly, given to the instant apprehension of truths through a combination of lateral thinking and intuition. The life she weaves around her at the Hollow is the middlebrow version of the highlife, made up of stylish eccentricity, a close-knit extended family, and lots of crossword puzzles:

'Why anyone ever comes to stay with the Angkatells, I don't know', said Midge. 'What with the brainwork, and the round games, and your peculiar style of conversation, Lucy.'[16]

As the trace of smugness in this statement might suggest, the novel celebrates this middlebrow paradise unashamedly, while still holding up the faint possibility that its games and evasions might conceal darker deceits. The variety of middlebrow intelligence and sophistication epitomized by Lucy Angkatell is contrasted to the highbrow intellectuality of her young cousin David, a gauche and spotty youth just down from Oxford, who is gently condemned by both the other characters and the narrative:

'One wishes that they could put off being intellectual until they were rather older. As it is, they always glower at one so and bite their nails and seem to have so many spots and sometimes an Adam's apple as well. And they either won't speak at all, or else are very loud and contradictory.' (p. 8)

The combination of familiarity with and slight contempt for the effortful intellectual attitudes of the highbrow epitomizes the note

---

[15] Alison Light, *Forever England: Femininity, Literature and Conservatism Between the Wars* (London: Routledge, 1991), 75.
[16] Agatha Christie, *The Hollow*, 1946 (London: Fontana, 1973), 7.

striven for by middlebrow literature in general. But it is the critic or abstract thinker who is the main target of middlebrow disapprobation: the creative artist, in contrast, is treated with automatic respect. So, *The Hollow* also contains another cousin of Lucy's: Henrietta, a driven, bohemian sculptor 'who does advanced things like that curious affair in metal and plaster that she exhibited at the New Artists last year' (p. 8). In order that their admiration of Henrietta's work does not appear too slavish, however, the middlebrow representatives are carefully selective in their aesthetic judgements:

'It looked rather like a Heath Robinson step-ladder. It was called Ascending Thought—or something like that. It is the kind of thing that would impress a boy like David. . . . I thought myself it was just silly. . . . But some of Henrietta's things I think are quite lovely. That Weeping Ash-tree figure, for instance.'

Contrary to Leavis's model of smug insularity, it was by just such meticulously careful positionings—and in terms of class as well as intellectual and aesthetic status—that the middlebrow established itself as a significant cultural force in this period.

Another blindspot in Leavis's understanding of the middlebrow occurs around the issue of pleasure. She is one of a number of commentators to reflect on the newly-fraught issue of 'escapist' reading, condemning novels that offer fantasy because 'a habit of fantasising will lead to maladjustment in actual life' (p. 54). She distinguishes from fantasizing another form of literary pleasure which, though not so actively dangerous, is still dubious: 'mental relaxation', 'under the head [of which] may be included detective stories, the enormous popularity of which (like the passion for solving crossword puzzles) seems to show that for the reader of to-day a not unpleasurable way of relaxing is to exercise the ratiocinative faculties on a minor non-personal problem' (p. 50). The trouble with this taste for Leavis is its lack of regulation—she compares the leisured reader of her time, who spends up to eight hours a day indulging in light reading, with the readers of the nineteenth century, who, recognizing the ill-effects of 'an inordinate addiction to light reading', restricted it, along with the drinking of wine, to the hours after luncheon. The social paradox, for Leavis, is that detective stories, in particular, are read by 'the professionally cultured' and 'scientific men, clergymen, lawyers and business men generally': 'those who in the last century would have been the guardians of the public conscience in the matter of mental self-indulgence' (pp. 50-1). There is a strong sense throughout Leavis's work of a reading culture abandoned by its appropriate arbiters, and left to flounder, rudderless.

The generality of such attacks on reading for pleasure throughout the 1930s and 1940s can be gauged from the exasperated tone taken by Somerset Maugham in a talk given on 'The Writer's Point of View' for the National Book League in 1951:

Now, I have little doubt that many of you who have been good enough to listen to me will object that to read merely for pleasure is nothing but what in recent years has come to be disparagingly known as escapism. It is. I don't know what bright critic conceived the idea expressed by that word, but it was seized upon by many people who should have known better and for some time to describe a book as escapist was roundly to condemn it. You will still see the word used by the less intelligent reviewers to whom it has never occurred that all literature is escapist. In fact that is its charm.[17]

Two writers who were particularly caustic about the excesses of 'trivial' writing were George Orwell and Virginia Woolf, yet, interestingly, they both elaborate on the pleasures of reading trashy literature. Woolf, who cherished a cultish lifelong passion for the novels of Charlotte M. Yonge,[18] wrote with feeling on the joys of the bad book in an essay on 'Hours in a Library' for the *Times Literary Supplement* in 1916:

And we soon develop another taste, unsatisfied by the great—not a very valuable taste, perhaps, but certainly a very pleasant possession—the taste for bad books. Without committing the indiscretion of naming names we know which authors can be trusted to produce yearly (for happily they are prolific) a novel, a book of poems or essays, which affords us indescribable pleasure. We owe a great deal to bad books; indeed, we come to count their authors and their heroes among those figures who play so large a part in our own silent life.[19]

Orwell makes the same point, employing a term he attributes to G. K. Chesterton—'the good bad book': 'the kind of book that has

[17] W. Somerset Maugham, *The Writer's Point of View* (London: Cambridge University Press, 1951), recording the text of the 9th Annual Lecture of the National Book League, delivered at the Kingsway Hall on 24 Oct. 1951, 9-10.
[18] See Quentin Bell, Angelica Garnett, Henrietta Garnett, Richard Shore, *Charleston Past and Present*, 1987 (London: The Hogarth Press, 1993), 156.
[19] Virginia Woolf, 'Hours in a Library', *Granite and Rainbow* (London: The Hogarth Press, 1958), 28.

no literary pretensions but which remains readable when more serious productions have perished'.[20] He includes *Raffles* and the Sherlock Holmes stories as pre-eminent examples of this sort of literature, and concludes that 'the existence of good bad literature—the fact that one can be amused or excited or even moved by a book that one's intellect simply cannot take seriously—is a reminder that art is not the same thing as cerebration' (p. 21). But it was a decade earlier, commenting in 'Bookshop Memories' on the gap between what people actually enjoy reading and what they think they should enjoy, that Orwell captured precisely the cultish pleasure in non-intellectual reading matter that had passed Queenie Leavis by, and which lies behind many accounts of reading in middlebrow novels themselves:

> For casual reading—in your bath, for instance, or late at night when you are too tired to go to bed, or in the odd quarter of an hour before lunch—there is nothing to touch a back number of the *Girl's Own Paper*. (p. 246)

As well as conjuring up a wonderful image, this remark shows an awareness of that sense of reading as a physical pleasure which plays a major part in the way women's middlebrow novels conceive of the relationship between themselves and their readers. We find it also in the many associations between reading and eating in this fiction—as, for example, in the repeated conversations about books with which E. M. Delafield's Provincial Lady attempts to enliven awkward dinner parties and silent family meals, and in the case of *Cold Comfort Farm*'s Flora who 'liked Victorian novels. They were the only kind of novel you could read while you were eating an apple'.[21]

Any attempt to define the middlebrow novel in this period must inevitably run up against the monolith of modernism. In one sense middlebrow fiction is the 'other' of the modernist or avant-garde novel, the bugbear continually reviled by highbrow critics and literary experimenters as corrupting public taste and devaluing the status of the novel. Yet the feminine middlebrow also provides the brimming bowl into which recent revisers of the modernist canon have dipped for new plums: Rose Macaulay, Antonia White, and Elizabeth Bowen are among the once squarely middlebrow writers who have recently been co-opted into a newly femininized modernist

---

[20] 'Good Bad Books', *Tribune* 2 Nov. 1945, in *The Collected Essays, Journalism and Letters*, iv: *In Front of Your Nose: 1945–1950* (London: Secker & Warburg, 1968), 19.
[21] Stella Gibbons, *Cold Comfort Farm*, 1932 (Harmondsworth: Penguin, 1983), 53.

history. For this revisionist project, modernism has traditionally been defined too narrowly because it has been unconsciously gendered masculine, and women writers excluded on the basis that their concerns with the domestic and the personal are inherently trivial. So Suzanne Clark's *Sentimental Modernism* (1991) argues that feminized discourses of emotion have been falsely excluded from the modernist project; Gillian Hanscombe and Virginia L. Smyers propose the term 'para-modernism' to extend the modernist literary phenomenon to a wide range of contemporary women writers, and Bonnie Kime Scott, editor of *The Gender of Modernism* (1990) goes as far as to suggest that 'the experimental, audience challenging, language-focused writing that used to be regarded as modernism' could be redefined as 'a gendered subcategory—"early male modernism", or "masculinist modernism"' of a much broader modernism that would allow the works of women their rightful place.[22] All these critics seek to elevate previously comparatively unregarded women novelists to the high status of modernists on the basis of experimental, symbolist, or anti-traditionalist elements in their work. While these attempts to reposition women writers within a 'serious' literary category are worthy ones, they are also problematic. 'Modernism' is a label that was applied retrospectively to the experimental writing of the early twentieth century, and would, of course, have meant little to writers at the time. We can renegotiate its definition endlessly, but it brings us no closer to seeing the literary map of the time as contemporaries would have seen it. Indeed, I would argue that the critical insistence, since the 1950s, on seeing the literature of this period solely in terms of modernism has significantly distorted our understanding. Rather than hack about at the definition of modernism in order to squeeze the women writers of the first half of the century into its confines, it seems to me more productive to employ the less slippery concepts of the highbrow or the avant-garde, which had specific, though continually contested, meanings for contemporaries. Equally, rather than extend the definition of the high-status highbrow to cover as much women's writing of the period as possible, I think it crucial to retain the sense of

---

[22] Suzanne Clark, *Sentimental Modernism: Women Writers and the Revolution of the Word* (Bloomington: Indiana University Press, 1991); Gillian Hanscombe and Virginia L. Smyers, *Writing for Their Lives: The Modernist Women 1910–1940* (London: Women's Press, 1987); Bonnie Kime Scott (ed.), *The Gender of Modernism* (Bloomington: Indiana University Press, 1990), 4.

cultural boundaries that dominated contemporary thinking about literature; it is only by exploring the heavily patrolled border between intellectual, experimental fiction and the commercial middlebrow that we will find the places where the distinctions between these categories begin to break down, and interesting things escape.

'Middlebrow' and 'highbrow' are far from impermeable categories, and many texts shifted their status from one to the other, or were uneasily trapped in the no-man's land in-between. The curious dialogue-laden novels of Ivy Compton-Burnett are a good example of the latter: from the time of their first publication they possessed a profoundly indeterminate status—abstruse, effortful, and formally innovative, but so obsessed with class and domesticity as to attract an instant reader-cult that undermined their claims to high seriousness. Verbally complex works, yet produced to an unchanging formula, and cranked out on a virtually biennial basis for five decades, Compton-Burnett's novels challenge the distinction between high and middlebrow fiction. Virginia Woolf took her seriously as a highbrow rival, recording in her diary in 1937 the sleepless nights produced by the contrast of the favourable reviews received by Compton-Burnett's *Daughters and Sons* and those for her own *The Years*, yet the Hogarth Press had turned down the manuscript of Compton-Burnett's second novel in 1929, with Leonard Woolf declaring that 'She can't even write'.[23] Profoundly original, but wedded to the culture of the pre-war period, Compton-Burnett's novels offered highbrow difficulty without the modernist ideological commitment to the future, and the middlebrow pleasures of a self-indulgent snobbery and the anatomizing of family life without any concessions to the notion of reading as relaxation. Other hybrid writers of the period include Enid Bagnold, whose 1935 *National Velvet* achieved best-seller status despite what Claud Cockburn has aptly described as its 'high surrealism', and Elizabeth Bowen, who combines caustic gossip about class and domesticity with a stylized, mannered exploration of profoundly separate subjectivities that has much in common with Virginia Woolf's similar project.[24]

The conventional construction of modernism has, of course, long celebrated Woolf as its lone female exemplar. While it would be

---

[23] Richard Kennedy, *A Boy at the Hogarth Press* (Harmondsworth: Penguin, 1972), 82.
[24] Cockburn, *Bestseller*, 181.

foolish to challenge her status as a profoundly original formal innovator, I would suggest that the gap between Woolf and her female contemporaries looked by no means as yawning in her lifetime as it has since appeared. Woolf herself repeatedly compared her work with that of other women novelists (such as Rose Macaulay and Rosamund Lehmann), evaluating their success and status against her own, and admitting jealousy at their talent in at least one case (that of Katherine Mansfield).[25] In at least some of her formulations on the nature and purpose of writing, she sees her own literary project as both specifically female, and shared by other women writers. In her essay 'Women and Fiction' of 1929, for example, she argues that contemporary women's fiction is 'far more genuine and far more interesting to-day than it was a hundred or even fifty years ago', because a lifting of some aspects of gender oppression has allowed women writers to extend their range from their own suffering to the lives of women in general.[26] The challenge, as she sees it, for the contemporary female novelist, is to represent the quotidian realities—both physical and psychological—of women's lives:

> Here again there are difficulties to be overcome, for, if one may generalise, not only do women submit less readily to observation than men, but their lives are far less tested and examined by the ordinary processes of life. Often nothing tangible remains of a woman's day. The food that has been cooked is eaten; the children that have been nursed have gone out into the world. Where does the accent fall? What is the salient point for the novelist to seize upon? It is difficult to say. Her life has an anonymous character which is baffling and puzzling in the extreme. For the first time, this dark country is beginning to be explored in fiction. (p. 82)

These challenges of representation, she claims, are repeatedly being met by recent women's fiction, which she praises for its honesty and courage, and its ability to speak in a specifically feminine voice but without bitterness: 'these qualities are much commoner than they were, and they give even to second- and third-rate work the value of truth and the interest of sincerity' (p. 82). On her own account, then, it is possible to read Woolf's fiction as part of a continuum with that of other women writers of the period, similarly searching for new means of representing women's changing historical circumstances.

[25] See e.g. *The Diary of Virginia Woolf*, ii: *1920–24*, ed. Anne Olivier Bell (London: The Hogarth Press, 1978), 57, 93, 138, 227, 314–15.
[26] 'Women and Fiction', *The Forum*, March 1929; republished in *Granite and Rainbow* (London: The Hogarth Press, 1958), 80–1.

Looked at in such terms, Woolf's work shares significant concerns with that of her contemporaries: the hypersensitivity to the minutiae of class distinctions, and the meticulous tabulating of the pleasures and disappointments of the domestic day that we find in a novel like *To the Lighthouse*, for instance, are both, as I will argue extensively elsewhere, central features of the aesthetic of the feminine middlebrow.

As such overlaps and hybridity suggests, the middlebrow cannot ultimately be distinguished from the avant-garde highbrow on a formal basis: some highly popular works were formally experimental; some extremely abstruse novels had a cultish mode of production; and the queen of high modernism shared many of the themes and concerns of the average middlebrow women's writer. In fact, both the middlebrow and the highbrow need finally to be understood not as formal or generic categories, but as cultural constructs.

Just as much was invested in the assigning of particular texts to certain intellectual categories, so a great deal of cultural capital was at stake in the identification of particular classes of readers. The highbrow was a largely self-proclaimed creature, a member of the intellectual class comprised of writers, critics, academics, and literary publishers. The highbrow reader, as is seen in the pronouncements of Queenie Leavis, and other self-appointed guardians of the intellectual torch such as T. S. Eliot, conceived of himself as occupying a besieged fortress, resisting the onslaughts of an increasingly consumerist mass culture. Reading, for the highbrow, was properly effortful intellectual work, and he despised the development of a thriving market in escapist and entertaining reading matter. As guardians of literature, the highbrows set themselves against the rapidly expanding lowbrow threat posed by radio, the cinema, pulp fiction, and cheap magazines. These clearly promised to marginalize the purely literary element in the culture of the nation—but so too did the incursions of the middlebrow onto the hallowed ground of literary taste and value. While the highbrow reader was self-identified, the middlebrow reader—like middlebrow texts—was less likely to embrace the label wholeheartedly. He was nevertheless identified, and eagerly pursued, by writers and publishers and by the burgeoning numbers of book clubs and lending libraries. The middlebrow, as a cultural phenomenon, is characterized precisely by its commodification—its endless flexibility in the face of the changing demands of the market. It is this feature that its highbrow critics most condemned—but it is also the reason that they, as we have seen in the case of Queenie Leavis, consistently underestimated it. Immediately responsive to shifts in public tastes, almost paranoically aware of the latest trends—both popular and intellectual—the middlebrow was able to continually reinvent itself, incorporating highbrow experimentation, language, and attitudes almost as soon as they were formulated, and combining them with a mass accessibility and pleasurable appeal. As Janice Radway, author of one of the very few critical analyses of the book club phenomenon, has remarked, the middlebrow commodified 'not only particular books, but the whole concept of Culture itself'.[27] High culture, with all its associations of class and status, was available to buy in the form of the average middlebrow novel, which promised its readers instant and easy access to the very intellectual counters the highbrow so jealously guarded.

Middlebrow fiction laid claim to the highbrow by assuming an easy familiarity with its key texts and attitudes, while simultaneously caricaturing intellectuals as self-indulgent and naive. E. M. Delafield's Provincial Lady series derived much of its humour from its protagonist's gentle exposure of the pretensions of snobs both social and intellectual. One such is her neighbour Miss Pankerton, who 'wears pince-nez and is said to have been at Oxford' and introduces herself as 'the most unconventional person in the whole world'.[28] Along with her effete intellectual friend Jahsper, she pursues the Provincial Lady with learned conversation through social gatherings and chance encounters, and is met with finally at the fancy dress party with which *Diary of a Provincial Lady* (1930) ends:

I am greeted by an unpleasant looking Hamlet, who suddenly turns out to be Miss Pankerton. Why, she asks accusingly, am I not in fancy dress? It would do me all the good in the world to give myself over to the Carnival spirit. It is what I *need*. I make enquiry for Jahsper—should never be surprised to hear that he had come as Ophelia—but Miss P. replies that Jahsper is in Bloomsbury again. Bloomsbury can do nothing without Jahsper. I say, No, I suppose not, in order to avoid hearing any more about either Jahsper or Bloomsbury. (p. 120)

---

[27] Janice Radway, *A Feeling for Books: The Book-of-the-Month Club, Literary Taste and Middle-Class Desire* (Chapel Hill: University of North Carolina Press, 1997), 249.

[28] E. M. Delafield, *Diary of a Provincial Lady* (1930), collected with other novels in the series as *The Diary of a Provincial Lady* (London: Virago, 1991), 98–9.

This is one of the earliest middlebrow references to Bloomsbury which, along with Virginia Woolf, its major exponent, become its key talismans of the highbrow.[29] By the time of the 1933 sequel, *The Provincial Lady Goes Further*, the protagonist has become a successful writer (clearly of middlebrow rather than highbrow books), and frequents smart literary gatherings at which she alternates between awed star-spotting and amused observation of the games of intellectual one-man-upship. So a novelist friend offers her interminable views 'on Bertrand Russell, the works of Stravinsky, and Relativity', many lively discussions are had about books none of the participants have read, and the Provincial Lady is alternately snubbed and bored by a range of literary luminaries ('London regained, though not before I have endured further spate of conversation from several lights of literature').[30] The anxiety of the highbrows to provoke shock is a particular feature of their representation: so participants at a Literary Conference in Brussels wax lyrical over *Lady Chatterley's Lover*, advising the Provincial Lady to detour via Paris on her way home in order to obtain the essential copy (p. 141), and a Bloomsbury literary gathering buzzes with the news that one of the guests has written a book that will 'undoubtedly be seized before publication and burnt' (p. 179). Stella Gibbons's 1932 *Cold Comfort Farm* makes similar mileage out of the pretensions of intellectuals in the person of 'Mr Mybug' (actually Meyerburg),[31] the repellent self-proclaimed genius who pursues the heroine Flora through the Sussex countryside, proclaiming about the phallic nature of the chestnut blossom. Mr Mybug is writing a life of Branwell Brontë, in which he claims that Branwell was the author of his sisters' books, and the devoted protector of his drunkard sister Anne. Like Delafield's Jahsper, he is a member of the

[29] In Rose Macaulay's 1926 *Crewe Train*, a novel which contains a number of thinly disguised parodies of the actual Bloomsbury set, the 'artistic, literary, political, musical and cultured' Gresham family are described as 'all right in Chelsea, though, except Humphrey, they were not quite fit for Bloomsbury' (p. 20). The works of Elizabeth Taylor repeatedly use Woolf as an intellectual counter: knowledge of *To the Lighthouse* forges a connection between Julia, the protagonist of *At Mrs Lippincote's* (1945) and the slightly seedy restaurateur she befriends; intellectually self-conscious adolescents discuss Woolf's destruction of the conventional novel in the 1951 *A Game of Hide-and-Seek* (though one of them has never heard of her); and the academic Mr Tillotson, languishing as a prisoner of war in *The Sleeping Beauty* (1953; London: Virago, 1982) had 'so lamented the death of Virginia Woolf that death might not have been all round him' (p. 56).
[30] *The Provincial Lady Goes Further*, 1932, in *The Diary of a Provincial Lady* (London: Virago, 1991), 143.
[31] A fact, we are told with slyly subtle anti-Semitism, 'not calculated to raise [Flora's] spirits' (*Cold Comfort Farm*, 108).

Bloomsbury set, whom Flora caricatures by interpreting their determinedly outlandish way of life as forced conventionality:

And was it quite fair to fling Elfine, all unprepared, to those Bloomsbury-cum-Charlotte-Street lions which exchanged their husbands and wives every other week-end in the most broad-minded fashion? They always made Flora think of the description of the wild boars painted on the vases in Dickens's story—'each wild boar having his leg elevated in the air at a painful angle to show his perfect freedom and gaiety'. And it must be so discouraging for them to find each new love exactly resembling the old one: just like trying balloon after balloon at a bad party and finding they all had holes in and would not blow up properly. (p. 112)

As the epitome of middlebrow sensibilities, Flora's disdain is carefully balanced: she expresses no shock at the antics of the free-living highbrows, rather a weary contempt, produced partly by over-familiarity: this is a world that holds no mysteries or glamour for her—she moves in social circles in which these 'types' are encountered all too frequently. The eternal literary standards of Dickens and (elsewhere) Jane Austen are her counters against the intellectual fripperies and fashions of the highbrow, which are presented as ephemeral by contrast.

By the time of the little-known 1949 sequel, *Conference at Cold Comfort Farm*, however, the content of highbrow texts is being taken more seriously by the middlebrow. In this novel the modernized farm is used as a conference centre for a group of International Thinkers, who include a Picasso-like painter called Peccavi and a sculptor who seems based on Henry Moore. The conference delegates are a-buzz with the latest literary sensation—a novel called *The Dromedary*:

The author was a Bessarabian who was (temporarily, his admirers trusted) in a Home. The book apparently dealt with one day only in the life of a perfectly ordinary Middle East dromedary, but by voraciously rummaging beneath its seemingly innocuous paragraphs, the International Thinkers had discovered that the Dromedary was really the Universe, and the contents of its three stomachs (raw, digested, and all ready) were the Past, the Present and the Future. The Arab who tended it was really Man. Ah, but who was the Chief Date, the incalculable and apparently sinister but sometimes apparently benevolent figure who, at every turn (and there were a good deal of turns), by-passed or flummoxed the Arab, Bhee? Combining as it did the emotions roused by a game of Hare and Hound with those inspired by the crossword puzzle in *The Times*, *The Dromedary* would have been considered by the International Thinkers well worth (had such a low thought ever entered their heads) the ten-and-sixpence demanded by its publishers.[32]

It is notable that Flora, too, has enjoyed this literary phenomenon, though her analysis of its pleasures places it determinedly with the distinctly middlebrow satisfaction of the crossword puzzle, and she insists on the element its highbrow admirers refuse to see—the book's nature as a commodity.[33] Another novel of 1949, Dodie Smith's *I Capture the Castle*, offers a similar portrayal of the highbrow as ludic. The story concerns the two adolescent Mortmain sisters, Cassandra and Rose, who live in a barely habitable castle with their father, a blocked writer, and their glamorous stepmother, a former artists' model. James Mortmain had written a celebrated novel many years earlier: 'a very unusual book called *Jacob Wrestling*, a mixture of fiction, philosophy and poetry', but had been unable to write anything else since.[34] He now spends his days cloistered in a room above the gate-house, reading detective stories and inventing complex games. The novel is set in the mid-1930s, which places the date of *Jacob Wrestling* as 1918, at the height of the modernist experiment, and significantly pre-dating James Joyce's *Ulysses* of 1922. Joyce is the obvious model for Mortmain's book—a fact that Smith herself acknowledged, stating that Joyce and Proust were the real begetters of the novel: 'strange forefathers for a book whose content may strike some people as suitable for *Peg's Paper*!'[35] As this comment suggests, *I Capture the Castle* seeks to achieve the classic middlebrow balancing act between the low pleasures of romance and simple narrative fulfilment and more elaborate intellectual satisfactions. While James Mortmain himself is a rather ridiculous figure, we are made to see the importance of his experimental writing through the respectful admiration of the American family who have inherited the nearby great house. Yet as with

---

[32] Stella Gibbons, *Conference at Cold Comfort Farm* (London: Longmans, Green & Co. Ltd., 1949), 108.

[33] Another text that caricatures the highbrow intellectual in terms of his fondness for word games is Margery Allingham's *More Work for the Undertaker* (1949), in which Lawrence, the strangest of the highly eccentric elderly Palinode siblings, who communicates entirely in riddles and obscure family references, is understood by the detective Albert Campion once he is revealed as the setter of crossword puzzles.

[34] Dodie Smith, *I Capture the Castle*, 1949 (London: Reprint Society, 1950), 4.

[35] Valerie Grove, *Dear Dodie: The Life of Dodie Smith* (London: Chatto & Windus, 1996), 165, 176.

Gibbons's invented experimental novel, the intellectual claims of Mortmain's work are presented in resolutely middlebrow terms. He finally manages to write his second novel when Cassandra resorts to the desperate measure of imprisoning him in the dungeon of their deserted tower with the Encyclopaedia Britannica and the collection of children's books and games that have become his daily reading. On releasing him, she is disappointed to discover that he has written nothing but 'the cat sat on the mat' and some children's puzzles, but this turns out to be the beginning of a great work, as Cassandra later sarcastically explains: 'Apparently I was all wrong about father. Apparently it is very clever to start a book by writing THE CAT SAT ON THE MAT nineteen times.' (p. 333). Familiarly pleasurable stories, and the sort of word games with which the middlebrow filled his increasing leisure hours are transformed into the heights of avant-garde literary attainment, allowing the middlebrow reader to feel both comfortably at ease with highbrow literature, and flatteringly superior to its clearly irrational creators. Having taken the sting out of the experimental highbrow, the novel even borrows some of its devices; notably an insistence on the materiality of text that begins in its division of the narrative according to the prices of the notebooks in which the narrator, Cassandra, records her thoughts and experiences ('The Sixpenny Book', 'The Two-Guinea Book'), and culminates (with an echo of her father's audacious narrative opening) in an inscription of the open-ended pain of unrequited love: 'Only the margin left to write on now. I love you, I love you, I love you' (p. 342).

Other middlebrow novels also imitate the experimental linguistic texture of the highbrow novels to which they refer. Margaret Kennedy's *The Feast* (1950), for example, a novel continually preoccupied with reading and its social and psychological effects, employs typographic idiosyncrasies to direct the reader's attention to the physicality of the various narratives it incorporates: reproducing the incompetent typing of the vicar composing his sermon, and the prose produced by the writer employing an old typewriter with no letter e; laying out words heard in a dream as free verse, and repeatedly interrupting the narrative with songs and quotations. The effect, as in much experimental fiction, is to direct the reader to the surface of the text, where a sort of allegorical detective puzzle is being played out, with a grizzly fate in store for a select band of the characters who emerge as living representatives of the seven deadly sins. Clearly middlebrow in its themes and approach, the novel nevertheless makes some significant intellectual demands of its readers, rewarding them with a wish-fulfilment ending that moves it decisively outside the bounds of realism and into the arena of fantasy.

Writers appear as characters in a startling number of middlebrow novels. They are partly present, as are other sorts of creative artists, to create an attractively bohemian atmosphere; but their representation also reveals significant features of the feminine middlebrow's understanding of contemporary literature. Perhaps surprisingly, in virtually every case the writers in question are male. They are also almost always highbrow, ranging from the Joycean father in *I Capture the Castle* to neo-Lawrentians in Margaret Kennedy's *The Feast* (1950), Angela Thirkell's *The Brandons* (1939), and Stella Gibbons's *Cold Comfort Farm* (1932). A particular caricature of the callow and arrogant young male novelist is ubiquitous: the charming and feckless Cullum in E. Arnot Robertson's eponymous novel of 1928 is one example, as is Roger Askew, a protégé of the publisher Paul in *Sweet Confusion*:

> Young Askew, after a few encounters on the stairs, had broken in upon him with the typescript of a novel which was no more publishable than the first efforts of young aspirants generally are. Yet it had seemed more hopeful than most. Amid the unrealities, the false accents, the clumsiness and the callow didactic tumult there were hints of quality to come. . . . Confronted by all this, it was easy to overlook the arrogance that lay beneath it, the pertinacious egotism that would feast upon a crumb of praise as though it were the whole loaf.[36]

The career of the typical young male novelist is pastiched by the worldly wise Mr Siddel in *The Feast*, who tells the ambitious Bruce (who has just completed his first angry-young-man work) that similar novelists 'generally write three books':

> The first is on the little victim theme. It has promise. It is well written. It gets astonishingly good reviews. It is very frank and tells how their childhood has been warped, either in a preparatory school or a public school, or both, or else in Wapping or on Cold Comfort Farm. At secondary and grammar schools they don't seem to go in for warping children nearly so extensively. I don't know why.[37]

---

[36] Norman Denny, *Sweet Confusion* (London: John Lane, 1947), 38.
[37] Margaret Kennedy, *The Feast* (London: Cassell & Company and The Book Society, 1950), 160.

The second is 'a comedy, a bitter comedy, and very *mondain*. With a continental background', and no one ever reads the third. Such dismissals indicate both an anxiety about the automatic respect accorded by the critical establishment to the self-consciously 'literary' outpourings of the average male novelist, and a simultaneous contempt for the lack of commerciality of such novelists. When women writers are represented in the feminine middlebrow, they are invariably highly professional, very successful, and extremely modest about their work. The Provincial Lady, who, in the first volume, is in awe of the success of her friend Mary, who is 'able to write stories which actually get published and paid for' (p. 30), devotes much of her later diaries to recounting the lack of respect accorded to her own literary efforts, despite their obvious commercial success. So she is patronized by intellectuals, and the vicar's wife informs her that she had often thought she would like to write a book—'Little things, she says—one here, another there—quaint sayings such as she hears everyday of her life as she pops round the parish—*Cranford*, she adds in conclusion' (p. 126). In Angela Thirkell's *The Brandons* (1939), the beautiful and sympathetic widow, Mrs Brandon, is besieged by various male authors wanting to read their works aloud to her. Blessed relief is afforded by her friend Mrs Morland, the only successful writer of her acquaintance, who refuses to talk about her novels for fear of boring people. Success is seen as going hand in hand with modesty:

'Oh, do you write?' Mrs Grant asked Mrs Morland.

'Only to earn my living', said Mrs Morland apologetically, for although her stories about Madame Koska's dressmaking establishment, where spies, Grand Dukes, drug-smugglers and C.I.D. officers flourished yearly, had a large sale, and she had arrived at the happy point where her public simply asked for 'the new Mrs Morland', instead of mentioning the name of the book, she thought quite poorly of her own hard-working talent and greatly admired people who wrote what she called real books.[38]

At a time when the number of women novelists was beginning to outstrip that of men,[39] the repeated representation of male novelists

[38] Angela Thirkell, *The Brandons*, 1939 (Harmondsworth: Penguin, 1950), 82.

[39] A fact that Ivy Compton-Burnett put down to the deaths of men in the First World War: 'Well, I expect that's because the men were dead, you see, and the women didn't marry so much because there was no one for them to marry, and so they had leisure, and, I think in a good many cases they had money, because their brothers were dead, and all that would tend to writing, wouldn't it, being single, and having some money, and having the time—having no men, you see.' (Kay Dick, *Ivy and Stevie* (London: Duckworth, 1971), 7)

as critically successful but callow and uncommercial indicates a clear sense among middlebrow women writers that their own work was judged differently from that of men, but also that a new and lucrative market had opened up for specifically female fiction.

Two types of literary institution came to a new national prominence in the years after the first world war: lending libraries and book clubs. Although private lending libraries had existed previously, it was during the war that they began the rapid expansion that would lead to a W. H. Smiths or Boots Booklovers' Library in every reasonably-sized town. Public library provision expanded also in this period, with an increase of books in stock from 15 million in 1924 to 42 million in 1949 and a quadrupling over roughly the same period of the number of 'service points' from which books were available.[40] There was a startling growth too in the cheap 'tuppenny' libraries run from local department stores, newsagencies, and tobacconists, which turned over a meagre stock of 500 or so books at a time.[41] Book borrowers divided fairly neatly on class lines: the working classes seem to have been the chief users of the tuppenny libraries and the main beneficiaries of the expansion in the public library service, while the middle classes utilized the more solidly established private libraries. Exemplary among these was the Boots Booklovers' Library which, although it was not the first of the private lending libraries (founded in 1899, it was considerably pre-dated by the W. H. Smith Circulating Library—1860, and Mudie's Library—1842) gained over its rivals both in its innovatory borrowing system and the styling of its library branches. Usually situated on the first floor of the stores, with picture windows overlooking the main street or square of the town, the Boots libraries offered a comfortable and elegant reading environment: decorated in the latest style, they offered an atmosphere resembling a club or country-house sitting room, in marked contrast to rivals W. H. Smiths, who tended to position their

---

[40] Joseph McAleer, *Popular Reading and Publishing in Britain 1914–1950* (Oxford: Clarendon Press, 1992), 49.

[41] Of these a disdainful Q. D. Leavis comments: 'In suburban side-streets and even village shops it is common to find a stock of worn and greasy novels let out at 2d or 3d a volume; and it is surprising that a clientèle drawn from the poorest class can afford to change the books several times a week, or even daily; but so strong is the reading habit that they do' (*Fiction and the Reading Public*, 7).

libraries in the basements of their stores.[42] The Boots libraries were intended as loss leaders, part of an enterprise to attract a middle-class clientele to what had previously been largely working-class pharmacies.[43] It was a highly successful move: while the upper middle classes were more likely to use one of the London libraries such as Mudie's or the Times Book Club, the rest of the middle class soon came to rely on Boots, to the extent that it acquired an iconic—and often parodied—status in the period as the supplier of books to the genteel.[44] Laura Jesson, the totemically middle-class heroine of the film *Brief Encounter*, has just been to change her library books at Boots before her transformative encounter on the station platform,[45] while Betjeman's 'In Westminster Abbey' locates the Boots library as a key signifier of a comfortable bourgeois existence:

> Think of what our Nation stands for,
> Books from Boots, and country lanes,
> Free speech, free passes, class distinction,
> Democracy and proper drains.[46]

Even within the libraries, a class distinction of which Betjeman's speaker would approve prevailed. Boots offered three different classes of membership 'to suit every type of reader': the expensive 'On Demand' subscription guaranteed the borrower that any book (as long as it was in circulation in the library as a whole) would be

---

[42] I am indebted for this and other information on the Boots libraries to Nickianne Moody, who is compiling an oral history archive of memories of the Boots Booklovers' Library. See her article 'The Boots Booklovers' Libraries', *Antiquarian Book Monthly* (Nov. 1996), 36–8.

[43] 'Jesse Boot, the founder of the chemist retail and dispensing chain came from a Nottinghamshire Methodist family. . . . The continued Wesleyan concern for the poor differentiated the Boots' shop from its competitors. Boots' policy was to buy in bulk in order to keep costs low and to sell medicines in poorer areas at the lowest possible price' (Moody, ibid. 36).

[44] Q. D. Leavis noted that the upper middle class used the Times Book Club and Mudie's, and the lower middle class Boots (*Fiction and the Reading Public*, 14). The Times Book Club, located at 42 Wigmore Street, was a lending library rather than a book club. Virginia Woolf was a member, with a subscription that entitled her to newly-published books on demand.

[45] Nicola Beauman memorably opens *A Very Great Profession: The Woman's Novel 1914–39* (London: Virago, 1983), her pioneering study of women's writing between the wars with this point. I am indebted to her work on literary depictions of circulating libraries in what follows.

[46] John Betjeman, 'In Westminster Abbey', *Old Lights for New Chancels*, 1940, *Collected Poems* (London: John Murray, 1958), 85.

dispatched to her local branch within a few days; the class A subscription offered access to all books in circulation, with new books supplied quickly but with no guarantees; while the class B subscriber had access 'to all but the newest books'—in practice having to wait six months before new books were available to her.[47] On Demand and Class A subscribers submitted booklists to the librarian, who would then attempt to reserve items on the list for the reader's next visit, or suggest suitable alternatives; the class B subscribers did not submit lists and searched for their own books. A great deal of emphasis was placed on the service aspect of the libraries, with librarians trained and examined in the art of meeting subscribers' reading requirements, and supplied with pamphlets such as the First Literary Course, which divided fiction into various categories—Light Romance, Family Stories, Detective Fiction, and so on. In an intriguing alternative to the modes of literary categorization offered by critics such as Connolly and Leavis, these varieties of fiction are explicated in terms of the type of subscriber who might favour each sort. So Light Romance is suitable for '[women who] say they like a "pretty book"' and Family Stories 'for those tired of romance . . . seeking . . . "a well-written book"'.[48] Novels were the chief literary commodity of the libraries, as is indicated by surviving booklists compiled by Boots' subscribers. One example from the early 1950s, stamped by the library when books had been supplied, is absolutely typical: the reader, who is named Rowlinson and has a class A subscription, lists among others *Family Story* by Leonora Starr, *Love in a Cold Climate* by Nancy Mitford, *Hunting the Fairies* by Compton Mackenzie, *Son of the Morning* by Gilbert Frankau, *Flowers on the Grass* by Monica Dickens, *Cost Price* by Dornford Yates, *Some Tame Gazelle* by Barbara Pym, *Nothing Serious* by P. G. Wodehouse, and *Frost at Morning* by Richmal Crompton.[49] It is an exemplary middlebrow selection, embracing thrillers, social comedies, family narratives, and up-market romances. She includes very little non-fiction, except for a couple of volumes of essays. The list illustrates very neatly the typical 'library book' of the period, indeed the phrase is actually employed in contemporary fiction to signify a

---

[47] Leaflet, undated but post-1930, setting out Terms and Conditions of Boots Booklovers Library, Box: Libraries 2, John Johnson Collection, Bodleian Library; Moody, 'The Boots Booklovers' Libraries', 37.
[48] Boots *First Literary Course* (1948), cited in Beauman, *A Very Great Profession*, 13.
[49] In Box: Libraries 2, John Johnson Collection, Bodleian Library.

particular type of (invariably middlebrow) novel; so Delafield's Laura in the 1927 *The Way Things Are* 'held her library book open upon her knee, and supposed herself to be reading it, whilst a merry phantasy careered round and round her mind'.[50] In Elizabeth Taylor's *The Sleeping Beauty* (1953) two middle-aged women friends lament their limited approach to life and culture:

They remained the same—two rather larkish schoolgirls. This they realised and it was the piteous part to them of growing old.
'We haven't changed enough', Isabella once said. 'We don't any longer match our looks. We've got lost and left behind.' 'We ought to take up something.' Evalie agreed. 'Not read the books we do. For instance, we never read books written by men, do we? Just library books all the time.'[51]

'Library books' here are books by women, a slightly guilty pleasure to be hidden from those you might want to impress (like an illicit box of chocolates for a dieter). For Taylor's women they cannot count as the 'something' one might 'take up'—they offer pleasure without improvement. It is striking that such dismissive sentiments are articulated in the fiction of precisely the sort of authors whose work 'went out well' in the circulating libraries, indicating an anxiety about the implications of this sort of mass success on their status as writers—and perhaps suggesting also a concern about the company their books were keeping on those promiscuously arranged library shelves. So Angela Thirkell, the author of cultishly popular social comedies, waxes amusing about bad thrillers and the typical library subscriber's idea of 'a nice book' in her 1939 *Before Lunch*:

'Your room looked so lovely and cool, and I read a bit of an awfully good book you left on the table where your plans are.'
'I am always needing nice books for my library list', said Mrs Stoner. 'What was it called, Daphne?'
'Something about Blood,' said Daphne. 'And there is an awfully good bit about where the detective gets on the track of an Argentine white slaver and the wardrobe suddenly turns round on a hinge and there he sees a girl's body hanging up by the heels and she had nothing on and has been dead for days. Oh, *All Blood Calling*, that's the name.'
Mrs Stoner said it sounded a very nice book and she would put it on her list.[52]

---

[50] E. M. Delafield, *The Way Things Are*, 1927 (London: Virago, 1988), 141.
[51] Elizabeth Taylor, *The Sleeping Beauty*, 1953 (London: Virago, 1982), 33–4.
[52] Angela Thirkell, *Before Lunch*, 1939 (Harmondsworth: Penguin, 1951), 126–7.

The subscriber's need to keep her library list continually replenished, and the librarian's need to ensure that subscribers left the library with a book—even if it was not really the one they wanted—encouraged a highly instrumental attitude towards literature. This may be one of the reasons for the marked hostility towards the circulating library that we find in much women's middlebrow fiction. Where we might expect middlebrow writers to embrace institutions that made their own works so widely available, instead we find repeated scenes in which poorly-educated librarians tyrannize their hapless subscribers; where the desired books are never available and readers are forced to accept unwanted alternatives. In Denis Mackail's 1925 *Greenery Street* the library attendant never has any of the books on Felicity's list, and instead offers her an unappealing selection from which she eventually makes a choice only through social embarrassment:

Attendant: 'Here are some of the latest, Mrs Foster.' (Felicity looks at the backs of these works, and fails to recognise either their titles or their authors.)
Felicity (politely, but disparagingly): 'I don't think I–'
Attendant (briskly): '*Prendergast's Property*—that's a very pretty story.'
Felicity (doubtfully): 'Oh . . . I never seem to like books where the people are called Prendergast.' . . .
(By this time, however, a small queue has formed behind her, which has the effect of weakening her critical judgement. The attendant realises this, and goes quickly ahead.)
Attendant: 'I think you'd like this, Mrs Foster. *Illumination*.'
(Felicity picks up *Illumination* and opens it. Nice short paragraphs, anyhow; and quite large print.)
Felicity: 'All right. That'll do for one.' (The queue shows fresh signs of impatience.) 'And—oh, very well. I'll take *The Transept* for the other. Perhaps my husband will like it.'
Attendant (more briskly than ever): 'Oh, he's sure to, Mrs Foster.'[53]

If it is not dictatorial librarians imposing their literary taste, it is fellow readers. E. M. Delafield's Laura is accosted in the local circulating library by her overbearing neighbour, Lady Kingsley-Browne:

'What are you going to get? Have you read *this*?' said her neighbour tiresomely, thrusting upon Laura's attention a novel with a title that she disliked, by an author whose works she never read. . . .

[53] Denis Mackail, *Greenery Street*, 1925 (Harmondsworth: Penguin, 1937), 115.

'What about the Georgian Poems for your other choice?'
Laura did not get very frequent opportunities of changing her books at the Quinnerton Library, and for motives of economy she did not subscribe to a London one. She had no wish to take Georgian Poems in place of one of the many new novels that she wanted to read. Nevertheless she presently found herself leaving the shop with this unwanted addition to her stock of literature. (p. 64)

One of the most striking features of this scene is the class dimension—Laura allows Lady Kingsley-Browne to bully her partly because of the weight carried by her superior class status, and the novel is careful to point out that Laura is of the class who might expect to make use of a London library if not prevented by the cost (new poverty, as discussed at length in the next chapter, being an acceptable—even status-guaranteeing—affliction of the upper-middle classes in the years after the First World War). Class is also a dominant preoccupation in the iconic description of a local circulating library in Elizabeth Bowen's *The Death of the Heart* (1938). The glamorous and lower-middle-class Daphne works as a library assistant at Smoot's—clearly Boots—where she is understood to bring a certain refinement to the establishment:

'They want a girl who *is* someone, if you know what I mean. A girl who—well, I don't quite know how to express it—a girl who did not come from a nice home would not do at all, here. You know, choosing books is such a personal thing; Seale is a small place and the people are so nice. Personality counts for so much here. The Corona Café is run by ladies, you know.'[54]

A key ingredient in the tone Daphne lends to the library is her refusal to read: 'It was clear that Daphne added, and knew she added, *cachet* to Smoot's by her air of barely condoning the traffic that went on there. Her palpable wish never to read placed at a disadvantage those who had become dependent on this habit' (p. 184). She exercises a malign cruelty over her mostly elderly subscribers, regarding them with 'a bold cold smile' (p. 185) and rejecting their timid conversational overtures. Under her tutelage, her colleague Miss Scott also begins to exercise the librarian's power of imposing undesirable literature on her readers:

[54] Elizabeth Bowen, *The Death of the Heart*, 1938 (Harmondsworth: Penguin, 1962), 157.

The lady who had not spoken was already dithering round a table of new novels. Her friend threw the novels rather a longing look, then turned strongmindedly to the cabinet of *belles lettres*. Raising her nose so as to bring her pince-nez to the correct angle, she took out a succession of books, scanned their title pages, looked through all the pictures, and almost always replaced them with a frustrated sigh. Did she not know that Daphne hated people to stick around messing the books about? 'I suppose there *is* something here I should really like?' she said. 'It's so hard to tell from the outsides.'

'Miss Scott', said Daphne plaintively, 'can't you help Mrs Adams?'

Mrs Adams, mortified, said: 'I *ought* to make out a list.'

'Well, people do find it helps.'

Mrs Adams did not half like being turned over to Miss Scott, who gave her a collection of well-known essays she was ashamed to refuse. She looked wistfully at her friend, who came back with a gay-looking novel and a happy face. 'You really oughtn't to miss these; they were beautifully written', said Miss Scott, giving poor Mrs Adams a shrewish look—in her subservient way, she was learning to be as great a bully as Daphne. (pp. 183–4)

If librarians like Daphne are bullies, the subscribers in such accounts are biddable sheep—too weak to choose the books they really want to read. The silliness of library subscribers, and the arbitrary nature of their taste in literature, is a repeated trope in the period. So, a writer in *The Book Guild Bulletin* in 1930 refers dismissively to 'the young ladies who throng the counters of Boots' libraries'.[55] Similarly, among a selection of typical readers (the bluff middle-aged man who would like a biography, the bespectacled blue-stocking who would like 'that new book of poems', and so on) characterized in cartoon form in an advertisement for book tokens dating from the early 1930s, the library user is represented as young, female, frivolous—and clueless about books: 'Jolly good! A Book Token! Here's my chance to have what's-his-name's new novel for keeps.'[56] What these middlebrow representations of the circulating library and its readers indicate most clearly is that—despite the deliberate reader-friendliness of the average middlebrow novel—writers were very uneasy about the type of reader their books were attracting. The fact that these satires at the expense of circulating

---

[55] George A. Birmingham in *The Book Guild Bulletin*, July 1930, quoted in Q. D. Leavis, *Fiction and the Reading Public*, 25.

[56] 'The Gift Problem. Last year's muddle... This year's solution', in Box: Book Clubs 1, John Johnson Collection, Bodleian Library.

libraries repeatedly focus on the power of librarians to force books on readers, and the lack of knowledge or taste of readers indicates the extent to which notions of literary discrimination and active readerly choice were central to the women's middlebrow novel's conception of itself.

If the circulating libraries offered a mass popularity that was embarrassing to some middlebrow authors, the other major new institutions of literary influence of the day—the book club and the 'Book of the Month' recommendations of the daily newspapers— offered fame and commercial rewards on an unprecedented scale to the authors whose work they selected. The book clubs in particular were extremely powerful institutions: the most influential of them all, the American Book-of-the-Month Club (founded in 1926) boasted in its literature of the literary reputations it had been responsible for establishing:

A Few of the Many Authors, *Now Famous* whose first successful book was introduced to the public by the Book-of-the-Month Club.

> *Anthony Adverse* was chosen as a book-of-the-month in July 1933. Prior to that, Harvey Allen was recognized as a poet, but was not nationally known.
>
> John Priestley is now well-known in this country: before our judges chose *The Good Companions*, in 1929, few readers here had ever heard of him.[57]

In Britain the Book Society (started in 1927), the Book Guild (1930), and many similar organizations were established in imitation of the Book-of-the-Month Club. Their selection committees of journalists, novelists, and reviewers would choose the books to be offered each month to the club members, at a significant reduction on the publishers' standard prices. The first choice would be dispatched to all members, with an option to return it and select one of the alternatives on offer. The promotional literature of the Book Club—one of many such ventures run by Foyles bookshop—is typical of the terms in which the book clubs sold themselves to readers:

Each month The Book Club chooses for its members an outstanding recently-published book. They are new, vital, enjoyable books (fiction and non-fiction) by the front-rank authors of our time. They are printed on good quality paper, and—VERY IMPORTANT—they are bound in The Book

---

[57] Advertising leaflet for the Book-of-the-Month Club, Box: Book Clubs 1, The John Johnson Collection, Bodleian Library.

Club's own special strong cloth binding with a dignified coloured jacket. These are we say with certainty books which you will be glad to read, proud to own; books which, for literary merit, appearance and production, are unequalled by any other book club scheme.... The Book Club brings these splendid books to you each month; keeping you abreast of the best fiction and non-fiction published; helping you to build up, at almost negligible cost, a first-class library of famous books.[58]

Eager to create the book-purchasing habit in a nation of book-borrowers, the book clubs sought to transform ephemeral best-sellers into 'modern classics', decking them out in 'dignified' uniform bindings, and employing a language designed to evoke a life of cultured gentility—'splendid books', 'a first-class library'. In fact, the main appeal of the book clubs was the outstanding savings they offered—the Book Club boasted that

> Members Buy Books Published at
> 7/6 8/6 10/6 and 12/6
> for 2/6 each.

These prices were too good to be missed, and readers joined the new clubs in their thousands. With a guaranteed mass readership, the book clubs could dictate terms to publishers and authors alike. Dodie Smith was dismayed when the American Literary Guild 'lower-brow than the Book-of-the-Month Club' ordered 550,000 copies of *I Capture the Castle*, dependent on her making certain changes to the text: 'I see' she wrote in her journal, 'how dangerous to the integrity of the author these book clubs are.'[59] With this sort of power, the book clubs were able to alter the literary landscape. Repelled by the taste of the selection committees, and taking personally the sneers at highbrows in the promotional literature, Q. D. Leavis nevertheless recognized the major cultural significance of the book club phenomenon:

By December 1929 the [Book Society] had nearly seven thousand members, and it is still growing, from which the quite unbiased observer might fairly deduce two important cultural changes: first, that by conferring authority on a taste for the second-rate ... a middlebrow standard of values has been set up; second, that middlebrow taste has thus been organised.[60]

---

[58] Publicity leaflet for The Book Club (Non-Political), run by W. and G. Foyle Ltd., 121 Charing Cross Road, in Box: Book Clubs 1, John Johnson Collection, Bodleian Library.

[59] Valerie Grove, *Dear Dodie: The Life of Dodie Smith* (London: Chatto & Windus, 1996), 179.

[60] *Fiction and the Reading Public*, 23–4.

The books selected by the various book clubs were not quite so homogeneous as Leavis's criticism implies—the Book Society, for instance, seems to have offered rather more 'literary' choices than the more straightforwardly populist books chosen by the various Foyles' enterprises (Virginia Woolf's *Flush*, Richard Hughes's *High Wind in Jamaica*, and Gertrude Stein's *The Autobiography of Alice B. Toklas* are some of the typical choices of the former, as against the Book Club's selection of Agatha Christie's *Dumb Witness*, Baroness Orczy's *The Turbulent Duchess*, and Pearl Buck's *This Proud Heart*)—but it is nevertheless clear that they represent a significant enterprise in controlling the reading matter of the British public. Once again Delafield's Provincial Lady offers a wryly self-deprecating response to this contemporary literary development:

November 14th.—Arrival of Book of the Month choice, and am disappointed. History of a place I am not interested in, by an author I do not like. Put it back into its wrapper again and make fresh choice from Recommended List. Find, on reading small literary bulletin enclosed with book, that exactly this course of procedure has been anticipated, and that it is described as being 'the mistake of a lifetime'. Am much annoyed, although not so much at having made (possibly) mistake of a lifetime, as at depressing thought of our all being so much alike that intelligent writers can apparently predict our behaviour with perfect accuracy.

Decide not to mention any of this to Lady B., always so tiresomely superior about Book of the Month as it is, taking up attitude that she does not require to be told what to read. (Should like to think of good repartee to this).[61]

Ruefully aware of being controlled, and somewhat embarrassed about allowing her reading to be dictated by selection committee, the Provincial Lady nevertheless succumbs to the lure of the book club; its influence on her circle is indicated by the report of a dinner party conversation in which the assembled company discuss their recent reading. They have all read *The Good Companions* and *High Wind in Jamaica*, clearly because—although the fact is not spelled out—they are recent Book Society choices. Awareness of the commercial success of books, and the role of book clubs in establishing it, plays a major part in the conversation:

We all say (a) that we have read *The Good Companions*, (b) that it is a very *long* book, (c) that it was chosen by the Book of the Month Club in

[61] *Diary of a Provincial Lady*, in *The Diary of a Provincial Lady*, 6.

America and must be having immense sales, and (d) that American sales are What Really Count. (pp. 10-11)

Although a powerful force in commodifying literature and perhaps responsible for inducing a uniformity of public taste, the book clubs also played an important part in democratizing both access to literature and definitions of literary value. This point is made directly in an account of the establishment of the Readers' Union—a book club that cannily sold itself as a union of readers against the commercial might of publishers:[62]

Perhaps it is as well to admit here that RU [Readers' Union] has never seen literature in the context, the rather Victorian context, of the fashionable novel, poetry, belles-lettres. We run a book club and not a literary club, for books are as large as life and life is larger than lit. . . . RU has always tried to reconcile the vulgar and the recondite, and has cherished the hope of a popular culture.[63]

Although the writer felt that this hope had in fact receded in the years between 1937 and 1958, there is a strong sense in which all the book clubs of the period were performing such acts of cultural remaking, formulating a middlebrow aesthetic by making the popular respectable and the obscure accessible. Although their effect was to ensure that large numbers of people read the same books, this also guaranteed that this literature became a talking point, a shared cultural reference against which their largely middle-class female readers could define themselves.

These reading institutions, in their various ways, construct reading as a communal activity, particularly for women. Books are read on the recommendation of others; they are enjoyed partly because of a cult status produced by other readers 'in the know'. This communality, I would like to argue, is also a key part of the way in which the women's middlebrow novel conceives of its readers. Reading is a fundamental trope in these novels, which demonstrate a continual preoccupation with different types of writing and different readerly relationships to it. Books are enjoyed, ridiculed, used as social and moral guides, as comfort objects, as symbols of class and status; they

---

[62] See pamphlets promoting the Readers' Union in Box: Book Clubs 1, John Johnson Collection, Bodleian Library.

[63] John Baker, *Low Cost of Bookloving: An Account of the First Twenty-One Years of Readers Union* (London: Readers Union, 1958), 12.

form bonds between people, or emphasize their differences. Reading, for the feminine middlebrow is a physical as well as an intellectual act: often compared to eating, it is a source of deep, sensual satisfactions, a self-indulgent pleasure, a means of escape as well as an affirmation of life choices. There is a determined intertextuality about this literature: novels continually refer to other novels, with the effect that an intricate network of connections is built up between texts. This has a number of consequences: as with the recommendations of librarians, the reader is introduced to other books that promise similar pleasures to that she is currently enjoying; it also allows the feminine middlebrow to establish its conventions, and direct the reader's expectations. Most significantly, it is one of the key means by which the very divergent women's middlebrow novels of the period established for themselves a shared generic identity.

Reading, within the middlebrow novel, serves a number of distinct purposes. Frequently, it is instructive, as in the classics earnestly appreciated by Angela Thirkell's adolescent characters in a number of novels, or the social education *Cold Comfort Farm*'s Flora offers her protegee Elfine by means of fashion magazines and the novels of Jane Austen:

> Elfine obediently resumed her reading aloud of 'Our Lives from Day to Day' from an April number of *Vogue*. When she had finished, Flora took her, page by page, through a copy of *Chiffons*, which was devoted to descriptions and sketches of lingerie. Flora pointed out how these graceful petticoats and night-gowns depended upon their pure line and delicate embroidery for their beauty; how all gross romanticism was purged away, or expressed only in a fold or flute of material. She then showed how the same delicacy might be found in the style of Jane Austen, or a painting by Marie Laurencin. (p. 136)

Such literary instruction is invariably treated with a gentle irony: Austen is tempered by *Vogue* and *Chiffons*, and the bouncing Lydia's enthusiastic discovery of Browning's poetry in Thirkell's 1937 *Summer Half* is presented as a youthful gaucherie:

> Browning had suddenly come into her life the night before, because the literature mistress had set a holiday essay on 'My favourite Browning poem, and my reasons for preferring it'. Lydia, to whom the poet was unknown, had contemptuously taken the volume of *Dramatic Lyrics* to bed with her, and fallen head over heels into it. Seeing Everard, Noel and Kate sitting under the tulip tree after breakfast, this seemed a good opportunity for a symposium on the subject that was filling her mind.

'I think', she announced loudly, as she sat down on the swing chair and began to rock herself to and fro, 'everyone ought to read Browning.'

'Quite a lot of them do', said Noel. . . .

She then, having an excellent verbal memory, quoted from the poet's work at such length that her hearers could hardly bear it.[64]

Political reading also comes under the heading of the instructive: Elizabeth Taylor's lonely Eleanor in *At Mrs Lippincote's* finds a new meaning in her life when she is taken under the wing of the members of a communist cell. Their reading comes from a very different canon than that found in the homes Eleanor has shared with her cousin Roddy and Julia, his fey, frivolous wife:

> Eleanor examined the titles of books on a shelf near the fire—*The Communist Manifesto*, *The Ragged-trousered Philanthropists*, some Left Book Club editions, *The Origin of the Family* and a book on birth control.[65]

Although the novel shows some respect for the determinedly unbourgeois existence of the communists, Eleanor's tentative involvement is mocked, particularly her new choice of newspaper, the radical *Daily Worker*, which she smuggles into the house and then disclaims when Julia finds it inadequate as a wrapping for butcher's meat.

The problem with instructive reading is its potential for earnestness: the biggest social sin, in the middlebrow imagination, is that of taking oneself too seriously. More approved is the act of reading for pleasure—this literature is full of images of abandoned immersion in books, from the Provincial Lady's slightly shame-faced indulgence in the classic books of her childhood to the complete physical involvement in her book of Teresa, the youngest of five eccentric sisters in Diana Tutton's 1953 *Guard Your Daughters*:

> [H]e turned to Teresa, who was bent over her book reading with absorption, eating toast at the same time, and with tears running down her cheeks and splashing on to her blue skirt. 'What are you reading, Teresa?' asked Gregory.
>
> 'It's a book by Broster,' she said politely. 'It's called *Sir Isumbras at the Ford*. It's *very* sad. I'm reading it for the third time.'
>
> 'And it still makes you cry?'
>
> 'Oh yes, I always cry.'[66]

---

[64] Angela Thirkell, *Summer Half*, 1937 (Harmondsworth: Penguin, 1951), 241–2.

[65] Elizabeth Taylor, *At Mrs Lippincote's*, 1945 (London: Virago, 1995), 65.

[66] Diana Tutton, *Guard Your Daughters*, 1953 (London: The Reprint Society, 1954), 8–9.

The psychological effects of reading are taken seriously, particularly during the war years, when a number of novels debate the relative merits of various types of reading. The publisher Paul in Norman Denny's 1947 *Sweet Confusion* (set in the run up to the war) concentrates on well-crafted detective stories which offer the consoling distractions of plot, rather than 'the sort of anxious, self-conscious, self-parading fiction which I regard as the bane of our present literature' (pp. 169–70). The Provincial Lady, an established novelist by the time of *The Provincial Lady in Wartime* (1940) has offered herself to the Ministry of Information as a propagandist, and been told that her proper war-work is the writing of fiction. She tries to reassure another frustrated writer of their social usefulness:

> Try to console J. L. with assurance that there is to be a boom in books, as nobody will be able to do anything amusing in the evenings, what with black-out, petrol restrictions, and limitations of theatre and cinema openings, so they will have to fall back on reading.
> Realise too late that this is not very happily expressed.[67]

There are a number of discussions in the course of the novel of the most comforting type of literature for war-time reading, with the Provincial Lady taking refuge in children's classics and Dickens and her fellow novelist portentously declaring that 'he personally finds the Greeks provide him with escapist literature. Plato.' (p. 412). Working in a canteen, the Provincial Lady is asked to recommend a book for a fellow worker:

> In times such as these, she replies very apologetically indeed, she thinks a novel is practically the only thing. Not a detective novel, not a novel about politics, nor about the unemployed, nothing to do with sex, and above all not a novel about life under the Nazi regime in Germany. (p. 434)

All contemporaneity is decisively rejected in this list, but luckily the Provincial Lady has a suitably escapist alternative, by an irreproachably middlebrow novelist:

> Inspiration immediately descends upon me and I tell her without hesitation to read a delightful novel called *The Priory* by Dorothy Whipple, which answers all requirements, and has a happy ending into the bargain.

[67] *The Provincial Lady in Wartime*, 1940; in *The Diary of a Provincial Lady* (London: Virago, 1991), 412.

Mrs Peacock says it seems too good to be true, and she can hardly believe that any modern novel is as nice as all that, but I assure her that it is and that it is many years since I have enjoyed anything so much. (pp. 434-5)[68]

'Delightful', 'happy', 'nice', with no enforced instruction or reference to the horrors of contemporary life: this is the middlebrow at its most self-indulgent, but its pleasures can now be triumphantly justified by its new function as comfort in the dark days of fear and uncertainty.[69]

As well as different reading purposes, the feminine middlebrow clearly identifies different types of reader. The lowbrow reader's entirely uncritical immersion in the alternative worlds of romance or adventure narratives is distinguished from the pleasant mood-enhancement sought by middlebrow readers such as the Provincial Lady's fellow worker. So in Angela Thirkell's 1939 *Before Lunch* it is a young and credulous maidservant who is the devoted reader of romance, interpreting her daily experiences in terms of its hectic logic: 'for had she not borne witness for her chosen hero, just like Glamora Tudor in *The Flames of Desire* when she told wicked Lord Mauleverer that it was really the Duke she loved'.[70] Also distinguished from the typical middlebrow reader is the ignorant or uncritical reader, who misses the point of the books she reads, or fails comically to appreciate her own limitations. The beautiful, stupid Rose Birkett, who features in a number of Angela Thirkell's Barsetshire novels, is a case in point—so utterly unread that she is under the misapprehension that 'there was a play called alternatively Shakespeare and Hamlet'.[71] The type of undiscriminating reader reviled by Orwell for their treatment of books as a commodity available by the yard is treated ironically in a number of novels. In E. Arnot Robertson's *Cullum* (1928) the youthful female narrator is trapped by a boring woman at a dinner party:

Mrs Cole settled herself by me on the sofa, and, unaware of my hatred of being touched, pawed my arm while she chatted with her restful vigour,

---

[68] *The Priory* is a genuine novel, described in very similar terms to those the Provincial Lady employs in the National Book Council's 1939 *Christmas Book Magazine*: 'an entrancing study in human relationships set in an old priory that sheds its benediction over a most charming story'.

[69] This new attitude to reading is also found in the advertising of book clubs—'Books Beat the Blackout' trumpets a utility-style leaflet for the Book Club, while another declares 'Wartime Service: Read to Relax' (Box: Book Clubs 1, John Johnson Collection, Bodleian Library).

[70] Thirkell, *Before Lunch*, 117.   [71] Thirkell, *Summer Half*, 141-2.

which allowed no time for replies; I had been thankful to it before. She had lately finished reading a book which she insisted that I must read; it was marvellously well written, quite too fascinating, she said, and though at the moment she could not remember the title she knew it was by the man who wrote *The Crock*—(or it might have been *The Arrow*)—*of Gold*. Anyway, it was by whichever of these authors had also written *Fortitude*. After ten minutes of description I was no longer surprised that, as I had noted at dinner, the attention of her family immediately strayed elsewhere as soon as she became enthusiastic over anything.[72]

In a novel in which the passionate central relationship between the narrator and the young novelist Cullum is founded on a mutual love of and respect for books, Mrs Cole's vague and uninformed attitude to reading marks her out as worthy of contempt. In the novels of Elizabeth Taylor, individuals are similarly characterized by their approach to reading: in her 1953 *The Sleeping Beauty*, for example, the middle-aged widow Isabella, described on the first page of the novel as 'flippant', offers an elaborate breakdown of her own taxonomy of reading, based on the physical posture of the person engaged in the act, and glaringly lacking in any sense of literary content:

'Where is [Lawrence] . . .?'
'He is upstairs in his room, sulking. What am I saying? Studying, I mean. Studying.'
'What is he studying?'
'Well, reading then. I always say "reading" when people are lolling in a chair, or lying on the sofa, or in the train. But studying when they sit up to a table.'
'What does he read?'
'Books and papers and magazines.' She turned her cuff back secretly to glance at her watch, thinking of the meal in the oven. 'And library books', she added.
'Pretty comprehensive.'[73]

It is by delineating such empty attitudes to reading that the feminine middlebrow gestures towards the sort of discriminating yet emotionally responsive reader that is its ideal.

A major distinguishing feature of this ideal reader is that it is female. The feminine middlebrow genders reading as a matter of course, repeatedly revealing men as inadequate readers. In *At Mrs*

[72] E. Arnot Robertson, *Cullum*, 1928 (London: Virago, 1990), 22.
[73] Taylor, *The Sleeping Beauty*, 4.

Lippincote's Julia tries to persuade her husband to take their young son a drop of wine in a glass of water with the declaration that ' "Young girls used always to drink it at bedtime. Look at Catherine Morland!" ' (p. 79); Roddy's bemused response is ' "I never knew her" '. It is because of her husband's failure to understand her many literary references that Julia begins an intellectual affair with his boss the Wing Commander, a man unique in his cultish, emotional responses to reading. A similar husbandly incomprehension besets Delafield's Provincial Lady:

> I am reminded, by no means for the first time, of Edgeworthian classic, *Rosamund and the Party of Pleasure*—but literary allusions never a great success with Robert at any time, and feel sure that this is no moment for taking undue risks.[74]

Any of her repeated references to children's classics is Robert's invariable signal to retire exasperated: he is a man so immune to the delights of literature that he cannot imagine why it is necessary to pack any books at all for a trip abroad (*Diary of a Provincial Lady*, p. 211). Other men, also, are revealed as obtuse about the sort of literary pleasures the feminine middlebrow valorizes, so a male fellow novelist reveals the degree to which his reading has left him emotionally untouched:

> Incredibly lovely September morning, with white mists curling above the meadows and cobwebs glittering in the hedges, and am reminded of Pip's departure from the village early in the morning in *Great Expectations*. Ask H. H. if he knows it and he says Yes, quite well—but adds that he doesn't remember a word of it. Subject is allowed to drop.[75]

It is H. H. who finds the Greeks and Elizabethan poetry the most appropriate reading for wartime: men are presented as cold and analytical in their approaches to literature; unable to access the childlike pleasures of abandonment of self to text. It is only male children who fully devote themselves to the books they read, like the schoolboys excitedly reading after lights out in Angela Thirkell's *Summer Half* (1937), or Julia's son Oliver in *At Mrs Lippincote's* (1945), who is passionately in love with Lorna Doone, and pays a weekly homage to her in the local library, kissing the books on either side when she has been borrowed by someone else (pp. 14–15).

[74] *The Provincial Lady Goes Further*, in *The Diary of a Provincial Lady*, 165.
[75] *The Provincial Lady in Wartime*, ibid. 392.

When men in this fiction do indulge in middlebrow reading, it is invariably detective fiction to which they turn. The blocked novelist father in Dodie Smith's *I Capture the Castle* (1949) has spent ten years closeted in his turret room, reading the latest detective novels as they are delivered to him by the local librarian; the father in Diana Tutton's *Guard Your Daughters* (1953), a writer of 'literary' detective stories, is acclaimed by another male character as '*the only, really, great* detective writer there has ever been' (pp. 80–1); and the publisher George in Norman Denny's *Sweet Confusion* (1947) is described 'settl[ing] himself in front of the drawing-room fire with Agatha Christie' (p. 199). In Christie's own detective stories, the male characters are often detective fiction buffs: in *The Hollow* (1946), the victim, just before his murder by shooting, had been reading a detective story which revealed that the police could identify which gun had been used by the marks left on the bullet—a clue that sets up the expectation of his having committed suicide, with the twist being that in fact it was his wife (a much less likely reader of detective fiction) who had gleaned this information to use in her murder of him. Similarly, in one of her most ingenious stories, the 1926 *Murder of Roger Ackroyd*, the narrating doctor, who is to be infamously revealed as the murderer, dismisses at the beginning of the novel the sort of intricate crimes found in the typical detective story. For the feminine middlebrow, as for Queenie Leavis, it is clear that the detective story forms an exception to the usual run of middlebrow novels; its ratiocinative elements offering the illusion of an active, intellectually engaged reading, rather than a passive abandonment, allowing the male reader to indulge in escapist reading without experiencing a feared loss of control.

For the woman reader as imagined by the middlebrow, such a loss of control is a major part of the pleasure of reading. Literature and life become inextricably intertwined, and experiences are understood in terms of the literary events they recall. It is her occupation of this imaginative realm that the Provincial Lady's husband finds so objectionable; a poor breakfast leads inevitably to literary reminiscence: 'how impossible ever to encounter burnt porridge without vivid recollections of Jane Eyre at Lowood School', and a family picnic reminds her of *The Daisy Chain*.[76] Similarly, in *I Capture the Castle*, Cassandra understands her life entirely in terms of literature,

---

[76] *Diary of a Provincial Lady* and *The Provincial Lady Goes Further*, ibid. 14; 218.

but realizes that she often significantly distorts it as a result: her gormless swain Stephen is 'rather like how I imagine Silvius in *As You Like It*', she decides, '—but I am nothing like Phoebe' (p. 9). Her sister Rose, impressing the rich new neighbours by her slow descent of the castle staircase in a newly dyed tea-gown, is compared by Cassandra to Beatrix in Thackeray's *Henry Esmond*: 'but Beatrix didn't trip over her dress three stairs from the bottom and have to clutch at the banisters with a green-dyed hand' (p. 56). Part of the process of growing up, for this novel, is the abandonment of fantasy, and the acknowledgement that life seldom fits the patterns of fiction. The most intense literary fantasizing is seen as the province of childhood—but as something that the ideal middlebrow woman reader retains access to. Julia in *At Mrs Lippincote's* has passed her intense literary identifications on to her young son, whose passion for reading is described in startlingly physical terms:

> Oliver Davenant did not merely read books. He snuffed them up, took breaths of them into his lungs, filled his eyes with the sight of the print and his head with the sound of the words. Some emanation from the book itself poured into his bones, as if he were absorbing steady sunshine. The pages had personality. He was of the kind who cannot have a horrifying book in the room at night. He would, in fine weather, lay it upon an outside sill and close the window. Often Julia would see a book lying on his doormat. (p. 14)

It is nostalgia for such totally engaged reading that animates much middlebrow women's fiction: Judy in *Sweet Confusion* longs to recapture it: 'I'd give anything to feel as sad and lovely as I did after reading *The Prisoner of Zenda* when I was sixteen' (p. 79), and the now-grown-up narrator of *Guard Your Daughters* recalls the total imaginative engagement of childhood games based on books:

> I took the short cut home across the Common, that had seemed so big and wild when we were children. It had a few patches of ling, and used to play the part of the Heather when we were being Alan Breck and David. (p. 1)

The tacit assumption in the latter passage that the reader will recognize the reference to Stevenson's *Kidnapped* is indicative of the degree to which feminine middlebrow fiction relies on its readers possessing a shared literary and cultural background. Continual reference to other books is, as already noted, one of the key ways in which the women's middlebrow novel establishes for itself a distinctive generic identity, with different types of literature invoking particular aspects of that identity. So Victorian novels (those of Dickens and

Charlotte Brontë, and—more surprisingly—Charlotte M. Yonge, appear very frequently) suggest an adherence to traditional narrative values, while contemporary highbrow texts impart a sense of cosmopolitan gloss to the average middlebrow novel. The contemporary shock-novel such as *The Well of Loneliness* and *Lady Chatterley's Lover* is used to suggest broad-minded tolerance and an openness to new sexual mores and psychological issues. Children's classics, most notably *Little Women* (mentioned in *The Provincial Lady in Wartime*, *A Game of Hide and Seek*, *Guard Your Daughters*, and *Sweet Confusion*) gesture towards a readership that retains the childlike openness to the reading experience, and a willingness to incorporate textual fantasies into the stuff of their lives; it also contributes to the cultish quality of the middlebrow—its concern to create a body of literature that offers hidden, esoteric pleasures to a readership in the know.

Curiously, references to other contemporary middlebrow texts are rarer—with the notable exception of *Cold Comfort Farm*, which seems to have established itself as a defining classic of the genre by the 1950s and is featured in a number of novels in a manner that assumes the reader's intimate knowledge. When 'middlebrow' novels are named, they are almost invariably of a particular sort—novels that occupy the frontier territory between middlebrow and lowbrow, and are consequently roundly despised by the middlebrow 'proper'.[77] Authors such as Berta Ruck, Gilbert Frankau, and Warwick Deeping are the chosen reading of the vulgar landlady Mrs Pinsett—'a great reader'—in *Sweet Confusion*: 'she had confided to Paul that when W. J. Locke died she had felt it as the loss of a personal friend. It did not seem necessary to know more about Mrs

[77] An entertaining distinction between the two types of middlebrow novel is drawn in a letter from Kingsley Amis to Philip Larkin (couched in the monstrously coy style he habitually employed for his closest friend) in which he asks Larkin to recommend some reading for his mother ('Gilb' and 'Pam Franco' are Gilbert Frankau and his daughter Pamela, both middlebrow novelists; 'ter ruck' is presumably Berta Ruck): 'My mother would like you to do a little service for her. She doesn't know the names of enough men and ladies who put down words for people to read, and this hampers her at Boot's because they always give her the wrong ones and she doesn't find this 8 till she gets them home. Could you therefore . . . suggest a few names? People she likes are: Hilda Lewis, Philip Gibbs, Ethel Mannin, W. S. Maugham ("as long as he isn't too near the bone")? Margery Lane, Gilb or Pam Franco, and the author of 'Rebecca' (I say this is P. Franco, but she doesn't think so). People she doesn't like are: Nay-oh-mee Jay-cobb, Rue-bee airs, [del.]—ter ruck. In other words, she likes writers who pretend to write well rather than those who don't bother to pretend' (*The Letters of Kingsley Amis*, ed. Zachary Leader (London: HarperCollins, 2000), 94).

Pinsett' (p. 41). The devastating finality with which her taste in literature can be used to both define and dismiss Mrs Pinsett is ultimately a product of class. The mechanisms by which such dismissals both inform and structure the feminine middlebrow in this period form the subject of the next chapter.

2

'Not Our Sort': The Re-Formation of Middle-Class Identities

> I definitely think of myself as middle class. It is difficult to say why. I had a typical middle-class education (small private school and local secondary school). I have a middle-class job and live in a middle-class district. But none of these things would make me middle class in themselves. If I had been clever enough to get a higher post or profession, or rebellious enough to choose a more attractive manual job, I should not thereby have changed my class. Nor should I change it by living in a different district. Besides, my education and job and residence (to a certain extent) were determined by the fact that my parents were middle class—so it is like the old riddle of the hen and the egg. Income has something to do with it but it is not in itself a deciding factor nowadays as many working-class people get higher pay than the lower middle class, and many upper-class 'new poor' get less.
>
> 56-year-old female civil servant, 1949[1]

IN the years after the First World War, the middle class became increasingly self-conscious. Its members began to question their own identity, the role of their class and its future in the nation.

---

[1] From a Mass-Observation survey in January 1949; reported in an unpublished manuscript by Mollie Tarrant for a book called *Class* (undated, but clearly post-1949), p. 8. The manuscript, which is in the archive, has some interesting comments from Tom Harrisson, founder of Mass-Observation. Mollie Tarrant was a long-time Observer, who went on to become a director of the M-O archive in the 1970s.

Founded by Harrisson in the 1930s, Mass-Observation was a large-scale sociological project, designed to create an archive of public opinion on a huge range of topics. Its reports were used by public administrators and academics, as well as by advertisers and manufacturers. René Cutforth in *Later Than We Thought: A Portrait of the Thirties* (Newton Abbot: David & Charles, 1976), gave a picture of the 'mass observer', who, 'with pencil and notebook, was everywhere: he would join a dole queue to find out what, if anything, was said in those sad processions. He would sit in the midst of holidaymakers at the seaside and take down their conversations. He would record the graffiti in railway station lavatories or the tea-time small talk at a diocesan conference' (p. 74).

Sociologists, politicians, novelists, and journalists asked what it meant to be middle-class and whether the middle class was in fact more than one class. It was frequently suggested that the middle class was dying out or, alternatively, that everyone was becoming middle-class. The Mass-Observation project, established in the 1930s to collect data on the public's responses to all aspects of contemporary life, focused repeatedly on these questions, anatomizing the feelings, prejudices, and self-images of its largely middle-class panels of diarists and Mass-Observers. File reports summarized the findings under headings like 'Social Climbing' (no. 1341, July 1942) and 'Notes on Class Consciousness and Unconsciousness' (no. 1683, May 1943). Panel members demonstrated an obsessive interest in what we might call middle-classness. Asked to explain what class (if any) she saw herself as belonging to, and why, the fairly typical respondent quoted at the start of the chapter, having decided that neither job, income, education, or family alone determines her class status, enters the murkier categories of tastes, leisure and social and domestic habits as class distinguishers:

I suppose it is rather a question of being born into a family and social group with particular customs, outlook and way of life—a group, that is (in my case) in which it is normal for the children to go to a secondary school, which usually chooses 'black-coat' or professional careers, but which can't afford university education or the higher professions; which has a certain amount of leisure and culture and expects to have time for such things as books, music and social activities, but does not go in for extravagant entertainment, expensive dinners at hotels, and so on; which chooses theatre seats in the balcony or pit rather than the stalls or gallery—which lives, generally, in dining room or lounge rather than in the kitchen or in various rooms for different times of the day, which speaks and writes generally correct English, is, generally speaking, thrifty. And so on![2]

This woman reveals herself an expert at what René Cutforth called 'the universal game [of] class judgement and assessment', possessed of numerous mental categories to which to assign minute

[2] Quoted in Tarrant, *Class*, 8. I read this respondent's attitude to class as part of a pervasive anxiety about status in the period, but for an alternative view of the motives of the thousands of volunteer Mass-Observers who recorded their experiences for the archive in the period, see Tom Jeffery's article 'A Place in the Nation: The Lower Middle Class in England', in Rudy Koshar (ed.), *Splintered Classes: Politics and the Lower Middle Class in Interwar Europe* (New York: Holmes and Meier, 1990), 70–96, in which he argues that involvement with Mass-Observation had 'a vital political dimension', consonant with belonging to the Left Book Club, for a proportion of the lower middle class.

differences of behaviour in herself and others.[3] Such a detailed mental map of class indicates both intense interest in the subject, and a paranoia about it. These twin notes of fascination and fear are present in virtually all discourses about the middle class in this period.

Prominent among those discourses was the women's middlebrow novel. While it is true that virtually all the literature of the time was intensely class-conscious, the feminine middlebrow was peculiarly devoted to the anatomizing of middle-classness. Indeed, as suggested in the previous chapter, a fundamental concern with middle-class identity and taste is one of the key factors that defines the feminine middlebrow. Although there are a few male middlebrow novelists who are strongly interested in the subtle shifts and tensions of contemporary middle-class identity, it is in the women's middlebrow novel that we find the most concerted analysis of what it means to be middle class. One reason that women novelists interested themselves more fully than men in the intricacies of middle-class identities may have been that the minute adjudication of class distinctions was still considered (as it had been throughout the eighteenth and nineteenth centuries) to be a feminine activity. In a period when they mostly did not work outside the home, the class position of middle-class women was still largely determined by their fathers or husbands. Without the means to actively alter their own class position, they therefore had a vested interest in talking-up that position, or at least maintaining the social status quo. Middle-class men, on the other hand, with more opportunities of raising their social status through career advancement or the acquisition of wealth, were less interested in the battle for social ascendancy that was waged on the level of manners, taste, and speech.[4] This gendered 'take' on class seems to have transferred itself very clearly to middlebrow literature, which (as discussed in the previous chapter) operated in terms of a fairly marked gender divide. The novels of E. F. Benson, who is one of

---

[3] Cutforth, *Later Than We Thought*, 34.
[4] Most male middlebrow writers (if, as discussed in the previous chapter, the notion is not a contradiction in terms in this period) are interested in classes other than their own: the aristocracy imagined by Evelyn Waugh and P. G. Wodehouse, the working class anatomized by George Orwell and Edward Upward are more typical subjects than the middle classes, though interest in the lower middle class does increase throughout the period. (Such interest had, of course, been very strong in the years before the First World War, with writers like Wells and Shaw focusing intently on the 'clerkly' class.)

the very few exceptions to the rule, actually work to support this sense of a preoccupation with middle-classness as a peculiarly feminine concern. In his Mapp and Lucia novels, Benson animates a world in which middle-class, middle-aged women have no other concerns than their place in a precisely graduated pecking-order. In the earlier novels, his country towns of Tilling and Riseholme are dominated by the formidably snobbish Miss Mapp and the pretentiously artistic Mrs Lucas (Lucia) respectively. When Lucia moves to Tilling in the third novel of the sequence (*Mapp and Lucia*), the polite games of social one-upmanship become naked war. Although there are men in this world, they are firmly annexed by the women, weapons in their battle for pre-eminence, rather than combatants in their own right. Everything is grist to the social mill, from the size and age of houses to success at bridge and the contents of the daily shopping basket. This is an upper-middle-class world, although one character gains status from the fact that his sister is married to an Italian count, and a few working-class characters lurk unnamed around the edges of the narrative. Servants, although notionally working-class, are in fact comically superior creatures with grand names such as Foljambe and Grosvenor, endlessly propitiated because their haughtiness confirms the status of their employers. The only lower-middle-class characters are the shopkeepers, who offer venues for the daily circulation of gossip. In fact, Benson's novels function as elaborate pastiches of the concerns of the feminine middlebrow, in which the day-to-day minutiae of domestic detail, social tensions, and servant trouble tip over into surrealism. So, the refusal of a recipe becomes the excuse for spying and leads to Mapp and Lucia being washed out to sea in a freak flood on an upturned kitchen table (*Mapp and Lucia*), while exclusions from dinner parties result in bitter long-standing feuds and elaborate schemes of revenge. Benson's exuberant fantasies offer us a condensed version of the feminine middlebrow, in which social self-improvement and the continual refining of middle-class identity are imagined as the primary concerns of both characters and readers.

One reason that the middle class was subject to such intense analysis from so many quarters is because it was becoming increasingly prominent in both social and political terms. The Edwardian aristocracy had been severely weakened by the First World War, with many of its sons killed, and its fortunes reduced by death duties and increased taxation.[5] The aristocracy survived the 1920s as 'a raree-show', with a 'much diminished round of coming-out balls for debutantes . . . and the fatuous goings-on of their younger generation, the bright young things . . . the staple diet of the columns in the popular newspapers.'[6] By the 1930s, with 'the upper class more or less relegated, like Red Indians, to reservations (mostly in Scotland)', public life, manners, and codes of conduct had passed largely into the hands of the middle class.[7] It is significant that more than half of all Cabinet posts in the years between 1916 and 1935, in both Labour and Conservative administrations, were held by middle-class politicians.[8] One inevitable consequence of this rise in power of the middle class was that some of its members rose above their own class altogether. The old aristocracy was to an extent replaced by a new plutocracy which had profited by the war, consisting mostly of businessmen and manufacturers, who intermarried with the old aristocracy and turned themselves into copies of the

[5] Some historians challenge the notion that the aristocracy were largely wiped out by the First World War: John Stevenson talks of 'the myth of the lost generation', and argues that the sale of much of their lands helped some aristocratic families to rationalize their financial positions and maintain their situations after 1918, but he notes that the proportion of landowners (that is, the old aristocracy) among the most wealthy declined in the years after 1918, with a new elite of manufacturers becoming increasingly powerful. (*British Society 1914–45*, 1984, (Harmondsworth: Penguin, 1990), 331–5). A. J. P. Taylor also argued that the aristocracy survived the war with much of their wealth intact, but that the war itself changed many of them, unfitting them for a life of leisure, and leading them into employment, mainly in finance and business. The effect, he claims, was the almost complete disappearance 'of the old cleavage between landowners and capitalists' (*English History 1914–45* (Oxford: Clarendon Press, 1965), 171–2). The conclusions we can draw from these arguments are that on the one hand a new, essentially bourgeois, elite of manufacturers continued in these years to encroach on the wealth and status of the aristocracy, as it had done since the 19th century (often, of course, consolidating its position by marrying into the class it was replacing) and on the other hand the remainder of the aristocracy itself was becoming increasingly bourgeois in its way of life.
[6] Cutforth, *Later Than We Thought*, 37. [7] Ibid.
[8] The figures are John Stevenson's. Less than a quarter of Cabinet posts were held by members of the aristocracy during these years, and slightly fewer by working-class ministers (the latter mainly during Labour administrations). This compares to the figures for Cabinets from 1886 to 1916, where half of the posts were held by aristocrats, and most of the rest by members of 'old' landowning families. A large number of new aristocrats were created during the post-war years: between 1911 and 1950 420 businessmen and politicians, almost all middle-class, were made peers. Stevenson cites this figure as evidence of the residual strength of the aristocracy after World War One, but I take it rather as evidence of the increasing power of the middle class. (Stevenson, *British Society 1914–45*, 342.)

class they displaced in power (George Orwell described the thus transformed elite as 'like the knife which has had two new blades and three new handles': utterly different, and yet still in some sense the same.[9]) As well as the aristocracy *per se*, the *rentier* class of 'old' landed families was greatly affected by the war and its economic aftermath.[10] This decayed gentry was typified in letters to the newspapers and political debates by the stock figure of the impoverished widow living on rents, and is found residing in 'high-class' boarding houses in the novels of Agatha Christie and E. F. Benson. The erstwhile gentry became unmistakably middle-class in the post-war years, sliding down the social scale to join the professionals who had previously formed the upper middle class, and increasing the numerous intra-class tensions and hostilities by their presence.

As significant as the fact of the reduction in the power and presence of the aristocracy was the contemporary response to these developments. It was the deaths of aristocrats that loomed largest in many accounts of the war:

In the retreat from Mons and the first battle of Ypres perished the flower of the British aristocracy . . . In the useless slaughter of the Guards on the Somme, or the Rifle Brigade in Hooge Wood, half the great families of England, heirs of large estates and wealth, perished without a cry.[11]

We find a similarly elegiac tone in many of the country-house novels of the period, which tap into a middle-class nostalgia for a largely fantasized aristocratic past.[12] Elizabeth Bowen's *The Last September* (1929), the early novels of M. J. Farrell (1920s and 30s) and, pre-eminently, Evelyn Waugh's *Brideshead Revisited* (1945) are among the works that re-create the Great House and its personnel in their dying throes. In what is Bowen's second novel, she details the frivolous lives of Anglo-Irish aristocrats in the 1920s, as the Troubles

---

[9] George Orwell, *The Lion and the Unicorn: Socialism and the English Genius* (1941), *The Collected Essays, Journalism and Letters of George Orwell*, ii: *My Country Right or Left, 1940–1943*, ed. Sonia Orwell and Ian Angus (London: Secker & Warburg, 1968), 69.

[10] Stevenson argues that the gentry were the greatest losers from the war, stating that 'of the gentry families existing in Essex, Oxfordshire and Shropshire in the 1870s only a third maintained their country seat by 1952'. (*British Society 1914–45*, 334).

[11] Charles Masterman, *England After the War* (1922), cited in Stevenson, *British Society 1914–45*, 331.

[12] The 'country-house novel' is a recognizable generic category in this period; indeed, it seems to come into being in response to the perceived destruction of the aristocracy. I use the term to indicate something distinct from the middlebrow, though many texts belong to both categories.

go on around them. The novel combines satirical social comedy with a nostalgia for a lost way of life and lost houses. It begins with a view of the Great House and its inhabitants that would be idyllic but for the anatomizing self-consciousness of the protagonist:

> About six o'clock the sound of a motor, collected out of the wide country and narrowed under the trees of the avenue, brought the household out in excitement on to the steps. . . . In those days, girls wore crisp white skirts and transparent blouses clotted with white flowers; ribbons, threaded through with a view to appearance, appeared over their shoulders. So that Lois stood at the top of the steps looking cool and fresh; she knew how fresh she must look, like other young girls, and clasping her elbows tightly behind her back, tried hard to conceal her embarrassment. The dogs came pattering out from the hall and stood beside her; above, the vast facade of the house stared coldly over its mounting lawns. She wished she could freeze the moment and keep it always. But as the car approached, as it stopped, she stooped down and patted one of the dogs.[13]

This world is already lost at the moment of description—it is located in a vanished past, 'in those days', though the events occur in the same decade in which the novel is published. It is also illusory, it can't be captured in a snapshot image as Lois wishes, because it is a carefully constructed front: her clothes a deliberate evocation of innocence, her gaze knowing. The house, the centre of this life, does not safely enclose its occupants, but coldly endures them. These Anglo-Irish aristocrats are caught in a moment of contradiction—socializing with the English army officers garrisoned in their town, but keeping the secret of the caches of weapons stored on their land by republican tenants. Simultaneously on both sides of a conflict they cannot quite take seriously, they inevitably come to grief. The English officer Lois wants to marry is killed in an ambush, and the novel ends with the house and others of its kind set alight, as its inhabitants have their side decided for them. The house—executed, rather than destroyed—seems almost to welcome its immolation: 'above the steps, the door stood open hospitably on a furnace' (p. 206). M. J. Farrell's Irish Great Houses are also ambivalent spaces, the 'island fortress[es]' of the Anglo-Irish aristocracy, within the demesnes of which they can lead their pastiche English lives of hunting, shooting, and fishing, they are also cruel places.[14] The lonely governess in *Full House* (1935) thinks of her employers' house

[13] Elizabeth Bowen, *The Last September*, 1929 (Harmondsworth: Penguin, 1987), 7.
[14] Caroline Blackwood in the Afterword to *Full House* (London: Virago, 1988), 317.

Silverue as 'a house of sorrow' and has 'a sudden overpowering sense that those who belonged to such a place could not escape from sharing in its sorrow' (pp. 219-20). Farrell's Anglo-Irish aristocrats retreat further and further into their unhappy homes, increasingly irrelevant as a class to the world around them, living on their memories of a more glorious past.[15] *Brideshead Revisited* is, of course, the apotheosis of the novel of the lost aristocracy—its fantasy of decadent grandeur so glutinous that even its author was later to find it an embarrassment.[16] Writing in 1959, Evelyn Waugh attributed the novel's heavily portentous tone to the fact that it was written during the Second World War: 'it was a bleak period of present privation and threatening disaster—the period of soya beans and Basic English—and in consequence the book is infused with a kind of gluttony, for food and wine, for the splendours of the recent past, and for rhetorical and ornamental language, which now with a full stomach I find distasteful.'[17] The novel views the destruction and dispersal of its aristocratic family from the perspective of the middle-class narrator Charles Ryder, who is taken over by the family of his friend Sebastian Flyte, and adopts their flamboyant existence as his own. On the verge of marrying Sebastian's sister Julia at the moment when her dying father proposes to disinherit his eldest son, Charles is in sight of inheriting Brideshead himself. Although Julia calls off the wedding Charles remains the symbolic inheritor, as the novel begins and ends with him as an officer billeted on the now-deserted house, touring its rooms, and remembering the family who are now all dead or self-cloistered from the world.

It is significant that Charles both adopts the values of his aristocratic friends (their Anglo-Catholicism, their aesthetic tastes) and survives them. He represents the middle-class annexation of aristocratic culture which played a significant part in establishing new codes of middle-class identity in the period. With the aristocracy an increasingly negligible force, the upper sections of the middle class

---

[15] Indeed, they are still there in the 1980s when, as Molly Keane, she revisits them in their self-imposed exile in *Time After Time* (1983).

[16] I discuss Evelyn Waugh, as I do other male writers elsewhere, partly to contextualize the concerns of the feminine middlebrow, and partly because any division of literature on gender terms can only be provisional: while it is true to say that there are broad distinctions in the way in which male and female middlebrow writers of the period treat the issue of class, such distinctions will clearly never be absolutely exclusive.

[17] Evelyn Waugh, 1959 Preface to *Brideshead Revisited*, first published 1944 (Harmondsworth: Penguin, 1980), 7.

hijacked the notion of gentility, which then became one of the most hotly contested of all class properties:

> The values attached to the notion of gentility were aristocratic rather than bourgeois and rested on a static ideal. As a code of honour, and strategy of exclusion, it valorised birth over wealth, background and upbringing over achievement. The gentleman was celebrated not for what he did but for what he was, the lady owed her authority to manners rather than money. But it was an adjustable code, adaptable to the purposes, and the social limitations, of those who espoused it, and in the inter-war years it seems to have served a compensatory function for that large section of the middle classes who believed they had come down in the world, and were denied the respect they were due.[18]

The middlebrow women's novel annexes aristocratic identities and values in a number of ways. Association with aristocrats gives middle-class characters what Raphael Samuel calls a 'borrowed prestige' (p. 28); as Charles gains glamour and authority at Oxford because of his links with Sebastian Flyte, so Harriet Vane in Dorothy L. Sayers's 1935 *Gaudy Night* gains in status in the eyes of others through her connection with Lord Peter Wimsey. The association through friendship has the disadvantage that it can appear craven on the part of the middle-class character, something Sayers meticulously avoids by having Harriet fall over herself to avoid contact with Lord Peter through a number of previous novels, before finally succumbing to his romantic pursuit in *Gaudy Night* only when he makes it clear that he views her as an intellectual equal (with other forms of equality thereby implied).

Safer is the family connection with aristocracy, which in no way threatens upper-middle-class pride.[19] This results in the staple character of the aristocratic mother, who has lost her class with her bourgeois marriage, but still retains the glamorous associations of her family's past. Angela Thirkell is extremely fond of this device,

---
[18] Raphael Samuel, 'Middle Class Between the Wars', Part II, *New Socialist* No. 10 June/July 1983, 31. (Part I was in No. 9, Jan./Feb. 1983, and Part III in No. 11, May/June 1984).

[19] Samuel notes that 'Middle-class people in the [inter-war] period, to judge from the evidence of autobiography, seem to have traced their pedigrees from above rather than below, making the most of their more elevated ancestors, while neglecting to remember those of more humble estate. Perversely, but in a way entirely consonant with, and indeed, determined by, an aristocratic scale of values, it became a matter of family pride to be able to claim one had 'come down' in the world, since the alternative, in a highly mobile society which nevertheless valorised fixity, would have been to admit being upstarts' (Ibid. 28).

which is typified in her 1934 novel *Wild Strawberries* by the artistic, wildly eccentric Lady Emily, daughter of an Earl and married to plain 'Mr' Leslie. The Leslie family's stylish eccentricity is bestowed on them by their mother, their respectable solidity by their father. Thirkell is clearly besotted by the charming, brilliant Lady Emily, whose description tallies markedly with the jacket photograph showing the author herself with upswept hair and lace mantilla: 'she had wound her head into an elaborate turban, very becoming to her handsome haggard face with its delicate aquiline nose, thin carved lips and bright dark eyes'.[20] The novel goes out of its way, however, to make it clear that Lady Emily's aristocratic status does not transfer itself to her children, placing this misconception in the mouth of a self-important French woman, who misunderstands the intricacies of the English class system:

> 'My husband is only Mr Leslie', Lady Emily began, but was cut firmly short by a torrent of words from Madame Boulle, who was firmly convinced after studying a Debrett which she had found in the vicarage, that Martin, in virtue of being an Earl's great-grandson on his mother's side, would naturally come into a baronetcy at his father's death. Lady Emily and Agnes tried to explain, but were overwhelmed by Madame Boulle's display of knowledge. It appeared that she had in her youth been a governess in English families of the highest distinction, and since her marriage had continually received scions of the nobility as paying-guests. (p. 133)

In fact, the Leslie family have no desire to claim aristocratic rank, being well satisfied with the leaven in the bourgeois lump provided by Lady Emily herself. Such a family background allows them to feel comfortably superior to both other members of the upper middle class and the aristocracy: they are more genteel than one (and demonstrably so, as their mother possesses her own title), and more practical than the other. It is notable that both other characters and Thirkell herself seem to feel that these aristocratic mothers are better taken only in small doses—they are dizzily other-worldly, and portrayed as comic rather than impressive in their devotion to the tracing of genealogies, and recalling of past splendours (these being the only points of characterization of the mother in another novel, *Summer Half* (1937)). In *To the Lighthouse*, the novel (as suggested in the previous chapter) in which she approaches closest to middle-brow concerns, Virginia Woolf places Mrs Ramsay in a similarly

---

[20] Angela Thirkell, *Wild Strawberries*, 1934 (Harmondsworth: Penguin, 1954), 16–17.

hybrid class position, bourgeois in life-style and attitudes, but descended from the aristocracy: 'for had she not in her veins the blood of that very noble, if slightly mythical Italian house, whose daughters, scattered about English drawing-rooms in the nineteenth century, had lisped so charmingly, had stormed so wildly, and all her wit and her bearing and her temper came from them, and not from the sluggish English, or the cold Scotch.'[21] This background leads Mrs Ramsay to feel 'half grudging, some respect' for 'the great in birth' (p. 14), but only because she shares their descent: it is made clear that she feels inferior to no one.

The figure of the toady, who applies himself to the cultivation of the aristocracy, is frequently employed to highlight by contrast the easy terms of equality felt by the central characters towards even the most exalted. So *Wild Strawberries* contains Mr Holt, who had devoted his life to 'the art of pleasing his superiors' (p. 41), studying gardening to ingratiate himself with upper-class ladies, and acting as a conduit of tantalizing gossip. A hangover from Edwardian days, Mr Holt is a sadly pathetic figure, becoming more of a bore as his looks and powers of entertaining diminish, passed around from house to house only out of the charity of his hostesses, and ignored and resented by their other guests. Nancy Mitford's *Love in a Cold Climate* (1949) centres on the fortunes of two toadies and their rival methods of ingratiation. This device allows her novel to ridicule snobbery, but also indulge in it; the opening sentence sets the tone with the announcement that: 'I am obliged to begin this story with a brief account of the Hampton Family, because it is necessary to emphasize the fact once and for all that the Hamptons were very grand as well as very rich.'[22] Lord Hampton's brother-in-law, Boy Dougdale, is the first of the toadies: passionately interested in the aristocracy 'his great talent for snobbishness and small talent for literature have produced three detailed studies of his wife's forebears' (p. 155). His rival is the flamboyantly camp colonial Cedric, a distant cousin in favour of whom the furious Lord Mountdore disinherits his daughter Polly when she marries the ageing Boy. Cedric's power of fascination lies in his passionate appreciation of the beauty and luxury of Hampton, and his ability to transform the

[21] Virginia Woolf, *To the Lighthouse*, 1927 (Oxford: Oxford University Press, 1992), 14–15.
[22] Nancy Mitford, *Love in a Cold Climate*, 1949, in *The Nancy Mitford Omnibus* (Harmondsworth: Penguin, 1986), 155.

Mountdores into creatures of cosmopolitan glamour. Mitford's novel is unusual in that the toadies triumph, and Cedric at the end triumphantly bears off to Paris not just Lady Mountdore, but also Boy, with whom he has fallen in love. The novel ends with the middle classes, as represented by the ghastly Borely clan, firmly routed, and appears to be offering a picture of the aristocracy enduring. But it is significant that it is Cedric who has breathed new life into the Mountdores by remaking them in his own image: the son of Lord Mountdore's black-sheep second cousin several times removed and his elderly Canadian nurse, Cedric is so déclassé as to be almost without class, and has reinvented himself as a European sophisticate. As in Mitford's other novels, the future for the remnants of the British aristocracy lies in self-imposed exile in France, not in their own country. Her aristocrats are clowns, their eccentricities played up for the delectation of the middle-class reader, their snobberies—and those of their author—always carefully comic.

Another sort of toady who figures in the feminine middlebrow is the servant. Angela Thirkell's *Summer Half* (1937) has several, notably a butler and a nanny. Simnet, butler for the headmaster of Southbridge school, was once a scout at an Oxford college, but left his post when the new Master started writing for the evening papers:

'There has been a sad come-down of late, sir, in Oxford. Presidents and Masters of Colleges courting publicity in a way that cheapens Us, sir.'[23]

Simnet's prestige is all borrowed, but he has the dignity of absolute self-assurance, having completely internalized the values of the aristocracy. His importance is that he can innocently make statements about class that the upper middle classes cannot make for themselves: thus it is he who underlines the protagonist's connection with the aristocracy: ' "I remember you well, sir, and the High Old Times, if you will excuse the expression, you and the Honourable Mr Norris used to have" ' (p. 42). He is so well imbued with upper-class values that he functions as a virtual guarantor of the gentility of others: ' "the moment I set eyes on you last Saturday week, I said to myself: That is Mr Keith . . . and he is a gentleman" ' (p. 42), yet because his characterization is knowingly in the comic-servant mould, we are asked to believe that concern with such class distinctions is beneath those to whom they are applied. Simnet is necessary

---

[23] Angela Thirkell, *Summer Half*, 1937 (Harmondsworth: Penguin, 1951), 42.

because, in the codes of gentility the middle class was in the process of assuming, a gentleman could not announce himself to be such without forfeiting his own gentility. The Keiths' old nanny serves a similar function, her devotion confirming the rank of the family:

> Mrs Twicker had the old Nanny's passion for gentry children, and welcomed them with as much joy as if they had once been babies in her charge. Of her own children, who were all out in the world, she never had thought much, owing to their parentage, though she had treated them with the impartial kindness due from the upper classes to the lower. (p.189)

This image of the old retainer, so strongly identified with the interests of her employers that her own independent life holds little interest for her, is a fantasy that held particular sway in the inter-war years as the servant class gradually disappeared (an issue discussed in detail in the next chapter). The grotesquery of this Aunt-Jemima-like figure can be attributed to the unconscious hostility that entered mistress–servant relationships in these years, as middle-class women became more and more frustrated with the reluctant service they obtained from the few servants that were still available. Nanny is a fantasy of a sort of glorified machine, without needs or interests of her own, entirely devoted to her employers, and endlessly available to reconfirm their gentility. Her devotion, like Simnet's snobbery, is not represented as something required by the upper middle classes: it is rather a benign eccentricity which they kindly tolerate. In fact, Nanny is hardly an employee at all: married to the gardener, she lives a kind of half-life on the edge of the estate, until reanimated by the arrival of 'gentry children'. The work she is occasioned by having visiting schoolboys as lodgers is represented not as a job, but as pure enjoyment: 'On Monday morning Mrs Twicker, who never let public holidays interfere with her pleasures, had the washing in soak by six o'clock' (p. 239).[24] The values Nanny admires in the gentry are significantly aristocratic rather than middle-class: 'the boys then

---

[24] We find a remarkable pastiche of this old retainer figure in the housekeeper, Matchett, in Elizabeth Bowen's 1938 novel *The Death of the Heart*. Passed on to Thomas and Anna from Thomas's mother, Matchett is a family servant of the pre-war variety, but she is devoted not to the family, but to its furniture, which she has cared for and loved for decades. For Bowen, such a genuine feeling for places and objects and their history is a mark of strength of character, and Matchett, unlike the vicious or stupid servants in other middlebrow novels of the period, is the moral centre of the novel. Possessed of formidable dignity, Matchett is the only point of solidity in the novel, showing up her employers' concerns as trivial and heartless, and rescuing the teenage protagonist, Portia, from despair at the end of the novel.

chopped wood for the copper fire, and lighted it with a ruinous expenditure of matches and paper which shocked and yet pleased Mrs Twicker, as showing that the gentry still possessed the combination of incompetence and wastefulness which she so much admired' (p. 239). What looks like a joke at the expense of the gentry is, in fact, an insistence that it is not yet middle class, though Nanny's desire for reassurance on this point indicates the fear of the inevitable fall.

The middle-class adoption of aristocratic values was about far more than social climbing: it was an indication that the middle class was in the process of replacing the aristocracy in social, political, and economic significance. We find a sense of middle-class social primacy reflected in a tendency to patronize the aristocracy: to view its remnants as entertaining misfits, social dinosaurs whose time has passed. This is a theme constantly repeated in *Punch*, that bastion of middle-class prejudices. In inter-war editions of the magazine, jokes and comments about class invariably turn on the contrast between middle-class and aristocratic life-styles, with the aristocracy always coming off worst. In the issue of 3 August 1938, there is a Thomas Derrick cartoon stretching over two pages, entitled 'HER PEOPLE / HIS PEOPLE', showing a young couple visiting each other's parents.[25] Hers are middle class and jolly, captured in the middle of tea round the sitting-room fire, with brothers lounging on the table, the mother cheerily brandishing a kettle, and everyone rushing forward to welcome the bemused young man. His are aristocratic, depicted in a chilly formal hall, looking down their noses and through their monocles at their son's girlfriend, watched over by an equally supercilious ancestral portrait on the wall. Where the middle-class family serve themselves tea, the aristocrats are furnished with a grand butler. Even the family pets reflect the class of their owners: the aristocrats' dog a haughty setter; the middle-class pets an eager Scottie and fawning tabby. The message is abundantly clear—the middle classes are relaxed, easy, and welcoming; the aristocrats cold, snobbish, and trapped in the past. A similar message is conveyed in a comic verse called 'Smartness' in the 2 November issue of the same year, which caricatures the lives of socialites: 'I envy those ones | With their fussed-over sons . . . The people, I mean, | In last week's magazine'. The lifestyle, pretensions, and language of the

[25] *Punch*, cxcv, 122–3.

upper class are roundly mocked, and the verse ends, scansion abandoned in an access of sincerity 'I wish I were able | To be one without being bored', summing up a profoundly middle-class sense of the superiority of a quietist, respectable, home-based existence.[26] We find a similar middle-class patronizing of aristocrats in a number of middlebrow women's novels. The ghastly Lady B. attempts to put down E. M. Delafield's Provincial Lady, who adopts a mocking attitude in response:

> Lady B. calls in the afternoon—not, as might have been expected, to see if I am in bed with pneumonia, but to ask if I will help at a Bazaar early in May. Further enquiry reveals that it is in aid of Party Funds. I say What Party? (Am well aware of Lady B.'s political views, but resent having it taken for granted that mine are the same—which they are not.)
>
> Lady B. says she is Surprised. Later on she says Look at the Russians, and even, Look at the Pope. I find myself telling her to Look at Unemployment—none of which gets us any further....
>
> Escort Lady B. to the hall-door, she tells me that the oak dresser would look better on the other side of the hall, and that it is a mistake to put walnut and mahogany in the same room. Her last word is that she will Write, about the bazaar. Relieve my feelings by waving small red flag belonging to Vicky, which is lying on the Hall-stand, and saying A la lanterne! as chauffeur drives off.[27]

The Provincial Lady always emerges best from such encounters because of her saving irony: her ability to laugh at herself is presented as the most endearingly unstuffy of middle-class values, and at odds with the pomposity and arrogance of Lady B. The Provincial Lady is never cowed by her aristocratic neighbour, and is seen to endure her irritating attentions rather than actively seek her out. Mrs Miniver, as Alison Light notes, is also gently mocking of the aristocracy: ' "How unpleasing, musically, is the sound of a pack of upper-class English voices in full cry"; though one numbers them among one's friends, the aristocracy are "museum pieces" who live their lives in "inverted commas" and shiver in badly heated, barnlike, homes.'[28]

---

[26] *Punch*, cxcv, 482.

[27] E. M. Delafield, *Diary of a Provincial Lady* (1930), reissued, with other novels in the series, as *The Diary of a Provincial Lady* (London: Virago, 1984), 35.

[28] Alison Light, *Forever England: Femininity, Literature and Conservatism Between the Wars* (London: Routledge, 1991), 129, quoting Jan Struther, *Mrs Miniver*, 1939 (London: Virago, 1989), 11. Light sees Mrs Miniver's mockery of the aristocracy as unusual: 'Mrs Miniver's patronage of the nobility must have been pure pleasure to her readers' (129), while I would suggest that she is actually expressing a representative middle-class disdain.

Raphael Samuel states that 'the intelligentsia of the [inter-war] period were captivated by the idea of "society", both in its metropolitan and its country-house phases', turning themselves into 'court-jesters of the Mayfair rich' and 'ventriloquists of its accents'.[29] The 'intelligentsia' he cites include Evelyn Waugh and Dornford Yates, Freddie Lonsdale and Noel Coward, all fairly popular (rather than highbrow) writers, and all men. While he may well be right about middlebrow male writers (and one can add others such as Wodehouse and Huxley to the list), female middlebrow writers were very far from being captivated by aristocratic excesses, but rather sought to annex certain aristocratic qualities and status for the use of the middle classes. Theirs is not a fawning literature, but rather a subtle denuding of the aristocracy: Agatha Christie's actresses and retired colonels moving into and modernizing the big country houses,[30] the Provincial Lady and Mrs Miniver laughing at their aristocratic friends, Angela Thirkell's professionalized gentry, all represent a middle class taking what it wants of aristocratic values and happily discarding the rest. In its confidence about this process, its absolute assurance of (upper-) middle-class social ascendance, the feminine middlebrow adopts a positively triumphalist attitude to class.

There was, however, another side of the coin: those who believed they had come down in the world were not only the decayed gentry, but those large numbers of the traditional middle class who had suffered economically as a result of the war. It was not only the extremely wealthy who were affected by the high rates of income tax, surtax, and death duties which were introduced during the war and maintained at nearly the same levels afterwards: a sizeable proportion of the upper middle class found their standard of living considerably reduced from its pre-war levels.[31] Those most afflicted were in the income bracket £300–£600 a year—'people such as head and senior teachers, bank managers, accountants, civil service

---

[29] Samuel, 'Middle Class between The Wars', Part II, 30.

[30] I am grateful to Alison Light for this point: she remarks that Christie's country houses 'seem mainly to interest the writer at the point at which they are no longer inhabited by aristocrats but are modernised by the middle classes.' (*Forever England*, 80).

[31] A. J. P. Taylor notes that 'a rich man paid 8 per cent of his income in tax before the war, one third of it after'. The less than startling net result, for the nation, was that 'between the wars taxation transferred something like 5 per cent of the national income from rich to poor, or perhaps rather less' (*English History 1914–45*, 176).

Executive Officers, and chemists and professional engineers in mid career'.[32] Increases in prices in the 1920s consolidated the problem, and the plight of the middle-class 'new poor' began to be documented. Writing in 1922 one commentator graphically depicted the economic fall of a section of the middle class: 'the general impression is of a whole body of decent citizens slipping down by inexorable God-made or man-made or Devil-made laws into the Abyss as if a table were suddenly tilted and all the little dolls or marionettes were sent sliding to the floor.'[33] The newspapers were flooded with letters in which middle-class people detailed the expedients to which poverty had reduced them:

My wife goes 'sticking'. That saves the expense of firewood. Our holidays are generally imaginary. That saves too. My wife gets bargains at remnant sales, and rhubarb in the garden does yeoman service. Also my wife murders her eyes with sewing, sewing, sewing. Saving is out of the question.

The maid has gone long since. A charwoman one day a week is hired, and all the washing is done at home. I clean the boots and wash up before nine o'clock office. I wash up after midday dinner. I mend most of the boots and shoes and cut the boys' hair . . . We are exhausting our stock of clothing, china, etc., and what renewals are made are the cheapest possible. . . . Food, always plain, is still plain—but now sometimes not enough—not enough milk, butter and fruit. I neither smoke nor drink intoxicants. Friends have sent cast-off clothing for the children . . .[34]

While it is clear that many members of the middle class found their standards of living significantly reduced in the years immediately after the First World War, prices fell and incomes rose in the later 1920s and 1930s, and most historians agree that the middle class as a whole was actually better off in the inter-war years than it had been previously.[35] In the years during and after the Second World War, however, middle class standards of living dropped once again, as a result first of wartime privations and second of the actions of the new Labour Government of 1945, which introduced

---

[32] Alan A. Jackson, *The Middle Classes 1900–1950* (Nairn: David St John Thomas, 1991), 27–8.
[33] Charles Masterman, *England After the War* (1922), 62–3. Quoted in Roy Lewis and Angus Maude, *The English Middle Classes* (London: Phoenix House, 1949), 78.
[34] Part of a symposium of letters published by the *Daily News*, quoted in Masterman, *England After the War*, 62–3, in Lewis and Maude, *The English Middle Classes*, 77.
[35] 'For the British middle classes, these fifty years (1900–1950) saw further refinements in comfort and privileges as their increasingly pervasive influence rose to new strength' (Jackson, *The Middle Classes 1900–1950*, 6).

compulsory national insurance, increased taxation, and ensured that 'for the first time in British history the brunt of an economic crisis [was] not borne by the workers'.[36] Contemporary statistics suggested that salary earners as a group were 20 per cent worse off in 1947 than in 1938.[37] Most Mass-Observation panel members reporting in the late 1940s felt they were considerably affected by the present cost of living, with only one in five owning themselves to be economically unscathed.[38] Again, there were fears of people losing class as a result of these economic privations: surveying the reports of panel members, Mollie Tarrant, the author of an unpublished book called *Class* for Mass-Observation, worried about the 'many middle class [people who] may now [be] arbitrarily displaced from the group which they still feel themselves [to] belong to, and whose mores they are still helping develop and establish'.[39]

Such anxieties about loss of financial status across the four decades from 1920 to 1959 may seem to undermine the notion of the increased prominence of the middle class in this period. As a number of contemporaries noted, however, the post-1918 middle class enjoyed a larger social and political significance regardless of any alteration in its members' economic circumstances: 'amid pressures, official and unofficial, political and economic, the middle classes not only continue to exist but to exert a prestige value out of all proportion to their powers as an economic group.'[40] For George Orwell, writing in 1941, wealth was no longer a prerequisite for power; the future belonged to the large class of managers and technicians which ran modern industry rather than to the old-style property owners.[41] Still more important than increases in authority and status, however, was the massive increase in size of the middle class in this period. It was somewhat augmented from above, as members of the upper class lost caste with property and incomes, but most significant was the influx from below. The number of salaried workers in private employment in the United Kingdom nearly tripled between 1911 and 1921 (from one million to two and three quarters, representing a rise from 12 to 20 per cent of the employed population). Civil servants more than doubled in number

---

[36] An American observer, Herbert L. Matthews, writing in the *New York Times*, 25 Nov. 1947, quoted in Lewis and Maude, *The English Middle Classes*, 95.
[37] Tarrant, *Class*, page unnumbered, ch. 3. This figure takes into account a 68 per cent rise in prices in the period.
[38] Ibid.   [39] Ibid. 4–5.   [40] Ibid. 3.
[41] Orwell, *The Lion and the Unicorn, Collected Essays, Journalism and Letters*, ii, 76.

between 1914 and 1921, and those in local government increased even more.[42] Most of these new 'white collar workers' were drawn from the working class; their middle-class status now determined by factors such as salaried employment, expectation of advancement, a pension, stability of employment, and 'respectability':

> These council school teachers, technicians, shop managers, sales managers, commercial travellers and, above all, clerks, usually came from a working-class background but once on the first rung of the middle-class ladder, they managed their financial affairs with care and frugality, so that they were able, ever more successfully, by saving and salaried job holding, to achieve secure middle-class status.[43]

This newly enlarged lower middle class had a striking effect on the landscape of the country, as it was its members who occupied most of the new suburbs springing up on the outskirts of every town and along arterial roads: 'all England became suburban except for the slums at one extreme and the Pennine moors at the other.'[44] These were the housing developments whose architecture was condemned by Osbert Lancaster as 'By-Pass Variegated', and which were roundly reviled by John Betjeman, but they changed the lives of millions of people in the years between the wars by providing them with electricity, gas, bathrooms, and indoor lavatories. For a number of contemporary commentators, these suburbs were the sign of a significant national transformation: travelling on his *English Journey* in 1933, J. B. Priestley found two old Englands— the shires and the industrial towns—but also an unexpected third England 'which appeared haphazard and in unexpected places, the England of the twentieth century, shapeless, unplanned, yet representing the ideal towards which all Englishmen unconsciously moved'.[45] This was the England of suburban ribbon developments, where birth rates were declining, everyone owned or aspired to own a motor car, and entertainment was provided by the wireless, dance halls, and 'the talkies'. George Orwell wrote of the same England in 1941:

> The place to look for the germs of the future England is in light-industry areas and along the arterial roads. In Slough, Dagenham, Barnet,

---
[42] Figures from A. L. Bowley and J. Stamp, *The National Income 1924* (1927), quoted in Jackson, *The Middle Classes 1900–1950*, 14; also from Taylor, *English History 1914–45*, 173.
[43] Jackson, *The Middle Classes 1900–1950*, 17.
[44] Taylor, *English History 1914–45*, 167–8.   [45] Ibid. 30.

Letchworth, Hayes—everywhere, indeed, on the outskirts of great towns—the old pattern is gradually changing into something new. In those vast new wildernesses of glass and brick the sharp distinctions of the older kind of town, with its slums and mansions, or of the country, with its manor-houses and squalid cottages, no longer exists. There are wide graduations of income, but it is the same kind of life that is being lived at different levels, in labour-saving flats or council houses, along the concrete roads and in the naked democracy of the swimming pool.[46]

Novels offer us remarkably few representations of the new, suburban lower-middle-class life, which we find most clearly depicted in autobiographical accounts such as John Osborne's *A Better Class of Person*.[47] Osborne's family were highly typical in their move from Fulham to the suburbs in the 1930s, and his descriptions of the 'Bankclerk's Tudor' and pebbledashed modernism of Stoneleigh provide us with fascinating details of a way of life that few others troubled to record (pp. 38–40). But Osborne's is the meticulous attention of the satirist: the sophistication of the cream and black decor in the Show House rented by his parents; the determined privacy and inwardness of the suburban way of life are elaborated with his trademark anger and contempt. Even the apparently blameless pleasures and rituals of his grandmother are treated with withering scorn:

She must have achieved almost exactly what she wanted: a nice Early Night, a nice Early Life. It was certainly easy, easy and empty of spirit. She personified the terrible sin of sloth at its most paltry. Not the sloth of despair in the face of God. Despair would be like staying up spiritually too late. Every afternoon of this replete lifetime of self-conceit and cosseting, a bit of toffee or butterscotch went down a treat with Warwick Deeping. (p. 48)

It is notable that it is his grandmother's standards of comfort and enjoyment that Osborne finds so risible, since it is precisely this access to leisure—the bourgeois right to relax—that the lower middle class had so recently acquired. Osborne's contempt for his own class, which looked so radical in his plays of the 1950s, can also be seen as simply a turning inward of the contempt felt by the upper middle class for the lower. His reviling of the smug contentment and small horizons of the new suburbs certainly echoes the responses we

---

[46] Orwell, *The Lion and the Unicorn, The Collected Essays, Journalism and Letters*, ii, 77.
[47] John Osborne, *A Better Class of Person: An Autobiography 1929–1956* (Harmondsworth: Penguin, 1982).

find in the middlebrow literature of the period. Although very few middlebrow writers depict lower-middle-class life in its own terms, a number express a thinly disguised loathing and fear of the encroaching lower middle classes. So Evelyn Waugh's *Brideshead Revisited* begins and ends with the spectre of 'the age of Hooper' destroying the centuries of labour that had built Brideshead. Hooper, one of Charles Ryder's platoon commanders, is 'a sallow youth with hair combed back, without parting, from his forehead, and a flat, Midland accent'. Despised by the colonel for his lack of discipline, and disliked by the men for his inefficiency and overfamiliarity, the lower-middle-class Hooper represents the future for Charles:

> In the weeks that we were together Hooper became a symbol to me of Young England, so that whenever I read some public utterance proclaiming what Youth demanded in the Future and what the world owed to Youth, I would test these general statements by substituting 'Hooper' and seeing if they still seemed plausible. Thus in the dark hour before reveille I sometimes pondered: 'Hooper Rallies', 'Hooper Hostels', 'International Hooper Cooperation', and 'the Religion of Hooper'. He was the acid test of all these alloys. (p.15)

Although Charles professes a vague liking for Hooper, the future he symbolizes is clearly represented as a grimly mediocre one. Hooper hardly exists as a character: he is necessary as a symbol because Waugh requires someone to blame for the loss of the aristocracy and its culture. Hooper stands for the thoughtless, cultureless hordes of the lower middle class, caught between classes, neither masters nor men, disorganized and over-casual, yet in the grip of a hopeless admiration for bureaucracy and commercialism:

> Though himself a man to whom one could not confidently entrust the simplest duty, he had an over-mastering regard for efficiency and, drawing on his modest commercial experience, he would sometimes say of the ways of the Army in pay and supply and the use of 'man-hours': 'They couldn't get away with that in business.' (p. 15)

We find a similar scapegoating of the lower middle class in Dorothy L. Sayers's *Gaudy Night*, in which the action revolves around a campaign of hate-mail in an Oxford women's college. The students are away at the time of the first incidents, so suspicion rests on the dons and the scouts. Harriet Vane, an ex-student of the college and a mystery writer, who becomes involved in the investigation, early rules out the scouts on the grounds that one of the notes contains a Latin tag with which working-class women could not possibly be familiar. Most of the novel therefore concentrates on the eccentricities and rivalries of the women academics, but the denouement reveals that the culprit was, in fact, a scout, Annie, who is crucially lower middle class. The daughter of the keeper of a genteel boarding-house, Annie had married a young academic who was one of her mother's tenants. He had killed himself when found out in an act of scholarly deceit, leaving Annie a widow with two small children, forced by necessity to work as a college servant. Her hate-mail and threats are directed at the woman responsible for exposing her husband's deceit. With its bourgeois-feminist agenda of proving that women can work together as scholars, the novel stigmatizes the 'womanly woman' who sublimates her own needs to those of her husband, equating such an ideology with that of Nazi Germany. Such retrogressive attitudes are seen as essentially lower-middle-class, with the upper-middle-class woman typically pursuing intellectual and professional independence. Virginia Woolf similarly separates the upper from the lower middle classes on the grounds of imaginative freedom: Mrs Ramsay despises her husband's young colleague Charles Tansley for his inability to 'feel right' about the idea of going to the circus. Although he opens his heart to her about the privations of his lower-middle-class childhood (father a chemist, nine brothers and sisters, 'he himself had paid his own way since he was thirteen'), Mrs Ramsay still holds back sympathy, judging his 'stiff parched words', and ultimately condemning him, in the most devastatingly final of upper-middle-class dismissals, as an 'odious little man' when he tells her son that it will not be possible to go to the lighthouse tomorrow.[48]

One of very few sympathetic representations of the lower middle classes in the fiction of the period is in Elizabeth Bowen's *The Death of the Heart* (1938).[49] The Heccomb household in Seale-on-Sea, where the teenage protagonist, Portia, is sent to stay when her brother and his wife go abroad for the summer, is assertively lower-middle-class. It is nominally headed by Mrs Heccomb, the ex-governess of Portia's sister-in-law, Anna, and is tyrannized over by

[48] Woolf, *To the Lighthouse*, 18–22.
[49] Elizabeth Bowen's work, with its writerly qualities and philosophical concerns, is located at the highbrow end of the middlebrow. Her novels nevertheless share many of the typical preoccupations and stylistic features of the feminine middlebrow.

the adult children of her late husband, a doctor. The first description of the house is through Portia's class-innocent eyes, but it nevertheless overflows with class signifiers:

> The sun porch, into which she hastily looked, held some basket chairs and an empty aquarium. At one end of the room, an extravagant fire fluttered on brown glazed tiles; the wireless cabinet was the most glossy of all. Opposite the windows a glass-fronted bookcase, full but with a remarkably locked look, chiefly served to reflect the marine view. A dark blue chenille curtain, faded in lighter streaks, muffled an arch that might lead to the stairs. In other parts of the room, Portia's humble glances discovered such objects as a scarlet portable gramophone, a tray with a painting outfit, a half-painted lamp shade, a mountain of magazines. Two armchairs and a settee, with crumpled bottoms, made a square round the fire, and there was a gate-legged table, already set for tea. It was set for tea, but the cake plates were still empty—Mrs Heccomb was tipping cakes out of paper bags.
>
> Outside, the sea went on with its independent sighing, but still seemed an annexe of the living-room. Portia, laying her gloves on an armchair, got the feeling that there was room for everyone here. She learned later that Daphne called this the lounge.[50]

The modern tiled fireplace, the locked show bookcase, and the shop-bought cakes are all fairly conventional signals of a lower-middle-class life-style. What is remarkable about this description is the degree to which it also captures the pleasure and comfort of this life-style; the room is full of the devices of leisure: the wireless, the gramophone (startlingly modern in its scarlet casing), magazines, and hobbies. This is a house for leisure in its very location: on the seafront, so that the sea itself seems part of the house and its pleasures. The inmates of the house are devoted to the pursuit of enjoyment, with Daphne and Dickie, Mrs Heccomb's stepchildren, following a round of impromptu dances (in the lounge, with the carpet rolled back), cinema visits, and walks and drives with crowds of friends. For Portia, accustomed to the cheap European hotels she had lived in with her mother, and the chilly grandeur of her brother's Regency house on the edge of Regent's Park, the Heccomb's Waikiki is a place not of vulgarity, but of unfamiliar comfort. The statement that Daphne called the living-room the lounge is multi-purpose: it is the clearest signifier of the Heccomb's lower-middle-classness for any reader who has been unable to read

---

[50] Elizabeth Bowen, *The Death of the Heart*, 1938 (Harmondsworth: Penguin, 1962), 134.

the more subtle indications; but it also figures the extent to which Portia is adrift in unfamiliar territory, having to learn the native usages. Most significantly, though, it returns to the word its fullest meaning: the room is called the lounge not because the Heccombs know no better, but because they lounge in it. The lower middle class is depicted in this novel as the class with the greatest talent for, and appreciation of, leisure: perhaps because they had so recently achieved it.

It is significant that it is Daphne who attaches the name lounge to the room, because it places this naming as an act of self-assertion. Daphne is an active apologist for her class, and harbours a strong dislike for Portia's sister-in-law, Anna, whom she hardly knows. The novel names this as a specifically class-based antagonism, directed at Anna because she is upper-middle-class. Daphne, we are told, 'had a grudging regard for the upper class' and 'delighted to honour what she was perfectly happy not to have', but 'she did not (rightly) consider Anna properly upper class' (p. 144). It is because Anna has privilege and property without the undeniable rank that would have clearly separated her from Daphne, that Daphne so resents her:

> She considered that Anna had got more than she ought. She thought Anna gave herself airs. . . . Had Anna had a title this might have been less bitter. (p. 144)

This dislike shapes Daphne's character: she deliberately defines herself in opposition to Anna: 'in so far as anything had influenced Daphne's evolution, it had been the wish to behave and speak on all occasions as Anna would not' (p. 144). This representation of an active lower-middle-class dislike and resentment of the upper middle class is virtually unique in middlebrow women's fiction, at least before the Second World War. In this regard, Bowen's novel is unusually sympathetic to lower-middle-class interests; it is notable, however, that once Daphne becomes hostile to Portia, that sympathy is removed. Horrified when Portia asks her why she has been holding hands with Portia's friend Eddie in the cinema, Daphne launches into a frenzied counter-attack, in which she reveals herself to be guilty of all the vulgarity and mean-mindedness of which she accuses Portia:

> Daphne's reaction time was not quick: it took her about two seconds to go rigid all over on the chaise longue. Then her eyes ran together, her features thickened: there was a pause in which she slowly diluted Portia's appalling

remark. In that pause, the civilization of Waikiki seemed to rock on its base. When Daphne spoke again her voice had a rasping note, as though the moral sound box had cracked.

'Now look here', she said . . . 'there's no reason for you to be vulgar. . . . I don't wish to blow my own trumpet, I never have, but one thing I will say is that I'm not a cat, and I'd never put in my oar with a girl friend's boy friend. But the moment you brought that boy here, I could see in a moment anybody could have him. It's written all over him. He can't even pass the salt without using his eyes. . . . I had no idea you were so *common*, and nor had Mumsie the least idea, I'm sure, or she wouldn't have ever obliged your sister-in-law by having you to stop here, convenient or not. (pp. 203–4)

It is a veritable explosion of the sort of language the upper middle class considered irredeemably coarse. To use words such as 'vulgar' and 'common' was in itself an act of vulgarity. It is the first time the novel has systematically caricatured Daphne's speech, and it is designed to remove all readerly sympathy for her. Even Daphne's features change as she becomes a sort of monster of bad taste. It is notable that it is Portia's innocent questions about her flirtation that provoke this remarkable response: what is being demonstrated is the stranglehold notions of gentility have over Daphne and her culture: she is quite happy to flirt with Eddie, but it rocks her values to the core to have it talked about. The upper-middle-class characters, in contrast, are much more open about their dalliances, because less concerned to prove a gentility that they largely take for granted. Although unusually willing to represent lower-middle-class culture on its own terms, even this novel represents relations between the upper and lower middle classes as fundamentally hostile. In this regard, the feminine middlebrow was profoundly at odds with the optimism of certain cultural commentators, who welcomed the expansion of the lower middle class as heralding the erasure of class differences.

For George Orwell, the new England he had identified was distinguished by its essential classlessness, its inhabitants were 'people of indeterminate social class: something that had never existed in England [before 1918]': they were 'the people who are most at home in and most definitely *of* the modern world, the technicians and the higher-paid skilled workers, the airmen and their mechanics, the radio experts, film producers, popular journalists and industrial chemists'. This new, modern class gave hope of the end of the class system: 'they are the indeterminate stratum at which the older class distinctions are beginning to break down.'[51] While writers such as Orwell and Priestley were excited by these developments, for many of the traditional middle class, the huge expansion of their class from below was very disturbing. Mollie Tarrant saw the increase in numbers as a dilution of the middle class, worrying that 'far more people are anxious to claim middle-class status than any economic criteria would allow', and, like Orwell, suggesting that the effect of the expansion was, paradoxically, to weaken the middle class:

> The middle classes, as historically understood, are experiencing a two-fold diminution at the present time: through restriction, where privilege has depended on the possession of capital, and inversely through political extension of group privileges to the nation as a whole.[52]

The Mass-Observation panel members whose attitudes she collated were also mostly fearful and confused about what was happening to their class, bemoaning 'the indecisive, amorphous character of middle class groupings at the present time', and the fact that 'class distinctions are far less marked than they used to be'. One heartfelt lament, couched in heavily class-laden language, sums up the paranoia felt by many middle-class people as old class certainties dissolved before their eyes: 'today we are all mixed up: the poor, the well-to-do, the vulgar, the refined, are everywhere' (p. 8). By the mid-1950s the feared dilution of middle-classness was more or less complete:

> The years around the middle of the century really did mark a turning point, after which things would never be quite the same again for the middle classes, their values and their way of life, even though some . . . characteristics . . . have endured. After the early fifties, the high standards of comfort were no longer the privilege of a visibly disparate minority, becoming much more widely spread; within a few more years, as one of Alan Ayckbourn's characters points out, almost everyone not already middle class appeared to be striving for that status in some degree.[53]

Far from giving up easily, however, the upper middle class went down into the swamp of egalitarianism kicking and screaming, its snobbery becoming both more intense and more rarified, as it sought to construct codes of belonging that the usurpers could not crack.

[51] Orwell, *The Lion and the Unicorn*, *The Collected Essays, Journalism and Letters*, ii, 77–8.
[52] Tarrant, *Class*, 7–8.   [53] Jackson, *The Middle Classes 1900–1950*, 6.

It was the paradoxical result of the massive expansion of the middle class that the divisions within the class became more marked. It becomes increasingly difficult, when considering this period, to speak of the middle class as a single unity: the conventional division into upper and lower middle class goes some way towards reflecting the actuality of class identities in a time in which, as Raphael Samuel has noted, 'the clergyman's widow, in reduced circumstances, would not make friends with the elementary school teacher, though she might have her round for tea' and where 'Barristers and solicitors inhabited separate universes, the one a refuge for impecunious gentlemen, the other a summit of ambition for the tradesman's brightest son'.[54] It would be more accurate, however, to see middle-class identity in these years operating not so much as a binary system but as a pyramidal structure, in which, as Evelyn Waugh puts it 'everyone thinks he is a gentleman . . . [and] everyone draws the line of demarcation immediately below his own heels'.[55] Middle-class identity and status became a matter of contest, and with numerous axes of division available, it was a contest that could never ultimately be decided:

Class was so inextricably bound up with notions of status that it is almost impossible to delineate the infinite gradations which might be applied. Occupation, background, education, habits of speech, dress and recreation could combine in kaleidoscopic fashion to produce an impossibly complex set of steps in the social structure.[56]

Even this pyramidal model does not fully explain the complexities of class identity in the period, as it implies that an individual had a fixed position that could eventually be ascertained through a complex analysis of a wide range of material and cultural factors. An individual's class position, in fact, depended very much on who was judging him. In understanding class identity in the period we might usefully bear in mind P. N. Furbank's contention that class is a system relying inevitably on the perspective of a classifier, whose judgements are necessarily relative. He asserts that rather than class-based language being neutral, it is invariably a transaction: by assigning someone to a class you are assigning yourself and your

[54] Samuel, 'Middle Class between the Wars', Part I, 30.
[55] Evelyn Waugh, 'An Open Letter to the Honourable Mrs Peter Rodd (Nancy Mitford) on a very serious subject', *Noblesse Oblige*, ed. Nancy Mitford, 1956 (Harmondsworth: Penguin, 1968), 67.
[56] Stevenson, *British Society 1914–45*, 342.

listeners to a class also.[57] Alison Light makes a similar point, arguing that 'being "middle-class" in fact depends on an extremely anxious production of endless discriminations between people who are constantly assessing each others' standing' and that to understand class in the period between the wars it is necessary to 'restore the feeling of temporality to class distinctions along with a sense of their fertility.'[58] Different sections of the middle class had different rules for inclusion and exclusion, and their own minutely graded snobberies and smugnesses: as Raphael Samuel points out, there were acute class distinctions felt between bank clerks and insurance agents; doctors and opticians; painters and writers.[59] Middle-class identity was therefore essentially fluid and shifting: 'there is no stable middle class identity, only different variations of unsureness and self-assertions, and different membership qualifications.'[60] René Cutforth best sums up the significance of the continual patrolling of intra-middle-class divisions that went on in this period:

> The universal game was class assessment and judgement, as it had been in England for a very long time. You presented your 'all present and correct' act for inspection and duly inspected the inspector. I think it's true to say, though it makes me sad to think of it, that for millions of people in England in the Thirties, to score well at this game was the chief reason for existence.... What made the game more complicated was that different middle-class sections played it by different rules. In the matter of what was done and what was not done, every white-collared Englishman daily walked a tightrope over a deadly chasm.[61]

Paradoxically, however, it was precisely because of the sprawling complexity of middle-class identities in the period that contemporaries retained a firm attachment to the binary model of a middle class split into upper and lower sections. In an era when almost every member of the middle class experienced grave anxieties about their class status, there was something deeply seductive in a mode of thinking about class that allowed you to confirm your own status by ruling others out. Hence the prevalence of phrases such as 'PLU' ('people like us'), 'not

[57] P. N. Furbank, *Unholy Pleasure or the Idea of Social Class* (Oxford: Oxford University Press, 1985), 14.
[58] Light, *Forever England*, 13.
[59] 'The middle class between the wars was less a class than a society of orders each with its own exclusion rituals and status ideology, jealously guarding a more or less self-contained existence, and exquisitely graded according to a hierarchy of ranks' (Samuel, 'Middle Class Between the Wars', Part I, 30).
[60] Light, *Forever England*, 132. [61] Cutforth, *Later Than We Thought*, 34–7.

our sort', and 'not one of us'. The meanings of 'upper-middle-class' and 'lower-middle-class' or their coded equivalents were entirely dependent on who was doing the categorizing. Very few people whom sociologists would categorize as lower-middle-class would have used the term of themselves; they would generally have described themselves as simply 'middle-class'. Conversely, virtually everyone who employed one of the many genteel euphemisms for 'upper-middle-class' considered themselves to belong to this category. Hence 'upper-middle-class' usually means 'people like me', and 'lower-middle-class' 'people I am anxious to distinguish myself from'. Despite the reductive and slippery nature of these categories, they remain vital to an understanding of middle-class identity in the period, as long as we retain a sense of their fundamentally provisional nature.

The factors by which class positions could be asserted and ascertained were legion, ranging from fairly solid material determinants such as income, property, work, education, accent, and family background, to the often crucial minutiae of taste, manners, dress, forms of entertainment, and tricks of speech. Sociologists both at the time and later have made repeated attempts to equate class status with a measurable combination of one or more of these factors, but without much success.[62] This is in part because the 'game' consisted in trumping opponents with increasingly rarefied signifiers of belonging, or alternately, in ruling out entirely the grounds on which they claimed to belong. Descent from an 'old' family, for example, could be used to trump wealth as vulgar and arriviste, while 'bad', casual manners counted in some circles as authentically haute-bourgeois and superior to an over-careful refinement that savoured of lower-middle-classness. The very act of discovering new class signifiers was often used to denote upper-middle-class insouciance, functioning as a sort of amusingly outré party game. Roy Lewis and Angus Maude, the authors of a 1949 survey of *The English Middle Classes* provide a probably tongue-in-cheek example at the beginning of their lengthy sociological and historical analysis, where they offer a formulation of class distinctions that is persuasive precisely because of its audacious reductiveness:

Before the war, when textile supplies and laundry facilities were more ample, it might perhaps have been held that the middle classes were composed of all

[62] See Furbank, *Unholy Pleasure or the Idea of Social Class* for an entertaining attack on these attempts as fundamentally misguided.

those who used napkin rings (on the grounds that the working class did not use table napkins at all, while members of the upper class used a clean napkin at each meal), and that the dividing line between the upper-middle and lower-middle classes was at the point at which a napkin became a serviette.[63]

The most successful extension of this game was Nancy Mitford's humorous but devastatingly influential prescription of 'U' and 'non-U' linguistic usages ('U' for 'Upper Class') in her 1956 essay 'The English Aristocracy'.[64] Here she adopts the analysis and terminology of a sociolinguist, Professor Alan Ross, to describe the English upper-class use of language as an exclusive code denoting membership of their caste. Crucially, she does not restrict membership of that caste to the aristocracy, arguing that due to the English system of primogeniture, the 'upper class' is significantly larger than that of the ennobled aristocracy. The division she wants to draw is, in fact, not between the aristocracy and the middle class in general, but one between the upper middle class and the other ranks of the middle class:

> Most of the peers share the education, usage, and point of view of a vast upper middle class, but the upper middle class does not, in its turn, merge imperceptibly into the middle class. There is a very definite border line, easily recognisable by hundreds of small but significant landmarks. (p. 37)

In its eagerness to draw that firm dividing line beneath the upper middle class, Mitford's teasing essay is precisely of its time. The Second World War had introduced both the inter-class camaraderie of service life and American cultural influences, which had contributed to the breakdown of the upper-middle-class cultural hegemony begun before the war. By the later 1950s, the lower middle class, typified by the bright grammar school boy, was clearly in the social ascendancy; Jimmy Porter was the new social as well as literary model, and the upper middle class was panicking in retreat.

Mitford's essay serves to confirm the primary place accorded to language in the range of exclusive class-signifiers with which the upper middle classes sought to bolster their social dominance. But language was a double-edged sword: code words could be learned and accents acquired by the determined social climber, a process greatly aided by the careful diction and received pronunciation of the BBC announcers of the period. In fact, by revealing 'U' usages

---

[63] Lewis and Maude, *The English Middle Classes*, 13.
[64] In *Noblesse Oblige*, ed. Mitford.

(though some are deliberately out of date), Mitford is contributing, probably knowingly, to this very process. A lower-middle-class reader, made privy to the crucial 'U' signifiers, could then count herself among those in the inner circle. It is a form of snobbery that works to undo itself. Alison Light makes a similar point about the paradoxical accessibility of rarified linguistic signifiers in the novels of Ivy Compton-Burnett, arguing that their use of language is an essentially modern phenomenon: 'it had at once the appearance of exclusivity and yet, like elocution lessons, was easily learnt.'

Like the modulated tones on the new wireless programmes, these voices in the air were modern productions ironically undercutting the relation between speaker and knowable social place, turning communication into the art of mimicry and claims to social status into a species of ventriloquy. They guaranteed too a kind of elevation whose snobberies were paradoxically open to all: all one needed to do was to speak with the right accent, to learn, as Compton-Burnett had done herself, to talk properly. (p. 47)

It was not out of perversity that those anxious to confirm their own upper-middle-class status by excluding others increasingly placed their trust in such ephemeral signifiers as language and manners: it was because other forms of social differentiation were rapidly disappearing.

The many changes to middle-class identity had a significant impact on middle-class culture in these decades. The traditional self-confident outward-looking ethos of the upper middle class had been eroded by the decline of empire as well as by economic factors. Now the traditional middle classes looked inward, retreating to the home, where they placed new emphasis on leisure, developing a cultish interest in bridge, crossword puzzles, and detective fiction. At the same time, the new, 'modern' middle-class culture of the suburbs was becoming increasingly dominant. This was a culture based on consumerism, funded by increased incomes and the new availability of mortgages and hire-purchase, centred on the motor-car and the cinema. For Orwell it was 'a rather restless, cultureless life, centring round tinned food, *Picture Post*, the radio and the internal combustion engine', yet for him it clearly represented the future.[65] With other commentators, he notes a levelling out in contemporary culture, with rich and poor increasingly wearing the same clothes,

---

[65] Orwell, *The Lion and the Unicorn*, *The Collected Essays, Journalism and Letters*, ii, 77–8.

and eating the same food. In particular, books, films, and radio programmes crossed class divides, uniting the nation with a common culture. Culturally as well as economically, everyone was becoming middle class. This was a fearful prospect for many of the upper middle class, particularly since it looked as if everyone was becoming *lower* middle class. They mounted their resistance to this levelling down of middle-class culture on a number of fronts, often by inverting the terms of social success as they had previously prevailed. In the face of increasing lower-middle-class prosperity, for instance, they elevated the thrift that was a newly essential part of their own lives from tiresome privation into elegant simplicity.[66] If the lower middle classes had money to burn, then how much classier it must be to refrain from spending, to patch your old clothes rather than buying new ones. Such turning of the tables on the massed ranks of the lower middle class was one of the major ways in which the upper middle class maintained what cultural authority it had in this period.

The middlebrow novel proved a significant arena for such conflicts. As Raphael Samuel has noted, an 'embattled sense of caste . . . seems not only to inform but actually to structure the literature of the time'.[67] The middlebrow novel in particular was one of the spaces in which there was an attempt to establish upper-middle-class concerns and values as hegemonic. While middlebrow novels were read by a wide cross-section of the middle classes, their authors were almost invariably upper middle class, or at least considered themselves to be so (in fact, the writing of fiction would virtually serve to confer upper-middle-class status). These writers needed to perform the complex balancing act of attracting readers from the whole of the middle class, while writing of the modes and manners of upper-middle-class life. The middlebrow novel accomplished this by functioning as a form of conduct literature, educating lower-middle-class readers in the rules of haute-bourgeois discourse and behaviour while simultaneously creating a sense of intimacy designed to make them feel already a part of that exclusive club to

---

[66] Mollie Tarrant notes that 'the frustrations of living in a servantless, rationed and queue controlled world . . . were not entirely without their compensations' for many of the traditional middle class: 'the simplicities of present day entertaining, shopping triumphs snatched from defeat, the juggling of ends and means, the increasing domestication of sons and husbands have been for many middle class women at least, gains rather than losses' (*Class*, 60).
[67] Samuel, 'Middle Class between the Wars', Part I, 30.

which they were assumed to aspire. The lower-middle-class reader was treated as if she was already conversant with upper-middle-class attitudes, manners, and prejudices, and because privy to this class's disdain for lower-middle-class 'vulgarities', was presumed not to be guilty of such herself. At the same time, she was given access to a number of those crucial signifiers that each class jealously guarded from those beneath it, in order that she could improve herself. Although invariably contemptuous of lower-middle-class characters within their pages, these novels were curiously generous to the bulk of their readers: they were seeking not to exclude them, but to transform them into passable simulacra of the upper middle class, and so ensure the continuity of the culture and values of that class. It is significant that the most extended snobberies in these novels are about *acquirable* class signifiers, such as language, manners, and behaviour, rather than social fixities such as occupation, family background, and education. In this regard they are simultaneously exclusive and accommodating, allowing anyone admittance to the upper-middle-class club as long as they are prepared to learn its rules.

In essence, the feminine middlebrow contributed to the creation of a whole network of newly defined common values and interests which served to unite the middle class, but also attempted to establish upper-middle-class concerns as culturally dominant. It also kept pace with the changing historical circumstances of this class. An examination of four representative women's middlebrow novels from each of the decades from the 1920s to the 1950s allows us to witness an increasing preoccupation with middle-class identities in general, and the cultural and social status of the upper middle class in particular. The mutating form of attitudes to middle-classness can be mapped even in the titles of these novels: Winifred Holtby's 1924 *The Crowded Street* is concerned with the social claustrophobia produced by an early twentieth-century bourgeois respectability that is still more or less Victorian in structure; the middle classes depicted less than a decade later in Rachel Ferguson's *The Brontës Went to Woolworths* (1931) are much less respectable, and a great deal more embattled, devoting themselves to subtle and elaborate games of one-upmanship, represented by the sort of highbrow slumming the title denotes. The Second World War, in Elizabeth Bowen's 1949 *The Heat of the Day* acts as a fiery crucible in which class identities and values are reassessed in the light of the pressing concerns of the immediate present; by the 1950s the upper middle class was in retreat, increasingly strident in the assertion of its values, and demonstrating the sort of paranoia denoted by the title of Diane Tutton's 1953 *Guard Your Daughters*.

The Crowded Street is, like many of Winifred Holtby's novels, semi-autobiographical. Set in Yorkshire, it spans a period from 1900 to 1920, depicting a world in which middle-class girls are slowly submerged beneath a weight of stultifying respectability, until offered a sort of freedom by the war. It is a world that still has parallels with the Brontës' Yorkshire of a century earlier, where middle-class girls must devote all their efforts to securing a husband, where the life of a spinster is one of shamed sequestration and trivial domestic tasks. Class is the overriding concern of the Yorkshire village of Marshington, where every inhabitant can be placed on a precisely calibrated scale of status by the middle-class women who devote every waking moment to campaigns designed to raise their own family's social position. The broad distinctions of class are instantly apparent, with houses and dress establishing clear lines of demarcation:

> Everyone, positively everyone, was there. The Avenue in ready-made crepe de Chine, and ditto suits; the village, in cotton voile and muslin and reachmedowns; the Houses, resplendent in charmeuse and foulard and, even occasionally, in morning coats.[68]

The lower-middle-class inhabitants of the Avenue are automatically excluded from significance by the self-appointed ladies who matter, who are themselves ranked in clear sequential order, with the old-gentry Neale family of unquestioned prominence as a result of their land and family connections.

The novel's protagonist, Muriel Hammond, lives under the heavy yoke of class-based constraints. Her mother, the offspring of a family devoted to the concept of Birth—'All Bennets had the gift of tracing genealogies by faith rather than sight. A naive confidence in the magic of Birth dignified a curiosity that arose not from snobbishness alone' (p. 25), is felt to have married beneath herself by choosing the son of a wealthy self-made tradesman. The young Rachel Hammond's efforts to 'recapture the social ground she had forfeited by marrying Dick Hammond's son' (p. 22) are described like a military campaign at the start of the novel:

[68] Winifred Holtby, *The Crowded Street*, 1924 (London: Virago, 1984), 259.

The death of her father-in-law had made it a little easier for Rachel Hammond to live down the origins of his son, but even by 1903 she still spoke with deference to Mrs Marshall Gurney, and never passed the new store on the site of the old oil-shop without a shudder. She kept her difficulties to herself, and no one but her sister Beatrice knew how great at times had been the travail of her soul. Beatrice alone stood by her when she ignored the early callers from the Avenue and the Terrace. No small amount of courage had enabled a young bride to refuse the proffered friendship of auctioneers' wives and the Nonconformist section of the village, when refusal might have meant perpetual isolation. Old Dick Hammond had been a mighty witness before the Lord among the Primitives; but for a whole year of nerve-racking anxiety his daughter-in-law sat in the new house that he had built, awaiting the calls of that Upper Marshington to whom Church was a symbol of social salvation, and Chapel of more than ecclesiastical Nonconformity. (p.23)

Establishing a significant class position is represented by this novel as a matter of determined social rejection and exclusion; of ruling others out in order that you might be ruled in, so one woman resigns from the Conservative Club Committee because another, a publican's wife, is elected Treasurer. The taint Rachel Hammond has to expunge from her husband is that of 'trade': as anathema to the genteel ladies of early twentieth-century Marshington as to their Victorian counterparts. But there are signs that the world is changing: the respectable doctor Mrs Hammond has lined up for her younger daughter instead marries the grocer's daughter, whose existence Mrs Hammond has never deigned to notice. Though depending on matters of family background and husband's occupation, class is also carried in a myriad of tiny signifiers: so the impregnable social status of the Neale family is indicated by the rusty awkward bell at Weare Grange which is 'one of the most powerful defences of that social fortress', and Muriel learns that attention to the smallest aspects of dress and behaviour is crucial:

It really mattered. To have a belt that fastened firmly onto one's new serge skirt. . . . She was travelling in a land of which she only imperfectly understood the language . . . and yet the eye of the All-Seeing could hardly have been more observant than the eye of People, who measured worth by the difference between a cotton and a linen handkerchief. (p. 44)

The ultimate aim for the upper-middle-class social climbers of Marshington is not to be seen as middle class at all. The culmination of Mrs Hammond's long climb is reached when she befriends 'an Honourable' and can at last dare to be rude to the Marshington ladies—'the relief, after so many years of restraint, was immense' (p. 96). The ladies' desire to escape the middle class is clearly understood by the local schoolteacher:

'Now girls', announced Mrs Hancock. She never called her pupils 'young ladies', having informed their parents that this savoured of middle-class gentility. They, anxious to fling off the least suspicion of resemblance to the class to which they almost all belonged, had approved with emphasis. (p. 31)

Class-consciousness and social climbing are seen as feminine affairs, and daughters are key to the successful pursuit of status, their lives consisting of little but grooming for marriage. The novel details the empty years in which Muriel, the Hammond's shy and awkward elder daughter, sits waiting for her life proper to begin, as all around her other girls achieve the 'sex-success' that is their only worth in the eyes of Marshington. Following the logic of this measure of female value, Muriel's younger sister rebels with a wartime affair with a soldier that results in her pregnancy, shot-gun marriage to another man whom she despises, immurement in the Wuthering-Heights-like environment of her in-laws' farm, and finally death before the child is born. Muriel herself follows the line of least resistance, not even taking up the war-work that offers escape to other girls. Her salvation finally comes in the figure of her more dynamic friend Delia, who offers her a home and post in London as her assistant. Delia works for the Reform League, an organization seeking to unite women of all classes in social and political work: 'a great society run by women . . . to try to draw all classes into social service, by clubs and settlements in every town where mill girls might meet with daughters of barristers or squires . . . to carry out political propaganda for the purposes of forcing through social legislation' (p. 243). It is significant that the Reform League overtly challenges the distinctions of class that have ruled—and ruined— Muriel's life so far. The crowning irony comes with her return visit home, when her new gloss of confidence and sophistication attracts Godfrey Neale, the great catch of Marshington, whom she has long hopelessly desired. With her new vision of a wider world she realizes that Godfrey's attraction lies mainly in his status and property, and refuses him, thus finally renouncing the values of the town. It is notable that the novel's feminism is precisely couched in terms of class, and that its fantasy is of a future in which women can unite across class divisions.

It is a future that has certainly not been attained by the 1930s, when attitudes to class have become distinctly less Victorian but, if anything, even more embattled. The upper-middle-class Carne family in *The Brontës Went to Woolworths* are seriously bohemian: the eldest daughter, Deirdre, works as a journalist and her younger sister is training as an actress. Their lives are considerably freer than those of Muriel Hammond and her sister, but they are still heavily circumscribed by family loyalties and rituals. The three sisters and their shadowy mother are intensely inward-looking as a family, devoting much of their time to the playing of elaborate fantasy games. They live surrounded by the creatures of their imaginations: as Deirdre explains, 'meals in our family are usually eaten amid a cloud of witnesses, unless there are visitors'.[69] These witnesses are fantasy images of real-life public figures, and include a music-hall comic, a pierrot, and—most importantly—a High Court judge, who eventually makes the transition from fantasy-status to reality when Deirdre befriends his wife at a charity fair. The novel makes little attempt to differentiate between fantasy and reality, and it takes several chapters for the reader to be sure that at least half the characters actually exist in the realm of fantasy. The family's despised and brow-beaten governesses never do fully grasp the intricacies of the game, and thus mark themselves as hopeless outsiders—classiness in this novel is defined almost exclusively in terms of superior powers of imagination.

The novel is notable for the overtness of its treatment of class, which is a key element in all of the Carne family's fantasies. They imagine Mildred Toddington, the wife of the judge, as of a lower class than her husband—'Mildred [is not] as top-shelfish as you think she is. After all . . . Brockley is anybody's name' (pp. 40–1)—and they enjoy conjuring up situations in which her solecisms grate on her husband's sensibilities. Class, except when it impacts closely on the life of the family, is an amusing game; indeed, part of the way in which the family's daring modernity is figured is in the ease, levity, and openness with which they address the whole subject. The middle sister Katrine, for instance, is thrilled at the prospect of going back-stage at the Music Hall because of the opportunity of hearing non-U language:

[69] Rachel Ferguson, *The Brontës Went to Woolworths*, 1931 (London: Virago, 1988), 28.

Katrine whispered ecstatically, 'Oh, will somebody say "Pleased to meet you" to us? 'All of them', I replied, 'and what the answer is, I haven't the faintest idea. It's like when people say "God bless you"; one doesn't know whether to say "Don't mention it", "Not at all", or "The same to you".' (p. 46)

The Carnes extend their fascination with the linguistic usages of other classes into an elaborate game, based on what they consider to be the verbal infelicities of their friend Freddie Pipson, a music hall comedian whom Deirdre has met through her journalism:

The latest Carne joke, it appeared, was to say 'Pleased to meet you', whenever they passed each other on the stairs, and to do what they described as 'pipsoning' at meal-times. Deirdre would say, 'If you'll pardon me, Mrs Carne, you're commencing to cut the beef wrongly, if you know what I mean', and Katrine would reply, 'If I'm not robbing *you*, may I ask you to pass the cruet?' then both together would enquire, 'Is your tea as you like it?' And even Shiel would call out, 'Don't spill it, Miss Carne; if I may pass the remark, whatever are you doing?' (p. 112)

Their governess's objection to the unkindness of this mockery is sternly countered by Deirdre's assertion that it is a mark of their affection for Pipson, but it clearly, also, reveals an obsessive concern with a whole host of class-dividers in linguistic usage. Although the issue is ostensibly one of different sorts of phatic utterances—'pleased to meet you' is merely a lower-middle-class version of the upper-middle-class 'how do you do'—what is most significant about this string of pipsonisms is the degree to which they express interest in others: warmth, concern, and engagement. There is a strong suggestion that they are incorrect because they indicate an over-involvement that runs counter to the increasingly strong notes of stiff unconcern and closely-guarded privacy that characterized the upper-middle-class life of the time.

The Carnes' relationship with Freddie Pipson results from the dedicated slumming that is a key part of their self-conscious bohemianism. Our first introduction to him draws attention primarily to his class, through Deirdre's expressions of supreme tolerance:

Comedians are far more elastic in their higher reaches [than chorus girls], and think of plenty of things, and are apt to collect artistic objects far above their station, and are usually thoroughly good sorts and not a bit the 'laddie type'.... Pipson is a wonder. He is the only justification I know for that dreadful phrase, 'One of Nature's gentlemen'. He has everything except birth, and if he ever marries, his wife will be a lucky and blessèd woman. (p. 44)

In fact, Deirdre's tolerance comes back to haunt her, for when Pipson gets Katrine a job in a revue chorus the two of them fall in love. In answer to Katrine's plaintive, 'Deiry, *could* one marry Freddie?' (p. 218), Deirdre replies with an outburst positively eugenic in its opposition to inter-class marriages:

I wrote: 'Katrine, my Plainest, it can't be done. We are both born snobs and disbelieve in marrying out of our class, and sooner or later you'd begin to resent the situation. I've seen some of his relations, you know, in the dressing-room. One of them is called Sidney, and looks it, and he says "Naow" and "Haow" and lives at Herne Hill. ... Your children would be a ghastly toss-up. They *might* be like us, but can you see a daughter with Freddie's nose?' (p. 219)

It is notable that the most serious objection to Freddie is not his own upper-working-class status, but the pseudo-gentility of his lower-middle-class relative Sidney: Deirdre's strongest dissuasion to Katrine is that Sidney would be on first name terms with her if she married Freddie. Deirdre makes her attack—which is, of course, successful—in the full knowledge of Freddie's charms—'Oh, what a husband and father and lover were there' (p. 221), and admitting that 'if there weren't so many Ifs about on both sides I'd have loved a week with him at sunny Bognor Regis in the past' (p. 220).

Flirtations with working-class men—a sort of sexual slumming—are one of the ways in which upper-middle-class girls enact a bohemian cool in these novels. There is a similar scenario in E. Arnot Robertson's 1933 *Ordinary Families*, where the closest childhood friendship of the middle-class Lallie is with a local boy, Ted Mawley, who shares her interest in wildlife. Her physical appreciation of Ted's beauty, born with her adolescence, is cut brutally short by her family's teasing about the time they spend together in a bird-watching hide:

And I remembered exactly how we had lain; and where my body had touched his—the young fineness of this had somehow become part of the rising tide of disgust and interest flowing through my mind—and the times when one or both of us shifted to relieve cramp and his head or hand had come in contact with mine ... A mould of nastiness grew over the bright recollection not only of this day but of many similar hours. The skin of his shoulder, whiter than mine, had little gold hairs and almost purple lights in it, I remembered from the summer, hating the memory. Oh, but Ted with his clod face and coarse hands was surely unthinkable in the way they were making me think of him![70]

The mixture of physical attraction and repulsion expressed here seems to be precisely a product of Ted's class and the differences between them. Like Deirdre, Lallie expresses the most active sexual desire she admits to in response to a working-class man. In both cases, sexual desire is apparently admissible because it is so impossible. But the middle-class girls in these scenarios crucially maintain the upper hand, never allowing the flirtation to become serious, as this could fundamentally challenge their own class status. Lallie is complicit in destroying her nascent feelings for Ted through the brutal family humour that focuses on their class differences, as she too can see the impossibility of the desire she has just recognized:

Father led the good-natured teasing, doing a funny love-scene in which Ted's amorous yearnings were bellowed in broad Suffolk dialect, and my replies called for a shy falsetto of refinement. Mother and I joined fervently in the laughter. And in laughter dissolved my long, untroubled friendship with Ted. (p. 165)

Such scenes, in which working-class men are both sexualized and dismissed, are in fact one of the very few ways in which the working class figures at all in middlebrow women's fiction. The only major exception is servants (the largely hostile depiction of whom is discussed in the next chapter). This omission is remarkable in a period that saw the General Strike, the rise of mass movements throughout Europe, and the birth of the Welfare State, all events that developed an already-existing middle-class paranoia about the threat represented by the working class. While many male writers were deeply preoccupied by the working class, their female equivalents seem to have reserved their paranoia for those whom they saw as more closely encroaching on their own class position.

The major class tension in Ferguson's novel, therefore, is that between the Carnes and the youngest daughter's governess, Agatha Martin. Agatha's class position is precisely in the middle of the middle class—she is the daughter of a lower-ranking army officer from Cheltenham. Deirdre thinks that she feels great sympathy for Miss Martin, imagining the sadness of the day when 'Captain Martin

---

[70] E. Arnot Robertson, *Ordinary Families*, 1933 (London: Virago, 1982), 163–4.

broke it to his daughters that they must clear out and earn', but her real feeling is irritation with Miss Martin's reproachful presence in the household—'will one never be allowed to possess oneself in peace?' (p. 18). She feels cursed by her sympathetic twinges towards the governess, and obliged to seek her out, but is eventually reassured to discover that 'the creature, cornered, simply isn't there' (p. 58). One of the subtleties of the novel is the fluctuating distance it establishes between its own and Deirdre's moral positions, so that Deirdre's snobberies are sometimes beguilingly honest, and sometimes gratuitously cruel. At the end of the novel, we are allowed access to Miss Martin's damning perspective on the Carnes, though the novel does not simply switch its sympathies at this point; we continue to feel, with Deirdre, the provoking nature of Miss Martin's flustered gentilities. More tellingly, in a novel intensely preoccupied with the figures of the Brontë sisters, it is Miss Martin, not the sophisticated and creative Carnes, who is in the end associated with the Brontës. Her family history echoes theirs as the daughters of an improvident father, forced to work as governesses. Her final fate of companionate social labour with her beloved curate is that which Jane Eyre avoids, but which Charlotte Brontë herself finally succumbed to. These parallels are supported by the fact that the Brontës themselves are interested in Miss Martin. Their ghosts contact her, not the Carne sisters, at a table-turning in Yorkshire, and visit the house in London to persuade her to leave her thankless job. Their allegiance with Miss Martin is one of class, something that Deirdre, seeing them as part of her own aristocracy of creative talent, simply fails to comprehend: 'Miss Martin certainly hadn't deserved this, confound her' (p. 194).

The distinction between Agatha Martin's class position and the Carnes' is further underlined by their attitudes to the class of others. In a notable episode, Miss Martin is revealed as simultaneously more snobbish and less adept at reading class than the Carnes. Freddie Pipson is again the instigator of profound class-based emotions:

> He had come to tea a week ago—driven up in an immense car, and had been treated altogether as an equal by his hostess and her daughters. Agatha had made the terrible mistake of liking him, in spite of his accent and grammar. He had been most attentive and polite, and by his abstention from bad language or calls for beer, had given her no clue whatsoever as to who or what he was . . . she assume[d] he was some business magnate of such longstanding that his beginnings were purged. (pp. 109–10)

Miss Martin is closer in class to Pipson, and therefore much more fearful of what he represents, imagining the beer and swearing that is for her the inevitable concomitant of a working-class man. Despite liking Freddie, she feels it necessary to the establishment of her own class position to make it clear that she has recognized the signs of his lower class status: 'Later, Agatha delicately approached the subject of the departed guest . . . "A charming man, but—would one say he was *quite* a gentleman?" ' (p. 111). But this is a game she cannot win: the very gentility of her hesitation allows her to be decisively wrong-footed by Deirdre's brash negative—' "Pipson? A gentleman? . . . he's a low comedian" ' (p. 111), which simultaneously asserts that his status is so self-evident as not to require comment, and establishes the Carnes as so sophisticated that they don't have to restrict their guests to those of gentle rank. The issue of class-consciousness thus serves to separate the Carnes decisively from Agatha Martin and the sort of studied respectability she represents. Their combination of snobbery and bohemian tolerance is established paradoxically as the most haute-bourgeois of social attitudes. In the intricacies of its class distinctions, their dependence on superior powers of imagination and taste rather than on solid material differences, *The Brontës Went to Woolworths* is part of a concerted upper-middle-class endeavour to permanently exclude the increasing numbers of the lower middle class; but in its hesitancies about the Carnes' snobberies, and its partial sympathies for their despised governess, it allows itself some distance from this most conservative of projects.

Elizabeth Bowen's 1949 novel, *The Heat of the Day*, is set during the Second World War, at a time when, it is conventionally believed, class barriers were broken down. Bowen's novel is, indeed, interested in the social promiscuity that resulted from the upheavals of the war, but class remains a significant index of characterization and instrument of plot. The setting is a London strangely deserted by the respectable, in which the single and eccentric of all classes mingle freely. The protagonist, Stella Rodney, a middle-aged widow with a son in the army, lives alone in a furnished flat, enjoying the freedom to conduct a love affair unobserved. Sexual and social liberation that could only be hinted at by Ferguson's characters is taken for granted by the denizens of this new, surreal London, living with the ever-present threat of death:

[A]mong the crowds still eating, drinking, working, travelling, halting, there began to be an instinctive movement to break down indifference while there was still time. The wall between the living and the living became less solid as the wall between the living and the dead thinned. In that September transparency people became transparent, only to be located by the just darker flicker of their hearts. Strangers saying 'Good night, good luck', to each other at street corners, as the sky first blanched then faded with evening, each hoped not to die that night, still more not to die unknown.[71]

Desperate to be known and acknowledged, the novel's characters hound each other in a curious chain of need, so the novel opens with the lower-middle-class Louie attempting to pick up the enigmatic Harrison at an outdoor concert, and then follows Harrison to Stella's flat, where he begins his campaign to infiltrate himself into her life. Stella, in turn, is devoted to her lover Robert, whose seemingly straightforward exterior turns out to mask dark secrets.

Despite the apparent relaxing of social distinctions, class is a significant element in the establishment of character in the novel, though notably only the characters of women. While women are precisely defined by the class position they inherit from their families, men are cut curiously free from class constraints, existing in a sort of existential present in which they reinvent themselves daily. Stella, whose 'extraction was from a class that has taken an unexpected number of generations to die out—gentry till lately owning, still recollecting, land' (p. 115) is notable for her reticence and self-control: 'the habit of guardedness was growing on her, as on many other people, reinforcing what was in her an existing bent: she never had asked much, for dislike of being in turn asked' (p. 26). In this she contrasts with the lower-middle-class Louie (whose parents had 'done well with their little business, or shop, at Ashford' (p. 16)), whose only remarkable feature is a large mouth, caked with lipstick: 'a mouth that blurted rather than spoke, a mouth incontinent and at the same time artless'. In the context of wartime paranoia ('Keep mum—she's not so dumb!' warned the posters), the art of keeping one's own counsel was strongly valued, but in fact reticence, along with other forms of verbal control, functioned as a key upper-middle-class signifier throughout the whole period.

If Stella and Louie represent the poles of middle-class identity, the family of Stella's lover, Robert, occupy the centre. The Kelways are not only the essence of middle-classness, but the essence of Englishness:

---

[71] Elizabeth Bowen, *The Heat of the Day*, 1949 (Harmondsworth: Penguin, 1962), 92.

The English, she could only tell herself, were extraordinary—for if this were not England she did not know what it was. You could not account for this family headed by Mrs Kelway by simply saying that it was middle class, because that left you asking, middle of what? She saw the Kelways suspended in the middle of nothing. She could envisage them so suspended when there *was* nothing more. Always without a quiver as to their state. Their economy could not be plumbed: their effect was moral. (p. 114)

If the term 'middle middle class' signifies anything (and we do find it used in the period), it is the Kelways.[72] Their comfortable, self-contained life-style combines the pleasure-seeking convenience culture of the rising lower middle class, and the solidity and retreat of the upper middle class. As always with Bowen's fiction, the most striking indications of character—particularly those of women—are carried in the highly detailed descriptions of houses. Holme Dene, the Kelway's Home Counties house, dates from 1900 and 'combine[s] half-timbering with bow and french-windows and two or three balconies'. This confused profusion is matched by the garden, which is 'furnished' with 'a tennis pavilion, a pergola, a sundial, a rock garden, a dovecote, some gnomes, a seesaw, a grouping of rusticated seats, and a bird bath' (pp. 110, 106). This unforgiving list signals affluence, a devotion to leisure, and a confusion of taste: an impression supported by the fact that 'Stella, who could not stop looking, could think of nothing to say' (p. 106). The interior is also a mixture of class signifiers—the main living room is referred to in lower-middle-class style as the 'lounge', but it contains some old mahogany pieces of furniture which denote a long family history of established middle-classness. The main quality that establishes the Kelways as solidly middle-class, rather than as belonging to the continually aspiring lower middle class, is their ineffable respectability. It is this ethical solidity that brings home to Stella the tastelessness of her visiting Robert's family while conducting an affair with him:

But what could be this unexpected qualm as to the propriety of their having come to Holme Dene? The escapade, bad enough in its tastelessness and bravado, had a more deep impropriety with regard to themselves. Nothing more psychic than Mrs Kelway's tea table, with its china and

---

[72] One of the respondents to Mass-Observation, considering the past characteristics of the middle class, writes of 'the essentially bad "genteel" [*sic*] manners of the former lower middle and middle-middle classes' (Tarrant, *Class*, 139). George Orwell's 'upper-lower middle class' is a similar elaboration of the conventional binary division between the two sections of the middle class.

eatables, interposed between them: the tea table, however, was in itself enough. (p. 114)

It is this respectability that is the fundamental divide between Stella and the Kelways: she is characterized as bohemian and loose-living in the context of their unshakeable moral certainties.

That there is something illusory about these certainties becomes increasingly clear. The Kelways' form of middle-classness centres crucially on the home, with domestic life privileged at the expense of the world outside. Yet this home is not as solid, psychologically, as it looks: for a start, it has been for sale for years, with no one interested in viewing it since before the war. Its inconvenience has been ratified by the war: 'we always have lived uncomfortably in this house; *now* it is possible for us to make a point of doing so' (p. 121), but it remains a testament to the family's disappointment in their dead father's judgement. It is simply one of a string of houses they have lived in, the names and locations of which read like a litany of middle-class life and pieties between the wars: '[Father] had his heart set on a house called Fair Leigh outside Reigate . . . I was born in a house called Elmsfield near Chislehurst; and between that and this we lived in another house called Meadowcrest, outside Hemel Hempstead' (p. 120). In these prosperous Edwardian suburbs, the houses named to evoke a lost countryside, a facsimile of gracious living took place, but the impermanence indicated by these successive moves separates the Kelways and their class from the old gentry class, with its fixity of place, whose pre-war lives they were imitating. The very form of the house is tricksy: 'upstairs, as elsewhere, it had been planned with a sort of playful circumlocution—corridors, archways, recesses, half-landings, ledges, niches, and balustrades combined to fuddle any sense of direction and check, so far as possible, progress from room to room' (p. 256), indicating a deceit at the heart of the life of the bourgeois family within its walls. The apparent openness and plain speaking of the Kelways is revealed as an elaborately maintained sham:

> The many twists of the passages had always made it impossible to see down them; some other member of the family, slightly hastening the step as one's own was heard, had always got round the next corner just in time. A pause just inside, to make sure that the coast was clear, had preceded the opening of any door, the emergence of anyone from a room. The unwillingness of the Kelways to embarrass themselves or each other by inadvertent meetings

had always been marked. Their private hours, it could be taken, were spent in nerving themselves for inevitable family confrontations such as mealtimes, and in working on to their faces the required expression of having nothing to hide. (p. 256)

In the final pages of the novel, Robert is revealed as a Nazi spy, ideologically committed to the destruction of his own culture and class; but paradoxically his family, pre-eminently middle-class in both its certainties and its deceits, is presented as the forcing ground for his treachery, the place where he learnt the techniques of the spy. His revulsion from his own class is provoked particularly by the essential femininity of its culture: Holme Dene is described as 'a man-eating house ... one of a monstrous hatch-out over southern England of the 1900s' (p. 257). The decline of an assertive model of masculinity after the First World War, and the concomitant rise of a brisk, no-nonsense form of femininity (issues that will be discussed in detail in the final chapter) had a decisive effect on middle-class culture, which became less sentimental but more than ever centred on the feminine sphere of the home. Mr Kelway represents a generation of men who feel themselves to be without a role:

Lock-shorn, without the bodily prestige of either a soldier or a manual worker, as incapable of knocking anybody about as he was of bellowing, Mr Kelway had been to be watched seeing out at Holme Dene the last two years of an existence which had become derisory. Prestige from his money-making, unspectacular but regular, had been nil; his sex had so lost caste that the very least it could do was buy tolerance. (p. 257)

Robert's Nazi sympathies and his systematic betrayal of his country are presented as his attempt to reintroduce a culture of masculinity, and to take revenge on a nation that has become indistinguishable from a particular form of feminized middle-class identity. We find an almost identical masculine revulsion from a middle-class culture defined as ineffably feminine in Angus Wilson's short story 'Mother's Sense of Fun', published in the same year as Bowen's novel.[73] In his first collection of short stories, *The Wrong Set*, Wilson pastiches the established themes of the feminine middlebrow in much the same way as E. F. Benson, though with a bitterness that is at odds with the latter's exuberant enjoyment. Self-conscious eccentricity ('Fresh Air Fiend', 'Crazy Crowd') and intra-middle-class tensions ('Saturnalia', 'A Visit in Bad Taste') are his main themes,

[73] In Angus Wilson, *The Wrong Set*, 1949 (Harmondsworth: Penguin, 1959).

but his stories differ from the women's middlebrow novels that are their source in the satiric distance from which their middle-class characters are viewed. The mother in 'Mother's Sense of Fun' is instantly recognizable for the reader of women's middlebrow novels: she has shades of Angela Thirkell's benignly eccentric mothers, the jokey good humour of the Provincial Lady, the smugness of Mrs Miniver. Seen from her son's perspective, she is insufferable:

> The sweet cooing which she used in moments of intimacy roused greater suspicion in him, for it called so openly for surrender. But his hostility was chiefly reserved for the high pitched jollity of her everyday speech, which, apart from being more aurally revolting, revealed her insensitive and bullying nature. All day long it seemed to shrill about the house in a constant stream of self-satisfied humour and obtuse common sense. (p. 169)

All of her careful upper-middle-class originality: her 'nice Bohemian refusal' to be dominated by household routine, her plain speaking about class, are despised by her son, who waits daily in an agony of irritation for her to utter her cosy clichés, and exercise her famed sense of humour. He feels so strangled by the essential femininity of life in her upper-middle-class house that he feels only relief when she dies unexpectedly, but finds himself trapped by her abrasively rational view of the world even after her death:

> He might be free in little things, but in essentials she had tied him to her and now she had left him for ever. She had had the last word in the matter as usual. 'My poor boy will be lonely' she had said. She was dead right. (p.182)

What texts like Wilson's and Bowen's indicate is the extent to which middle-class culture (particularly that of the upper middle class) had become associated by the late 1940s with a certain form of pragmatic, rational femininity. The reaction of the literary establishment against upper-middle-class culture in the 1950s was in part a reaction also against the model of femininity that had grown up in the years before and during the Second World War.

Despite its lingering attachment to the categories of class as a mode of description, *The Heat of the Day* unmasks the solid middle-class respectability represented by the Kelways as pathological, and discredits Stella's haute-bourgeois bohemianism, which has led her into a relationship with Robert. The novel ends not with Stella, but with Louie, who is pictured standing with her illegitimate baby in a bombed-out wasteland, watching swans flying overhead.

In this bleak image there is a sense of a future in which the lower middle class will need to remake the nation, displacing the Kelways and their damaging combination of smugness and psychological restraint in the process.

By the 1950s, Louie's class was clearly in the ascendant, and the keynotes of upper-middle-class discourse had become a paranoid watchfulness and a desperation to defend the last vestiges of its cultural supremacy. In Diane Tutton's 1953 *Guard Your Daughters*, the upper-middle-class family at the novel's centre lives a life of self-deluding retreat. The five adolescent Harvey sisters live in a William and Mary manor house with their father—a famous writer of highly literate detective stories—and their reclusive, artistic mother, who has developed a mania about her daughters' safety. As a result, they are forbidden to go to parties or meet men. The eldest has managed to find a husband while teaching a Sunday school class, but the rest are reduced to annexing strange men and inviting them home under false pretences, where they are 'mobbed' by all the sisters. Convinced of the classiness of their eccentric way of life, the sisters are very proud of the oddness of their family. The middle child, Morgan, who narrates the story, tells, for instance, of the occasion when they had 'startled the audience at a local amateur dramatic show by sweeping in—all seven of us—in evening dress, headed by Father and Mother who looked like royalty' (p. 64).[74] The family's primary quality is hyper-class-consciousness: when the eldest sister returns to tell the others about married life, for instance, the issue of class distinctions is at the forefront of their concerns:

'Tell me some more, dearest. What are the other people like?'
'Rather lace-curtainy, a lot of them. They think I'm very badly brought up because I don't say pardon and I do say sweat.'
'Well, don't let them corrupt you.'
'I wouldn't dare. Father'd have something to say.' (pp. 24–5)

This passage demonstrates a problem that the upper middle class faced particularly strongly in the 1950s: their own cultural and linguistic usages were no longer assumed to be correct, and gentility was now being claimed from both sides of the line dividing upper from lower middle class. Cultural hegemony has been lost to the extent that Morgan feels envy for her eldest sister's shiny new house,

---

[74] Diane Tutton, *Guard Your Daughters*, 1953 (London: The Reprint Society, 1954), 64.

'with its bright paint and labour-saving gadgets', and particularly for her stainless steel sink, until reminded by another sister that such a life is really to be pitied: ' "Poor old Pandora. Lost in trackless Suburbia" ' (p. 160). It is notable that the husband who has taken Pandora to the wastes of suburbia is as upper-middle-class as the Harveys themselves: the lower middle classes are felt to be so different as to be virtually a separate species, with whom the likes of the Harveys could not mate. This is made clear when Morgan tries to pick up men at the cinema:

> During the advertisements which followed, the building was quite light and we were able to study the head and shoulders of the young man in front. His jacket was of greenish tweed, his head well-shaped, his hair fair and glossy with a slight wave. He had nice ears and the back of his neck was truly delicious. I raised my eyebrows at Teresa and she nodded violently. I stubbed out my cigarette, took a fresh one, and leant forward. 'Excuse me', I cooed, 'have you a match?'
>
> The young man turned round, and for a sublime moment I compared him to David Niven. Then he spoke, and I knew that all was lost. 'Pardon?' he said, 'I didn't quite catch?'. (pp. 73–4)

The impossibility of this young man rests entirely in his language: one 'non-U' word has ruled him out for ever.

The Harvey girls' class-consciousness is as strong in the other direction: although considering themselves 'fairly upper-class', they are secretly overawed by their neighbour, the aristocratic Susanna Malfrey, and try to emulate her disdainful manner. Attending a cocktail party at her parents' house, they are overwhelmed with self-consciousness, and the awareness of having committed a series of dreadful *faux pas* (one of them wears the same dress as her hostess, and takes her host for the butler). Yet despite these indications of a sense of inferiority, they insist on viewing the Honourable Susanna as an equal, noting that the bookshop proprietor 'bowed as low [to Susanna] as if she'd been a Harvey' (p. 111), and laughing at her ignorance and superficiality. Such behaviour is a manifest attempt to elevate themselves, in imagination, at least, out of the middle class entirely, in order to avoid the tainting associations of the lower middle class.

As with Rachel Ferguson's Carnes, the Harveys adopt the haute-bourgeois pose of treating class as an elaborate joke, and thus indicating their own insouciance. Morgan's greatest social success with Susanna's sophisticated set is achieved by the comic song she invents, composed of vulgarly hearty expressions for drunkenness: 'Oh squiffy elated and staggery-bye | Back in a moment and mud-in-your-eye' (p. 203), which manages to be simultaneously daring in subject matter and snobbish in approach. Morgan and her sister Thisbe occupy themselves at the daunting cocktail party with a mock conversation in which they pretend to be lower-middle-class housewives in a competitive conversation:

> 'We must be quite twin souls, Miss Postletwaite, for I'm like that about books. Give me a good book, I say to my hubby, and let the world wag on.'
> 'How very wise you are, Mrs ——'
> 'Plock.'
> 'I beg your pardon?'
> 'Mrs Plock, dear. PLOCK. Plock.'
> 'Not Block?'
> 'Oh no, indeed. The Blocks are quite a common family—barbers, my dear. Very well to do, of course, but so, *so* arrivistes.'
> 'The Block-Heddes, on the other hand—'
> 'Oh, quite a different matter, my dear. A very old family indeed, and all in the Army.' (p. 169)

The joke is in the class pretensions of a section of society they consider quite beyond the pale (in the notion of a barber as well to do but arriviste) and in the aping of lower-middle-class linguistic signifiers ('pardon' and 'hubby'). As far as this novel is concerned, language is the only significant class signifier: family background, housing, and occupation are assumed, rather than stated, and there is an absolute confidence that you can tell all you need about a person the moment they open their mouth.

It is on such flimsy grounds that the family mount their defence against encroaching egalitarianism. Their class's fear of the future is acted out by the mother, whom everyone, it emerges in the double-twist of the ending, has always assumed to be mad. In fact she is revealed to be sane and manipulative, pretending insanity in order to keep her daughters always at home. This wish to keep her daughters with her would have been a perfectly reasonable desire before the First World War, but can only be seen as either insane or cruel within the logic of the mid-century. The novel ends with the family dispersed, the daughters living in London, training for careers, absorbed into a post-war world where class, if not negligible, is at least determined anew by the efforts of each generation.

The feminine middlebrow emerges as fundamentally ambivalent about middle-classness. One of the strongest defenders of an upper-middle-class value-system, part of its popularity as a literary form was due to the fact that it provided a means for the excluded to acquire crucial signifiers of belonging. Its snobberies are presented as a guilty pleasure, and its encoding of class values makes the reader who cracks the codes complicit. Yet even in the 1930s and 1950s, when fear of the encroaching lower middle class was at its height, these novels retain some distance from their own reactionariness, opening up spaces from which we can view their exclusions and games of one-upmanship as cruel and pointless. The product of a time of intense middle-class anxiety, they offer a temporary palliation of the real-life stresses produced by continual class-consciousness, by allowing every reader the satisfactions of being upper middle class.

3

Imagining the Home

ENTERTAINING the Honourable and supercilious Suzanne Malfrey to tea, the Harvey sisters in Diana Tutton's 1953 novel *Guard Your Daughters* test their guest's imaginative faculties with a question:

'If you're reading a novel . . . when it describes a house—hall, drawing-room and so on—what do you see?'[1]

Suzanne fails the test ignominiously, declaring obtusely that she sees nothing but the book itself; but the question of the ways in which the home is imagined is a crucial one for the middlebrow women's novel of this period. Repeatedly, in such novels from the 1920s to the 1950s, domestic space is described in obsessive, coded detail. Essentially, the feminine middlebrow constructs the home as a text to be read for its ideological import. In this contention, I follow Nancy Armstrong's suggestion in 'The Rise of the Domestic Woman',[2] where she sees such an imagining of the home and its material objects as constituting a 'grammar' (begun, she claims, in eighteenth-century conduct books for women, and continued in the eighteenth- and nineteenth-century domestic novel) that

> opened a magical space in the culture where ordinary work could find its proper gratification and where the very objects that set men against one another in the competitive market place served to bind them together in a community of domestic values. (p. 136)

As established in Chapter 1, the modernist literary project which displaced a fully realized material environment in favour of subjective experience left a gap which the middlebrow novel filled. The inheritors of the tradition of bourgeois domestic writing that Armstrong discusses are the women's middlebrow novels of the first

---

[1] Diane Tutton, *Guard Your Daughters*, 1953 (London: The Reprint Society, 1954), 195–6.
[2] In Nancy Armstrong and Leonard Tennenhouse (eds.), *The Ideology of Conduct: Essays on Literature and the History of Sexuality* (New York and London: Methuen, 1987).

half of the twentieth century. But if the Victorian bourgeois home was the source of a feminine identity designed to soothe and soften the culture's aggressive materialism, then we find that model of the home in the process of disintegration in the feminine middlebrow. If solid material and psychological values can be read off from the grammar of household objects in the eighteenth and nineteenth centuries, so too can the collapse of such a metaphysics be traced in the ever-changing homes depicted in the domestic literature of the twentieth century (a literature that encompasses cookery books and hostess manuals, women's magazines and market-research reports, as well as the middlebrow novel).

The Harvey sisters' question to Suzanne Malfrey is significant because it lays stress on the act of imagining the home, and judges the ability to so imagine as a mark of both literary and human sensibility (Suzanne is spoilt and affected, and her failure to answer appropriately serves to close the book on her personality). The home in the period, unlike the more firmly codified eighteenth- and nineteenth-century bourgeois interiors discussed by Armstrong, is never a given; it requires imagining into being, and its creation is an index, particularly, of the characters of the women who create it. This calling into being of the domestic space is advanced as the central purpose of many of the women's magazines launched in the period. The editorial of the founding issue of *Good Housekeeping* in March 1922 explains that

> House decoration changes with other fashions, and the house-proud woman likes to know what is being done in big and little houses. . . . These things . . . will be described month by month in GOOD HOUSEKEEPING, so that the house itself shall always have that up-to-date look that other women recognise. For though women are supposed to dress themselves to please their men-folk, they deck their houses most often for each other.[3]

It is here both a woman's duty and her delicious indulgence to produce a continually evolving domestic sphere, and this endeavour is, notably, sold to her by the manipulation of an anxiety about the judgement of other women. The home is constructed in this period in a relation to the outside world that is simultaneously anxious and exhibitionist—a duality that will be explored further with reference

---

[3] 'The Reason for Good Housekeeping' (March 1922) in Brian Braithwaite, Noëlle Walsh, Glyn Davies, compilers, *Ragtime to Wartime: the Best of Good Housekeeping 1922–1939* (London: Ebury Press, 1986), 11.

to the subject of 'entertaining' so obsessively treated in the literature directed at the hostess.

The home was repeatedly reimagined in the years following the First World War, not just by novelists and journalists, but by government agencies, the building industry, and manufacturers. The poor health of conscripts during the war (by 1918 four out of ten were declared unfit for any kind of military service)[4] had been largely blamed on pre-war housing conditions, and after the war a massive campaign of slum clearance and the building of 'Homes Fit for Heroes' was embarked on. Throughout the inter-war years, and after the Second World War, successive governments subsidized new building work, and laid down minimum specifications of size, airiness and convenience. Housing was seen as an issue particularly concerning women, with the Ministry of Reconstruction established in 1917 appointing an all-women committee to report on housewives' housing requirements, and women's organizations such as the Women's Housing Council Federation and the Women's Cooperative Guild campaigning for better housing for the working classes. While the state-controlled measures were largely concerned with working-class housing, the housing needs of the middle classes also underwent a significant reassessment during these years. The large Victorian houses occupied by many of the middle classes were increasingly felt to be expensive and inconvenient to manage. Speculative building, and newly available building society mortgages, combined with falling house prices and low interest rates throughout the late 1920s and 1930s led many middle-class people to exchange their old homes for new. These factors also enabled many to become owner-occupiers for the first time, and were responsible for propelling many working-class people into the ranks of the newly middle class. In all, four million new houses were built in the inter-war years, one million of them council houses on new estates. Of the rest, most were located in the suburbs that were expanding around every town. Reviled as smug and philistine by urban sophisticates, these suburban houses became the heartland of a new middle-class existence. Through their physical distance from urban centres, the new working-class housing estates and middle-class suburbs contributed to an increasing isolation of women within the home. This was palliated by a concerted drive to make

[4] Deirdre Beddoes, *Back to Home and Duty* (London: Pandora, 1989), 90.

the home more and more attractive to the housewife, with major exhibitions (Ideal Home, Kitchen Front, Modern Homes, and so on) throughout the inter-war years, and during and after the Second World War, tempting the domestic woman with products designed to ease her labour and beautify her home. Manufacturers used Mass-Observation surveys and other forms of market research to repeatedly quiz housewives on their ideal kitchen and bathroom, and their changing tastes in paint colours and furnishings, aiming to sell their products by initiating a virtually continual transformation of the domestic environment.

The middlebrow women's novel echoes the contemporary sense of a domestic sphere in a state of flux. In many novels the home is foregrounded, becoming the central concern, an emblem of difficult and disturbing change. The action of Lettice Cooper's *The New House* (1936) encompasses one day in the lives of an upper-middle-class family—the day on which they move from their large, inconvenient house, which is to be knocked down and replaced by a housing estate, to the new house of the title. Housing, and its immediate contemporary importance, is the central theme of the novel, and a number of houses are depicted: the old house with its stately beauty corrupted by the windowless attics intended for its servants; the 'new house', thankfully not actually new, but the 'charming' lodge of another large house, now a convalescent home; and the genuinely 'new' villa, inhabited by the family's son Maurice and his wife Evelyn. It is in considering this house that Rhoda, the novel's protagonist, makes explicit the identification of women and houses that informs the novel:

'It's a nice little house. Delia hasn't seen it yet. It's better than–'
   Rhoda stopped herself. She had been going to say that it was better than a nasty modern villa, but had remembered in time that Maurice's house was a modern villa, and in her opinion might almost be described as nasty. An obscure impulse prompted her to make amends to what she really disliked about his house.
   'How is Evelyn?'[5]

Although the novel makes full use of such metaphoric identifications between women and their homes, its guiding imperative derives from a more rigorously materialist analysis of the condition of the nation.

---

[5] Lettice Cooper, *The New House*, 1936 (London: Virago, 1987), 63–4.

This analysis recognizes that the houses of the rich should give way to the housing estates needed by the poor. In terms of such an analysis, the desire of women to gain an identity from their homes is pitiful and retrogressive. Mrs Powell, the mother, sees herself as a willing slave to her home (although, in fact, most of the work has been performed by her servants and her daughter):

> Doing [only] what was necessary seemed to Mrs Powell to be less than right. A house to her had always been something to fuss over and slave for, a thing which should be encouraged to demand sacrifices, and, by so doing, increase your sense of virtue. (p. 156)

The novel's central dynamic, as in a number of other middlebrow women's novels, is in Rhoda's need to escape such self-enslavement. The question of whether she will actually manage to break loose from the domestic environment and gain the bright new future of secretarial work and a lodging in London is ultimately left unanswered.

Another novel that centres itself literally and metaphorically on a house is Elizabeth Taylor's *At Mrs Lippincote's* (1945). The house in question is not, however, the protagonist's own, but belongs to the elderly Mrs Lippincote. This displacement is emblematic of both the social and psychological disruptions of wartime, and of a distance between the fey bohemian sensibility of the heroine Julia and the stuffy Victorianism of Mrs Lippincote and her house:

> The house had a closed smell. A little light came through some blood-red glass at the front door. Through an archway hung with plush, she came to the kitchen. It was like the baser side of someone's nature. Beyond the plush curtains, the house put aside all show of decency. Here, there was no doubt about the suggestion of damp. Beads of moisture lay upon the walls. She rattled curtains across the window and put on the light.
> This room, she supposed, represented what was fitting and decent for the working class. On this side of the arch, varnished deal was preferred, wallpaper of brown and pink flowers, a brown tablecloth reaching to the floor and a plant with thick grey velvet leaves. Then down a hollowed stone step into a brick scullery where a refrigerator whirred and water dropped bleakly and with regularity into a bowl. She opened a cupboard and was frightened by a soup tureen the size of a baby's bath. In another cupboard a dozen meat dishes of very slightly varying sizes, white with a wreath of inky flowers, the glaze thread with faint sepia cracks.
> 'That is how Mrs Lippincote set up house', she told herself.[6]

---

[6] Elizabeth Taylor, *At Mrs Lippincote's* (London: Peter Davies, 1945), 8–9.

As well as being identified with its female owner, the house itself acquires both personality and agency: putting aside show of decency behind its plush curtains in imitation of the contemporary model of Victorian sexual hypocrisy. Its very structure is conceived of in terms of psychology—with the kitchen its id. The blatant damp of this part of the house is partly a materialist assertion of the inconvenience of older houses, but it also echoes Virginia Woolf's tongue-in-cheek characterization in *Orlando* (1928) of the Victorian era as a time of creeping dampness.[7] By turning on the light Julia effects a metaphorical illumination of the dismal, psychologically stultified past. Her fear of the soup tureen is both a mark of her charming lack of seriousness and of her refusal of the commitment to domestic labour it represents. She is repeatedly demonstrated to be a bad and slovenly cook, more interested in the life of the imagination than that of the kitchen. Her only effective act of a 'domestic' nature in the whole course of the novel is the reorganization of the furniture to produce light, clear rooms free of the oppressive freight and detail of the Victorian interior. This action, crucially, is envisaged by both her and the text as a game—most unlike the ponderous, lifelong endeavour represented by the soup tureens and the phrase 'set up house'. Even Julia's preoccupation with the details of Mrs Lippincote's life—she pores over her wedding photographs and considers reading her letters—serves to separate her from the domesticity that determined and limited the older woman: her curiosity names that life as over and finished, transmutes it, like the traumatic domestic imprisonment of the Brontës, which also fascinates her, into an engagingly gruesome story.[8]

Yet this novel offers nothing so unequivocal as a complete rejection of the domestic. Despite her role as domestic rebel, Julia, like Mrs Lippincote, is intimately associated with the home. Later in the novel, she and the house become virtually one, as she is transformed almost to furniture by her utility dress:

Julia had one beautiful frock. It was made of striped bolster ticking, black and white, and in its stiff folds she looked like Mrs Siddons. Standing at the

---

[7] Virginia Woolf, *Orlando*, 1928 (Oxford: Oxford University Press, 1992), 217–21.
[8] For an intriguing discussion on the subject of letters—their writing, reading, and not reading—in this novel see Jenny Hartley, *Millions Like Us: British Women's Fiction of the Second World War* (London: Virago, 1997), 136–7.

mirror with the rose-pink room behind her, she was pleased with herself. But not with the room, she decided, turning round. (p. 78)

Julia and the room are capable of direct comparison—she is dressed well, in furnishing fabric; the room is not yet dressed. What this connection of woman and house represents is a reversal of the old-fashioned domestic model of the woman serving the home. The house needs to be brought up to date, to become worthy of the modern woman who inhabits it, and it is this updating of both the house and the ideology associated with it that becomes one of the key concerns of the middlebrow women's novel after the First World War.

In both *At Mrs Lippincote's* and *The New House*, the harshest indictment of the despised Victorians in the eyes of the modern female observer is the poverty of the provision they made for their servants. This points to the intense preoccupation with servants and their treatment in the culture and literature of the years following the First World War. These years were witness to one of the most decisive social changes for centuries—the decline of a servant class. This decline was an obsessive concern for the bourgeoisie in the years between the wars and crucially affected the patterns of the lives of both working and middle-class women.

Most contemporary commentators and later historians see the First World War as the root cause of this social change. Working-class women became accustomed to the independence, camaraderie, and higher wages of the munitions factories, and were extremely reluctant to return to domestic service after the war. As Robert Graves put it:

[A]ny girl who had earned good wages in factories, and had come to like the regular hours, the society of other workers, and the strict but impersonal discipline, was reluctant to put herself under the personal dominion of 'some old cat' who would expect her to work long hours for little money, but show complete subservience and dispense of all former friendships or amusements.[9]

In response to this reluctance, the government took concerted measures immediately after the war to attempt to push working-class women back into service. A weekly benefit was paid to ex-munitions workers for thirteen weeks; to obtain this they had to attend daily at

[9] Robert Graves and Alan Hodges, *The Long Week-end: A Social History of Great Britain 1918–1939*, 1940 (Harmondsworth: Penguin, 1971), 40–1.

a labour exchange and be available for work. The problem came in the definition of work:

Officialdom viewed domestic service as fit work for practically any woman who signed on: the women had other ideas. Over and over again in these years and later women were denied benefit for refusing posts as domestics. The shortage of domestic servants, labelled by the middle class the 'servant problem', had become acute: middle-class women, who had been prepared to put up with lack of help during the war, were no longer willing to do so. It was considered an outrage that unemployed women would be living it up on their donations whilst mistresses struggled, servantless, at home.[10]

The government solved the problem to a degree by withholding benefit from women who refused domestic jobs—many of which were offered at derisory wages.[11] Partly as a result of Government measures, domestic service remained in the inter-war period the largest single source of employment for workingclass women, as it had been before the war.[12] Middle-class paranoia was justified to an extent, however: there was a decisive shift in the attitudes to service among the working classes over the period from the 1920s to the 1950s. By the time of the 1951 census, only 1.2 per cent of private households in Great Britain had one or more servants, compared with the 4.8 per cent (England and Wales) given in the previous census of 1931.[13] As Christopher Driver observed of the early 1950s, when the change was complete:

[M]iddle class houses continued to be cleaned, at least in part, by persons other than their owners. But no longer did these persons live in, or work full time, as cooks and housemaids. (p. 14)

We find in the magazines, cookery books, and fiction of the years between the wars what amounts to an hysterical worry among the middle classes about the decline in the numbers of servants, and the difficulty of getting—and keeping—good ones. Working-class women were no longer the biddable creatures they had been before the war: as a cook-general remarks in Agatha Christie's *Three-Act*

[10] Beddoes, *Back to Home and Duty*, 51.
[11] J. Beauchamp gave a figure of 12s 6d to 15s a week as a common payment for a maid in *Women Who Work* (London: Lawrence & Wishart, 1937), p. 74.
[12] Deirdre Beddoes gives the following figures: 'In 1911, 39 per cent of working women were in service; in 1921 service still accounted for 33 per cent of all working women and by 1931 the figure had risen to 35 per cent' (*Back to Home and Duty*, 61).
[13] Christopher Driver, *The British at Table: 1940–1980* (London: Chatto & Windus; The Hogarth Press, 1983), 14.

Tragedy (1935) ' "with the young ones you can't get the training—their mothers don't give it to them nowadays" '.[14] The sense of being tyrannized by their servants that was expressed by many middle-class women, is epitomized by the complaint of a writer in *Women's Leader* 1 April 1920:

There is no freedom with unwilling service, ill performed, higher wages demanded than can be paid, principles of cleanliness and orderliness violated, appearances having to be kept up and rigid rules adhered to for fear 'the girl will give notice'. It is tyranny.[15]

The problems of getting, training, and keeping maids loom large in women's magazines of the 1920s and 1930s. Articles on this subject are stern on the need to treat maids well: 'Running a Home (part II)' in *Good Housekeeping* of May 1925 advises the reader with two servants that 'the duties of the maids should be made interchangeable as far as possible; in this way each maid has more freedom without inconveniencing the family.'[16]

Necessities are made virtues also in an article in the same magazine for April 1923, where it is suggested that valuable space could be saved in 'the small town house' if non-resident staff were employed. The article presents some revealing tonal oscillations: beginning with an emphasis on space-saving for the middle-class family, moving on to praise of the class and manners of the typical daily maid ('frequently she is a woman of a competent and superior type, the wife, perhaps, of a disabled soldier, obliged to return to service in this form, and highly recommended by the better-class registry which supplies her'), recommending an improvement in the conditions under which servants could be employed ('it is not an inconsiderable piece of social work to-day to make of domestic service a more pleasant profession'), delicately avoiding the allocation of blame when talking of the poor conditions endured by servants in the past ('[domestic service] has broken down mainly because it asked too much and gave too little'), and ending, notably, with an appeal not to the high morals, but to the parsimony of the prospective employer:

The mistress of daily servants will find first and foremost that the morning

---

[14] Agatha Christie, *Three-Act Tragedy*, 1935 (London: Pan Books, 1983), 69.
[15] Quoted in Beddoes, *Back to Home and Duty*, 61.
[16] Braithwaite et al., *Ragtime to Wartime*, 40.

and evening journey infuse a new tone and vigour into the daily round. Not only is it healthy, but it gives variety and makes for cheerfulness. She will find, too, that where everything has to be done within hours, the day's work will tend to be better arranged and generally better done.... But best of all compensations (if any are needed), as the door closes finally the chancellor of the domestic economy may sigh with contentment, for she knows that below stairs everything invites inspection.... And she knows, too, that the kettle will not boil again until to-morrow, that the kitchen teapot will remain on its shelf, and the tea undisturbed in its tin.[17]

The key ambivalence that operates in this article is a result of the felt need to disguise, even between fellow members of the middle class, the desperation to retain servants under an apparently deep concern for their welfare. It is an oft-repeated note in the discourses on this subject after the First World War. In addresses to servants themselves an equally awkward tone is struck. In their 1933 book on the art of hostessing, Doris and June Langley Moore include a section of 'Instructions to Parlourmaids', where, after four pages of detail on the particular services demanded by modern social life— the serving of cocktails, for instance—they proffer the following persuasion of the usefulness to the parlourmaid herself of a good training:

Practice makes perfect, and by the time you are able to serve an elaborate dinner without a blunder, to receive visitors in a manner that spares them all embarrassment, to deliver messages tactfully and accurately, and to remember names—apart from all your mere routine duties—you will be fit to work in a very grand and stately house where you will doubtless meet a number of very grand and stately chauffeurs, footmen, valets, and butlers, and gamekeepers, any of whom should be glad to marry a girl with such a splendid array of domestic accomplishments. (That is, if they are not married already. Men so often are.)[18]

The very uneasy shifts between snobbish assumptions about the class aspirations of the maid, inept persuasion of the likelihood of such being realized, and the chumminess of the final rueful parenthesis epitomizes the difficulty of communication between maid and mistress that seems to have been triggered in the post-war period.

The domestic novel of this period is also full of moments of

---

[17] Ibid. 15.
[18] June and Doris Langley Moore, *The Pleasure of Your Company: A Text-book of Hospitality* (London: Gerald Howe Ltd., 1933), 238–9.

incomprehension between the two classes of women who inhabited the middle-class home. The noble savage Denham in Rose Macaulay's *Crewe Train* (1926) fears the maids in her new married home and is in her turn despised by them:

> Winifred and Laura, the maids, were alarming. They would ask questions to which their mistress knew no answer, sometimes about food or drink, sometimes about household arrangements.
> 'I don't know,' Denham would gruffly say. 'Do whatever you like about it.' Or she would have a shot at the right answer, and see from the domestic's countenance that she was right off the target. Winifred and Laura did not think much of their mistress, and no wonder. She was so obviously not 'used to having things nice'. She saw no difference in merit between linen sheets and cotton, between pearls and glass beads, between silver and cheap plate. . . . She was not, no, certainly she could not be a lady.[19]

The possibility of servants making such judgements of one's lifestyle and class accounts in part for the repeated theme of mistresses worrying that they will not live up to their maids' high standards. But what this worry also highlights is a profound and increasing discomfort among the middle classes about the keeping of domestic servants at all. Such discomfort can be traced to the increasing ease of domestic work achieved with the advent of mechanical aids such as vacuum cleaners, washing machines, and refrigerators—such appliances were in fact frequently advertised as replacement servants in the literature directed at the middle-class housewife (as in the 1930s' advertisement for a combination clothes washer, rinser, wringer, ironer, and vacuum cleaner marketed as 'Atmos: the mechanical housemaid'). There is also the strong possibility that such expressions of embarrassment are a neat way of disguising beneath liberal sentiments the fact that most middle-class families could no longer afford servants, whether or not any were available for hire.[20]

The reader is interestingly positioned by passages such as that

---

[19] Rose Macaulay, *Crewe Train* (London: E. Collins Sons & Co. Ltd., 1926), 152.

[20] '[I]n fact most families that had once kept servants could no longer do so, and facilities for housewives to run their homes themselves with a minimum of effort were fast being introduced from the United States, where the same reluctance for domestic service had always existed. "Labour saving" devices in cooking, washing-up, cleaning, laundering, a far wider choice of tinned and bottled fruits, refrigerators, mass-produced clothes, invisible-mending services: all these were offered and taken up readily' (Graves and Hodges, *The Long Week-end*, 41).

quoted from *Crewe Train*. We know that Denham is by birth a lady, and, more importantly, the novel has by now courted and won our support for her as a free and modern spirit, above such categorizations by class. The effect is to make us uncomfortable about the servants' limited perspective, and wary of the prospect of submitting ourselves to their scrutiny. But Rose Macaulay proceeds to go one better, reflecting on the middle-class comforts made possible by such judgemental intruders into the home:

> Tea came in, with lots of buttered scones, and a new cake. After all, that was something, tea and hot scones coming in for themselves like that, not having to be produced with labour by oneself. There was something in servants; only the nuisance of having them about, making so much unnecessary fuss in the house, easily weighed down their advantages. (p. 223)

Macaulay's ironic depiction of the way in which the middle-class discourse on servants between the wars often attempted to minimize the difficulty of their presence by reducing them to the sum of the services they performed—tea and scones 'coming in for themselves' is echoed with a manifest lack of irony in the opening pages of that classic of bourgeois complacency, Jan Struther's *Mrs Miniver* (1939): 'She rearranged the fire a little, mostly for the pleasure of handling the fluted steel poker, and then sat down by it. Tea was already laid: there were honey sandwiches, brandy-snaps, and small ratafia biscuits; and there would, she knew, be crumpets.'[21] The servants remain unmentioned throughout the initial chapter in which Mrs Miniver returns to reaccustom herself with the small, ineffable pleasures of home. The crumpets, in fact, appear about to be conjured up by her own prescience.

E. M. Delafield treats middle-class concerns in relation to servants with humour in her *Diary of a Provincial Lady* (1930), where her diarist undergoes genteel torments in her dealings with her servants:

> March 4th—Ethel, as I anticipated, gives notice. Cook says this is so unsettling, she thinks she had better go too. Despair invades me. Write five letters to Registry Offices.
> March 7th—No hope.
> March 8th—Cook relents, so far as to say that she will stay until I am

---

[21] Jan Struther, *Mrs Miniver*, 1939 (London: Virago, 1989), 2–3.

suited. Feel inclined to answer that, in that case, she had better make up her mind to a lifetime spent together—but naturally refrain.[22]

The repeated advice of magazine columnists on the art of retaining servants is offered by the ghastly Lady B., the bane of the protagonist's life:

> Meet Lady B., who says the servant difficulty, in reality, is non-existent. She has NO trouble. It is a question of knowing how to treat them. Firmness, she says, but at the same time one must be human. Am I human? she asks. Do I understand that they want occasional diversion, just as I do myself? I lose my head and reply No, that it is my custom to keep my servants chained up in the cellar when their work is done. This flight of satire rather spoilt by Lady B. laughing heartily, and saying that I am always so amusing. (p. 41)

Eventually the Provincial Lady is forced to accept a most unusual servant—a superior house-parlourman called Howard Fitzsimmons, engaged by her husband. The reader is left to suppose that Fitzsimmons is not a 'real' servant—for one thing, he responds to orders with a cheery 'Right-oh!'—but his reasons for taking the job are never explored and he soon departs. As is usual in this fiction, women are portrayed as being more sensitive to class distinctions than men—her husband fails to see why it is so 'impossible' that the servant should be called Fitzsimmons. The purpose of this curious figure is perhaps to indicate the decline of a genuine 'servant class' to the extent that impoverished middle-class men are all that is available. The narrator's attempts to find a suitable mode of address for her new employee expose contemporary middle-class behaviour in response to their servants as cowed and absurd, but the novel's sympathies nevertheless remain firmly with the servant-employing class, to whom it exclusively addresses its laments: 'Servants, in truth, make cowards of us all' (p. 97).

An intriguing real-life example of the cowardice, hard-heartedness and sheer embarrassment servants induced in their employers during these years is provided by Virginia Woolf's protracted attempts, recorded in her diary between 1924 and 1934, to rid herself of her maid Nelly. She repeatedly gears herself up to 'deliver sentence of death', as she puts it, and then backs down. Her

---

[22] E. M. Delafield, *Diary of a Provincial Lady*, (1930), reissued with other novels in the series as *The Diary of a Provincial Lady* (London: Virago, 1991), 40–1.

descriptions of her mixed feelings of contempt, pity, and frustration sum up the vexed mistress–maid relationship:

> This is written to while away one of those stupendous moments—one of those painful, ridiculous, agitating moments which make one half sick & yet I don't know—I'm excited too; & feel free & then sordid; & unsettled; & so on—I've told Nelly to go; after a series of scenes which I won't bore myself to describe. And in the midst of the usual anger, I looked into her little shifting greedy eyes, & saw nothing but malice & spite there, & felt that that had come to be the reality now: she doesn't care for me, or for anything: has been eaten up by her poor timid servants fears & cares & respectabilities.[23]

A corrective to such a typical dismissal of a servant's own concerns (even if it is an atypically honest one) is provided in *The New House*, which offers one of the most extended analyses of the new servant–mistress relationship, minutely exploring Rhoda's feelings about the cook, and then the cook's feelings about Rhoda to systematically expose Rhoda's misconceptions as well as her well-intentioned sympathies. Rhoda, more sensitive and less robust than her mother, whose relationship with her servants is unproblematically authoritarian, recognizes the fundamental separation between the servants' part of the house and the family's: 'She always felt shy when she penetrated to that downstairs world. The life lived so near to them and so far apart from them was a dark continent, full of unexplored mystery' (p. 100). Her consciousness of the otherness of the servants springs, paradoxically, from the partial breaking down of class barriers in the years between the wars, and is contrasted with her mother's matter of fact, pre-war sense of the servants as domestic appliances:

> Mrs Powell would be very kind to a servant who was ill or in trouble, but she could never quite feel that they were independent human beings. It astonished her that they should be unwilling to sacrifice an afternoon out for her convenience. When they had birthdays and were given presents of bath salts, powder-puffs, and coloured beads, she commented on it to Rhoda with surprise. What did they want out of things like that? Regarding them at the bottom of her heart as automata, she handled them with assurance and precision, while Rhoda was secretly afraid of asking too much, and got a far more unwilling and inefficient service. (p. 101)

---

[23] *The Diary of Virginia Woolf*, iii: *1925–1930*, ed. Anne Olivier Bell (London: The Hogarth Press, 1980), Thurs. 8 Aug. 1929, 240.

To counteract its apparent recommendation of Mrs Powell's methods, the text shifts immediately to a report of the cook's lack of ease in the presence of Rhoda, eliciting sympathy for her, and contradicting Mrs Powell's perception of her as an automaton:

> As Rhoda came into the kitchen, the ease of cook's body changed to stiffness, and a mask fell over her face. She stopped crying. She did not dislike Rhoda—at the moment she was sorry to part from her—but Rhoda was on the other side. As soon as she came into the room Annie Hargreaves became cook. Rhoda knew it, and minded more than Annie Hargreaves. Here was a woman only a few years older than herself, living in the same house with her, full, no doubt, of hopes and fears and sorrows and wishes, and as far apart from her as a foreigner who did not speak English. It seemed absurd. (p. 101)

Although sympathetic, this is still Rhoda's perspective. Her fellow feeling for the cook is qualified by that 'no doubt'. At first it appears that this is as far as Cooper will go towards representing the experience of the other within the middle-class home, but two pages on we return to Annie Hargreaves, immediately after hearing Rhoda's curious envy of the independent life of the younger maid, Ivy, in comparison with the constraints of her own. Rhoda's naive sense of her own hard luck—'I've been caught in a trap because I've been brought up in a fairly prosperous family. People like me ought to be born poor, and start earning our livings early; it would be the best chance for us!' (p. 103)—is sharply contradicted by Annie Hargreaves's musing on the disappointments and limitations of her own life:

> She would have a bit of a rest now, but it couldn't be more than a week or two, because her people were all miners. They couldn't do without what she sent them. . . . Forty next month, and in service since I was fourteen. Please may I slip out to post a letter? Would you like the chicken hashed or done in a fricassay? . . . You get sick of other people's houses. (pp. 103–4)

Another attempt to bridge the gap between mistress and maid was made by Monica Dickens (granddaughter of Charles), who worked as a cook and housemaid for some months in order to write a book about her experiences. The result, *One Pair of Hands* (1939), entertainingly exposed the realities of life below stairs to its middle-class readers, detailing the petty snobberies of mistresses and deceits of maids, graphically describing the descent into stupidity that results from total exhaustion, and demonstrating that even the kindest of employers tended to think of their servants as alternately automatons and 'screamingly funny' music-hall turns.[24] Despite revealing the thankless life led by most maids, Dickens remains convinced that there is a future for domestic service if it can only be reformed. The epilogue to the novel has her speaking of her experiences as a servant to an audience of middle-class housewives at a home exhibition. She stresses the need for established conditions of service, and for proper training for domestic servants, echoing the urgings of many other campaigners that domestic labour should be transformed into something more scientific and respected. A more accurate indication for the future of domestic service, however, is given by the note on which the novel ends, as her departing audience discuss how boring they had found her lecture, or confess that they had slept through it: because the middle-class woman was unable or unwilling to pay higher wages and provide more congenial conditions of employment, the Second World War saw the last servants leaving middle-class homes, and not returning.

Diane Tutton's Harvey sisters in *Guard Your Daughters*, like most of the novel's readers by 1953, do much of the housework. The family had had servants when the girls were children, who are mentioned only in passing. The daily woman, Mrs Phillips, is their only domestic help at the time of the novel's action, and Morgan, narrating a year later, finds that she can remember her only very faintly:

I used to see her every day for years and years, and I used to joke with her, a sort of false heartiness meant to keep her in a good temper, but she never made any impression on me at all. Surely I must be a very egotistical and horrible person? (p. 159)

This question clearly expects an answer in the negative, but the profound—if unconscious—snobbery Morgan goes on to demonstrate is hard to ignore. Mrs Phillips is most memorable, it seems, for her accent—'she speaks in a pinched way and has only one vowel sound—a short i' (p. 159)—which Morgan and one of her sisters had used in childhood as the basis of a secret language called Philish which, to their great amusement, is incomprehensible to Mrs Phillips herself. It is more than coincidence that the most active snobbery in response to the otherness of the servant is found in a

[24] Monica Dickens, *One Pair of Hands*, 1939 (London: Michael Joseph Ltd., 1952).

book written after the middle-class battle to keep servants has been conceded lost. There is no longer any need to propitiate, and the unconscious hostility can at last be aired.

The decline of domestic servants in the middle-class home throughout the inter-war years, and their almost total disappearance after the Second World War clearly had a momentous effect on the life of the middle-class woman within her home. Because she had to do housework, a burgeoning number of woman's magazines, cookery books, and hostess manuals insisted that housework was now stylish. An examination of these sources makes it clear that an effective ideology of the domestic began to direct itself at middle-class women in the 1920s. It was an ideology composed of a number of elements—most notably professionalism, competition, simplicity, and display. The barrage effect of this ideology is indicated by the sheer scale on which it was introduced. At least sixty new women's magazines were started in the years between 1920 and 1945.[25] A considerable number were expensive monthlies aimed at the middle-class woman, such as *Good Housekeeping* (founded 1922), *Woman and Home* (1926), *My Home* and *Modern Home* (both 1928). As their titles suggest, their major emphasis was on helping the middle-class woman to run her home without servants; their main message was that the home was the centre of a woman's attention, the source of her identity.

It was also in the inter-war period that a new sort of cookery book began to appear in increasing numbers. Where the cookery books of the pre-war period had been either Beeton-esque tomes, or cheaply produced guides to economy cooking, the new cookery book was fashionable. Written by society hostesses and famous restaurateurs, expensively produced with elegant typefaces and specially commissioned art work, these books offered a new vision of domesticity as elegant and creative rather than a tedious drudgery.[26] Many of these cookery books politely elide the issue of the probable absence of servants, assuming that the housewife is passing the recipes on to her cook, but tactfully providing her with the information she needs to do

[25] Cynthia White, *Women's Magazines 1693–1968* (London: Michael Joseph, 1970); cited in Beddoes, *Back to Home and Duty*, 14.
[26] Examples include *Minnie, Lady Hindlip's Cookery Book* (1925), Lady Jekyll's *Kitchen Essays* (1922), Ruth Lowinsky's *Lovely Food* (1931), Mrs Philip Martineau's *Caviar to Candy* (1927), Quaglino's *Complete Hostess* (1935) and *Lady Sysonby's Cook Book* (1935).

the work herself (witness the neatly double-edged title of Catherine Ives's 1928 book *When the Cook Is Away*). The emphasis is not on the *necessity* of middle-class women now carrying out their own domestic labour, but on the stylishness of their choosing to do so. Thus 'Quaglino' encouragingly remarks in his 1935 book *The Complete Hostess* that 'in England for the last twenty years the public has been taking more interest in food and cooking. It is not just the Upper Four Hundred. Everybody is showing more keenness about it.'[27]

Cooking was now sold as a high-status leisure activity, a mode of self-display and self-improvement too interesting to be left to servants, even if there were any to be had. At the same time, there was an increasing movement towards the professionalization of housework through the domestic science movement, which set up training colleges to teach girls the principles of time-management, economy, and nutrition. Housework was to be approached as a job, the kitchen ordered like a factory. This concept of housework as a science was heavily employed by the manufacturers of new domestic equipment such as gas cookers, vacuum cleaners, and refrigerators, who promised that these gadgets would transform the home into a high-tech paradise (so in the 1920s husbands were exhorted to 'Give her Pleasure—Give her Leisure—Give her an ELECTROLUX for Christmas').

The drive for simplicity was another element of the new domestic ideology: menus were shortened, with the average number of courses for a grand dinner dwindling from the pre-war seven or eight to a more modest four or five. Superfluous 'Victorian' meals like tea and supper were increasingly dropped and furnishings became sparser and simpler in shape. Utopian schemes for labour-reducing modern living were devised, like *Good Housekeeping*'s article in June 1923 which offered a design for 'The Servantless House', with built-in furniture and rounded corners to walls to eliminate dust, and tiling and enamelled surfaces for easy cleaning in kitchen and bathroom.

The desires to compete with others, and to display the home as modern and fashionable were repeatedly manipulated by writers and advertisers throughout the period. A 1930s advertisement run in *Good Housekeeping* shows the housewife being assured by a grand salesman that ' "in good class houses, madam, we invariably fit

[27] Quaglino, *The Complete Hostess*, ed. Charles Graves, 1935 (London: Hamish Hamilton, 1936), 9.

Triplex Grates" ', while a 1950s advertisement in the same magazine for gas cookers exhorts the reader to 'imagine the look on our friends' faces when they see our RENOWN six'. Cookery writers offered meals for particular occasions on which the housewife might need to impress her guests: Lady Jekyll, specializing in the art of delicate patronage in her 1922 *Kitchen Essays* gave suggestions for menus for 'country friends for a Christmas shopping luncheon' and 'food for artists and speakers', while Ruth Lowinsky, society hostess, and wife of surrealist painter Thomas, offered in *Lovely Food* (1931) special occasion menus of such heightened specificity that they might well be thought to be tongue-in-cheek: 'for a father-in-law, who comes prepared to judge you as either the laziest housekeeper in England, or the most extravagant' and 'a slightly more pompous dinner for ten people who think they know all about food, but actually know only what they like'.[28] Some writers were quite overt about the ways in which housewives might use domestic success to improve their social status: 'there are many ambitious young hostesses today, in flats, in small houses, in suburban villas, who want to know more about Good Food, for their own and their friends' pleasure, and possibly—and who will blame them?—with an eye to social advancement.'[29]

While these various elements of fashion, professionalism, and competitive display are all apparent in a variety of domestic discourses throughout the period from the 1920s to the 1950s, we can trace particular historical developments in the ideology of the relationship of the middle-class woman to her home. In the 1920s and 1930s, the keynote of the message was to persuade her that domestic labour is high status and fashionable, with notions of professionalism and economy being secondary though still significant. With the onset of the Second World War, the message changed, and the ideology of the Kitchen Front concentrated on housework as war work. Efficiency, economy, and duty were the watchwords, and display and competition were put aside—indeed, were often treated as positively treasonable. After the war, once it became clear that servants would not be available again, the ideological barrage

[28] Lady Jekyll (Agnes), *Kitchen Essays with Recipes and their Occasions*, 1922 (London: Collins, 1969), 68, 91; Ruth Lowinsky, *Lovely Food* (London: Nonesuch Press, 1931), 8, 12.
[29] Ambrose Heath, *Good Food: Month by Month Recipes* (London: Faber & Faber, 1932), 15.

ceased to be so class-specific. It could now safely be assumed that all women would undertake housework, and the address uniquely to the middle-class woman was no longer needed. Instead, the emphasis was increasingly on technology and its time-saving attributes, and on modernity as a key quality of the home. In brief, in the period from the 1920s to the mid-1950s the middle-class woman is constructed by domestic discourses as first the fashionable housewife, then the dutiful housewife, and lastly the modern housewife.

We find middle-class women's changing attitudes to the domestic tasks that were newly their responsibility represented also in their fiction, but rather more problematically than in other discourses of the domestic. The novel, of course, rarely works univocally, and the women's middlebrow novel of this period is significant in that it offers its readers resistances to the new ideology as well as means of adjusting to it. Lettice Cooper's *The New House*, with its democratist values, sees the new model of middle-class women performing their own domestic labour as a significant social advance over the old days of service. The unlikeable Evelyn, daughter-in-law of Mrs Powell, is presented as unusual in not taking pleasure in her new tasks. Cooper's novel, like many others, presents the same sort of detailed list of household duties as were produced in women's magazines and in fuller form by the experts behind the scientific housework movement. These lists indicate, among other things, the sheer newness of the idea of performing one's own household tasks, and also serve to stress the importance, complexity, and seriousness of the job:

Evelyn talked of herself and Maurice as hard up, because they had two inexperienced young maids, could not afford to redecorate the house when she thought it necessary, and had to spend an unambitious summer holiday with her mother in rooms at the sea. Her friends, most of them other young matrons, were also 'hard up', some of them a little more so, some of them a little less. One or two had no maids, or they had a nurse for the baby and did the cooking. They all cooked, made clothes, repapered rooms, and enjoyed it, boasting freely and gaily about their experiments. Evelyn joined in the talk but she did not really enjoy it. She found very little pleasure in such activities. She wanted to have things, not to do them. She did not think it was fun to scratch up a meal for unexpected visitors. What she did, she did well. She did not, like her cheerful young friends, bake a lop-sided cake that was sad in the middle, and offer it, laughing and apologetic to her guests. She made a good cake, but she would rather have bought an expensive one. (p. 55)

If Cooper is optimistic that the new ideology is part of a democratizing process in which the middle classes are at last beginning to pull their weight, other texts in the 1930s were not so sanguine: both Rose Macaulay's *Crewe Train* and E. M. Delafield's *Diary of a Provincial Lady* were concerned to challenge, or at least to ironize, the growing assumption that middle-class women should find the meaning of their existence in actively caring for the home.

Denham in *Crewe Train* is a one-woman riposte to the pro-domestic ideology. A child of nature, Denham is rescued from a European bohemia and brought to England to be civilized. The civilizing force is to be her cousins—a large and self-consciously eccentric family of intellectuals, who would be the narrative focus in most other middlebrow novels of the period. Here, however, their pretensions are ruthlessly exposed by Denham's innocent regard. One of the first things we learn about her is her radical disregard for the conventional proprieties of the housewife:

Denham saw no kind of reason why she should help with activities which she had no desire to have performed, for her part, she would as soon have the house dirty as clean, so why bother? (p. 8)

Later, when her aunt brings cleaning stuffs with which to alleviate the squalor of Denham's newly acquired cottage-with-cave, Denham is taken aback:

Denham looked at her aunt in speculative surprise. Funny, knowing a person for over a year and still thinking she couldn't let the sink get messy and discoloured. Her attempts at the higher life must have been more successful than she had supposed.
'I shall be pretty busy, there', she said darkly. 'I shan't have a lot of time for the sink.'
'Indeed you won't. I know what camping in a cottage without servants is. The danger is that one does house chores from morning till night.'
Denham felt that danger to be remote. (p. 180)

The humour in the novel is in the conflict between the uncivilized Denham and her bohemian relatives, whose unconventional pose is revealed as a rule-laden sham in the light of Denham's utter disregard for any proprieties. In this passage, Denham's confusion of the higher life with a desire to scrub sinks is indicative. Even

Denham herself, however, is eventually both tamed and silenced by the overwhelming demands of the bourgeois home. Her mother-in-law, an active, adventuring woman, who spends much of her time abroad with her husband on archaeological digs, deals the final blow by providing Denham with a detailed timetable of activities suitable to the cultured and domestic young wife. Her treatment of domestic work and household management as 'work' in a professional sense, something requiring brains and organizational skills is a central plank in the new ideology of middle-class domesticity (it is discussed in notably similar terms by the graduates of Shrewsbury College in Dorothy L. Sayers's 1935 *Gaudy Night*):

'It's not an easy business, running a house and servants; you've got to put brains into it, if it's to be done well. . . . the more intelligent a woman is, the more brains she ought to bring to bear on her home. The Cambridge and Oxford Colleges are excellent training schools for housewives.'[30]

Crewe Train ends with the free-spirited Denham reeling under the weight of the improving timetable provided for her, which involves flower-arranging and learning Greek as well as continual supervision of the servants. Macaulay's irony is directed at what looks very much like a return, under the banner of modernity, to the cultured, domestically responsible Victorian wife, but it is significant that she leaves her heroine caught finally in the toils of this ideology.

The *Diary of a Provincial Lady* also looks with some irony at the new cult of the domestic. Although her life consists of a round of domestic trivialities, the Provincial Lady has no particular commitment to domestic ideology, as she realizes when talking to a friend:

Barbara says that it is sometimes very difficult to know which way Duty lies, that she has always thought a true woman's highest vocation is home-making, and that the love of a Good Man is the crown of life. I say Yes, Yes, to all of this. (Discover, on thinking it over, that I do not agree with any of it, and am shocked at my own extraordinary duplicity.) (pp. 53–4)

The most endearing of her characteristics is the Provincial Lady's incompetence as a housewife. The implication, perhaps, is that it is not a job worth doing, therefore it is not done well:

Look for Robin [her son] and eventually find him with the cat, shut up into totally unventilated linen cupboard, eating cheese which he says he found on the back stairs.

[30] Macaulay, *Crewe Train*, 304, 306.

(Undoubtedly, a certain irony can be found in the fact that I have recently been appointed to new Guardians Committee, and am expected to visit Workhouse, etc., with particular reference to children's quarters, in order that I may offer valuable suggestions on question of hygiene and general welfare of inmates. . . . Can only hope that fellow members of the Committee will never be inspired to submit my own domestic arrangements to similar inspection.) (p. 58)

The challenge here to the still-surviving ideology of amateur good works performed by the bourgeoisie is effective.

Such criticisms, however, though trenchant are ultimately pessimistic: both Denham and the Provincial Lady remain at the end of the novels firmly contained by their despised domestic roles. These novels represent the limit of the feminine middlebrow's overt resistance to the pro-domestic ideology. Other novels adopt a different, more covert, agenda: revising and recasting that ideology in forms designed to prove considerably more attractive to the sophisticated middle-class reader. Most crucially, they claim a woman's ability to 'home-make' as an art form, offering the middle-class housewife an imaginative allegiance with the bohemian creative artist as a compensation for the unfamiliar labour that is now to be her lot. We can see this claim being established in the much-repeated textual accounts of house decoration, cookery and hostessing, and in the descriptions of the plucky housewife coping with the new bourgeois poverty that afflicted many of the middle class in the 1940s and 1950s.

The upper middle classes in particular underwent a significant drop in standard of living in the war years, and found that the situation did not improve when the war ended. A Mass-Observation Bulletin entitled 'Middle Class Belts' described in 1948 this group as one for whom 'the adjustment of inadequate incomes to the cost of goods and services has involved not only steady reduction in standards of living, but something like an all-round retreat from the market'.[31] Statistics cited by one author in 1949 claimed that salary earners as a group (as opposed to working-class wage earners) were 20 per cent worse off in 1947 than in 1938, taking into account a 68 per cent rise in prices in the period.[32] Most middle-class respondents to Mass-Observation surveys in the 1940s and early 1950s felt that they were considerably affected by the present cost of living. These reduced

[31] Mass-Observation (M-O) Bulletin 20, Sept. 1948.
[32] Mollie Tarrant in an unpublished manuscript for Mass-Observation called *Class*, written in 1949 or shortly thereafter (ch. 3, no page number).

circumstances found their clearest articulation in the increasing fashion for parsimony and thrift. Mass-Observation panel members report cutting back on drink, cigarettes, entertainments, and books, and there is often a sort of perverse satisfaction in the lengths to which they are forced to go:

We are losing most of the things that made life gracious in the past. We have already given up a resident maid, changing our clothes three or four times a week, and, by degrees, keeping open house to our friends.[33]

This changed ethos is demonstrated by the curiously iconic status acquired in this period by a particular institution: the Woolworths store. Designed to cater to the needs of the working classes, it attracted increasing numbers of presumably self-conscious middle-class patrons, intent on obtaining bargains. Its astounding cheapness for its new middle-class patrons is indicated by a 1920s Bateman cartoon showing a fashionable woman standing impatiently in the middle of a Woolworths store, its counters entirely denuded, its staff amazed and aghast: the title—'The woman who spent £10 in a Woolworth store'.[34] Robert Graves described the influence of Woolworths on both working- and middle-class life in the years between the wars:

Woolworth's stores were the great cheap providers of household utensils and materials. There had been a few '6½d. Bazaars' before the war, but the Woolworth system was altogether new. It worked by small profits and quick returns in a huge variety of classified and displayed cut-price goods. ... the firm never had any difficulty in engaging unskilled sales-girls at a low wage; for 'the local Woolworth's' was increasingly the focus of popular life in most small towns. And the name of Woolworth was a blessed one to the general public; wherever a new branch was opened, the prices of ironmongers, drapers and household furnishers in the neighbourhood would drop two-pence in the shilling. The middle class at first affected to despise Woolworth's goods, but they soon caught the working-class habit and would exclaim brightly among themselves: 'My dear—guess where I got this amazing object—threepence at Maison Woolworth! I don't know *how* they do it.'[35]

[33] A housewife quoted in M-O File Report 3088, Feb. 1949, 'Keeping Up With the Jones's.
[34] Reproduced in H. M. Bateman: *The Man Who ... and Other Drawings*, ed. John Jensen (London: Methuen, 1975). In his *English Journey* (London: William Heinemann Ltd., 1934) J. B. Priestley remarked that 'you could almost accept Woolworths as [the] symbol' of Modern England (p. 402).
[35] Graves and Hodges, *The Long Week-end*, 172-3.

Precisely this tone of middle-class jollity in the face of Woolworths and the parsimony it represented for them is found in June and Doris Langley Moore's *The Pleasure of Your Company* (1933):

> Guessing competitions can be very ingenious. We have been to a party at which the guests were asked (a) to wear, visibly but inconspicuously, one article from Woolworth's, and (b) to commit one breach of etiquette in the arrangement of their dress. Prizes were awarded to those who were quickest in detecting Woolworth products and sartorial errors respectively, and marks were deducted from the score of players who made bad guesses. There were many *faux pas* which had, of course, to be forgiven in the extenuating circumstances. (p. 127)

This association of Woolworth's objects and breaches of etiquette in dressing (by implication things already going out of usage and therefore difficult to detect) unconsciously captures a key moment of transition in middle-class life and behaviour, as traditional bourgeois values give way under the exigencies of economic privation to a casualness that is virtually bohemian. We find this linking of Woolworths with middle-class eccentricity and bohemianism in a number of middlebrow novels. The store appears, with a range of significances, in the titles of several books: Karen Brown's *The Girl From Woolworths* (1930), Rachel Ferguson's *The Brontës Went to Woolworths* (1931) and Barbara Comyns's *Our Spoons Came From Woolworths* (1950). Karen Brown's story, written and published in America, employs Woolworths to indicate a form of working-class employment that allowed a girl some financial and social independence. The English usages are more complex. For Rachel Ferguson, writing in the early 1930s before the full onset of bourgeois poverty, the point of her title is in the conjunction between practicality (Woolworths) and the imaginary (the Brontës), but also in the gap between the dour limitations of the Brontës' nineteenth-century middle-class poverty, and the plucky adventuring of contemporary middle-class forays into Woolworths. The title's full significance only becomes apparent in the final pages of the novel. The youngest child of the Carne family who is at the novel's centre has been terrified by encountering the ghosts of the Brontës—roused by her elder sisters' table-turning. To save her sanity the down-to-earth family friend Lady Toddington—until now aloof from the fantasizing indulged in by the Carnes—domesticizes the Brontës:

'I saw the Brontës yesterday!', said Lady Toddington, 'In Woolworths . . . And Charlotte bought a hair-net. Mauve. Quite hideous, poor girl.' . . . 'Emily had one of her difficult turns right in the middle of the haberdashery.'[36]

The domestic commonplaces represented by the stock of a Woolworths store—hairnets and haberdashery—are the literal stuff of sanity for Ferguson's novel, capable of anchoring a fantasist to the real and the quotidian. It is therefore striking that the protagonist Deirdre elaborates on Lady Toddington's saving fantasy with an addendum that brings the Woolworths store firmly back into the arena of class, emphasizing the amusing social slumming it represents for the middle classes:

'Charlotte wrote to Miss Nussey: "It was a queer shop, much favoured with their custom by a class which I do not think to be our own. The attractions . . . are lights, variety of articles displayed, music, cleanliness and warmth (from whence obtained I do not know), but providing an evident lure to these families who know no better. . ."' (pp. 253-4)

For Barbara Comyns, the buying of spoons from Woolworths figures a fall into bohemian poverty which is at first amusing but later turns sour. At the start of the novel the narrator offers one of those scenes of setting up house that are so common in the middlebrow novel. They are so common because the scene they represent needed continual reimagining: in a situation of such rapid social and economic change the milieu into which a middle-class woman moved on marriage could be startlingly different to that of her parents, without her having married outside her class. It is Comyns's narrator's marriage to an artist that precipitates her into creative poverty:

A carpenter made us some little stools because I like sitting on stools better than anything else. We painted all our furniture duck-egg green with a dash of sea green; we had the paint specially mixed for us.[37]

This is poverty only in the sense of necessary contrivance: there is no actual deprivation involved, even though they have to buy their divan on hire purchase and have difficulty keeping up the payments. The significance of the novel's title is revealed later in this account of the acquiring of household goods:

[36] Rachel Ferguson, *The Brontës Went to Woolworths*, 1931 (London: Virago, 1988) 252-3.
[37] Barbara Comyns, *Our Spoons Came From Woolworths* (London: Eyre & Spottiswoode, 1950), 12.

We had a proper tea-set from Waring and Gillow, and a lot of blue plates from Woolworths; our cooking things came from there, too. I had hoped they would give us a set of real silver teaspoons when we bought the wedding-ring, but the jeweller we went to wouldn't, so our spoons came from Woolworths, too. (pp. 12–13)

This is clearly emblematic of the narrator's loss of social status—with the absence of silver cutlery a mark of the gentility she has forfeited by marriage. The writer of working-class life Margaret Eyles had decades earlier mocked precisely this sort of uncomprehending middle-class fictional account of poverty in *The Woman in the Little House* (1922), declaring that 'the average author knows nothing of the grey, steady hardship of working-class life; he knows plenty about poverty, but it is a gay sort of Bohemian poverty with sporadic flashes of prosperity—the sort of poverty that dresses perfectly for lunch at the Savoy with some important person, and cheerfully pawns its beautiful clothes to buy fish and chips for lunch tomorrow!'.[38]

The bourgeois poverty of the latter part of this period had a significant effect on modes of entertaining, encouraging a greater informality, and reducing some of the element of social competition that hospitality had previously contained. A Mass-Observation file report in 1949 called 'Keeping Up With the Jones's' contended that food shortages were inducing people to give up formal entertaining in favour of casual meals for only their closest friends, and remarked that many people were glad of the excuse to retire from the competitive social arena.[39] This is in marked contrast to attitudes to entertaining in the inter-war years, when it is treated with great seriousness in magazines, cookery books, and the increasing numbers of practical manuals exclusively devoted to the subject. Some significant tropes emerge in its treatment in these years. The first is a desire to establish and maintain a complex set of rules to govern social interaction. Invariably presented as a product of common-sense, kindness,

---

[38] M. L. Eyles, *The Woman in the Little House* (London: Grant Richards Ltd., 1922), 101. René Cutforth also offers an insight into the very different levels of poverty represented by Woolworth's legendary cheapness: 'Woolworths was exciting, like a treasure chest. You could set up housekeeping from Woolworths; and with cups and saucers at twopence apiece you catch a ghastly glimpse of the life-style of the unemployed, who spent so much of their time making cups from condensed milk tins, and patching up the kettle with the same material' (*Later Than We Thought: A Portrait of the Thirties* (Newton Abbott: David and Charles, 1976), 29–30).

[39] M-O File Report 3088, Feb. 1949, 'Keeping Up With the Jones's'.

or efficiency, these rules are never admitted to be divisive in class terms, although, of course, that is precisely their purpose. Thus June and Doris Langley Moore introduce their 1933 manual *The Pleasure of Your Company: A Text Book of Hospitality* with an assurance that class is the furthest thing from their minds in discussing etiquette and 'hostessing':

> Our ambition was to give this person [their 'ideal reader . . . a rather intelligent person trying to live with dignity and grace'], and those who were most like him, something more *comfortable*, something less imbued with the principle of snobbery than the other books we have read on the same subject. Those which we have come across usually contain numerous statements to the effect that certain things are 'only done' in the provinces, or the suburbs, or the servants' hall, as the case may be. Such statements seem to us very offensive and absurd, and we have tried not only to avoid writing anything like them, which was easy, but even to refrain from private discussion upon those narrow lines.[40]

One might think they protest too much, and indeed, almost immediately they are offering anecdotes about the stupidity of servants in the face of sophisticated plans for entertaining:

> We once brought two dozen grenadillas [passion fruit], and gave instructions to our cook to scoop them out and serve them with the sweets, at a rather ambitious little dinner of our own. She had never seen anything like them before, and, with a stupidity which had, perhaps, entered into league with her strong resentment of innovations, she threw away the inside of the fruit, and served only a dishful of empty shrivelled husks. Our dismay and the astonishment of our guests may be imagined. (p. 37)

This brief passage clearly illustrates both of the dominant features of the inter-war instructive discourse on entertaining: a profound social anxiety—which motivates the extreme hostility directed at the cook; and a strong streak of exhibitionism—hence the exotic fruit and the 'ambitious' dinner. We find other ambitious dinners represented repeatedly in the occasions for which food writers give suggested menus: Lady Jekyll, for instance, invites us to:

> Turn your thoughts to a tropical week-end in July or August, when you might expect a jaded Cabinet Minister or a depressed financier, a critic from the Foreign Office or an epicure from the Guards Club, and try them with this *Salle d'Agneau à la Miramer*. It is not exactly a cheap dish, but

---

[40] J. and D. Langley Moore, *The Pleasure of Your Company*, i.

we are told to cast our bread upon the waters and that we shall find it after many days: it might conceivably induce a rich legacy from a bachelor uncle. (p. 7)

It is notable that the guests are here imagined as a potentially hostile and judgemental audience, requiring elaborate—and expensive— propitiation. The act of entertaining, of bringing others into the home and displaying it to a more dispassionate gaze, is obviously always likely to provoke some anxiety, but in the discussion of the subject in cookery books and in the manuals of this period designed specifically to alleviate such anxiety, the profusion of details, rules, and suggestions seems likely to have increased the paranoia of the hostess.

In the women's middlebrow novel, in contrast, we find that from the 1920s onwards, scenes of entertaining are repeatedly represented as dramatically informal, in a way that anticipates the instructive discourses of twenty years later. Although the elements of fear and display are both present, they are displaced and re-formed through the middlebrow novel's singular embracing of the bohemian and the casual. Thus in Margaret Kennedy's 1924 bestseller *The Constant Nymph*, the wild-child Teresa is finally recognized by her uncle as the 'natural' partner of his artist son-in-law Lewis (married to the ultra-correct Florence) because of her casual and unaffected enactment of the role of hostess:

Presently it occurred to him, with a slight shock of surprise, how very well Teresa fitted into the picture. She seemed almost like Lewis's belonging. She had made one or two quite pertinent remarks; that was natural, since they were on ground which was familiar to her. But her chief business was to minister to them and this she did rather nicely; her hospitality had no polish, but it was suitable, somehow, to the company. She made a fresh pot of tea and, finding that Dr. Dawson had missed his lunch, she fetched up some corned beef. Charles, watching how she slapped it down on the table with a kind of off hand geniality, thought she would have made a very good barmaid. Then it struck him that it was her co-operation which had given Lewis the air of being so pleasing a host. He could imagine the pair of them entertaining with the greatest success, not in this house but in some queer, unmistakable house of their own.[41]

Florence, in contrast, brings a constraint to the evening when she enters, making the corned beef and kitchen knives look obviously

[41] Margaret Kennedy, *The Constant Nymph*, 1924 (London: Virago, 1992), 228–9.

out of place, and offering that sort of charm and politeness that stresses differentials in rank while appearing to overlook them: 'she was most charming to everybody, and especially kind to the young organist because he was insignificant and had a provincial accent' (p. 229).

A disregard like Teresa's for the conventions is presented as 'genuine' and unaffected in a surprising number of middlebrow novels. *Crewe Train*'s rebellious Denham naturally has something to say on the polite conventions of the dinner party:

> Presently they gave little dinners themselves. Denham said, 'Wouldn't it save a lot of time and trouble and plates and things if we put all the food on the table at once and let them take what they wanted?' (p. 137)

Such rejection of what Constance Spry called 'sugar-tongs manners'[42] is precisely what we would expect of Denham; what is interesting is that her cousin Evelyn recognizes this suggestion as a workable, even fashionable idea, but advises Denham against undertaking it until her membership of her social group is established:

> 'You mustn't try to be original yet, Denham dear. You don't know well enough yet how to keep the rules to break them safely. You must wait a bit, and meanwhile do things like other people. You see, when you break social rules, you should always seem to be *ahead* of fashion and convention, not lagging behind them, do you see what I mean?' (p. 137)

Breaking the rules, then—as demonstrated by Nancy Mitford's acknowledgement that the conventions of 'U' language are sometimes deliberately ignored by 'U' speakers as a joke—can be the clearest means of demonstrating that you know them but are too important and free-spirited to be bound by them.[43] Such contraventions are often presented in the feminine middlebrow as a modern avoidance of formality—they are also clearly a way of demonstrating a lack of intimidation when faced by those potentially judgemental guests. Thus in *At Mrs Lippincote's* Julia disarranges the over-expectant room before her party:

> [The room] waited. Chairs and sofas held out empty arms imploringly. Roses stood at attention. Ashtrays were disposed too carefully....

---

[42] Constance Spry and Rosemary Hume, *Hostess* (London: J. M. Dent & Sons, 1961), 29.
[43] Nancy Mitford, 'The English Aristocracy', *Noblesse Oblige*, ed. Nancy Mitford, first published 1956 (Harmondsworth: Penguin, 1968), 40.

> Roddy, coming in, couldn't see that it was all wrong. He stood there with two aspirins in the palm of one hand and a glass of water in the other. He wished all the guests would arrive at once, bursting in with exuberance, and in no time at all become semi-intoxicated. As a host, he liked things easy.
> Julia had more courage. The aspirins shocked her. She took them from him and dropped them into a rose-bowl, together with the water. 'Never let guests feel they have come at the beginning,' she said. 'It's true someone *must* be first, but *we* are here. So bring some drinks and let's begin.' She took an armful of cushions and threw them from a distance into the chairs, and then pulled one of the roses to pieces, scattering the petals. (pp. 78–9)

Although presented as welcoming of her, this behaviour is also part of the novel's continual reiteration of the theme of Julia as a rebel against conventionality. The gesture of destroying and scattering the rose, in particular, is designed to display a lack of domestic concern to her guests.

The girls in *Guard Your Daughters*, in contrast, greet the arrival of one guest for supper with scurrying panic, but also use the occasion as an opportunity to display their family in all its bohemian unconventionality. The discussion of what to serve Gregory, the unexpected visitor, for supper—a meal the family never eats—runs for six pages, with the unlabelled tins of food sent by overseas admirers of their father's writing ransacked for suitable ingredients for a '*recherché*' meal. Reduced by genteel poverty and rationing to such expedients as serving proper soup only to their parents and their guest, and water and gravy browning to themselves, the girls find their efforts considerably complicated by the fact that they must not arouse their father's suspicions of their intentions towards their guest, which might cause him to remark on the fact that the meal is unusually good. Throughout *Guard Your Daughters*, the Harvey girls are torn between a desire to seem 'normal' and a pride in their familial eccentricity—which they fully believe to be the acme of classiness. They are perhaps the clearest example of a conflict that operates in the middlebrow women's novel of this period between a desire to display the home and family as original and ideal and a fear of failing to conform to the rules of bourgeois society. We can find the source of this ambivalence in the complexity of middle-class identity in this period (as discussed in the previous chapter), where membership of the upper middle classes is denoted by an insouciance and a disregard for convention that can at any moment be revealed as a brittle façade when the individual is faced with someone more insouciant and unconventional than herself.

The bohemian middle-class woman in these novels cooks foreign food, thus establishing herself as sophisticated and broad-minded, avoiding the traditional English insularity which was increasingly seen as belonging to the denizens of suburbia. Monica Dickens (established as a reckless bohemian by her choice of occupation, her acting, and *outré* behaviour such as holding a secret cocktail party in the basement kitchen in which she is employed) cooks mainly French dishes for her employers, having had lessons in French cookery in London and when being 'finished' in Paris; while the sophisticated Florence in *The Constant Nymph* retires to the kitchen as her marriage collapses in ruins about her to prepare a *zabaglione* as an original dish to astound her guests.

Such uses of foreign recipes are not the startling anticipations of post-Second-World-War domestic trends that they might appear. A number of food writers began in the inter-war years to give recipes for dishes from the European and mediterranean peasant and bourgeois culinary traditions that were later to be more widely disseminated by the work of Elizabeth David. The trend was initiated by a young French intellectual, Marcel Boulestin, who came penniless to London in 1906, escaping the clutches of Colette's Svengali-esque husband Willy, whose assistant he had been. Boulestin stumbled on food writing by accident, achieving startling success with his first book, *Simple French Food for English Homes* in 1923.[44] While the English had long been familiar with the stuffy *haute cuisine* of banquets and hotels, Boulestin offered them something new with his descriptions of the economy, simplicity, and charm of ordinary French cooking. He gave recipes for *Cassoulet, Confits d'Oie* (preserved goose), and numerous stews and pâtés, and depicted the culinary traditions of the French peasantry in a prose dripping with nostalgia:

On a summer evening, they sit on low chairs outside the house, just by the door, holding a plateful on their knees. The day's work is over, the last lazy cow back in the stable after a last mouthful at the hedge. The twilight is blue and peaceful, only disturbed occasionally by the guttural song of some

[44] This was followed by cookery articles for most of the major newspapers and journals, the opening of his first restaurant in 1925, and the founding of a cooking school that was attended by society ladies and their cooks. In 1937 he became the first-ever television cook.

frogs in the ditch. The earth smells. But its perfume is not, to them, as sacred as that of the soup.[45]

Such sentimental evocations seized the imaginations of the public, and foreign recipes became increasingly de rigueur, with many food writers following Boulestin's example.[46] We find one of the earliest literary responses to this importation of the domestic rather than the professional cookery of Europe in the writing of Virginia Woolf. Woolf and Boulestin moved in the same intellectual social circles (she wrote to him in April 1935 declining an invitation to dinner, but reporting that her cook Mabel was enjoying her lessons at his restaurant)[47], and Woolf and her set were among the first to adopt the new taste for the ordinary food of the Continent. In her diary of the 1920s, she writes of the new sort of food they were enjoying in the more relaxed (often servantless) surroundings of their country house at Rodmell: 'the result is always savoury—stews & mashes & deep many coloured dishes swimming in gravy thick with carrots & onions.'[48] This food sound very like the famous *Boeuf en Daube* which is the central symbol of creativity and the domestic affections in the 1924 *To The Lighthouse*—Woolf's most concertedly domestic novel. This dish, prepared from an old French recipe of Mrs Ramsay's grandmother's, is designed by Mrs Ramsay to meld her guests into as harmonious a whole as the *daube* does its separate meats and flavourings. Significant ironies attach themselves to this splendid dish, with its 'confusion of savoury brown and yellow meats, and its bay leaves and its wine', notably the fact that it is the cook, and not Mrs Ramsay herself, who has spent three days on its preparation.[49] Nevertheless, it stands for the nurturing domestic spirit of Mrs Ramsay, which the text simultaneously celebrates and relegates to the past. It is significant that the *Boeuf en Daube* is both a foreign and a peasant dish: yet again the bohemian is intimately associated with bourgeois domesticity.

[45] X. Marcel Boulestin, *Simple French Cooking for English Homes* (London: William Heinemann Ltd, 1923), 10–11.
[46] e.g. Alice Martineau, *Caviar to Candy* (1927), Ambrose Heath, *Good Food* (1932), *Lady Sysonby's Cook Book* (1935), Constance Spry, *Come Into the Garden, Cook* (1942).
[47] *The Letters of Virginia Woolf*, vi: *Leave the Letters Till We're Dead*, ed. N. Nicholson and J. Trautmann (London: The Hogarth Press: London, 1980), no. 3007a.
[48] *The Diary of Virginia Woolf*, ii: *1920–1924*, ed. Anne Olivier Bell (London: The Hogarth Press, 1978), Wed. 7 Jan. 1920, 3.
[49] Virginia Woolf, *To The Lighthouse*, 1924 (Oxford: Oxford University Press, 1992), 135.

The taste for foreign food that gained currency throughout the inter-war years was abruptly halted by the onset of the Second World War. Cookery writers who had previously written widely of European food suddenly resorted to a little-Englandism. (Ambrose Heath, for example, who offered a recipe for the French fruit pancake *clafoutis* in his 1932 *Good Food*, gave a virtually identical one in his 1941 *Kitchen Front Recipes and Hints*—except that here it was safely Anglicized by being presented as hints about saving on the sugar ration by putting bits of fruit in a Yorkshire pudding batter.[50]) It was suddenly seen as unpatriotic to cook un-English food. In this context, the use made by Elizabeth Taylor's Julia of foreign recipes in the middle of the war is positively foolhardy:

> Two tearful nights and the excitement of the day had tired her. She wished that she might go to bed, instead of preparing food for other people.
> 'It doesn't matter what sort of meal it is', she decided, smashing eggs recklessly into a bowl, smearing the omelette-pan with garlic.
> 'I have an excuse for everything that goes wrong.' . . . she ladled rich brown onion soup on to fried bread, offered cheese, sipped. . . . with a wry mouth, she glanced at Roddy, wondering what it was she was sipping and if it were turning her teeth black. She tipped it quickly into her soup. . . .
> 'A meal in itself,' said the Wing Commander, cracking open a bread roll with a loud report.
> Julia fetched in the omelettes and a dish of beans.
> 'There is something so foreign about your cooking,' said Mrs Mallory kindly, not quite knowing what it was—the sensation of garlic in her mouth.
> Roddy thought Julia was in a reckless mood. Her cooking endorsed this. (pp. 153–4)

The significance of foreign—French—food in this context is that it clearly doesn't count as 'proper' food of the sort prepared by a dutiful homemaker. Instead, it is dangerously reckless, and the recklessness of her cooking is here seen to attach itself to Julia's personality: the meal is read as abandoned both in the slap-dash manner of its preparation and in its symbolic significance as a mark of Julia's desire to abandon her role as domestic provider.

Just as domestic novels in this period employ food and cooking as a significant set of tropes, so cookery books use references to literary

[50] *Good Food: Month by Month Recipes*, 138–9; *Kitchen Front Recipes and Hints: Extracts from the first seven months' early morning broadcasts by Ambrose Heath* (London: Adam and Charles Black, 1941), 54–5.

texts to establish a sense of the cultured identity of their readership and to suggest that cooking could, like reading, be both an art and a leisure activity. Boulestin, in particular, peppers his books with literary quotations. Woolf's *Boeuf en Daube* recipe is frequently referred to in cookery books of this period: it is given, for instance, by Ambrose Heath in *Good Food* (1932) and by Patience Gray and Primrose Boyd in *Plats du Jour* (1957). It is also discussed by the guests at Julia's 'foreign' dinner party. Heath calls Woolf's description of the dish 'a little rhapsody', and takes issue with the fact that Mr Bankes eats his portion with a knife and fork when 'epicures . . . would maintain [that] only a spoon should be used' (p. 185). Gray and Boyd are more reverential, although their confusion of Mrs Ramsay with Mrs Dalloway suggests that the reverence is for what has already, by 1957, become accepted as a literary classic, rather than for a much-loved favourite.[51]

Julia is a good example of the fey, educated housewife to whom food writers such as Ambrose Heath sought to appeal with recipes from literary classics. She informs her dinner guests that her baked apple recipe derives from *Villette*, adding that ' "I like to get my recipes from good literature" ' (p. 155). She too refers to Woolf's recipe as a classic, quoting its description with relish. The discussion of food that occurs around the *Boeuf en Daube* in *To the Lighthouse* is in fact a significant source for similar conversations in Elizabeth Taylor's novel. Mrs Ramsay and her guests concur on the wastefulness of the English cook compared to the imaginative frugality of her French counterpart:

> Of course it was French. What passes for cookery in England is an abomination (they agreed). It is putting cabbages in water. It is roasting meat till it is like leather. It is cutting off the delicious skins of vegetables. 'In which', said Mr Bankes, 'all the virtue of the vegetable is contained.' And the waste, said Mrs Ramsay. A whole French family could live on what an English cook throws away.[52]

Julia, clearly failing to recognize his echoing of Woolf's novel, takes issue with precisely this position when it is expressed by Mr Taylor, the lower-middle-class restaurateur she has befriended:

---

[51] Patience Gray and Primrose Boyd, *Plats du Jour, or Foreign Food* (Harmondsworth: Penguin, 1957). 168.
[52] Woolf, *To the Lighthouse*, 136.

When he had sipped quietly a little longer, he said, as if he were quoting the words:
'The English cook is a terrible combination of wastefulness and meanness. She would throw into the dustbin what a French family would make a meal from. . . .'
'Yes, we know all that', said Julia impatiently. 'Personally, I think they're welcome. I loathe that French family gathered round the dustbin and having a high old feast from potato peelings and fish-bones decorated with carrot tops.' (p. 102)

Julia's refusal of the stylish bohemian symbol of the French domestic culinary tradition, when she has represented precisely such bohemianism throughout the novel, and continues to do so, figures the extent to which the association of the bohemian with the bourgeois housewife has become established—to the point of cliché—by 1945.

A more direct association with the bohemian creative artist is offered to the middle-class woman through the activity of house-decoration, the woman decorating her home being another much-repeated scene in the feminine middlebrow. It is notable that rather than echoing the particular decorative fashions of the year in which a given novel is either written or set, descriptions of the middle-class woman's transformation of her domestic interior across the period operate in terms of a surprisingly consistent set of tropes. Most dominant is the way in which the modernity of certain women is encoded in terms of their use of colour in decoration. In *The Constant Nymph* (1924), the cultured Florence decorates her London house with a contrived simplicity designed to speak of her aesthetic sophistication:

the dining-room . . . was washed white, with an oak cottage dresser and blue plates. There was a gate-legged table, polished almost black, with a lustre dish on it full of golden oranges. The chimney piece was bare save for a Russian ornament of brilliant enamels which blazed through the sombre-tinted room. (pp. 194–5)

Her young cousins, the uncultivated offspring of an eccentric composer, fail to appreciate Florence's aesthetic vision; finding the house poor and bare. Unused to formal rooms of any sort, their own expectation is of a stately Victorian grandeur fitting to their notion of Florence's exalted status and wealth. The fact that Florence has based her decor on that of their childhood home—a dilapidated chalet on an Austrian mountainside—makes her taste even more incomprehensible to them. What the description of Florence's house tells the reader, however, is that she is a modern. The simplicity of the white walls, oak dresser, and blue plates in part conveys this information, but the modernity is principally carried in the description of the room's isolated spots of glowing colour. The keynotes of the bowl of oranges and the Russian ornament allow us to name this style as one influenced by the Russian Ballet aesthetic that had taken Europe by storm in the 1910s, and which had been one of the major elements that informed the Art Deco style developed in the 1920s:

> Before one could say Nijinsky the pale pastel shades that had reigned supreme on the walls of Mayfair for almost two decades were replaced by a riot of barbaric hues—jade green, purple, every variety of crimson and scarlet, and, above all, orange.[53]

Florence's insertion of elements of this new craze into her restrained peasant-inspired interior demonstrates her to be tasteful, but not a slave to fashion. Her modernity is tempered by her perfect gentility—which is one reason why she is such a terrible wife for the tempestuous Lewis. *The Constant Nymph* is unlike later books in associating the modern in decoration primarily with the most conventional woman. Teresa, the free-spirited child who is Lewis's 'natural' partner, is one of those who fails to appreciate Florence's decor but, significantly, the text connects her also to the modern aesthetic when she is given money for her birthday and buys an orange lustre bowl, approved by Florence as ' "very beautiful" ' (p. 248). Her uncle is surprised ' "that Teresa should ever own anything as concrete as a bowl" ' (p. 248), and in fact she owns it only briefly, because Lewis breaks it, declaring that:

> 'Bowls lead to houses. Houses are mainly to keep bowls in. If Tessa had a house she could buy as many bowls as she liked. She'd be done for. As it is, she should beware.' (p. 249)

The episode has served to establish Teresa as both a modern spirit, attracted by the pagan glow of the orange, and as the anti-bourgeois of Lewis's fantasy, not to be bounded by the walls of a house. In this she has much in common with *Crewe Train*'s Denham, for whom, as we have seen, the house and its service is an alien creed. The women in almost every other middlebrow novel from the 1920s to

---

[53] Osbert Lancaster, *Here, of All Places: The Pocket Lamp of Architecture* (London: John Murray, 1959), 126.

the 1950s, however, are contained by the domestic and express their rebellious spirits within, and in terms of, its codes.

Pure, strong colour and carefree peasant influences in decoration are the marks of the freest modern spirit in Rosamund Lehmann's first novel *Dusty Answer*, published in 1927. Here this modern woman is Jennifer: the third great love of the protagonist Judith:

> Jennifer was half asleep with her head upon the window-sill. The bowl of fruit burned in the dimness. How like Jennifer was her room! Yellow painted chairs, a red and blue rug on the hearth, cowslips in coloured bowls and jars, one branch of white lilac in a tall blue vase; the guitar with its many ribbons lying on the table; a silken Italian shawl, embroidered with great rose and blue and yellow flowers flung over the screen; wherever you looked colour leapt up at you; she threw colour about in profuse disorder and left it. Her hat of pale green straw with its little wreath of clover lay on the floor. A wide green straw would remind you of Jennifer to the end of your life. . .[54]

The bowl of fruit burning in the dimness echoes the similar image in *The Constant Nymph*, and in this case carries a greater narrative significance, because it is this copper bowl that Jennifer leaves her friend as a memento when she drops out of Cambridge to embark on a full-blown lesbian affair with the Radclyffe-Hall-like Geraldine. The bowl is used to represent Jennifer's life and vitality—as is her college room. Repeatedly in the feminine middlebrow, the woman's ability to transform her surroundings is read as an index to her personality and creativity. The felicitous carelessness and generosity with which Jennifer 'throws' colour names her as an adventuring, abandoned child of the present. The shy, old-fashioned Judith, in inheriting Jennifer's bowl is supposed to have inherited also some of her fire and life. In this case, the decor of the room is not so clearly fashionable—its influences are more Tyrolean than Art Deco, but its modernity is clearly figured in its boldness, and in its palette of primary colours.

That such colours signal bohemianism is indicated by 'Quaint Irene', E. F. Benson's caricature of the creative artist, who appears in his 'Mapp and Lucia' novels of the 1920s and 30s: Irene, a lesbian who dresses in men's clothes, has a studio with a pink porcelain stove, scarlet roof, magenta walls, and blue floor, and is at one point

[54] Rosamund Lehmann, *Dusty Answer*, 1927 (Harmondsworth: Penguin, 1986), 140.

seen sitting on a hammock suspended outside her first floor bedroom, painting her window-sill in squares of black and crimson.[55] Delia, the younger, braver sister in *The New House* employs a similar palette in imagining the flat she and her fiancé will decorate:

> Delia knew what she wanted for her flat, despised Evelyn's pouffes and cretonnes, and meant to have plain, pale wood, with bowls of jade and orange, or great heaps of cushions, raspberry red, silver green, and the deep, blue-purple of anemones. (p. 11)

Delia's aesthetic vision, like Jennifer's and Florence's, is rigorous in its rejection of the traditional and safe, strong in its simplicities. It again functions as a shorthand for her personal qualities. Her sister Rhoda thinks longingly of the house of her married friend Ursula, who defies convention in putting people first, tidiness second, and is imagined 'at present feeding her babies with porridge in the room in Hampstead which she had painted deep yellow, because it got so little sun' (p. 52). In the feminine middlebrow the employment of unconventional paintwork often functions—quite without irony—as an indication of moral fibre. Rhoda herself, trying to attain the strength to reject her stultifying life as her mother's domestic prop, gains access to this modern imaginary through the feminine activity of flower arranging:

> Arranging bowls of flowers was her passion. By choosing strange colours and putting them together, combining the vivid discords in a brilliant harmony, she expressed and satisfied a deep, unsatisfied longing for charm and colour. She ran out into the garden and picked, apparently at random, but really with design, a dark red rose, the scarlet flowers of a geum, a handful of flame and gold nasturtiums, a spray of early Michaelmas daisy, shafts of golden rod, a cluster of wine-coloured pansies . . . (p. 220)

Flowers, as the most ephemeral form of decoration, tend to be employed to represent the tentatively rebellious urges of the more conventional women—often, to serve the interests of reader-identification, the narrator or the protagonist. Thus Morgan, the most gullible and home-loving of the parentally-duped sisters in the 1953 *Guard Your Daughters* is accorded a similar skill with colour 'discords' in flower arrangements:

---

[55] E. F. Benson, *Miss Mapp*, 1922 (London: Black Swan, 1984), 27, 81–2; *Lucia's Progress*, 1935 (London: Black Swan, 1984), 124.

I like to mix a lot of improbable colours, and to add a few more flowers when the bowl looks full. I think of this, rather priggishly perhaps, as 'orchestration', and the conjunction of orange and crimson, for instance, jogs my nerves like a good discord. (p. 192)

This is a composite modernity, non-specific in its elements. The term 'discord' directs us to music rather than to art or literature; the ubiquitous orange here still signals the modern, but without any particular cultural or aesthetic associations. By this date modernity is figured unequivocally in the bold and the simple. In the 1945 *At Mrs Lippincote's*, Julia modernizes the house of Victorian-hangover Mrs Lippincote with a few deft touches. We realize quite how much of the novel's approval of Julia's character and actions is tied up in her ability to remake her surroundings when Mrs Lippincote herself, paying a long-awaited visit, tacitly approves the changes:

Once Julia had gone, Mrs Lippincote's restraint went too. Her eyes, like fish in a tank, went to each wall, to every corner, dived to the darkness beneath the sofa, vaguely discerned the warming-pan lying there, and returned to the surface, as it were, every time she heard a movement in the house, a footstep, or the clink of crockery. She tried to analyse—and dislike—the difference in the room and could do neither. What had been a colour scheme was broken up. A dark red cushion from the dining-room and an emerald green one from upstairs lay on the pink sofa. Sunflowers (in the drawing-room!) and scarlet carnations were arranged in the same vase. Mrs Lippincote shifted uneasily, but warily in her chair. (p. 164)

Yet again fauve colours are the index of the modern, and it is a woman who shakes up the past with a sure hand and eye, jogging the nerves with bracing discords. Thus the home and the domestic figure metaphorically not as a haven from the new, but as its source.

The modernity of the home in the feminine middlebrow is notably one it borrows from the creative arts: there is a marked lack of interest in those technological advancements that represented the modern home for advertisers and journalists. In this respect, as in so many others, the woman's middlebrow novel acts as a corrective to the terms of the dominant pro-domestic ideology. So, bourgeois poverty is transmuted into classy unconventionality, and cooking and entertaining allow the expression of a bohemian casualness and disregard for traditional formality. What the feminine middlebrow offers its readers is the opportunity to reorder and rename the elements of the domestic ideology that was increasingly dominating their lives, and in so doing, to reimagine the values that defined their class identity. Bohemianism, casualness, and an expressed disregard for the conventions are allowed to displace—but not altogether *re*place—the more traditional elements of propriety, emotional restraint and class-consciousness. The gradual disappearance of servants consigned the middle-class woman to a life of domesticity, but the middlebrow novel reimagined that life in order to offer her a shared cultural fantasy of a middle class freed to a degree from the restraints it had traditionally imposed upon itself.

4
The Eccentric Family

> How I loathe that kind of novel which is about a lot of sisters. It is usually called *They Were Seven*, or *Three—Not Out*, and one spends one's entire time trying to sort them all, and muttering, 'Was it Isobel who drank, or Gertie? And which was it who ran away with the gigolo, Amy or Pauline? And which of their separated husbands was Lionel, Isobel's or Amy's?'
> Katrine and I often grin over that sort of book, and choose which sister we'd be, and Katrine always tries to bag the drink one.
>
> *The Brontës Went to Woolworths* (1931)[1]

THE feminine middlebrow encountered elsewhere in this study concerns itself with redefining the significance of the home and of reading for the middle-class woman and in actively revising conceptions of class politics, gender roles, and sexuality.[2] All of these concerns coalesce in what seems to me both the oddest and the most characteristic preoccupation of the women's middlebrow novel in this period: its sense of the family as a profoundly eccentric organization. Repeatedly, a particular sort of family is foregrounded and emerges, under the spotlight, as a bizarre institution—idiosyncratic rather than normative; a place where social values are challenged rather than inculcated. The family becomes a fundamentally ambivalent space, functioning for its (largely female) members as a source of both creative energies and destructive neuroses, simultaneously a haven and a cage. The families in these novels are depicted as other than the society outside their front doors—they are eccentric, self-conscious units, establishing a familial identity through private games and invented languages. They are also ex-centric, with the focus of narrative attention invariably being the children's generation, rather than the ostensibly powerful adults. Apparently unable to cut loose from the parental home to establish new families of their own,

---
[1] Rachel Ferguson, *The Brontës Went to Woolworths*, 1931 (London: Virago, 1988), 7.
[2] The last two concerns form the subject of the final chapter of this book.

these near-adult children play out, with increasing desperation, their infantile roles. Such eccentric families form the focus of a significant number of the novels already discussed in this study: *Cold Comfort Farm*, *The Brontës Went to Woolworths*, *Guard Your Daughters*, *I Capture the Castle*, *Ordinary Families*, *Dusty Answer*, *Sweet Danger*, *The New House*, and *Crewe Train* are just a selection of those which evince some aspect of this trope. Often unfashionably large, invariably inwardly-directed, and positively self-congratulatory in their neuroses, the families in such novels elicit in their readers a compelling combination of fantasy-identification and repugnance.

One key feature of the sprawling, dysfunctional middlebrow family is its dramatic unlikeness to the conventional nuclear family that was becoming increasingly normative in post-war Britain. Surprisingly early—by the mid-1920s—the statistically average middle-class family had reduced in size from the typical six children of the Victorian period to just over two.[3] The main reason for this striking decline in family size was the increasing use of systematic birth control, which had begun among the middle classes in the 1870s, and was already fairly widespread before the First World War.[4] From the 1920s onwards, and under the influence of pioneers such as Marie Stopes, contraception became more generally available and highly publicized, with the result that the two-child family

---

[3] Jane Lewis (ed.), *Labour and Love: Women's Experience of Home and Family, 1850–1940* (Oxford: Basil Blackwell, 1986), 3; Jeffrey Weeks, *Sex, Politics and Society* (London: Longman, 1981), 187.

[4] Billie Melman, *Women and the Popular Imagination in the Twenties: Flappers and Nymphs* (London: Macmillan, 1988), 6.

Of course, the increased availability of contraception and the dissemination of birth control information were not alone responsible for the striking decline of family size in the twentieth century. The change could only have been effected by an accompanying shift in social values that made a small family desirable and hence contraception respectable. John Stevenson, in his history of *British Society 1914–1945* (London: Allen Lane, 1984), suggests that the factors motivating this ideological development were the marked decline in the infant and child mortality rate from the 1870s onwards—which made larger families for 'insurance' purposes less necessary—and the increased expense of bringing up a child which was produced for the working classes by the restrictions on child labour and the raising of the school leaving age, and for the middle and upper classes by the increased necessity of public or grammar school education to ensure the child's future in an ever-more volatile class structure. He also cites the increased expense and restricted availability, for the middle and upper classes, of domestic help, commenting that 'nothing perhaps more concentrated the minds of many middle-class families upon the necessity of limiting family size than the difficulties of obtaining domestic help in the nursery' (p. 158). (We find this concern illustrated fictionally by the frantic efforts of P. L. Travers's Banks family to find a nanny in the 1910s, and to keep the treasure—Mary Poppins—once they find her.)

had become the social norm across all classes by 1940.[5] This new small family, called by A. H. Halsey 'the basic demographic development of the twentieth century'[6] had far-reaching effects on 'living standards, the status of women and children, and attitudes towards home and family'.[7] It is all the more striking, therefore, that this family is emphatically not the one repeatedly represented in the woman's middlebrow novel, where we find instead the multitudinous, unfashionable, uneconomic family that belonged to the Victorian past. The Radlett family in Nancy Mitford's 1945 novel *The Pursuit of Love* has seven children, the Harveys in Diana Tutton's 1953 *Guard Your Daughters* have five daughters, Antonia Forest's Marlow family, who appear in the seven or so children's books she wrote between 1948 and the mid-1960s boasts eight children, and there are six Lamprey children in Ngaio Marsh's *Surfeit of Lampreys* (1941). Other novels concerned with at least four siblings are Rose Macaulay's *Told By An Idiot* (1923), Evelyn Waugh's *Brideshead Revisited* (1945), E. Arnot Robertson's *Ordinary Families* (1933), Rebecca West's *The Fountain Overflows* (1957), Margaret Kennedy's *The Constant Nymph* (1924), Josephine Tey's *Brat Farrar* (1947), Virginia Woolf's *To the Lighthouse* (1927), and most of the novels of Ivy Compton-Burnett. Still others concern themselves with extended multi-generational families of a type already unusual by 1918: Stella Gibbons's *Cold Comfort Farm* (1932) and Rosamund Lehmann's *Dusty Answer* (1927), with its family of cousins, are notable examples. The fact that the family in much fiction after 1918 is so at odds with its real-world counterpart has remained unnoted by most literary critics. Alison Light, for instance, claims that one of the features of the 'modernist conservatism' she finds endemic in the fiction of the 1920s and 1930s is 'an

---

[5] There were some attempts to correct the trend in the years after the Second World War, but as Jeffrey Weeks notes, they were largely unsuccessful: 'The large family remained generally unpopular, despite blandishments from Church, state and propagandists. The Archbishop of Canterbury, addressing the Mothers' Union in 1952, voiced a widespread offical view that "One child deliberately willed as the limit is no family at all but something of a misfortune, for child and parents. Two children accepted as the ideal limit do not make a real family—a family only truly begins with three children". But such emotional attempts to suggest the pathology of the small family cut little ice. A Gallup poll for the News Chronicle in 1944 suggested that the ideal family size was three, but even this, as Mass Observation pointed out, was barely above replacement level. At the same time, commentators observed a widespread hostility towards propaganda for large families' (*Sex, Politics and Society*, 233).
[6] Cited in Stevenson, *British Society 1914–1945*, 143.   [7] Ibid.

attack on the Victorian family which transferred allegiances to the modern couple and the small family'.[8] While this is certainly true of the material developments in this period, it is a far from accurate description of its fiction. The question to be addressed is why, in fact, precisely the opposite is true—why middlebrow fiction, unlike its readers, manifestly failed to transfer its allegiances to the new small family and all that it represented. This chapter will consider the large, inwardly-directed family as a locus for many of the dominant concerns of the feminine middlebrow.

The initiating text in this middlebrow cult of familial eccentricity must be Margaret Kennedy's 1924 best-seller, *The Constant Nymph*, with its focus on the offspring, wives, and hangers-on of Albert Sanger, an English composer who has renounced his own country in favour of a wandering life:

> He roved about from one European capital to another, never settling anywhere for long, driven forwards by his strange, restless fancy.... His preposterous family generally accompanied him. Few people could recollect quite how many children Sanger was supposed to have got, but there always seemed to be a good many and they were most shockingly brought up. They were, in their own orbit, known collectively as 'Sanger's Circus', a nick name earned for them by their wandering existence, their vulgarity, their conspicuous brilliance, the noise they made and the kind of naptha-flare genius which illuminated everything they said or did. Their father had given them a good, sound, musical training and nothing else. They had received no sort of regular education, but in the course of their travels, had picked up a good deal of mental furniture and could abuse each other most profanely in the *argot* of four languages.[9]

The most significant feature of this representation is the family's bohemianism, figured in their gypsy-like roamings, their artistic talent, and above all their lack of conventional good manners—their vulgarity and swearing separate them from the rest of their class, their very existence seeming an affront to middle-class proprieties. This novel is a key example—in fact, an originator—of the active flirtation with bohemianism that is so significant a part of the aesthetics of the women's middlebrow novel. Though the passage, in the voice of the shocked bourgeois observer, is vague about the matter, there are, in fact, seven Sanger children. Caryl and Kate, the two

---

[8] Alison Light, *Forever England: Femininity, Literature and Conservatism Between the Wars* (London: Routledge, 1991), 214.
[9] Margaret Kennedy, *The Constant Nymph*, 1924 (London: Virago, 1992), 2–3.

THE ECCENTRIC FAMILY 153

eldest, are the result of their father's first marriage to a singer. Antonia, Teresa (Tessa), Sebastian, and Paulina are the children of Evelyn Churchill, an English gentlewoman seduced and then married by Sanger. His youngest child, Susan, is the offspring of his mistress Linda, a vulgar slattern taken up by Sanger after Evelyn's death. The children are characterized by the novel in positively eugenic terms according to the class of their respective mothers: the Australian first wife—'clean, respectable, middle class, hard working and kind' (p. 27)—produced responsible, mature, essentially bourgeois children, Caryl and Kate who 'propped up the crazy household between them and were privately agreed as to its dreadfulness' (p. 35), while the children of the aristocratic Evelyn are passionate and highly strung—'from her they had inherited quick wits and considerable nervous instability' (p. 18). To complete the societal microcosm, the mistress Linda is of obscure origins—'it was believed that she had once been the daughter of a tobacconist at Ipswich' (p. 24)—and her daughter is appropriately common, and despised as such by her older siblings and her father. There is absolutely no irony in the novel's establishment of a class system within the family, or in its assignment of moral worth according to this system: the contempt with which the seven-year-old 'Soozanne' is treated is fully condoned, being justified in terms of her musical pretensions:

Susan needed no encouragement. She was delighted with any sort of notice. She climbed on to the dais, pushed back her yellow curls, and began to warble in a shallow, sugary treble. Her facility, self-confidence and inaccuracy were on a level with the amazing vulgarity of her performance.... Sanger himself was inclined to fear that her push and her unscrupulous showiness would carry her further than the others and establish her as the star of the family. Hence his animosity; he could not bear that she should eclipse the patient, industrious talent of Caryl and Kate, or the fine brilliance of Evelyn's children. He scowled heavily all through her song. (pp. 57–8)

In the context of the haute-bourgeois fear of encroachment from the classes below that was discussed in Chapter 2, Susan's pushiness, lack of taste, and over-weening confidence make perfect sense. So, too, is the decadent nerviness of the aristocratic Sanger children comprehensible in terms of that combination of admiration and patronage with which the inter-war upper middle class viewed the remnants of the upper classes.

It is these wild, undisciplined 'Churchill' Sangers in whom the novel is most closely interested, particularly the warm-hearted, sensitive, and insightful Tessa and her beautiful, reckless elder sister Antonia. The novel views these girls with the lascivious eye of an elderly roué, remarking of Antonia that 'to the experienced eye her promise was infinite' (p. 35). The novel's various plots revolve around the precocious sexuality of the two girls: a highly titillating theme that clearly accounted for a great deal of the book's remarkable popular success, and on the subject of which it is markedly ambivalent. It appears to concur with Lewis Dodd, a friend of their father's, who contemplates the nature of Teresa and her sisters in deterministic terms:

[Teresa] was barely two years younger than that sister whose history she would inevitably repeat. Paulina, too, was fashioned for the same fate. Unbalanced, untaught, fatally warm-hearted, endowed with none of the stolid prudence which had protected the more fortunate Kate, they were both likely to set about the grimy business of life in much the same way. He knew what company they kept; lust, a blind devourer, a brutish, uncomprehending Moloch, haunted their insecure youth, claiming them as predestined victims. (pp. 68–9)

The girls are here cast as inevitable sexual victims, but whether of their own or other people's lust is unclear: the text both denounces their sexuality as decadent and destructive, and celebrates it as the ultimate in classy bohemian unconventionality.

At the start of the novel, when she is sixteen, we learn that Antonia has just returned from Germany, where she had gone, without telling her family, in the company of Jacob Birnbaum, a Jewish friend of Sanger's. She reveals that she has taken Jacob for her lover, although she affects to despise him. Tessa is shocked at the revelation, but because of Birnbaum's unprepossessing looks, rather than Antonia's behaviour: ' "I wonder at your taste, Tony. He's so fat!" ' (p. 39). Antonia's choice is particularly shocking because of Birnbaum's race. *The Constant Nymph* is notoriously anti-semitic: the children call this cultured financier and artistic patron 'Ikey Mo' and harp constantly on his large nose. Antonia, when she discovers that he has offered to pay for her education (having already seen to the sexual side of it) expresses her outraged contempt in racial terms: ' "I won't have his money. He's a dirty Jew. . . . He's beneath my notice." ' (pp. 117–18). Their cousin Florence disguises her racial contempt with liberal tolerance: 'the young Jew remained, but

THE ECCENTRIC FAMILY 155

he was not really so bad' (p. 109). Although we see his hurt at the children's cruel jibes, the novel is not really interested in Birnbaum's perspective—like the fat, vulgar Russian Trigorin, he functions as a stock character, chiefly employed to demonstrate the extreme bohemian tolerance of the Sanger family in associating with such outsiders at all.

Antonia, although clearly the most sexually transgressive of the sisters, is allowed to escape the ultimate results of brutish appetite by marrying Birnbaum, while it is the technically innocent Tessa who suffers the traditional literary fate of the fallen woman. The central focus of the novel is Tessa and her life-long devotion to the much older Lewis Dodd. On Sanger's death Florence, an English cousin of the children of his second marriage, arrives at the Karindehütte, Sanger's chaotic Tyrolean chalet, to take the children home to England. She and Lewis fall rapidly in love and are married. The second half of the novel traces the inexorable decline of their marriage in England, the children's escape from their English boarding schools, and Lewis's eventual realization that Tessa is the one he has always loved. Although the narrative evinces great sympathy for Tessa, Kennedy is careful to stack the cards heavily against any possible happy resolution of her dilemma. When Lewis finally declares himself she refuses out of loyalty to Florence to countenance a relationship with him. It is Florence's vicious verbal attack on Tessa following Lewis's revelation of his feelings that changes her mind. They elope together, but are not allowed to enjoy the fruits of their sin: Tessa dies of a heart attack, trying to open a window on their first evening in a Belgian pension. With a retribution as damning as anything meted out to erring heroines by Victorian moralists such as Mrs Henry Wood, the novel ingeniously combines sexual titillation with a high moral tone.

Its ambivalent moral attitudes clearly played a part in the great popular success of *The Constant Nymph*.[10] As Claud Cockburn has argued, it is the combination of sexual licence and an openness

---

[10] Some indication of the novel's success and status is given by the many literary luminaries who offered plaudits on its first publication: George Moore, A. E. Housman, Thomas Hardy, and Arnold Bennett all congratulated Kennedy; Karen von Blixen wrote from Kenya to her family in Denmark to recommend it; and it formed the basis of a shared code employed in letters by Cyril Connolly and one of his friends from Eton to communicate their most emotional experiences. (See Violet Powell, *The Constant Novelist: A Study of Margaret Kennedy 1896–1967* (London: Heinemann, 1983), 67, 69–70, 73.)

about matters of desire and passion with the distancing, sanitizing effect of the bohemian, partly 'foreign' family—not like the reader's—that made the book simultaneously arousing and safe.[11] An example of the text's active titillation of its readership is in the episode in which Sanger confronts Antonia for the first time since her illicit sojourn with Birnbaum. The novel here buys into the sadistic-pornographic satisfaction so dominant in that other key best-seller of the immediate post-war years, Edith M. Hull's *The Sheik* (1919), with its raped and eventually joyfully compliant English heroine.[12] Sanger announces that he had intended to beat Antonia when she returned home, but that ' "it's too much trouble" ' (p. 49). He then promises to ' "institute a disciplinary system" ', which will involve him ' "thrash[ing] all the girls for half an hour every morning" '. This task, he proposes, could in fact be shared out among their brothers:

'If the men of this family co-operate, we may manage to introduce a little order into the household. Caryl shall beat Kate.' (p. 50)

The girls require this proleptic punishment ' "for their incontinent behaviour" ', a sexual reference that is made explicit by their stepmother, who announces sourly that Jacob had better beat Antonia, as ' "he's been keeping her this past week" '. Punishment is heavily eroticized, and is divorced from any particular crime—it is in the nature of girls, it is implied, to require physical chastisement. All of this sails very close to the overt eroticization of beatings, whippings, and pain found in *The Sheik*. But something else is happening here, something that arguably played a large part in the massive popularity of *The Constant Nymph*—we are given a picture of family relations in crisis. The implied violence and sexualization of family life are only prospective—indeed, couched as a joke—but they hover as possibilities for the rest of the novel. More tellingly, the scene actually serves to underline Sanger's failures as a strong parent: far from punishing Antonia for her sexual misdemeanours, he cannot summon up the energy even to be shocked. It is the manifest failure of this family to function according to either the ideals, inherited from the Victorians, of discipline and firmly hierarchized structures, or

[11] Claud Cockburn, *Bestsellers: The Books that Everyone Read 1900–1939* (London: Sidgwick & Jackson, 1972).
[12] *The Sheik* made use of exotic foreign settings to a similar—though more flamboyant—end of safely sanitizing distance.

the more modern conceptions of psychologically-informed loving comprehension that is its most striking feature. It is in this way, more than any other, that *The Constant Nymph* influences the many family novels of the next thirty-five years. The family in this novel, and in most of those that follow it, is essentially dysfunctional.

It is also essentially other than the society around it, divorced from many of its concerns, or representing them in a parodically distorted form, as in the internal class system operating in the Sanger family. Initially, this family sees itself as at one with the world: there is no gap between the environment of the Austrian chalet and the larger world of bohemian travelling musicians that is its backdrop, and the family moves easily from one sphere to the other, incorporating numerous outsiders effortlessly into their group identity:

[T]hey had, as yet, hardly learnt the difference between private and public life; the transitions between the two had been, in the old days, much less abrupt. They had been used to live, as it were, without reticence, transferring themselves noisily from the racket of their home to the racket of the Opera House without any appreciable change of atmosphere. There had been none of these secret toilets and preparations, these studied issuings forth into the larger world. (p. 273)

It is only when the children are transplanted to England that they begin to conceive of their family as separate from the world outside it; and it is with this experience of otherness, paradoxically, that the family unit becomes firmly structured:

Florence was not long in discovering that the Sangers in London were more formidable than the Sangers in the Tyrol. In their house she had never felt so much of a stranger among them as she did now in her own; they seemed to have become a family, so much more corporate and defined. Christmas was scarcely over before she began to be aware that she had imported, not three friendless orphans, but an alien community, foreign and inimical to her way of life. She began to be very eager to get rid of them. (p. 203)

It is notable that it is in the class- and rule-bound environment of the English upper middle class that the eccentric family begins to define itself as other. But, in the paradox that is central to my study, it is nevertheless *of* that class, and precisely marketed to appeal to it. Thus, contrary to Anita Brookner's rather curious assertion, in her introduction to the Virago edition, that the female reader's sympathies are for the genteel, cultured Florence, deceived by her husband's insane desire for a nymphet, the novel in fact works very strongly to direct the reader's sympathies towards Tessa and her selfless, self-knowing love.[13] It plays deliberately with the attractions posed by the bohemian, anti-bourgeois nature of the Sanger family for its respectable middle-class readers, focalizing the family through the shocked eyes of the upright, dignified Florence, but ensuring that unlicensed passion rather than polite respectability triumphs imaginatively.

To a large extent *The Constant Nymph*, and many of the novels it influenced, buy into the distorted values of the family groups they examine. They do, however, allow points of elision or exaggeration through which the reader can glimpse the oddness of such values. These novels play, with various degrees of consciousness and effectiveness, with the tensions between identification and repugnance elicited in the reader by the eccentric family. A key technique used by a number of novels to create an ironic distance between the reader and the eccentric family is the employment (as with Florence) of a partial outsider to focalize the family. So in Ngaio Marsh's *A Surfeit of Lampreys* (1941) and Nancy Mitford's *The Pursuit of Love* (1945), both very typical eccentric family narratives, we are introduced to the family by a rather shy only child, who envies the camaraderie and allowed misrule of the eccentric family, but is uneasy about their replacement of external social values with their own. This partial outsider is the reader's representative, placing a check on the family, offering an ironic and corrective distance, often taming their eccentricities before they can collapse into misrule. This figure also allows for an elaboration of the profound, if paradoxical, attraction the eccentric family seems to exert in this period. In Rosamund Lehmann's first novel, *Dusty Answer* (1927), for instance, the protagonist Judith falls in love with the family next door, a fey, confident group of first cousins who appear and disappear throughout her teenage years. She attempts to form relationships with each of the three male cousins in turn, finding each inadequate because it is the family as a unit that she is really attracted to. She ends the novel alone, having learnt that no one can be relied on: the togetherness represented by the eccentric family exposed as a chimerical fantasy. In those novels that offer the reader no point of focalization outside the eccentric family, that

---

[13] Anita Brookner, Introduction to *The Constant Nymph* (London: Virago, 1983; 1992).

THE ECCENTRIC FAMILY 159

family emerges at its most disturbing. *The Brontës Went to Woolworths* depicts its Carne family through the self-satisfied voice of Deirdre, the eldest daughter, who regards the imaginative excesses of her family as perfectly proper, but is gradually revealed to be offering a profoundly unreliable perspective. The text thus invites the reader to read it against its apparent grain. It is a device that here and elsewhere (for example in Diane Tutton's feyly disturbing *Guard Your Daughters* of 1953) allows for an effective deconstruction of the narratives that construct family identity, revealing them as deeply duplicitous, and often concealing areas of profound psychic distress.

The Constant Nymph lies visibly behind many later middlebrow family novels, and is echoed with the sort of conscious intertextuality that, as discussed in Chapter 1, is employed by the feminine middlebrow to constitute for itself a generic identity. A significant example is Rose Macaulay's *Crewe Train* (1926), which uses the earlier book's plot of the bohemian against the civilized world, though it reverses *The Constant Nymph*'s polarity between individual and society—portraying one un-formed, uneducated girl exposing the conventionality of a creative, eccentric family of artists and intellectuals. Such echoes are more than simple borrowings. Publishing her novel only two years later, Macaulay could hardly have expected the similarities between it and Margaret Kennedy's sensational bestseller to go unnoticed. *Crewe Train* functions as an ironic commentary on *The Constant Nymph*, replacing its lurid portrayal of the Sanger's bohemian life-style with the tomboyish adventurings of its heroine Denham. Most notably, it treats with heavy irony the classy, bohemian, and self-regarding family that is at the centre of so many novels up to the 1950s:

Audrey always said that Evelyn [her mother] looked decadent, like a Beardsley woman shingled. Audrey was proud of her mother for not looking ordinary and undistinguished and middle-aged. She herself was just a pretty and pleasant-looking girl; but Evelyn had a cachet. Noel's head and face had the delicate, clear beauty of a cameo, and Guy had his elegance and his whiskers and Humphrey a kind of sad, tormented, clever look. Beside looking well, they were artistic, literary, political, musical and cultured. So, as families go, they were all right in Chelsea, though, except Humphrey, they were not quite fit for Bloomsbury.[14]

[14] Rose Macaulay, *Crewe Train* (London: W. Collins Sons & Co. Ltd., 1926), 19–20.

The beautiful and extraordinary mother, the cultivated and creative life-style, the distinguished and artistic appearances, the dangerous frisson of sexual radicalism suggested by the reference to Beardsley, and most of all the sense of a unified family identity are key tropes in the representation of the eccentric family. The tongue-in-cheek Bloomsbury reference sounds like a dig at Macaulay's rival Virginia Woolf, and indeed, later on in the novel, the cultured Greshams host a party to which Tibetan lamas and Sudanese dancers are invited as a spectacle for their friends. The similarity to Leonard Woolf's internationalist activities can hardly be accidental, and it is significant that the Greshams come out of the affair very badly.[15] A similarly knowing ironizing of the eccentric family is offered right at the start of *The Brontës Went to Woolworths*, in the passage that forms the epigraph for this chapter. Deirdre's flamboyantly stated contempt for the family narrative—'How I loathe that kind of novel which is about a lot of sisters'—cunningly mocks what might well be seen as the novel's own genre, thus simultaneously establishing the generic status of the eccentric family novel, and going one step further in bold insouciance to demonstrate both this novel's and the Carnes' superior idiosyncracy. In this opening announcement the reader-hooking sensationalisms of *Constant-Nymph*-like novels are both bagged and trumped by *The Brontës Went to Woolworths*, as Deirdre describes her family's habit of transforming trashy literature into the stuff of shared fantasy: 'Katrine and I often grin over that sort of book, and choose which sister we'd be, and Katrine always tries to bag the drink one.' Their taste for the sordid elements in the type of novels Deirdre parodies serves to mark the Carnes out as unconventional and daring, while their fantasy remaking of such narratives establishes them as the type of ideal middlebrow readers discussed in Chapter I.

Where *The Constant Nymph* saw familial eccentricity as the province of bohemian outsiders, the increased popular awareness of psychological theories over the course of the intervening decade means that E. Arnot Robertson's *Ordinary Families* (1933) is concerned instead to unveil the oddities and tensions lying beneath the surface of highly

---

[15] Leonard Woolf was deeply committed to the advancement of international understanding and wrote energetically on international affairs, imperialism, and the League of Nations.

conventional family life.[16] Her ordinary family consists of parents and four children, who are all hearty outdoor-types, and at first the novel seems to be an adult version of Arthur Ransome's children's books, with lots of boating, bird-watching, and fair-play. This image, though, is gradually revealed to be created and maintained by an elaborate family politics. The story is told, looking back from adulthood, by Lalage (Lallie) Rush, one of the youngest of the children. She observes her family with the acuteness of the secretive child, and also with the sardonic perspective of the adult; a device that combines the insider and the outsider perspectives, offering the reader both nostalgia for a childhood idyll, and the bitter awareness of its false idealization.

It is a novel intensely interested in the *idea* of the family. Lallie is early aware of the ways in which a 'family identity' regulates the behaviour and attitudes of the children and serves to mark her family off from others. Considering whether to push her annoying younger sister Margaret into a pond, Lallie decides not to, as it would end in a water-fight and, contrary to family tradition, she dislikes getting wet. She is swayed, though, by the fact that such behaviour is a part of her family's official character—'it was the sort of thing that the Rush children were expected to do, and I fancy this weighed with me for a minute or two' (p. 18). The pressure towards this shared and normative family identity is strong. Lallie, 'uncomfortably aware of not being, inside, anything like as Rush as I should have chosen to be' (p. 28), provokes a neighbour into amused horror at her proposed night-sail, purely in order to hear her attribute such rashness to the Rush family character. In fact, Lallie wants to go not for the discomfort or danger, but to watch the stars—a taste absolutely antithetical to the rugged, unsentimental family character. Her sense that her family is defined by a rigorously maintained group identity is confirmed by their neighbour Mr Quest: ' "your family has an official sense of humour, hasn't it? Like the Cottrell's official sensitiveness towards Art and Such" ' (p. 175). The Cottrells and Mr Quest's family form, with the Rushes, the centre of a middle-class community, and each defines itself in terms of its relation to, and difference from, the other families. Thus, the Cottrell and Rush children 'were brought up fast friends for the convenience of [their] parents, who gained by dumping [them] all together in one house or the other, an occasional respite from family life' (p. 23).

[16] E. Arnot Robertson, *Ordinary Families*, 1933 (London: Virago, 1986). The popular take-up of psychoanalysis in this period is considered in Ch. 5.

Falling for the official myth of their friendship, it is years before the children realize how much they actually dislike each other.

The way in which eccentricity functions as a sort of social commodity for families in many of the books under consideration is acutely registered by Lallie thinking about her father's persona. They meet socially an American chemist, 'whose brother, it appeared, had been on a scientific expedition up the Amazon many years before, and still vividly remembered meeting father':

> I could picture that encounter from what was being said—the once-trim little American steamer stuck in a floating morass of flowering weed . . . And then the canoe with the half-naked man in it, skimming through openings in the damnably scented vegetation that blocked their passage: their excited attempts to hail this gold-skinned god in Brazilian-Spanish and the local Indian dialect. And his answering, 'Where are you from? . . . No, this is the Parana . . . you'll have to go back two hundred miles . . . My name's Rush . . . did you hear before you left who won the America Cup last year?'
> Genuinely, I knew, the fate of the America Cup contest of the previous year would have been one of father's first interests on meeting white men again after months in the Chaco. But what satisfaction he must have derived, immediately afterwards, from realizing just how odd this interest really was! (pp. 117–18)

The novel's focus, here as elsewhere, is not so much on the precise details of the Rush family eccentricity, as in the psychological rewards offered by feeling oneself to be unusual. Familial eccentricity is seen to be the norm, with the Rush family representative in its oddities. Unlike Rachel Ferguson and Margaret Kennedy, whose novels glory in their protagonists' differences from other less creative families, Arnot Robertson understands family life, in itself, as odd. Lallie herself tries to solve the paradox of her family's simultaneous typicality and strangeness:

> 'Oh, but Dru, ours isn't an ordinary family!' I protested, thinking first of our Rushness, and then of the cross-currents that ran under the surface smoothness of our communal life—the growing antagonism between father and Roland, between mother and Dru, one prompted by resentment of a successor, and the other by the resentment of having none, the queer inverted jealousy of another's failure: and then of my feeling for Margaret, who remained enchanting to me however often, trying to get in touch with that rare something which I believed must lie behind such loveliness, I came up against the blank wall of an alien mind, and drew away baffled and for a time resentful. No, surely ours could not be an ordinary family. (p. 138)

It is the stupid but beautiful Margaret who solves the problem, and accounts also for the novel's whole interest in the subject: ' "I suppose all families are like ours, really. Not ordinary when you know them" ' (p. 138). It is this unveiling of the strange and unlikely beneath the brisk politeness of English middle-class life that is the novel's ultimate purpose.

The dark currents running slowly beneath the bubbly surface of family life are the concern here, as in both *The Constant Nymph* and *The Brontës Went to Woolworths*. The destructiveness of family teasing is demonstrated particularly in the case of the lumbering elder daughter, Dru, who is so convinced by family accusations of her fatness that she becomes reclusive. There are increasing tensions, as demonstrated in the above quotation, between the two elder children and the parents of the same gender: an understanding of family dynamics casually informed by the increasing popularity of the ideas of Freud. The most fundamental elements of family life are made strange through the focus of Lallie's perception, so her mother's desire to feed her is converted into neurosis through a zoological metaphor:

Like most maternally-minded women, mother was unconcerned about the spiritual welfare of those she loved as long as she could personally ensure that they over-ate several times a day. I thought of an incident described by a naturalist in one of my most cherished books, the record of an adult wasp attendant on a wasp-grub, both of which were kept without food for a period, during which the wasp grew more and more agitated on behalf of its hungry charge. Finally it bit off the grub's hind leg, offering it solicitously to what remained. Just the sort of devoted wasp, I felt, that mother might have been. (pp. 95–6)

Such comparisons problematize the whole nature of maternal affection, representing it as disturbed, in a manner consonant with the distanced behaviourist ideal of motherhood that increasingly dominated contemporary thinking. The attitudes and values of their universally admired father are also systematically debunked, with his robust treatment of his children emerging as increasingly foolhardy, as when he insists that they go to sea during a heavy gale: 'Ronnie grumbled at father as audibly as he thought safe in Sootie's hearing, expressing the blasphemous conviction that in his efforts to raise a tough family father would do us all in, one of these days' (p. 70). His much-vaunted sense of fair play leads him to be perversely unfair to his own children, with whom he is furious when they win all the events in the Regatta he organizes. More unconventionally, he chooses to give his adolescent daughter a detailed account of his sexual exploits as a young man and the affair he had in South America with a local girl. Much of the novel's concern is with the everyday drama of the child's gradual coming to awareness of its parents as separate personalities from itself, with their idiosyncracies and faults experienced as betrayals because so recently unsuspected. Parents, in the end, are seen as fundamentally unknowable by their own children:

> These were . . . the two persons in all the world most irrevocably barred from my confidence, by the fact of their relationship, whenever we chanced to speak of anything that really mattered. All strangers were potentially closer to me than either of them, not because they were uncongenial people—fundamentally they were not—but because they were my mother and father, in whose intimate, unknowable lives I had once played so quaint a part. (Is that, too, always the same in ordinary families?) (p. 197)

It is this lack of intimacy which makes, in the novel's terms, such a deceit of sentimental depictions of the family. And yet those who represent modern attempts to reform the family are if anything seen as more objectionable than the Rushes. The aestheticism of the Cottrells, which is one alternative to the Rushes' hearty restraint, is dismissed as producing precocious, self-conscious children. The Rush attitude to parenting is contrasted with the fashionable modern ideas of the psychologically-informed parent at one of the Cottrell's intellectual parties. There a 'timid looking woman novelist, who seemed to crouch for protection behind her one fierce feature, horizontal front teeth' (p. 105) assumes the moral highground with her assertion that it is unfair to have children ' "unless you're prepared to recognize that motherhood's a full-time job mentally, even if it isn't physically" '. Mrs Rush's response is bemused:

> 'Well—I suppose—Do you mean . . . ?' Mother, who had found it a full-time job physically, and had never given a thought to its moral responsibilities, was soon out of her depth. . . . Then mother was asked by the novelist how many children she had had. Wriggling out of a direct answer, 'I've got four', she said, slightly grateful for the first time, probably, for the death of two of us in infancy. It did reduce the number to what, in this company, seemed more tolerable proportions. (pp. 105–6)

Despite the exposure of Mrs Rush's maternal inadequacies, the deaths of her children, and the repellent appearance and manner of the 'advanced' woman novelist ensure that readerly sympathies are directed to the former. For Arnot Robertson the experience of family life is intrinsically painful, and fashionable theories offer no palliatives.

The political correctness of intellectuals is a common theme for mockery in the middlebrow novel, but, as argued extensively elsewhere in this study, the bohemian casualness of the artistic community was becoming increasingly attractive to the bourgeoisie, particularly in the 1920s and 1930s. The novel effects a very typical middlebrow compromise, where the posturing Cottrell offspring are despised for their effete ways, but the Rush children indulge in a 'tease' that marks them out as as fully bohemian as their victims. Excluded from a Cottrell party due to a feud between the two families, Dru and Roland dress in rags and stand outside the Cottrell's gate, welcoming their celebrity guests with offers of Dru's body and dirty pictures for sale: 'the pair were bent on showing the Cottrells that though we might not talk of such things as a rule, we knew just as much about Life as their friends did, and there was therefore no excuse for our exclusion' (p. 112). An imaginative creativity that also aligns her with apparently anti-bourgeois conventions is manifested in Lallie's childhood taunting of Margaret with an elaborate story about her having been adopted:

> I told her that she was not really my sister; she did not belong to us at all .... the main theme on which I harped was that she had been taken from out of an orphan home for me to play with . . . I followed it up by saying carelessly that I had only to say the word at home and she would go back.... In order to prolong this savory moment to the utmost I loaded it with as much repetition as Margaret would stand. Credulity grew in me as it did in her while I added subsidiary details. One of them, of which I was proud enough for it to stick in my mind, was that I myself had picked her out from the other babies in the home and begged my kindly parents to let me keep this one as against a rival choice of their own: a good touch, that. (pp. 18–19)

It is significant that Lallie's act of transgressive creativity should work precisely against the institution of the family. Her cruelty, amusing though it is, has stark repercussions for her. The beautiful Margaret manages—quite unconsciously—to damage every secret pleasure and every relationship Lallie has. The novel ends with Margaret visiting Lallie and her new husband, and, with a single glance, arousing his desire, so that Lallie, yet again, disappears into her shadow. Such intense, irresolvable cruelties, the novel suggests, are at the heart of family relationships: even the most ordinary families are eccentric.

A tension between the ordinary and the extraordinary is also central to Nancy Mitford's *The Pursuit of Love* (1945), which examines the chaotic, adventurous family life of the aristocratic Radletts through the eyes of their more conventional cousin, Fanny, focalizing the extreme behaviour of the eccentric family through a character much closer in attitudes and background to the likely reader.[17] This familiar approach is particularly interesting in this instance, as the novel is transparently autobiographical, telling the story of the Mitford family, whose scandalous exploits had already made them notorious. Nancy Mitford plays fictional games with the members of her family, combining the personalities and experiences of several of her siblings in one fictional character, exchanging her sisters' husbands, and—most significantly—defusing the worst of the family scandals through humour.

The Mitfords are one of the most famous real-life eccentric families of the twentieth century. Their fame, and our detailed knowledge of their lives, derive, like that of the Sitwells and the Stephens from a literary production of their family life as mythos. In the case of the Mitfords, much of this work was performed by the press, as it reported the scandal of Jessica's elopement with the communist Esmond Romilly (a nephew of Winston Churchill), and that of Unity's close relationship with Hitler. Both profoundly shocked respectable 1930s society with their political allegiances and sexual behaviour, and it is therefore curious that Nancy chose to transform their experiences into the stuff of humorous popular romance so soon after the events. The fact that Unity had shot herself in the head on receiving the news that England had declared war on Germany makes Nancy's jeu d'esprit seem even more tasteless. I would contend, however, that her purpose was to do more than milk family tragedy and shame for fictional effects—the result of her novel was to transform the exploits of her sisters into eccentricities only slightly more exaggerated than those thought perfectly proper in the English aristocracy. In marketing her family as wild, strange, but essentially benign eccentrics, Mitford defuses that opprobrium

---

[17] Nancy Mitford, *The Pursuit of Love*, 1945 (Harmondsworth: Penguin, 1970).

that had attached itself to the family after Unity's cavorting with the German Nazi party, the 'state' visit to Hitler of Lord and Lady Redesdale (the Mitford parents), and Diana's marriage to Oswald Mosley. It is Nancy Mitford's unique and peculiar achievement to have turned all this national treachery and political extremism into the stuff of gentle middlebrow comedy—and this in the final year of the war. The Nazi associations are almost entirely removed in her fictional account, with the few remaining being not with the Radletts (Mitfords) but with the vulgar banking family into which Linda first marries. The Kroesigs (probably modelled on the Guinnesses—Diana was first married to Brian Guinness) are admirers of Hitler, and receive a motor tour when they visit him, as had Lord and Lady Redesdale when Unity and Diana took them to meet the Führer in 1932. The Kroesigs are fairly marginal figures in *The Pursuit of Love*, and have the excuse of being German: Mitford's own family disgrace is thus notably displaced. Jessica's elopement to Spain during the Spanish Civil War is given to the heroine, Linda, who thus combines in one person all the shocking adventuring carried out by Jessica, Unity, and Diana Mitford. The novel takes seriously the suffering Linda witnesses in the refugee camps, which it perhaps intends to stand in for those other, more terrible, camps of which it hardly speaks:[18]

> By this time the camps were quite decently organised; there were rows of orderly though depressing huts, and the men were getting regular meals, which, if not very appetizing, did at least keep body and soul together. But the sight of these thousands of human beings, young and healthy, herded behind wire away from their womenfolk, with nothing on earth to do day after dismal day, was a recurring torture to Linda. She began to think that Uncle Matthew had been right—that abroad, where such things could happen, was indeed unutterably bloody, and that foreigners, who could inflict them upon each other, must be fiends. (p. 118)

Uncle Matthew's profound insularity is presented throughout the novel as one of the keynotes of his character, and it is asserted here in order to annex his xenophobia in the service of an anti-totalitarian position: a clear attempt to distance the Mitford family from its notorious association with fascism.

---

[18] There is a very brief reference in the final pages of the novel, when Uncle Davy remarks that his (presumably German-Jewish) physician, Dr Meyerstein, has 'been in a camp for years' (p. 190).

Nancy Mitford would seem to have had a strong investment in creating a picture of a familial eccentricity characterized by charm and benignity, but in fact, her portrait of the Radletts is often as disturbing as Rachel Ferguson's account of the morbid and snobbish Carnes. In the opening chapter, for instance, we are offered the spectacle of Uncle Matthew's 'child hunts':

> My Uncle Matthew had four magnificent blood-hounds, with which he used to hunt his children. Two of us would go off with a good start to lay the trail, and Uncle Matthew and the rest would follow the hounds on horseback. It was great fun. Once he came to my house and hunted Linda and me over Shenley Common. This caused the most tremendous stir locally, the Kentish week-enders on their way to church were appalled by the sight of four great hounds in full cry after two little girls. My uncle seemed to them like a wicked lord of fiction, and I became more than ever surrounded with an aura of madness, badness, and dangerousness for their children to know. (p. 10)

The passage provides a clue as to how Mitford manages to depict the Radlett family as both transgressive of social and moral codes, and deeply likeable—she characterizes those codes as middle-class. Uncle Matthew's aberrant and potentially disturbing behaviour is paradoxically defused for the reader by the objection of the 'Kentish week-enders'. Both Kent (by this date a bourgeois commuter county) and 'week-end' (later to be included in Mitford's own list of proscribed non-U words denoting social vulgarity) represent a narrow-minded suburban constraint that marks Uncle Matthew out, in contrast, as stylishly eccentric and pre-eminently aristocratic. Mitford is careful, though, to make her exclusive circle of crazy aristocrats accessible. The 'Hons Society' founded by the Radletts is not confined to the children of Lords—their favourite groom, for instance, is an honorary Hon:

> It was not necessary to have been born an Hon in order to be one. As Linda once remarked: 'Kind hearts are more than coronets, and simple faith than Norman blood.' I'm not sure how much we really believed this, we were wicked snobs in those days, but we subscribed to the general idea. (p. 15)[19]

---

[19] Significantly, Jessica Mitford, one of the founders of the real-life Hons society (Nancy was much too old to join) claims in her 1960 autobiography, *Hons and Rebels*, that her sister gives an inaccurate account—that 'Hons' had nothing to do with their being the offspring of a Lord, but actually derived 'from the Hens which played so large a part in our lives'. (Jessica Mitford, *Hons and Rebels*, 1960 (Harmondsworth: Penguin, 1962), 13.) If we believe Jessica, who also, given her radical politics, has a vested interest in her own account, it appears that Nancy altered the facts of her family history to create an image of an active and enjoyable snobbery.

More significantly, the hegemonic authority of the aristocracy is carefully tempered by the persistent identification of Fanny as middle class. Although actually of exactly the same class as the Radletts—'I was an Hon, since my father, like theirs, was a lord' (p. 14)—her Uncle Matthew insists that Fanny is being brought up as middle class because she goes to school instead of having a governess, and uses expressions such as 'notepaper' and 'mirror' rather than 'writing paper' and 'looking glass'. If the aristocratic Fanny is condemned as middle class, the reader can read such a slur as simply a feature of the eccentricity of her uncle, and except herself from similar calumny. The list of exclusionary 'U' words actually works as an invitation, simultaneously welcoming the reader already aware of them into the club, and teaching the parvenu the Open Sesame. As discussed in Chapter 2, such constructions of class work by simultaneously instructing the reader in the usages of the class above her own and allowing her to pretend to herself that she already knew them.

The idea of the family as overtly and deeply shocking is central to Mitford's conception of the Radletts. The children are fascinated by the idea of wickedness, and revel in the whispered scandals they've overheard about Fanny's parents. Linda, in particular, is deeply envious of Fanny's possession of a much-married, repeatedly adulterous mother. Fanny's revelations about, for instance, her mother's abortions are greeted with the 'perpetual refrain'—' "You are so lucky, having wicked parents" '. Linda herself sets out on her own career of wickedness early:

> There was much worse drama when Linda, aged twelve, told the daughters of neighbours, who had come to tea, what she supposed to be the facts of life. Linda's presentation of the 'facts' had been so gruesome that the children left Alconleigh howling dismally, their nerves permanently impaired, their future chances of a sane and happy sex life much reduced. (p. 6)

An absolute disregard for the bourgeois gentilities that outlawed an open discussion of sex and bodily functions runs throughout the narrative. A pubescent Linda joins in the dinner-party conversation about whether chickens experience pain laying eggs with the remark that ' "it's only about like going to the lav" ' (p. 30); some years later she announces her pregnancy with the laconic ' "I am in pig" ' (p. 81). The children, at the start of the novel, are 'much preoccupied with sin' (p. 7), and engage in fascinated speculation about Oscar

Wilde and the nature of his outrage. All of this openness about the sexual serves to mark the family out as precisely not bourgeois; as possessing a healthy disregard for mincing euphemisms that is in part attributed to their country upbringing (hence the chickens and the pig imagery), but mostly to an aristocratic self-confidence and culture of plain speaking. The novel assumes that the reader will tolerate, indeed admire, their brazenness because of their impeccably upper-class status.

It is this class dimension that is used to establish a particular sort of familial eccentricity—one that humorously disregards the socially acceptable to speak deeper truths. Thus, one of the first things we are privy to in the novel is the Radlett children's breathless anticipation of their parents' deaths:

> There was the unforgettable holiday when Uncle Matthew and Aunt Sadie went to Canada. The Radlett children would rush for the newspapers every day hoping to see that their parents' ship had gone down with all aboard; they yearned to be total orphans—especially Linda, who saw herself as Katy in *What Katy Did*, the reins of the household gathered into small but capable hands. The ship met with no iceberg and weathered the Atlantic storms, but meanwhile we had a wonderful holiday, free from rules. (p. 6)

Because this is a collective fantasy it therefore gains credence as more than an individual aberration. Its literary dimension—the identification with *What Katy Did*—works to make the destructive fantasy fey rather than disturbed. We are more inclined to read it as an amusing indication of the children's involvement with books, or their collective egotism, than as a sign of mass hysteria or a corrupt family unit, but the passage nevertheless creates an uneasy sense of real hostilities beneath the surface of family life. This sense underlies the novel, but it remains covert. Jassy, one of the younger sisters, devotes herself from early childhood to building up her 'running-away fund', but we never really know why. Uncle Matthew's erratic violence is never seen to have serious consequences, but it is acknowledged that his behaviour is legitimated only by his class position:

> Had they been poor children they would probably have been removed from their roaring, raging, whacking papa and sent to an approved home, or, indeed, he himself would have been removed from them and sent to prison for refusing to educate them. (p. 13)

Indeed, Uncle Matthew—'this violent, uncontrolled man' (p. 13)—is seen as the central reason for the extreme oddities of his family: 'nature . . . provides her own remedies, and no doubt the Radletts had enough of Uncle Matthew in them to enable them to weather storms in which ordinary children like me would have lost their nerve completely' (p. 13). Thus, the Radletts are creatures of extreme and violent passions, clearly at odds with the conventional world around them:

> The Radletts were always either on a peak of happiness or drowning in black waves of despair; their emotions were on no ordinary plane, they loved or they loathed, they laughed or they cried, they lived in a world of superlatives. (p. 13)

Their emotional unconventionality means that the Radletts don't bother to edit their emotional responses. Linda takes the contemporary code of detached, restrained maternity to extremes when she rejects her first child with casual disdain: ' "I can always tell if I like people from the start, and I don't like Moira, that's all. She's a fearful Counter-Hon, wait till you see her" ' (pp. 82–3). As with every other occasion on which the darker eccentricities of the Radletts are aired, however, Nancy Mitford provides an alternative interpretation of the event in order to retain our sympathies. When Aunt Emily reveals that Linda had almost died giving birth the latter's casual coolness about her baby emerges as a plucky refusal to discuss the danger she had been in. In fact, bad and indifferent mothers are the norm rather than the exception in this novel. Fanny's mother, the Bolter, abandons her daughter as a baby, and remains only intermittently in touch. Linda continues to despise the infant Moira as she grows up, leaving her with her ex-husband when she—following in her aunt's footsteps—elopes with another man. Even Aunt Sadie, the mother of the Radlett children, although benign in comparison with her husband, is represented as an unusually detached, uninvolved mother. The large size of the Radlett family is put down not to maternal instincts, but to bad planning on her and Uncle Matthew's part—they 'lived in a perpetual state of surprise at having filled so many cradles, about the future of whose occupants they seemed to have no particular policy' (pp. 13–14). The multiplication effect works to suggest that most families are in some ways inadequate. This idea is supported by Linda's excited revelation of a scandal at the heart of her husband's deeply respectable and tedious family:

'Tony... had a sister called Moira who died, and what d'you think I found out (not from him, but from their old nanny)? She died because Marjorie whacked her over the head with a hammer when she was four months old. Do you call that interesting? And they say we are an uncontrolled family—why even Fa has never actually murdered anybody, or do you count that beater?' (p. 82)

A child's murder of her sister is, as Linda insists, a far worse aberration than anything that has occurred in the Radlett family: the implication is that the Radletts' wildness is actually a safety-valve that prevents such tragedies occurring. This brief account also suggests a self-consciousness on Mitford's part about the idea of the eccentric, violently emotional family. This is confirmed by a reference to what begins to look like the Ur-text of this genre, *The Constant Nymph*. Worrying about the prospective marriage of her guardian, Aunt Emily, (because she imagines all men to be emotional tyrants like Uncle Matthew and her own father) Fanny is teased by her cousin Louisa with *The Constant Nymph*—'she read aloud the last chapters, and soon I was dying at a Brussels boarding-house, in the arms of Aunt Emily's husband' (p. 24). As well as indicating Mitford's sense of her text as part of a progression of novels concerned with emotionally aberrant families, this intertextual reference points to another link with earlier narratives of the eccentric family—the characters' active engagement with fantasy, particularly that produced by reading. Like the opening references to 'books about a lot of sisters' that positions *The Brontës Went to Woolworths* as both part of, and ironically aware of, the fiction of family disorder, this imaginative connection with *The Constant Nymph* gestures towards the romance elements to come in *The Pursuit of Love*. It also, however, stresses the novel's difference from Margaret Kennedy's heightened melodrama—for Fanny's new uncle is not another passionate rebel like Lewis Dodd, but a charming, effeminate hypochondriac, comically given to diet fads and miracle cures. Where Kennedy's novel takes seriously the bohemian excesses of its eccentric family, Mitford labours to render her own family's much darker eccentricities safely comic.

While the eccentric family imagined repeatedly by middlebrow women's fiction in the years following the First World War is an essentially new creation, it is modelled on two totemic Victorian literary families, one fictional, one real: the Marches from Louisa M. Alcott's

Little Women, and the Brontës. Both are awarded iconic status by the feminine middlebrow; referred to with intimate familiarity by numerous novels, they are employed to establish the parameters of depictions of the literary (and liter*ate*) family.

Alcott's *Little Women*, as noted in Chapter 1, is among the most popular of novels with the characters of the feminine middlebrow. Enthused over by *Sweet Confusion*'s Judy (' "my favourite book, my very favourite!" '), it is employed in that novel to suggest the charming catholicity of taste of the ideal middlebrow woman reader.[20] In Elizabeth Taylor's 1951 *A Game of Hide and Seek*, an intellectual couple turning out a cupboard full of old books to donate to the Liberal Party jumble sale squabble over whether to include *Little Women*, with the wife refusing to countenance its loss, although she owns another copy. The contested book was given to her by an aunt and she plans to keep it for her daughter; the other was a present from her mother: ' "She used to read it to me after tea. We both cried dreadfully." '[21] Alcott's novel has a multi-generational appeal, and here clearly stands in for an inheritable tradition of female solidarity and readerly pleasure. The Provincial Lady has another of those episodes of literary misunderstanding which serve to mark her isolation from others in her domestic sphere when she suggests to her husband and aunt that *Little Women*'s devoted family servant, Hannah, forms a telling contrast to their own erratic Cook. Her husband, as usual, has no knowledge of the novel and 'looks appalled when I say that Hannah is a character from the classics'. Her Aunt Blanche, who has at least read the novel, confuses Hannah with Aunt March and declares that ' "anyway, books are no guide to real life" ', thus separating herself catagorically from the knowing but enthusiastically immersed women readers celebrated by the feminine middlebrow: those who appreciate the emblematic power of certain fictions to map the tribulations of their daily lives.[22] The cult authority of Alcott's novel, particularly in the first half of the twentieth century is indicated by Elaine Showalter's list of famous women who have acknowledged the impact of *Little Women* on their lives—it includes Gertrude Stein, Adrienne Rich, and Simone

---

[20] Norman Denny, *Sweet Confusion* (London: John Lane, 1947), 46.
[21] Elizabeth Taylor, *A Game of Hide-and-Seek* (London: The Book Club, 1951), 102–3.
[22] E. M. Delafield, *The Provincial Lady in Wartime*, 1940, collected with other novels in the series as *The Diary of a Provincial Lady* (London: Virago, 1991), 460–1.

de Beauvoir.[23] In *What Katy Read*, their 1995 study of 'classic' girls' stories and their influence, Shirley Foster and Judy Simon note the exemplary role played by *Little Women* for generations of both American and English female readers, arguing that its power resides in its recognition that acquiring an adult feminine identity is not natural or instinctual, but 'a learned and often fraught process':

> In its ability to promote a double set of value systems, the book maintains a precarious balancing act, simultaneously providing for its readers a positive image of the values of home and female domesticity *and* arguing for the importance of creative independence for women.[24]

This simultaneous endorsement of both conservative and radical models of adult femininity is clearly one reason for the novel's great appeal to the readers and writers of the women's middlebrow novel at a time when gender identities were in a state of confused flux following the transformative traumas of the First World War. I would contend, though, that the very particular model of the *family* offered by the novel is an equal source of the powerful attraction it wielded for women in this period. Although its official ideology is one which extolls the passive, domestic, emotionally repressed woman (in the person of Marmee), the action of the novel actually valorises the emotional and—increasingly—economic self-sufficency of the March sisters, who employ their creative talents and ingenuity to support the family in the absence of their father. It is the image of the family as an essentially female space that is one of the most significant ways in which *Little Women* influences later middlebrow family fictions, where the fathers are so often either literally or emotionally absent. The idea of siblings defined by individual talents (Meg's embroidery, Jo's writing, Beth's music, and Amy's drawing) is also echoed in many later novels. A key example is Diane Tutton's *Guard Your Daughters* (1953) (already discussed in Chapter 2), in which the Harvey family, like Margaret Kennedy's Sangers and Rose Macaulay's Greshams, is primarily defined through the creativity of its members. The father is a celebrated writer of literary detective stories, the mother an artistic and aristocratic-looking recluse, and the girls are, respectively, maternal, poetic, musical, domestic, and

---

[23] Elaine Showalter, *Sister's Choice: Tradition and Change in American Women's Writing* (Oxford: Clarendon Press, 1989), 42.

[24] Shirley Foster and Judy Simons, *What Katy Read: Feminist Re-Readings of 'Classic' Stories for Girls* (Iowa: University of Iowa Press, 1995), 87.

bookish. The daughters, although all but one are grown up, continue to live at home, enjoying a life made up of trivial domestic satisfactions: sisterly chat in the bathroom as all bathe in turn, an impromptu game of French cricket and ludicrous culinary contrivances when an unexpected guest arrives for supper. It is a quite conscious reworking of *Little Women*; as is confirmed by a significant referencing of the earlier novel: when Cressida, the second-youngest sister, prepares to go on a visit, the behaviour of her siblings is governed by a desire to echo the conduct of the March sisters when Meg prepares for her first ball (the novel notably fails to clarify the events echoed, assuming that its readers will be intimately acquainted with Alcott's text):

> I decided to be handsome about it, and asked Cressida which of my clothes she would like to borrow. Thisbe had already lent her a skirt, and I didn't want to be outdone. I was prompted, too, by affectionate memories of *Little Women*. Theresa may also have been thinking of that, for she bundled all her handkerchiefs out on to the floor and chose the two most elaborate for Cressida's use.[25]

Guard Your Daughters does more than simply echo the earlier text, however—its deconstructive rewriting reveals the impossibility of such benign family dynamics in the modern world of psychoanalysis and nascent female autonomy. Where Alcott's girls—even the boyish and ambitious Jo—come gradually to an accommodation with the values of their domestically conformist mother, Tutton's daughters come to realize that their own mother's attempts to control their behaviour stem from much more disturbing roots. When Cressida runs away from home, the mother is propelled into a nervous collapse:

> Mother dropped the letter to the floor, stood up, and shrieked. Oh, if only I could forget it! It was a long, high shriek, that went higher, and as she shrieked she beat with her hands on the door behind her—her own bedroom door. Her eyes were turned up and there was froth on her lips. (p. 221)

The reader has already picked up the subtextual suggestions of Mother's mental instability, and it now emerges that her daughters have been dreading such an event for years. Specialists are called from London, and after long consultation they pronounce Mother

[25] Diane Tutton, *Guard Your Daughters*, 1953 (London: The Reprint Society, 1954), 158.

not mad at all: she has been cynically faking it all these years to control her husband and daughters. A further revelation for the girls is that all of their father's huge book-royalty payments have been saved towards the buying and equipping of a private nursing home for the sole use of his wife, should her illness progress. He has quite deliberately restricted his daughters' lives and educations in order to avoid provoking his wife into a mental collapse. Although Morgan very quickly turns away from the full horror of the situation into the saving fiction of her mother's development of a gradual mania as the result of this indulgence, the myth of familial harmony has been completely exploded. By the end of the novel there is nothing left of the family. The girls are dismissed to various trainings in London in order that their mother can recover quietly and, as Morgan says, 'we shall never really be a family again' (p. 246).

It is perhaps because the positive images of domestic harmony offered by *Little Women* seem ultimately unrealizable to the modern middlebrow—though the more attractive for that unattainability—that the antithetical familial model of the Brontës holds such sway, offering a means of exploring the neurotic entanglements of family life for women. The Brontës function as powerful cultural icons in a number of novels. In Stella Gibbons's *Cold Comfort Farm* (1932), Dodie Smith's *I Capture the Castle* (1949) and E. M. Delafield's *Diary of a Provincial Lady* (1930), the reader is assumed to have a close familiarity with the lives and works of the Brontë family. In other novels, notably Elizabeth Taylor's *At Mrs Lippincote's* (1945) and Rachel Ferguson's *The Brontës Went to Woolworths* (1931), the Brontës are a central textual element, at once enjoyably grotesque figures from an increasingly remote Victorian past, and emblems of some of the key concerns of middle-class women in a rapidly changing present.

The use of the Brontës in the feminine middlebrow is illustrative of a contemporary obsession. The Brontë Museum at the Haworth Parsonage opened in the 1920s, and photographs of the opening, displayed in the museum today, show a massive crowd more reminiscent of a political rally than a cultural event. In 1933 three pseudo-historical plays about the Brontë family ran simultaneously in London.[26] Numerous fictionalized biographies were published,

---

[26] Robert Graves and Alan Hodges, *The Long Week-end* (Harmondsworth: Penguin, 1971), 292.

including E. Thornton Cook's *They Lived: A Brontë Novel* (1935), Hilda White's *Wild Decembers: A Biographical Portrait of the Brontës* (1957), and Roberta Trigg's *Haworth Idyll: A Fantasy* (1946).[27] The last imagines the experience of children attending the school at Haworth Parsonage that Emily and Charlotte envisaged but never secured—an effective example of the productive confusion between fact and fiction often produced when the Brontës were contemplated in this period. The tone of all three accounts oscillates sharply between the sentimental and the grotesque, indicating the twin pulls the biography had for contemporary imaginations. This period also sees a rise in critical research on the Brontës' works and lives. An interesting example is a collection of letters and memoirs, *The Brontës, Their Lives Recorded by Their Contemporaries* which was compiled and introduced by E. M. Delafield and published in 1935 by Leonard and Virginia Woolf at the Hogarth Press and serves as a useful indication of the range of the Brontës' appeal at this time—from the middlebrow whimsey of the former to the high-cultural seriousness embodied by the latter. Comparatively little of the interest in the Brontës focuses on their writing—instead, it is the family itself, and its supposedly tortured, isolated life that fascinates reader and writers.[28] The Brontës, of course, are the original eccentric family, and it is my contention that much of the Brontëphilia we find in this period is motivated by a simultaneous attraction to and repulsion from the model of the family they represent.

In the middlebrow use of the Brontës, the same topoi reappear continually: the social and geographical isolation of the family, the claustrophobia of their domestic life, and their use of literature as an escape, particularly through their joint creation of imaginary worlds. The Brontës were in many ways the perfect middlebrow subject: available for both serious analysis and gossipy speculation; their works clearly of high literary status, but also intimately familiar to many middle-class women through repeated adolescent

---

[27] E. Thornton Cook, *They Lived: A Brontë Novel* (London: John Murray, 1935); Hilda White, *Wild Decembers: A Biographical Portrait of the Brontës*, 1957 (New York: E. Dunton & Co., 1958); Roberta Trigg, *Haworth Idyll: A Fantasy* (Richmond Virginia: Whittet & Shepperson, 1946).
[28] Patsy Stoneman has, though, interestingly demonstrated the ways in which the plots of *Jane Eyre* and *Wuthering Heights* were reworked repeatedly in this, as in other periods in her *Brontë Transformations: The Cultural Dissemination of Jane Eyre and Wuthering Heights* (Hemel Hempstead: Harvester-Wheatsheaf, 1996).

rereadings.[29] Indeed, familiarity with the Brontës' lives and works is used in a number of novels as a test of the personal, intellectual, and social worth of individuals. They are a frequent reference point for E. M. Delafield's Provincial Lady as she attempts to rise above the frustrations of her domestic routine with literary references and parallels which prove meaningless to her stolid husband. In Elizabeth Taylor's *At Mrs Lippincote's*, knowledge of the Brontës firmly divides the sheep from the goats. Julia, the protagonist, her fey and charming son, Oliver, and her husband's enigmatic boss, the Wing Commander, are all Brontë addicts, swapping information and speculation about the family's life stories with intense pleasure. Julia's disappointing and adulterous husband and his annoying cousin fail to understand this fascination, writing it off as provocatively whimsical in this time of war. In this novel, interest in the Brontës denotes a certain sophistication, a recognition that life holds more than the rigours of the quotidian round. There is the assumption that the reader, also, will pick up the Brontë references—that such knowledge and interest in fact *defines* a certain sort of woman: middle-class, intellectually curious, intimately engaged with her reading. The Brontës *represent* reading in some iconic sense, denoting the pleasurable excess of the ideal middlebrow woman reader over-identifying with what she reads. The Brontë references are part of that elaborate intertextuality in the middlebrow women's novels of this period (discussed at length in Chapter 1), whereby they establish themselves, through a web of cross-reference and echo, as a sort of sub-genre, and in so doing establish a distinct identity for their readers. This intertextuality is rarely a 'dead' echo—it is produced through an elaborate engagement with other texts on the part of both characters and the text itself. An example is a debate, carried on in a number of novels, on the relative merits of the works of Jane Austen and the Brontës in defining worlds in which one would like to live. The debate is articulated directly in Dodie Smith's 1949 novel *I Capture the Castle*:

'Did you think of anything when Miss Marcy said Scoatney Hall was being re-opened? *I* thought of the beginning of *Pride and Prejudice*—where Mrs Bennet says "Netherfield Park is let at last". And then Mr Bennet goes over to call on the new rich owner.'

[29] In this regard it is worth noting that the pre-eminently middlebrow Daphne du Maurier published a biographical study entitled *The Infernal World of Branwell Brontë* in 1960 (just outside the temporal boundary of this work).

'Mr Bennet didn't owe him any rent.' I said.
'Father wouldn't go anyway. How I wish I lived in a Jane Austen novel!' I said I'd rather be in a Charlotte Brontë.
'Which would be nicest—Jane with a touch of Charlotte, or Charlotte with a touch of Jane?'
This is the kind of discussion I like very much but I wanted to get on with my journal, so I just said: 'Fifty per cent each way would be perfect', and started to write very determinedly. Now it is nearly midnight. I feel rather like a Brontë myself, writing by the light of a guttering candle with my fingers so numb I can hardly hold the pencil.[30]

In fact, the plots of the sisters' lives are determined by the literary models they here select. The elder, Rose, faces the Austen dilemma of a choice between two men, with initial hostility towards one turning into love. Cassandra, the narrator, (who notably shares the name of Jane Austen's sister) is referred to by the Vicar as 'the insidious type—Jane Eyre with a touch of Becky Sharp', and has the Brontëesque fate of unrequited love.

In Stella Gibbons's *Cold Comfort Farm*, also, a conflict between an Austen and a Brontë world view is played out. Our attention is directed to the Brontës early, when Flora Poste, the urban sophisticate, is warned by the pub landlady of the presence of an intellectual in the depths of rural Surrey:

'A book-writer... He's doin' one now about another young fellow who wrote books, and then his sisters pretended they wrote them, and then they all died of consumption, poor young mommets.'
'Ha! A Life of Branwell Brontë', thought Flora. 'I might have known it. There has been increasing discontent among the male intellectuals for some time at the thought that a woman wrote *Wuthering Heights*. I thought one of them would produce something of this kind, sooner or later.'[31]

Gibbons here follows the real-life Brontë controversies of the 1930s, when a number of writers advanced just such a theory. Mr Mybug, when Flora meets him, expounds his ideas more fully:

'They were all drunkards, but Anne was the worst of the lot. Branwell, who adored her, used to pretend to get drunk at the Black Bull in order to get gin on tick for Anne. The landlord wouldn't let him have it if Branwell hadn't built up—with what devotion, only God knows—that false reputation as a

---

[30] Dodie Smith, *I Capture the Castle*, 1949 (London: The Reprint Society, 1950), 24.
[31] Stella Gibbons, *Cold Comfort Farm*, 1932 (Harmondsworth: Penguin, 1983), 75–6.

brilliant, reckless, idle drunkard. The landlord was proud to have young Mr Brontë in his tavern; it attracted custom to the place, and Branwell could get gin for Anne on tick—as much as Anne wanted. Secretly, he worked twelve hours a day writing *Shirley* and *Villette*—and, of course, *Wuthering Heights*. I've proved all this by evidence from the three letters to old Mrs Prunty.' (p. 102)

There is clearly a sense here of the Brontës as the province of women, grotesquely misread by male intellectuals who attempt to usurp them. As Flora snobbishly muses: 'one of the disadvantages of almost universal education was the fact that all kinds of persons acquired a familiarity with one's favourite writers. It gave one a curious feeling; it was like seeing a drunken stranger wrapped in one's own dressing-gown' (p. 105). And so the Brontës are marked out not only as female territory, but as upper-middle-class—not properly belonging to those classes that were the main beneficiaries of that almost universal education.

Cold Comfort Farm as Flora first encounters it is Brontë-world, a giddy amalgam of Brontë pastiches: so the flighty Elfine is a version of Cathy; the darkly-brooding Seth is a type of Heathcliff, and their mad mother, Judith, is a sort of Bertha Mason. The fun of the novel is that Flora herself belongs to a Jane Austen novel, and tidies up their lives with the energy of an Emma—and with much more success (marrying Elfine to the local squire, sending Seth to Hollywood as a film star, and engaging Judith a psychoanalyst who transfers her obsessions onto old churches). In Gibbons's parody, the Brontë-plot is consigned to the past: the modern world requires the open rationalism of an Austen.

The most sustained middlebrow response to the Brontës occurs in *The Brontës Went to Woolworths* where, as already mentioned, the Brontës function as both ideas and as characters—ghosts who contact the family during a seance and later visit their home. The Carnes' parallel with the Brontës is suggested throughout the novel, and the Brontës also represent both the attractions and the dangers of the co-operative creation of fantasies that can become more necessary than reality. The Carnes, in their 'making out' are echoes of the Brontës, and it is clear that a similar fate threatens to that of Emily, unable and unwilling to leave the worlds of her childhood imaginings. The Carne family fantasies are presented as appealing in their fey excesses; a certain giddy surrealism animates, for instance, the idea that their dog, Crellie, is a gruff Kiplingesque army veteran who in the course of a much-travelled life once spent a period as the Pope. At the same time, a nagging sense of psychic damage underlies the fantasies. Deirdre has been unable to marry because she was in love with Sherlock Holmes, and their mother, when the girls were children, had dressed them in their best clothes to meet the ghost of their father. By the end of the novel fantasy is seen as unequivocally dangerous, particularly for Shiel, the youngest child, who has an uneasy grip on the differences between the two worlds her family inhabit. She is terrified by the Brontës' ghosts—as creatures half-way between the two worlds—and to save her sanity they have to be domesticated. It is the down-to-earth Lady Toddington (the wife of the judge Deirdre has transformed from fantasy figure to friend-of-the-family) who finally achieves this, describing how the day before she had seen the Brontës shopping in Woolworths.

Throughout the novel the Carnes express a sense of intimacy with the Brontës and their works. Deirdre, for instance, is convinced that Emily is 'harassed' by the positioning of her portrait in the National Portrait Gallery, and tells her ' "My dear, I can't do anything about it" ' (p. 34). However, when the Carnes holiday in Yorkshire, they are too busy being miserable to visit Haworth, and they fail to recognize the signs that they are being haunted by the Brontës. (These signs include a drunken red-headed boy in the local pub, a dog called Keeper who befriends their dog, and annotations in Charlotte Brontë's hand on the manuscript of Deirdre's novel.) In fact, as already discussed, the person who actually gets to meet the Brontës is their despised governess, Miss Martin, who is egged on by their ghosts to leave her job and go and work with the man she loves—a curate with more than a touch of St John Rivers about him. Deirdre resents this privilege bitterly, but the family solve the problem of being overlooked by the Brontës by 'bagging' them, and remaking them in a fantasy version. They are incorporated into the elaborate family fantasies, expressing opinions about the flirtation of the middle sister with a 'low' comedian: ' "Emily . . . treats it with a marble contempt, but Charlotte says that where one loves, one takes" ' (p. 222), and it is announced that ' "Emily is writing a new book called Swithering Depths" ' (p. 230): the Brontës are reduced to safely parodic figures. The robust Lady Toddington, having abandoned Elizabeth Gaskell's *Life of Charlotte Brontë* as ' "all such a *fuss!*" ' (p. 167), feels herself free to simply invent Brontë history and behaviour, dismissing Charlotte and Emily as ' "a couple of dreary bores" ' (p. 214). Her husband tries to redeem the Brontës' neglect of the Carnes by suggesting that they were attracted to the family rather than to Miss Martin—' "Hasn't it occurred to you that Charlotte and Emily were drawn to you, as a family, by a happiness they never had themselves?" ' (p. 211). On one level these attempts represent a modern remaking of the Brontës, claiming the attractive parts of their mythology, and dismissing the rest. But the text doesn't quite validate these rewritings: the Brontës' unhappiness lives again in the neglected Miss Martin, and the flamboyant Carnes don't quite survive her assessment of the awfulness of families: 'show[ing] one face to each other and another to the stranger within their gates' (p. 182), which condemns them as both unpleasant and—much worse from their perspective—typical. The Brontës serve as an emblem for the middlebrow eccentric family, but they reveal it as snobbish and self-congratulatory, a place where creative fantasies spill over easily into neurosis.

Part of the fascination with the Brontës in Ferguson's novel is with the grotesque elements of their lives. Judge Toddington displays a cultish interest in the Brontë relics in the Parsonage, and revels in the extremes of their experience, praising it as superior to their works:

'The Brontë family has been, like Switzerland, too much stamped over, and virtues have been discovered in all their work which I, personally, won't admit it always possessed. But what a family! Even if they'd never written a line, what a story! Isn't it all artistically complete that there isn't a quotable line recorded of Anne? Wasn't there a sort of fate which ordained that she, of all the family, should be buried away from home, dying, meek, futile on that Scarborough sofa . . . and Branwell, drugged and drunk dying, erect, in his best suit, out of bravado?' (p. 128)

There is a similar taste for the grotesque in *At Mrs Lippincote's*, with Julia fascinating her impressionable young son—who has already peopled the locked attic tower of their rented house with a frenzied Mrs Rochester—by describing a particularly macabre relic she has seen at the Parsonage:

'Once I saw Emily Brontë's comb, a very nasty-looking comb too. She dropped it off the horsehair sofa the moment she died and it fell on the fire. Charlotte grabbed it, which seems an odd thing to have bothered about doing with her sister dying. There it is to this day, a bit burnt. One of the most horrible things I ever saw.' (p. 18)

The Wing Commander impresses Julia by having seen the Pensionnat Heger, and he later visits Anne's grave in Scarborough, and muses on the fact of her bones lying beneath his feet. The stress is on the Brontës as gruesome relics: although they are depicted in middlebrow women's fiction with a gossipy familiarity and intimacy, their fascination lies as much in their *distance*—in the gap between their world of damp, graveyards, and repression, and the bright modernity of the years after world war one. Throughout these novels there is a jokey attempt to keep the Brontës in their place, to ward them off, but they keep returning. As such hauntings suggest, the Brontës function for the feminine middlebrow as both inspiration and warning: they serve as a model of the potential of the feminine creative imagination, and the power of intense familial bonds to both license and support it, but also as a grotesque example of the limitations of the domestic environment as a source of women's identities.[32]

The neurotic intensity of family life suggested by the Brontë paradigm makes the eccentric family a fertile subject for the detective fiction of the period. Notably, some of the best-known of the novels of the 'Golden Age' detective writers focus on crimes occurring within just such families: Ngaio Marsh's *A Surfeit of Lampreys* (1941), Josephine Tey's *Brat Farrar* (1949), Margery Allingham's *More Work for the Undertaker* (1949), and a number of the novels of Agatha Christie, including *Appointment with Death* (1938) and *Crooked House* (1949). We find very knowing depictions of eccentric families particularly in *More Work for the Undertaker* and *A Surfeit of Lampreys*: the Palinodes in the former are the typical family of the type enjoyed by the feminine middlebrow, but grown old. Younger sister Jessica dresses like a tramp, with grass in her shoes and an old motoring veil tied over a square of cardboard on her head, and devotes herself to the art of living on one-and-six a week; elder sister Evadne is a regally authoritative intellectual; and brother Lawrence communciates 'in crossword

[32] The Brontës also feature interestingly in two novels that fall outside the scope of my study. Antonia Forest's *Peter's Room* (1961) is part of her series of children's books about the Marlowe family which began in the 1940s as fairly conventional school stories and gradually mutated into something much more complex. In this novel the younger Marlowe children and their friend Patrick spend a vacation living out an elaborate fantasy inspired by the Brontës' imagined lands of Gondol and Angria. The result is that the benign world of unending summers typical of classic children's literature threatens to collapse into insanity as anarchic desires are licensed by the fantasy. Brontë-inspired imaginings are also dangerous in Jane Gardam's 1973 teenage novel *The Summer After the Funeral*, in which the protagonist decides that she is a reincarnation of Emily Brontë.

puzzle clues with an occasional unsolvable family reference thrown in'.[33] Two other siblings are dead, presumed murdered by one of the family. Reduced to penury, the Palinodes live on in their once-grand house:

'The district's gone down like a drunk in thirty years and the Palinodes with it. Used to have their carriage once, supported local tradesmen as if they were squires in the country. Now a dear old variety gal turned lodging-house keeper owns their house. Mortgage fell in, she inherited, her own place got bombed, so she moved over with some of her own boarders and took the Palinode family in her stride.' (p. 30)

The novel is well aware that the Palinodes are literary clichés, and provides them with a range of eccentricities lurid enough to tip them over into surrealism, while at the same time various minor characters stolidly insist that the family is perfectly normal: ' "Eccentric? Not unless brains are eccentric. They're a very good family" ' (p. 47). The detective plot, as is usually the case with Allingham, is so contorted as to be fanciful, and the major interest is in characterization. What the novel reveals particularly in its parodic excesses, is the degree to which such literary families are class fantasies, depictions of an idealized gentry at the moment that it effectively ceased to exist. Peculiar they may be, but the Palinodes maintain a scrupulous code of local patronage and support in their London 'village': ' "My father believed in employing local people. They may not be the best, he said, but they are one's own." ' It is presented as a noble attitude, but even the loopy Jessica realizes that it is fantastically outdated: ' "We Palinodes have carried one kind of squirearchy to its ridiculous conclusions, that's all. I shall forgive you anything as long as you never find us sad" ' (p. 138). In the amorphous chaos that is post-war London, such touching faith in old hierarchies and loyalties is in fact positively dangerous—one of the Palinode siblings has been murdered by their trusted bank manager, who slipped poison into the glass of sherry they still expected to take with him when visiting his offices. It is no accident that so many of the detective stories which focus on the eccentric family date from the period during or just after the Second World War: it is in these years, as established in Chapter 2, that the upper middle class finally relaxed its tenacious grip on the cultural hegemony. The

---

[33] Margery Allingham, *More Work for the Undertaker*, 1949 (Harmondsworth: Penguin, 1954), 61.

THE ECCENTRIC FAMILY 185

middlebrow fictions of these years function as elegies for this lost authority, and in their portraits of social dinosaurs like the Palinodes these detective novels both celebrate and mourn a potent upper-middle-class fantasy.

The same fantasy is presented just as deliberately, but with considerably less irony in Ngaio Marsh's *A Surfeit of Lampreys*, in which the charming, feckless, and impecunious family of Lord and Lady Lamprey are seen through the admiring eyes of New Zealander Roberta Grey, who befriends them during their brief experiment with running a sheep farm. Their unusualness, we are assured, is a product of context: 'In New Zealand the Lampreys were a remarkable family. Titles are rare in New Zealand and the younger sons of marquises are practically non-existent.'[34] The implication, of course, is that members of the aristocracy are so common in England that every reader will be perfectly familiar with them. It is the same device used by Nancy Mitford, Evelyn Waugh, Angela Thirkell, and others to make their fictional aristocracy the possession of the middle-class reader. The narrative focalization of the over-awed Roberta serves to confirm the Lampreys' excesses as representatively English. Over and over again the eccentricities of the Lampreys are underlined for us—by the text, by those who come into contact with them, and by the Lampreys themselves: ' "we no doubt seem a very unbalanced family" ' suggests Lady Charles (p. 141); ' "delightful lunatics" ' insists the family doctor (p. 171); ' "by this time you must have decided that we are a fantastically unconventional family" ' Lord Charles apologizes (p. 224). As Chief Detective-Inspector Alleyn, investigating the gruesome murder (with a meat skewer through the eye) of Lord Lamprey's elder brother in the lift of the Lampreys' apartment block, concludes: ' "the Lampreys showed great industry in underlining their eccentricity" ' (p. 224). The actual nature of their eccentricity is fairly tame, certainly when compared to the strange habits of the Palinodes or the elaborate fantasizing of the Carnes. The two eldest children perform a Maori war-dance from the dock to welcome Roberta to England (' "oh yes. Very funny" ' comments one of her fellow passengers lamely (p. 24)); they ring up a journalist friend of theirs when their uncle is murdered in order to give him the scoop; and they greet every extremity, including threatened

---

[34] Ngaio Marsh, *A Surfeit of Lampreys*, 1941 (Harmondsworth: Penguin, 1959), 7.

bankruptcy and murder, with a string of rather weak jokes. The text maintains an illusion of distance from the family through the somewhat cynical perspective of Alleyn, who warily resists their much-touted charm, and dismisses the suggestion of their doctor that he will end up falling for them himself: ' "That conjures up a lamentable picture, doesn't it? The investigating officer who fell to doting on his suspects" ' (p. 170). But in fact the novel only gains its suspense by manipulating the readers' sympathies so that we hope none of the charming Lampreys is guilty of murder, while fearing that they are. The novel does manifest a degree of self-consciousness about its own snobberies and improbabilities, but largely as a device to gain the reader's complicity: so the revelation that the wife of the murdered uncle dabbles in black magic is greeted by the cynical police surgeon with incredulity—' "Oh no, really!" cried Dr Curtis. "It's a little too much" ' (p. 169)—thereby undercutting the reader's own sense of disbelief. Similarly, the fecklessness of the family, whose idea of economizing is ' "enjoying quite *cheap* things like driving about England and staying at second-rate hotels and going to Ostend for a little cheap gamble instead of the Riviera where all their friends are" ' (p. 41), is rendered acceptable in the face of the mean-minded torrent of abuse his brother directs at Lord Charles when approached for a loan.

Although we might think the Lampreys are a dying breed, the novel marks them as survivors. Triumphantly proved innocent of the crime, they inherit the vast family estates, and immediately start worrying that death duties will impoverish them. Just as Mitford's and Thirkell's aristocrats are 'bagged' for the middle classes, so the Lampreys are to be sufficiently transformed to accommodate a more egalitarian future—the eldest son will get a job, and marry Roberta, thus thinning the esoteric stock with some good middle-class common sense.

While Marsh and Allingham represent in fantasy-mode those classes that belonged essentially to the pre-First-World-War period, Agatha Christie embraces the modern, meritocratic, and suburban middle classes. As Alison Light has persuasively argued, Christie's fiction is unusual in the period for its 'comparative freedom from much of the rancour and discontent about an expanding middle class which motivates her fellow writers':

Christie's interest in the domestic life of the middle classes is ecumenical. Her 'big houses' can easily include a gabled Tudorbethan house in a stockbroker belt or new suburb and very little narrative energy or pleasure is drawn from anger at social pretension.[35]

The Leonides family in *Crooked House* live at Swinly Dean 'the well-known outer suburb of London which boasts three excellent golf courses for the city financier'.[36] Led by patriarch Aristide, a Greek businessman who has made his money in numerous shady-but-legal enterprises, the family consists of Sophia, the fiancée of the narrator, and ' "one brother, one sister, a mother, a father, an uncle, an aunt by marriage, a grandfather, a great-aunt, and a step-grandmother" ' (p. 7). Aristide's first wife had been of impeccable county stock, the daughter of a Master of Fox Hounds; his second is ' "a young woman out of a tea-shop" ' (p. 19), married when she was twenty-four and he seventy-seven. The multi-generational family live under the one crooked, much-gabled roof as a result of the Blitz, with Aristide's two adult sons (the only survivors of a family of eight children) reduced to positions of childlike dependence. When Aristide is murdered the spotlight falls on the family, and their idiosyncracies begin to seem sinister. As in *A Surfeit of Lampreys*, the fall-guy set up by the text is the outsider within the family—in both cases the wives of the victims. Much of the character of the Leonides family is revealed in the ruthlessness with which they try and lead the investigation in the direction of the hapless Brenda; as Sophia suggests, there are a number of varieties of ruthlessness in the family—the casual violence of Aristide, who had stabbed two men in a brawl in his native Smyrna, and then the 'rectitude and arrogance' of the fox-hunting, military types on her grandmother's side. The novel is preoccupied with notions of heredity, with 'defects or chinks' (p. 95) within the family, with the chief investigating officer (father of the narrator) insisting that a descendant who inherited both the ruthlessness of the de Havilands and the unscrupulousness of the Leonides would be trouble. We are given portraits of the family particularly from the children's generation, who view their elders with an analytical contempt: Sophia coolly lists the emotional neuroses of her parents and aunt and uncle, while her younger brother caricatures them with the revulsion of adolescent embarrassment:

---

[35] Light, *Forever England*, 76; 77.
[36] Agatha Christie, *Crooked House*, 1949 (London: Fontana, 1959), 7.

'My goodness, this house is the absolute limit! Mother always haring up and down to London and bullying tame dramatists to rewrite plays for her, and making frightful fusses about nothing at all. And father shut up with his books and sometimes not hearing you if you speak to him. I don't see why I should have to be burdened with such peculiar parents. Then there's Uncle Roger—always so hearty that it makes you shudder. Aunt Clemency's all right, she doesn't bother you, but I sometimes think she's a bit batty.... But it is a queer household, don't you think so?' (p. 126)

As with the repeated declarations of the Lampreys' eccentricity, such descriptions insistently foregound the peculiarities of the family, offering them as tempting tit-bits to lure the unsuspecting reader into snapping up the wrong criminal. In our readerly detection, we are accompanied by the comical figure of the youngest Leonides, Josephine, who—rather like the continually jesting Lampreys—sees the murder investigation as the opportunity for an elaborate game.

Where other writers attempt to carve out a future for their eccentric families in the post-war world, Christie is fully aware of the deeply anachronistic nature of such families. Her novel performs an act of merciful surgery, severing the extended family into its constituent parts, and allowing them their freedom. So scientist Clemency is finally able to detach her husband from his neurotic commitment to the family business he has incompetently run into the ground; and Aristide, from the grave, deals a death blow to the English code of primogeniture by leaving his entire fortune, and thus the role as head of the family, to his granddaughter Sophia. The ultimate insistence on the unnaturalness of the extended family comes in the revelation that the murderer is the child Josephine, who has killed her grandfather because he would not let her take ballet lessons.

The same devastating deconstruction of notions of childish innocence is at the heart of Josephine Tey's masterpiece, *Brat Farrar*. A classic of assumed identity, the novel focuses on the Ashby family—consisting of Aunt Bee and the children of her dead brother: son Simon, eldest daughter Eleanor, and twins Ruth and Jane—and their small manor house of Latchetts.[37] Resembling Arnot Robertson's Rushes rather than Margaret Kennedy's Sangers, the Ashbys are resolutely English in their quiet and dignified way of life and their preoccupation with horses; an established part of their local community, with a long and respectable history:

[37] Josephine Tey, *Brat Farrar*, 1949 (Harmondsworth: Penguin, 1987), 11.

No queens had come to Latchetts to dine; no cavaliers to hide. For three hundred years it had stood in its meadows very much as it stood now; a yeoman's dwelling. And for nearly two of those three hundred years Ashbys had lived in it. (p. 11)

Unlike the Ledinghams of Clare, the prominent local aristocrats, 'prodigal of their talents and their riches', the Ashbys have achieved nothing of grandeur, but 'the great house in the park was a boarding-school for the unmanageable children of parents with progressive ideas and large bank accounts', while 'the Ashbys stayed at Latchetts' (p. 12). The Tory fantasy of an unchanging gentry, securely rooted in an idyllic English landscape is threatened by the incursions of an interloper, Brat Farrar, a foundling newly returned from an adventurous itinerant life in America, who is encouraged by a ne'er-do-well son of the Ledingham family to pose as Patrick Ashby, who had disappeared a decade ago as a child. If the escapade succeeds, Brat will disinherit Simon, Patrick's younger twin, and become master of Latchetts. Remarkably, given its lyrical attachment to the Ashbys and all they represent, the novel encourages the reader, from the first, to root for Brat.

Like *Crooked House*, this text employs notions of heredity as a mode of explanation, but where the ideas were fairly gestural in the former—' "I shouldn't worry your head about heredity. It's too tricky and complicated a subject" ' the head of the investigation tells his narrating son, and with him the reader (p. 95)—they are of crucial importance here. The Ashbys conform to a very distinct physical type—'fair, small-boned, long-headed' (p. 11), and the pattern is stronger than individual variations, as the family solicitor comments, looking at a photograph of the ten-year-old Patrick: ' "the family likeness is very strong. At that age they are just young Ashbys aren't they? Without any great individuality" ' (p. 48). Employing the same assumptions they bring to the breeding of horses, the family therefore cannot accept that Brat, who looks even more like Simon than the original Patrick did, is not one of them. Significantly, Brat also, who is doubtful about going through with the deception, does so because he is convinced that he must be an Ashby, an idea he debates somewhat melodramatically with himself:

'But what has Latchetts to do with me?'
'You ask that? You with your Ashby face, and your Ashby bones, and your Ashby tastes, and your Ashby colouring, and your Ashby blood.'
'I haven't any evidence at all that—'

'And your Ashby blood, I said. Why, you poor little brute of a foundling, Latchetts is your belonging-place, and you have the immortal gall to pretend you don't care a rap about it!' (p. 72)

Like those classic orphan and foundling narratives *Tom Jones* and *Oliver Twist*, the story appears to suggest that anyone can 'pass' in the upper echelons, provided he is decent and good-hearted, but in fact is deeply wedded to the notions of an inherited gentility that will 'out' whatever the circumstances. It is notable that Brat's outlook accords precisely with that of the Ashbys—the novel has no interest in exploring clashes of culture or class. He understands immediately why his aunt and sister would wish to prevent Simon from marrying the daughter of a perfectly respectable tenant farmer, and he feels the same disdain for their vulgarly made-up and obtrusive household help as the Ashbys do (despite, in another life, having bedded nameless women behind ranch bunk-houses). The novel's response to the 'new' classes is not the paranoia of many of the other middlebrow fictions of the period, but simply a patrician contempt. Of their daily help—referred to gaily as the ' "latest moron" ' (p. 19)—we are told

Lana came from the village, and had gilt hair and varnished fingernails and the local version of the current make-up. She 'obliged' only because her 'boy-friend' worked in the stables. She would sweep and dust, she explained when she first came, because that was 'all right', but she would not wait at table because that was 'menial'. Bee had longed to tell her that no one with her hands, or her breath, or her scent, or her manners, would ever be allowed to hand an Ashby a plate; but she had learned to be politic. (p. 74)

Lana is repellant in her modernity, her cheap fashionableness—contrasted with the fixed verities of the Ashbys—and in her power to dictate the terms of her employment. Bee's vengeful response is devastatingly dismissive, but it is notable that Lana never gets to hear it. Although the novel's confidence in the Ashbys' ability to survive in the modern world is unswerving, it is clear that—like the Lampreys—they need an injection of new blood to enable them to face out the future in Welfare-State Britain. It is this that Brat, with his independence from the tightly-knotted web of English class, can provide.

Like *Ordinary Families*, the novel's concern is with the strangenesses at the heart of the most unexceptional families. As a local reporter remarks ' "the world's Press is composed of family affairs"' (p. 91). What Brat discovers about the Ashbys is that at the age of thirteen the charming Simon had calmly killed his twin and thrown his body into a quarry, in order that he and not Patrick would inherit Latchetts. We would think that such a revelation would challenge the Ashbys' ineffable smugness about their heritage, but in fact it allows everything to be sorted out most satisfactorily, with Simon conveniently falling to his death while attempting to push Brat down the same quarry, and Brat recognized by an Ashby great-uncle as clearly the son of Walter, an Ashby cousin. Eleanor, who has been grappling with what she thought were incestuous feelings for Brat, can now hope to marry him, and his quiet responsibility and feelings for both horses and the estate's dependents will replace Simon's irresponsible self-centred flamboyance. The novel's powerful fantasy of class authority is bolstered by a belief in the family that is virtually religious in its lineaments and intensity: where heredity throws up a chink in the line, fate will supply a replacement, and the family will go on.

All of these employments of the eccentric family in detective fiction rely on a central conception of the family as simultaneously natural and unnatural—as neurotic and perverse almost by definition, but also inevitable and inescapable. It is an ambivalence also at the heart of the work of perhaps the arch-delineator of familial peculiarity— Ivy Compton-Burnett. In her fiction over five decades Compton-Burnett told essentially the same story, of neo-Edwardian homes in which large extended families tear each other to pieces day-after-day in a language of mannered savagery. Death, incest, murder, take place in these homes, but usually off-stage, while the incessantly chattering beaks of the families continue to peck bits of flesh off each other. Nothing is too horrific to be turned into a family jest, and the most important thing is to score off a relative with a carefully turned phrase. Parents are tyrants and children are debased prisoners, and the home is not a sanctuary but a place where tortures are practised and refined. Compton-Burnett's world is that of the gentry but—as Alison Light has compellingly argued—it is a gentry that never existed, one dislocated from its context and history. Her families have no social place, no connection to the villages or counties outside their manor-houses; their lives are essentially inward, reworkings of the domestic claustrophobia of Compton-Burnett's own upbringing in middle-class Hove:

Able at last to leap into a more aristocratic past, Compton-Burnett's imagination made something modern and radical of it: an indictment of domestic hypocrisy and a frank attack on the late Victorian family as the place of unhealthy secrets and repression. These were the tensions contained within the four walls of a suburban childhood and the boundaries of family life not as it was lived by the squirarchy but by the inmates of the private house. If the cult of the country house provided the stage, it was nevertheless the dramas of Hove which were re-enacted.[38]

Typical of her major themes and methods is *Parents and Children* of 1941, which focuses on the three generations of the Sullivan family living in the same house: Sir Jesse and his wife Regan, their son Fulbert, his wife Eleanor, and their nine children, ranging in age from three to twenty-three. The dominating emotions are Eleanor's bitterness at having to live in the home of her in-laws, always in a subordinate position; her highly-charged ambivalent feelings for her children; and their various degrees of resentment of her. Unlike other eccentric family narratives, where individual siblings are characterized in terms of their occupations and idiosyncracies, in Compton-Burnett's novels—where no one ever *does* anything—it is place within the family that provides identifying characteristics. The children are arranged in groups of three by age, to aid the reader's and—it is strongly implied—their mother's memory. The grown-up children are Luce, Daniel, and Graham: Luce is the sanctimoniously controlling elder sister, given to quiet recommendations about the behaviour of others, and prone to rueful laughter; the brothers have both just finished their Cambridge degrees, and are defined by their relationship to each other, as Daniel extends a single joke of pretending to believe Graham is mentally deficient into an entire way of life:

'I suppose Graham must come to meals,' said Daniel. 'There ought to be some other way of managing about him.'
'We must eat to live,' said Fulbert.
'But is that necessary for Graham, Father?'[39]

The 'school-room children' are fifteen-year-old Isabel, thirteen-year-old Venice, and James, twelve. Isabel is possessed of a penetrating sardonic intelligence, and devoted to her beautiful younger sister. James

[38] Light, *Forever England*, 38.
[39] Ivy Compton-Burnett, *Parents and Children*, 1941, in *A First Omnibus* (Harmondsworth: Penguin, 1994), 409.

is defined by his isolation within this group and the family as a whole, and by the fact that he is the only one presently at school, though on most occasions he manages to avoid attending. The nursery children are Honor and Gavin, ten and nine, who 'live for each other' (p. 437) and three-year-old Nevill, the only child whose spirit has not yet been broken by the power-struggles of family life, the endearing charm of whose utterances is rendered horrific by the inevitability of his fate. The plot, as it gradually emerges through the tapestry of gnomic utterances, is almost Shakespearean, involving the apparent death of Fulbert in South America and Eleanor's near-marriage to Ridley, the double-crossing family friend Fulbert has put in charge of his affairs. Particularly shocking is Eleanor's eagerness to move to a small house with Ridley, leaving the children with their grandparents.

One of the monstrous mothers Compton-Burnett is particularly adept at depicting, Eleanor expresses her feelings for her children in a constant barrage of nit-picking and emotional blackmail, allowing them absolutely no privacy. One of the most telling scenes is when she opens a letter her husband has sent to Isabel, completely assured in her right to do so. Using the only weapons Compton-Burnett accords her child characters, Isabel exposes her mother's arrogant hypocrisy with devastating candour and clarity:

> 'It is a pity you do such second-rate things', said Isabel, in a slow voice. 'It is a mean way of using power.' . . .
> 'Come, come, my child. You would have shown me the letter would you not?'
> 'I might have had no choice. But I should have read it myself first. There would have been a semblance of free will. Decency would not have been outraged.' (p. 552)

Having handed her children over to nurses and governesses, Eleanor has only an awkward formal relationship to them—their real love and respect belongs to those paid to look after them. The diametric opposite of the timorous, oppressed governesses of Rachel Ferguson, Miss Mitford is dignified and intelligent. Free from the power complexes that beset the family, since—unlike the Sullivans—she inhabits the house from choice, she observes the day-to-day life of the family from very much the perspective of the reader:

> Miss Mitford sat down to await the end of the scene. She did not leave it, because of its human appeal. She was the happiest person present, as she was more often than was suspected. She did not let pity for her employer

or pupil mar her interest. Pity had come to be the normal background to her mind, and other feelings arose irrespective of it. (p. 555)

The nurses too are superior beings, providing the younger children with the love and security not forthcoming from their mother. These servants are fantasy figures on the same lines as Mary Poppins, offering imaginative compensation for the inadequacies of the Edwardian upbringing, as well as some slight textual relief from the overpowering claustrophobia of familial life.

Another weight of negativity is added by the fact that the Sullivans are not alone—their small world is peopled with other, rather similar families. The family of the deceitful Ridley, the Cranmers, consisting of father Paul, sister Faith, and stepmother Hope, converse in tones as barbed as, though slightly more jocund than the Sullivans; while at the gates of Sir Jesse's estate live his wards, the Marlowes, a brother and two sisters. These latter are actually positively happy compared to the other families; brother and sister relationships, in the world of Compton-Burnett, are often celebrated as an ideal form of family life—one without the parents.[40] Although not fuelled by the bitter strife of the other families, the Marlowes are nonetheless appropriately eccentric, rather in the manner of the more benignly represented families in some of the novels examined earlier, and—like the Lampreys, the Carnes, and so on—are extremely proud of the fact:

'I wonder if we are as odd as we think we are', said Susan.
'We can only hope so', said her sister, 'and continue to do our best.' (p. 521)

Lacking occupations, or any other focus for their attention, the characters make the family their sole object of study—both their own and families in general. Aphoristic summations of the natures of families are common:

'Dear, dear, the miniature world of a family! All the emotions of mankind seem to find a place in it.'

---

[40] '[T]he novels imagine a whole series of semi-incestuous unions and celebrate the brother and sister relationship as quasi-marital. They betray not just a sense of continuing childhood solidarity, but also a desire to side-step the sexual and social expectations of being grown-up. The fiction is full of middle-aged brothers and sisters who have elected for celibacy and to live together. It seems an ideal solution to irreconcilable needs, providing a way of prolonging family life and of avoiding its worst consequences' (Light, *Forever England*, 43–4).

THE ECCENTRIC FAMILY 195

'It was those emotions that originally gave rise to it', said Daniel. 'No doubt they would still be there.' (p. 539)

Even the servants, who speak the same encrypted language as the family, harp on the topic. The most striking case is Mullet, the nursery maid, who entertains the children with elaborate tales of her own family and their rapid social decline—' "I often think of them, moving in their shabby gentility about their second-rate social round, always with that air of having come down in the world, which a truer dignity would lay aside" ' (p. 571). Her tale of the new poor is consonant with those many laments discussed in Chapter 2, but her story is a carefully constructed fantasy. Compton-Burnett plays bizarre games with the contemporary structures of class by placing this narrative in the mouth of a lower servant, destabilizing our sense of the realities of class identities. A further effect is to create a nightmarish sense that there is nothing outside the family. The servants must have very different families of their own, but such devices impede our abilities to imagine them. The action of the novel works inexorably to reinforce this notion: the Cranmers are virtually tied to the Sullivans, by dint of Ridley's near-marriage to Eleanor, and it is revealed that the Marlowes are actually Sir Jesse's illegitimate children. The walls close in, the family is all there is, and no one's going anywhere.

While detective novels rely on an ambiguity about just who, if anyone, in the family is actually insane, Compton-Burnett declares that the family itself is mad. Peculiar though her fiction is, it simply offers in an extreme form the ambivalence at the heart of all of these novels—a sense of the eccentric family as both fundamentally damaged and strangely compelling. Although these families might appear to belong to the past, they are actually profoundly modern creations, surreal rereadings—as the use of the Brontës and *Little Women*, and the novels of Compton-Burnett make clear—of Victorian family structures and ideologies; turning the traditional family inside out to reveal it as a deeply pathological and anti-social structure. In so repeatedly imagining a world in which the family is at odds with the society around it, the feminine middlebrow expresses a strong ambivalence about contemporary life. The inability of so many adult children in these novels to leave the family home perhaps functions as a symbolic reflection of the condition of many middle-class women in the first half of the century—immured in their homes by restrictions of employment, and the operation of a powerful pro-domestic ideology. Equally, the embattled self-containment of these eccentric families is emblematic of the increasingly besieged state of the upper middle class in these years. Yet the fact that the games, fantasies, consoling fictions, and illusions of grandeur employed by the members of the eccentric family to make palatable their self-entrapment are presented as so appealing is an indication of the degree to which the feminine middlebrow resisted those approaching freedoms that it also desired. It is no accident that we find very few such fictional representations of the family in the years after 1960: as middle-class women entered the work-force in increasing numbers, and cultural norms were finally prised from the grip of the upper middle class, the fantasy of the eccentric family at last lost its appeal.

5

A Crisis of Gender?

> When the guns fired in August 1914, did the faces of men and women show so plain in each other's eyes that romance was killed?
>
> Virginia Woolf, *A Room of One's Own* (1929)

FOR the generation that fought in it, and for those who came after, the Great War changed everything. As it became clear to most that the war was a bitter fiasco, old truths and authorities were called to account, and the sentimental pieties of the past challenged. The effect on gender roles was decisive: the traditional masculine values of honour, martial prowess, and emotional restraint were severely compromised by the futility of the mass-slaughter and the trauma that followed, while the delicate flower of English womanhood was transformed by the heavy labour of jobs in munitions factories and stints as ambulance drivers. The result was the formation, in the years immediately following the war, of new codes of masculinity, and a concomitant shift in the qualities associated with the feminine. The new man of this moment rejected the old masculine values of gravitas and heroism in favour of frivolity and an effete and brittle manner. The new woman took on the practicality and emotional control once the province of the male: she was competent, assured, and unemotional. These figures are significant new social stereotypes, repeatedly lamented, celebrated, and anatomized in the pages of the press over the course of more than a decade, and peopling most forms of contemporary fiction. Wodehouse's effete and dapper Bertie Wooster and the hearty golf-playing girls from whom he flees; the brittle and self-deprecating detective heroes of Dorothy Sayers and Margery Allingham, and the resolutely independent women who are finally bestowed on them; the cynical bright young things satirized by Aldous Huxley and Evelyn Waugh: these are just the most obvious manifestations of a redefining of gender roles that transformed the novel of the period. They raise questions not only about revised constructions of gender, but also of sexuality, as asexuality and homosexuality become increasingly common features of the characterization of both males and females.

It is these revised gender conventions that established the generic conventions of the middlebrow women's novel. As Woolf's rhetorical question implies, the new gender roles brought with them a radical reassessment of romance—the romance that had been at the centre of previous literary conventions. A new language is evolved in which romance is figured primarily by reticence: evasion rather than declaration becomes the new textual currency of love. Hero and heroine roles are fundamentally transformed, while shifts in attitudes to motherhood and marriage lead to an obsessive questioning about the trajectories of women's lives. Anxious to be modern, but nervous of censorship or even prosecution, the middlebrow women novelists of the post-war period picked their way carefully through the minefield of sexual description, evolving a respectable discourse for the representation of the previously unmentionable.

That both real-life and fictional gender roles were revised in the years immediately following the First World War is generally accepted by both historians and literary scholars, but despite this critical consensus, few have asked how long these revised identities prevailed. The tenacity of the new constructions of gender will be tested through an examination of a range of novels from the 1940s and 1950s. Although the Second World War briefly shook up gender conventions once again, I will suggest that in middlebrow women's fiction, the reimposition of traditional modes of femininity that is supposed to be a major feature of the culture of the 1950s was neither new nor pervasive. Rather, the texts of the post-war period see the fruition of notions of gender developed in the 1930s and retain, to a degree, the cultural ambivalence about gender that had been a feature of the years immediately following the First World War.

It was abundantly clear to contemporary commentators that the war had changed masculinity fundamentally. The most common explanation was 'shell-shock': the idea that proximity to exploding shells could produce a range of symptoms from insomnia and volatile moods to mutism and amnesia. However, as Elaine Showalter has persuasively argued, many of the 80,000 men who had sought medical help for the condition by the end of the war had not been under fire, and many more developed the condition after the war was over, suggesting that (as doctors began to realize) they were actually suffering from a neurosis produced by the acute stress of war.[1] Among the symptoms often reported, particularly among the upper- and upper-middle-class officers, were anxiety attacks, uncontrollable outbursts of emotion, and an alternation between depression and a restless desire for pleasure: responses that were profoundly at odds with the stiff upper lip ethos of their upbringings, and which would previously have been gendered feminine.[2] These are the features that most often occur in fictional accounts of the victim of shell-shock, perhaps the most archetypal being Dorothy Sayers's Lord Peter Wimsey who was ' "blown up and buried in a shell-hole" ', an experience that precipitated him into ' "a bad nervous breakdown" ' for two years and initiated a subsequent ' "impenetrable frivolity of manner and a dilettante pose" '.[3] A similarly detached, worldly-wise manner is adopted by Julian, one of the family of cousins loved by the protagonist Judith in Rosamund Lehmann's 1927 *Dusty Answer*. Returned unwounded from the conflict in which his brother was killed, he is nevertheless psychologically damaged: jaded and without direction, devoted to the pursuit of empty pleasures. Such brittle frivolity is clearly understood to disguise an excess of emotion. It is their openness about their emotional responses to the horrors of their combat experiences that so shocks the two old soldiers—relicts of earlier conflicts—who overhear the war reminiscences of the male protagonists in E. Arnot Robertson's *Four Frightened People* of 1931:

> The Colonel and his friend sat up and seemed to bristle. They gazed meaningly at each other with their disagreement temporarily overlooked, and then stared at the slightly disfigured young man who had not, in their eyes, earned the right to be openly afraid. Their thoughts were almost visible—*What* was England coming to when her young men publicly owned themselves cowards. . . .
>
> Colonel Chayning made an indescribable sound in his throat. He and his friend rose as one and left us, their differences forgotten—what was

---

[1] Elaine Showalter, *Hystories: Hysterical Epidemics and Modern Culture* (London: Picador, 1997), 72–5.

[2] Showalter interestingly notes that while officers experienced mainly emotional disturbances, the ordinary soldiers were more often found to be suffering from 'conversion hysterias', in which physical symptoms such as limps and paralyses were produced by severe stress.

[3] Dorothy Sayers, *Gaudy Night*, 1935 (London: Hodder & Stoughton, 1987), 444.

England coming to when her young men *publicly proclaimed themselves brave*?[4]

As the novel's woman narrator notes, the old soldiers belong to a world now lost—where 'the cult of personal courage which the war killed . . . was at its height as the well-bred Englishman's religion' (p. 58). The new men who are her contemporaries, in contrast, think in terms not of moral absolutes, but of nervous systems under stress: to them 'courage and cowardice were the reactions of the same man's nerves, when they were untried and young in fear, and when they had been worn down gradually, less by the dread of death than by the strain of continuing to exist in conditions which the old men understood only officially' (p. 59). The old campaigners are moral dinosaurs, their values meaningless in the traumatized post-war world; while the damaged, consciously valueless and self-trivializing masculinity of the younger men is established as paradoxically more heroic. It is this reversal of values that allows the newly emotional, psychologically wounded man to become the masculine prototype for the middlebrow woman's novel for at least the next decade.

The fictional herald of this new masculinity is Rebecca West's 1918 novel *The Return of the Soldier*, in which the wealthy Christopher returns from the front with his memory of the last fifteen years erased. Eager to restore him to himself and his magnificent house are his beautiful wife Kitty and his cousin Jenny, both of whom are in love with him. Also devoted to him is Margaret Allington, now a lumpen and jaded suburban housewife, once the innkeeper's daughter whom he had loved in his youth. The man at the centre of all this female adoration is curiously absent—a highly conventional being both in the romantic idealism of the youth he defensively relives, and in the mature decency of the adult self he flees: 'he himself, seen in the novel only through the uncritical eyes of love, is not an interesting character; he is the epitome of English masculine fineness, virtue and charm, a love object.'[5] Christopher is desired by virtue of his victimhood: both Jenny and Margaret respond to his psychological woundedness with a powerful maternal instinct. In Margaret's case, this nurture is represented as spiritual in its ability to heal the traumatized mind:

[4] E. Arnot Robertson, *Four Frightened People*, 1931 (London: Virago, 1982), 61–2.
[5] Victoria Glendinning, Introduction to the Virago edition, 1980, 1.

It means that the woman has gathered the soul of the man into her soul and is keeping it warm in love and peace so that his body can rest quiet for a little time. That is a great thing for a woman to do.[6]

The war has rendered Christopher childlike, and so the women who truly love him respond as mothers, ferocious in their need to protect him; it is only his frivolous wife who refuses this role, bemoaning instead the sexual desire with which he used to respond to her, so Jenny finds her 'holding a review of her underclothing': '[Kitty] continued to look wanly at the frail luminous silks her maid brought her, as a speculator who had cornered the article for which there had been no demand might look at his damnably numerous, damnably unprofitable freights' (pp. 126–7). It is notable that there are no actual children in this world—both Kitty and Christopher, and Margaret, have lost boys at a year old, and the sunlit nursery of the great house remains forever empty, leaving the space of childhood for the weakened returning men to occupy. Despite the fact that he is clearly happier remaining in his saving fugue, Jenny and Margaret collude with Kitty and the psychologists to restore Christopher to his mature self, because otherwise 'he would not be quite a man' (p. 183). The controlled, distant masculinity of the pre-war days is briefly recovered under hypnosis, when Christopher forgets the abandoned bliss with which he contemplated the dowdy Margaret and remembers Kitty, who he talks of 'with the humourous tenderness of the English husband' (p. 138). He fully assumes the straightjacket of this buttoned-up gender role in the horror of the conclusion when, restored to himself, he walks towards his waiting property:

He wore a dreadful decent smile; I knew how his voice would resolutely lift in greeting us. He walked not loose limbed like a boy, as he had done that very afternoon, but with the soldier's hard tread upon the heel. (p. 187)

Now condemned to remember 'that flooded trench in Flanders under that sky more full of flying death than clouds . . . that No Man's Land where bullets fall like rain on the rotting faces of the dead' (p. 187), Christopher has been 'returned' by the self-sacrificing Margaret, who showed him the favourite toys of his dead son. He is forced to full knowledge of the death of the nation's sons by the memory of that of his own. In this novel, men are children, children are dead, and

[6] Rebecca West, *The Return of the Soldier*, 1918 (London: Virago, 1980), 143–4.

women are mothers to their men. Except in the case of Kitty, the bereaved mother who unperturbed uses her dead son's nursery—carefully preserved by her husband—as a room in which to dry her hair, and who greets the terrible sight of her damaged husband with the exultant whisper ' "He's cured!" ' (p. 188). It is the Kittys of this world, the novel suggests, who force men into unnatural and painful roles; it is women like Jenny and Margaret who will try to rescue them through an apprehension of their inner selves.

It is not just Christopher's soul that preoccupies Jenny, but his body also:

He was so wonderful when he was young; he possessed in great measure the loveliness of young men, which is like the loveliness of the spry foal or the sapling, but in him it was vexed into a serious and moving beauty by the inhabiting soul. (p. 104)

The shift in the power balance between the sexes has left women free to eroticize men: it is paradoxically because they view them with a fierce maternal affection that Jenny, and the other women who like her have waited to snatch their men from the war, can now represent them as the objects of physical desire, rather than eternally its subjects. In Rosamund Lehmann's *Dusty Answer* (1927), the girl protagonist, Judith, is intensely aware of the physical attractions of men. Passionately drawn to the family of cousins who periodically visit the house next door and enliven her lonely childhood, Judith becomes emotionally involved with each in turn. Her childhood favourite is the charming Charlie, whose attractiveness consists in a classical beauty that tips over into femininity—'he had a lovely straight white nose, and a girl's mouth with full lips slightly apart, and a jutting cleft chin'—and so poses no sexual threat to the still immature Judith.[7] As with the women in Rebecca West's novel, Judith's primary response to Charlie is nurturing—in her fantasies 'he fell into awful dangers and she rescued him; he had accidents and she carried him for miles soothing his groans. He was ill and she nursed him, holding his hand through the worst of the delirium' (p. 13). It is no coincidence that the boy who elicits this Florence Nightingale response is the one doomed to die in the war: like West's Christopher, he is made desirable by virtue of his victimhood.

While Charlie's beautiful body is forever foredoomed to be broken, sturdier male bodies elicit a different aesthetic of desire. So

[7] Rosamund Lehmann, *Dusty Answer*, 1927 (Harmondsworth: Penguin, 1986), 13.

A CRISIS OF GENDER? 203

Judith responds to men according to their abilities as dancers and tennis players, and frankly assesses the improved physique of one of the cousins when she first meets him again as an adult:

He was still a little red, a little coltish and untidy, but his figure was impressive, with powerful heavy shoulders and narrow hips; and the muscles of his thigh and calf bulged beneath his trousers. (p. 70).

For this novel, the body is an important index of new freedoms—freedoms both to imagine and to act. Stumbling towards her new horizons as an independent modern woman, Judith accords bodily pleasures equal weight with intellectual achievements, sharing a love of physical exertion—running and climbing—with her college friend Jennifer, and delighting in the look of active bodies. She defines her feelings for Roddy, the tricksy and elusive cousin with whom she falls most deeply in love, in terms of bodily movement:

She smiled at him, thinking how she loved the feel of her own body moving obediently, the satisfaction of achieving a perfect stroke, the look of young bodies in play and repose,—especially his . . . (p. 81).

Masculine bodies are viewed with a similarly anatomizing gaze in *Four Frightened People*, in which young doctor Judy Corder and three companions abandon a plague-infested ship and are forced to trek across the Malay jungle in a desperate attempt to regain civilization. Judy's profession allows her to maintain a cool distance from conventional feminine concerns and attitudes, and she views men's bodies with a calm appraisal, while at the same time dismissing the gender from which she is so anxious to disassociate herself: 'I was thinking idly how physically unworthy of the thin-flanked, hard grandeur of the young male is the utilitarian female in almost all forms of life' (p. 33). The emphasis on flanks and hardness, as with the muscles that bulge through male trousers in *Dusty Answer*, is a provocative flirtation with overt sexual description, as well as a conscious reversal of the standard cultural assumption that it is only the female body that is available for erotic contemplation. It is a woman's desirous contemplation of a male that forms the transitional moment in Dorothy Sayers's *Gaudy Night* (1935)—itself a transitional text in her oeuvre as it is in this novel that the previously somewhat effete Lord Peter Wimsey is categorically transformed into a sex symbol. The novel, which Sayers called 'not really a detective story at all, but a novel with a mild detective interest of an almost entirely psychological kind', centres on Harriet Vane, the woman whom Wimsey saved from the gallows in a previous book, and with whom he had long been unrequitedly in love.[8] Asked to solve a case of poison-pen letters in her old Oxford college, Harriet calls Peter in late in the day, and they take time out from their investigations to punt on the river. It is during this trip that her perception of him changes:

Accepting rebuke, he relapsed into silence, while she studied his half-averted face. Considered generally, as a facade, it was by this time tolerably familiar to her, but now she saw details, magnified as it were by some glass in her own mind. The flat setting and fine scroll-work of the ear, and the height of the skull above it. The glitter of close-cropped hair where the neck-muscles lifted to meet the head. A minute sickle-shaped scar on the left temple. The faint laughter-lines at the corner of the eye and the droop of the lid at its outer end. The gleam of golden down on the cheek-bone. The wide spring of the nostril. An almost imperceptible beading of sweat on the upper lip and a tiny muscle that twitched the sensitive corner of the mouth. The slight sun-reddening of the fair skin at the base of the throat. The little hollow above the points of the collar-bone.

He looked up; and she was instantly scarlet, as though she had been dipped in boiling water. Through the confusion of her darkened eyes and drumming ears some enormous bulk seemed to stoop over her. Then the mist cleared. His eyes were riveted upon the manuscript again, but he breathed as though he had been running.[9]

Moving closer and closer, the text and Harriet pore together over the details of Peter's physiognomy, eroticizing it by the breathless attention of their regard. It is Harriet who is overwhelmed with passion; Peter who averts his gaze, chest rising and falling like a heroine of Gothic romance. The point of the passage, as well as marking a crucial turning point in their long-laboured relationship, is to legitimize the continually frivolous Wimsey as an object of readerly desire—to at last take him seriously.

These male bodies eroticized by a frank female regard are manifestly the products of the immediate post-war adjustment in gender power relations. But these admiring gazes point also to the fact that masculinity remained a potent cultural force for many inter-war women's middlebrow novels—a force for women to emulate as well

---

[8] Letter to Muriel St Clare Byrne, 8 Sept. 1935, *The Letters of Dorothy L. Sayers: 1899–1936: The Making of a Detective Novelist*, ed. Barbara Reynolds (London: Sceptre, 1996), 352.

[9] Dorothy Sayers, *Gaudy Night*, 281.

as adore. Conventional femininity is dismissed by the female protagonists of a number of novels: so *Dusty Answer*'s Judith sees herself as a 'trifling female creature' (p. 9) in comparison to the heady masculine glamour of the boys next door, and Judy Corder in *Four Frightened People* remarks coldly that she has 'no objection in general to the subservience of the female to the male (almost invariably her superior in every matter in which the two are comparable, in my experience)' (p. 130). Corder excepts herself—partially at least—from her general condemnation of femininity: her career as a doctor freeing her from the sentimentality she finds typical of the average woman. This is underlined by the aggravatingly bracing older woman who Corder and her two male companions reluctantly allow to accompany them when they flee the ship: Mrs Mardick remarks in veiled criticism of Judy that 'she . . . had always thought that a medical training must be somewhat blunting to any woman's natural sensitiveness and sympathy' (p. 125). In this curious novel's terms this is high praise, underlined by the fact that it comes from the mouth of an individual so relentlessly jolly in the face of all adversity that the other three finally abandon her to her fate alone in the jungle. Judy's own femininity—the mode which the text tacitly approves—is defined precisely in opposition to the sensitivity and sympathy Mrs Mardick extols as natural. The former rejects the conventional ambitions of her sex, defining herself as other than 'the satisfied wives and mothers' (p. 181), travelling independently and feeling free to take lovers outside marriage. Although she consciously acquires masculine attributes such as courage and emotional restraint, the novel is careful to distinguish this rational, assured femininity from a simple aping of the masculine—Judy views with mild contempt the 'stalwart mathematical mistress' on board ship:

She was one of those close-cropped gruff girls who are so much more aggressively boyish than any normal boy: she missed few opportunities of impressing on one how hard her rather small hands were, how muscular her not-too-developed calves. This kept every man in her vicinity aware of her essentially female presence and was, as Stewart said, hitting below the belt, even hers, which she wore drawn tightly round her hips, in order to make their narrowness apparent. What, in fact, it chiefly accentuated was their entirely unmasculine contour and bulk. (pp. 25–6)

The post-war fashion for unfeminine bodies and dress is mocked as paradoxically drawing attention to female physical attributes, but the tom-boyish teacher is also condemned, a page later, for her intrusion of scientific knowledge into a flirtatious conversation, and for her failure to use face powder: 'this was not a climate where women out for admiration could afford to be as boyish as all that' (pp. 26–7). There is only room in this text for one exceptional woman—all other forms of deviation from the norm have to be dismissed as just another variant on conventionality, so the lady novelist met with on the ship home is typical of 'professional women, who boast to one another of their cooking and their ability to renovate evening dresses and their visits to Ideal Home Exhibitions—being carefully non-peculiar' (p. 338). Even Judy herself does not entirely escape the general tone of contempt for women, who are dismissed in biological as well as cultural terms: when the strain of the trek through the jungle overwhelms her, she accounts for it as pre-menstrual tension:

> I knew that I was being idiotic; I was expecting the usual curse of my sex, which came to add another minor trouble to my lot the next day, and (as with most women) the turmoil in the blood beforehand and at the time inclined me to be unreasonable if I was subjected to any strain. My one slight advantage over other women was that I recognised this. (pp. 146–7)

In this novel's terms, the exceptional woman is one capable of outriding her biology. Men are allowed weaknesses, both psychological and physical, as a result of their war experiences, but the woman capable of evolving beyond the weakness of her gender can allow herself no such leeway.

This combination of a notional feminist politics with an almost visceral contempt for women in general is found in a surprising number of middlebrow women's novels of this date. *Gaudy Night* (as already discussed briefly in Chapter 2) concerns itself with the question of women's higher education, and whether it is possible to combine it with marriage and family. Set in a fictional Oxford women's college, it explores prejudices about single professional women—embittered, lonely, lesbian?—only to explode them. The detective element is provided by a series of violently abusive anonymous letters sent to various members of staff, which ex-student Harriet Vane is asked to investigate as a consequence of her having helped Lord Peter Wimsey with the solutions to other cases. Suspicion falls variously on the three distinct groups within college: dons, students, and scouts (college servants), but the latter are early ruled out by the Latin tag pinned to the gowned and hanged figure discovered in the chapel. A number of feminist, eccentric, or simply resentful women dons fall under particular suspicion, but they and their way of life are triumphantly vindicated by the ultimate discovery that the culprit *was* a scout—a lower-middle-class widow fallen on hard times after the suicide of her husband, a doctoral candidate who had been exposed as falsifying his research by one of the women dons. Her unlikely access to Latin phrases is thus explained away, and the viciousness and perversity that Harriet feared was the dark underside of this community of single intellectual women is placed instead with an uneducated married mother. The novel's agenda of legitimizing women's education and access to the professions would seem to be secure—except that it is in fact profoundly ambivalent about these issues. The guilty scout, Annie, echoes Harriet's own fears about the collegiate life when she denounces the assembled Senior Common Room at the novel's denouement:

'There's nothing in your books about life and marriage and children, is there? Nothing about desperate people,—or love—or hate or anything human.' (p. 427)

She portrays the women academics as succubi, feeding off men rather than nurturing and supporting them; refusing to do their ' "proper job in the world" ' (p. 428) of bearing children and caring for a home. Significantly, Annie hits at the root of the post-war change in gender roles by blaming Wimsey and men like him for this new breed of independent women: ' "It's men like you that make women like this. You don't know how to do anything but talk" ' (p. 428). Annie is given a powerful and articulate argument, though the other characters dismiss it as simply insane and it produces in Harriet a violent—though temporary—revulsion not from the intellectual life but from the idea of marriage. These dismissals are markedly overdetermined, with the novel so anxious about the possible validity of Annie's attack that it proleptically undermines the grounds of her argument by the insertion of a comic interlude between the college porter and a decorator's foreman:

'Young ladies', Padgett was heard to say, 'will 'ave their larks, same as young gentlemen.'
'When I was a lad', replied the foreman, 'young ladies was young ladies. And young gentlemen was young gentlemen. If you get my meaning.'
'Wot this country wants', said Padgett, 'is a 'Itler.'
'That's right', said the foreman. 'Keep the girls at 'ome. . . .' (p. 114)

In fact, the novel itself decides that a number of the girls would be better off at home. Many of the women of Harriet's generation of undergraduates, met with at the Gaudy with which the novel opens, have married and abandoned the expectations their education had established for them. The present generation of undergraduates are portrayed as giddy and irresponsible, more interested in boys than study. One such is dismissed by one of her friends in terms that set marriage and women's higher education firmly at odds: ' "She's no business to be up at Oxford at all, really. A nice domestic life with a man to be devoted to is what she really wants" ' (p. 141). The text's guiding assumption is that only the truly exceptional woman can manage to combine marriage with her own intellectual and professional interests, and that 'ordinary' women are to be patronized, pitied, or actively despised. The novel evinces a general irritation with women en masse, as if femaleness undiluted is profoundly unnatural, so Harriet, entering Hall for the evening meal, is struck by the sound:

'Strike' was the right word. It fell upon one like the rush and weight of a shouting waterfall; it beat on the ear like the hammer-clang of some infernal smithy; it savaged the air like the metallic clatter of fifty thousand monotype machines casting type. Two hundred female tongues, released as though by a spring, burst into high clamorous speech. She had forgotten what it was like, but it came back to her to-night how, at the beginning of every term, she had felt that if the noise were to go on like that for one minute more, she would go quite mad. . . . now it shattered her unaccustomed nerves with all and more than all its original violence. (pp. 26–7)

Femaleness is rendered artificial and violent by virtue of its multiplication: the threatened dilution of Harriet's uniqueness by the presence of hundreds of other intellectual women is warded off by the representation of them as either eccentric spinsters or a cacophonous mob. Intriguingly, we find precisely the same representation of Oxford women students in *Dusty Answer*, when Judith contemplates her fellows with trepidation and disgust her first night in Hall:

Trips. Labs. Lectures. Dons. Vacs. Chaperons. The voices gabbled on. The forks clattered. The roof echoed.

'Ugly and noisy', muttered Judith. 'Ugly and noisy and crude and smelly . . .' You could go on for ever.

There were eyes staring from everywhere, necks craning to look at her . . .

She studied the row of faces opposite her, and then more rows, and more, of faces. . . . Accepting, revealing faces they were, with no reserves in them, looking at each other, at things—not inward at themselves. But just a herd, when all was said: immature, untidy, all dull, and all alike, commonplace female creatures in the mass. (p. 110)

It is no accident that we find such repelled depictions of masses of women in the aftermath of the First World War: these images are the cultural products of a generation where maleness was in short supply, and the more desirable for that scarcity; a generation who would very often define feminism in terms of the ability of individual women to transcend their gender, rather than represent it.

These striking new gender representations are in large part responsible for the form of the feminine middlebrow: when these exceptional, competent, masculinized women come together with the brittle, emotional, eroticized men of their choice, a whole new language of romance is forced into being. A prime example is Margery Allingham's 1933 *Sweet Danger*, a novel comparable to *Gaudy Night*, as it too provides its author's series detective with a long-term love-interest. Like Sayers's Lord Peter Wimsey, Allingham's Albert Campion is the epitome of post-war masculinity as enjoyed by the feminine middlebrow: a jokingly evasive aristocrat (he outranks Wimsey on two counts, being rumoured to be the scion of one of the finest families in the land, but stylishly refusing to use a title), his mildness of manner and foppish appearance disguise his courage and startling intelligence. In *Sweet Danger*, as in Allingham's other detective stories, an exuberantly convoluted and melodramatic plot (in this case involving a tiny and mountainous Balkan state lost for a century, international spying, a mad country doctor practising witchcraft on his patients, and the recovery of an Earldom and a priceless missing crown) covers a surprisingly acute analysis of contemporary mores.[10] Campion's frivolity is threatened for the first time in *Sweet Danger* by his meeting with the adolescent Amanda Fitton—red-haired, bravely independent, and passionately interested in radios and engines. One of the most extreme examples of a heroine encroaching on masculine areas of competence, Amanda becomes an aeronautical engineer in a later novel (the 1938 *The Fashion in Shrouds*), so borrowing a touch of the heady glamour

[10] Allingham's novels from the 1920s to the 1950s offer a picture in microcosm of a society moving from the brittle frivolity of the immediate post-war years, through the mounting anxiety of the 1930s to the multiplying paranoias and identity crises of the Second World War.

that surrounded female flyers like Amy Johnson and Amelia Erhardt—'no image of woman's emancipation caught the public imagination more than that of the aviatrix'.[11] As with Harriet Vane in Sayers's novels, Amanda takes on the role of Campion's side-kick, helping him to set up diversionary tactics to foil the lurking villains. Their relationship is figured in almost entirely comradely terms throughout the novel, and yet the reader is expected to pick up the strong emotional subtext. This subtext is conveyed not in terms of what is said, but what is unspoken: reticence in such fiction becomes the key guarantor of emotional and—especially—romantic authenticity. This romantic reticence is established as the modern way in contrast with the much more conventional love-match between Campion's stuffy friend Guffy Randall and Amanda's very domesticated elder sister Mary. Their adherence to conventional gender roles is gently mocked both by the novel—'Mary . . . had spent the morning devoted to household affairs with the sweet womanly abstraction which Mr Randall admired'—and by Campion and Amanda, who greet the formers' growing attachment with some levity:

'By the way, have you noticed Guffy and Mary? I think it must be because she's led such a secluded life and has been starved for companionship of her own age, don't you?'

'Without a modicum of disrespect for my old friend, Mr Randall,' said Mr Campion judicially, 'perhaps so. Er—life's very beautiful, isn't it?'

'Speaking as a soul not yet mated, nerts,' said Amanda.[12]

The development of a bantering shorthand is one of the ways in which Amanda and Campion's very different love affair is established for the reader: their cynical distance from old-fashioned romantic pieties and their refusal of overt emotion paradoxically signal their higher romantic seriousness. The reticence is as much the text's as the characters', so Amanda's parting from Campion at a moment of high drama and strong danger carefully balances romance and its opposite:

She rose cautiously to her feet, slipped the gun in her jacket pocket, and turned towards the house. Then, looking back suddenly, she stopped and kissed him unromantically on the nose.

[11] Deirdre Beddoes, *Back to Home and Duty: Women Between the Wars, 1918–1939* (London: Pandora, 1989), 32.
[12] Margery Allingham, *Sweet Danger* , 1933 (Harmondsworth: Penguin, 1987), 179; 198. OED glosses 'nerts' as an alternative to 'nuts' as a slang exclamation of derision.

'That's by way of *pourboire*, in case we don't meet again', she said lightly. (p. 207)

Amanda here adopts the casual heroism of the cinematic hero, striding off to do battle with the forces of evil, revealing his deep emotional attachment in the very gestures he employs to make light of it. It is notable that her romantic reticence takes a different form from Campion's: where he evades deep feelings with his trademark veneer of affable vacancy, she employs a profoundly unfeminine directness that leaves no room for flirtatious ambiguity. It is the sixteen-year-old Amanda who makes the first incontrovertible moves as she lies wounded at the end of the novel, breaking through Campion's layers of emotional reserve with her devastating candour, and promising herself to him in six years' time. The language in which his emotional capitulation is couched is an intriguing blend of *Boys' Own* adventure and the grand passion, signalling the new ground on which the modern heroine was establishing herself:

> Mr Campion sat where he was for a long time, staring out across the room. His face was expressive, a luxury he scarcely ever permitted himself. At last he rose slowly to his feet and stood looking down very tenderly at this odd little person who had come crashing through one of the most harrowing adventures he had ever known and with unerring instinct had torn open old scars, revived old fires which he had believed extinct. (p. 251)

This is the new romantic fantasy for the middlebrow women's novel: that a competent, comradely girl can crack open the brittle carapace with which the war-wounded man protects his raw emotions, and coax them into the light of day. We know this as romance, not by its declarations and outpourings of emotion, but by its telling elisions, its sly refusals of sentiment, so that the tiniest give-away slips in language and address convey the strongest of feelings. These codes of emotional reticence have subsequently become so naturalized, particularly by their adoption as cinematic conventions, that we may find it hard to see them as innovations, but they represent a decisive shift in the fictional representation of romantic love.

We find these evasive codes employed repeatedly in women's middlebrow fiction between the wars. In *The Return of the Soldier* they structure the narrative, so that the narrating cousin never actually declares the passionate love that governs all of her responses to the soldier, and avoids depicting (indeed, covers her eyes and avoids seeing) the central scene of the profoundly emotional reunion between Christopher and his boyhood lover. She turns away from strong emotion, including her own, as if it was deeply vulgar, but nevertheless recognizes the primacy of the bond between the suburban Margaret and Christopher over the polite neutralities of the marriage to which he will eventually return. Ultimately, though, the text reveals declarative romantic passion as something that belongs to the past—a soft-focus pre-war fantasy that has to be renounced in the new harsh light of the modern world. It is this fantastical chimera that *Dusty Answer*'s lonely only-child Judith pursues in the glamorous next-door family, particularly in the elusive Roddy, for whom she constructs an elaborate—and false—personality, reading his evasiveness as mystery and his self-centredness as vulnerability. The novel functions on one level as a *Bildungsroman* in which the idealistic Judith must learn the inadequacy of her romantic illusions. Her one, long-awaited night of passion with Roddy she assumes to be the start of a relationship that will naturally lead to marriage, but he sees it as a trivial dalliance. In a reversal of conventional sexual morality he is so shocked when she sends him a love-letter the next day that he cannot bring himself to speak to her for years. Judith's mistake is not, as with the fallen literary heroines of previous generations, to give herself to a man, but to try to talk about it afterwards. Emotional outpourings, rather than sexual experience, are the new taboo. Hardened by this rejection, Judith tries to throw herself into the sophisticated relationships of the inter-war world, so that when another of the next-door cousins, the devoted Martin, declares his love for her, she feels, coolly, 'a faint relief and satisfaction' (p. 239), and briefly plans to marry him, despite feeling nothing for him. Later, she cavorts on the Mediterranean with the cynical and worldly-wise Julian, and takes seriously his suggestion that she should become his mistress. His expression of his feelings is couched in a contemporary language that eschews the romantic in favour of a direct violence of feeling that presents itself as deeply authentic because of its uncontrolled nature:

'Well *damn* you, don't you see I love you myself?' he cried in a perfect fury. 'Here I am, alone with you for a paltry ten days—after waiting years, mind you, *years* for my opportunity, and I find you moping and moaning over your lost schoolgirl illusions. Good God! Haven't you the guts to snap your fingers at a fellow who can't be bothered with you? Aren't you attractive and intelligent? Can't you laugh? Aren't there plenty of others? What am I here for? Go to the devil for a bit—I'll help you. I'll see you through it. But *don't moan.*' (pp. 268–9)

What Judith ultimately, and painfully, learns is that all romantic love is an illusion, and that she is finally alone. In the novel's bleakly satisfying conclusion she accepts that 'the futile obsession of dependence on other people' leads only to pain, and that 'this was to be happy—this emptiness, this light uncoloured state, this no-thought and no-feeling' (p. 303). Rosamund Lehmann's first novel, written in her early twenties, *Dusty Answer* achieved tremendous critical acclaim and popular success on its first publication. While in part the result of its daring treatment of sex, its reception also reflected the novel's innovative tone and philosophy, its capturing of the self-conscious cynicism of the first post-war generation, for whom romance was just one of the many illusions destroyed by the Great Trauma.[13]

This avant-garde cynicism is the dominant note in *Four Frightened People*, where romance is treated sardonically even at the moments of greatest erotic tension. The two men who accompany Judy and the annoying Mrs Mardick on their flight into the jungle are Judy's cousin Stewart and a somewhat pedantic civil servant, Arnold Ainger. The sexual potential of this situation is clear to Judy from the start:

I realised detachedly, as if this only affected someone else, that should we reach conditions primitive enough, both men, irrespective of my attractions (if any) would want me as a woman, and I should want one of them very strongly, and not the other. (p. 122)

Her clear-sighted, anti-romantic assessment marks her out as an essentially modern woman, who combines a masculine directness with feminine sexuality. She is also aware that such passion will be produced by extreme circumstances and 'probably we shall all three feel very silly about it when we get back to our own world, where the emotion will evaporate' (p. 123). Judy's breed of new woman believes in sex but not in romantic love—attitudes both confirmed and complicated by the progress of the narrative. From the novel's

---

[13] Lehmann received thousands of letters of praise, including ones from Galsworthy and Compton Mackenzie (who declared, 'My mantle has now fallen upon you'). In the *Sunday Times* a reviewer announced that 'This is a remarkable book. It is not often that one can say with confidence of a first novel by a young writer that it reveals new possibilities for literature'.

opening, romance is represented as something to be openly discussed, but never taken seriously; so Judy jokingly announces to her cousin that ' "You wouldn't recognise Romance if you met it. You've been in love with me, off and on, for years, and you do nothing about it" ' (p. 14). During the course of their arduous trek through the jungle, Judy's predictions come true: she and Arnold Ainger fall for each other, and Stewart is consumed with jealousy. On one level the scenario is that of one of the trashy 'triangle drama' novels Mrs Mardick reads (p. 22), but Judy's sardonic refusal of sentimentality ingeniously manages to both offer the reader romantic fulfilment and persuade her that she is above such tacky literary beguilements. Judy's increasingly deep feelings for Ainger she dismisses as an irrational response to circumstance, taking the ultra-modern line that romantic love is an illusion produced by chemical reactions and accidents of circumstance:

> Made as I am, in another age I should certainly have loved some other man as well as I now love this man. It is not real, then, my love—this focussing of all my desire on that one person. And this hankering in me which seems part of the substance of my being is a disturbance only in my brain and blood because I am young and vitally alive: his personal qualities have not engendered it. Not because my lover is what he is, but because I am what I am, is he so beloved. Then his loss is nothing irreplaceable. It is not real, my love. (p. 150)

Logically compelling though her reasoning is, Judy clearly protests too much—her argument is a bulwark against her thwarted desires, and only partially effective: 'poor comfort these thoughts were as a rule: to-night they were vaguely consoling, I was so tired' (p. 151). In the logic of the new anti-romantic discourse, such denials figure deep attachment, while neatly sidestepping any possible accusations of mawkishness. Just as Stewart and Judy openly discuss the nature of their feelings for each other, so she and Ainger are scrupulously honest in their acknowledgment of their growing attraction and discussion of the practical difficulties of consummation. Judy responds to Ainger's enquiry of whether she is in love with Stewart with devastating candour: ' "No." I added slowly, "with you, Arnold! At least, I want you" ', a self-correction which is confirmed by her declaration, at the end of the book, that although she and Ainger became lovers during the trek, they only fell in love later, on the boat taking them home. This love ultimately triumphs, when Ainger's wife divorces him, leaving him and Judy free to marry; though being cited as co-respondent means that she loses her career in the process. It is this conclusion of true love won—and appropriately paid for—that renders the text's daringly bohemian attitudes safely anodyne for the enjoyment of the conventional reader.

The texts discussed thus far, with their vulnerable men, competent women and inverted codes of romantic representation have largely concerned themselves with the pre-marital state; marriage, in middlebrow women's fiction, produces a rather different dynamic, being typically seen not as the apotheosis of romance but its antithesis. E. M. Delafield's Provincial Lady novels (discussed elsewhere in this book) turn this paradox to gentle comedy; in an earlier novel, *The Way Things Are* (1927), the disillusionment of the middle-class suburban wife is presented much more starkly. Thirty-four-year-old Laura Temple, the novel's protagonist, is married with two young sons, and preoccupied with the question of whether she really loves her husband Alfred. Their courtship had been a temperate affair—'she had never lost her head, nor Alfred his'—more a matter of expediency than of passion:

> Laura now admitted to herself—what she had not admitted to herself at the time—that she had been rather anxious to be married, just when she first met Alfred.
>
> The war was over, and there had been a question of her returning home, which she did not want to do, and so many other people seemed to be getting married. . . . She wanted the experience of marriage, and she was just beginning to be rather afraid of missing it altogether, because so many of the men belonging to her own generation had gone.[14]

Married life, as Laura experiences it, is a continual round of coping with inadequate servants and difficult children—domestic responsibilities she cannot share with her taciturn, undemonstrative husband. Starved of romance, or even of fulfilling companionship, she dreams of passion: 'she wanted a life—an emotional life—of her own' (p. 8). So far, so conventional, but Delafield does not allow Laura even the comfort of imagining that her discontents raise her above the common herd—she knows herself to be entirely typical:

> Laura, for the sake of her own self-esteem, strenuously ignored the fact that in all probability she was sharing this desire with a large number of middle-class, middle-aged Englishwomen all over the country. (p. 8)

[14] E. M. Delafield, *The Way Things Are*, 1927 (London: Virago, 1988), 6–7.

Unlike the lives enjoyed by the daring, highly educated women in some of the novels discussed earlier, this insular, quietly unsatisfactory existence is assumed to be very close to that of the putative reader. Indeed, Laura herself is a voracious reader, compensating for the lack of romance in her life by 'read[ing] an immense number of novels, half unconsciously identifying herself with the central character in each' (p. 91). Unlike the emotionally damaged, volatile men found in the modern romances, Laura's husband is emotionally sterile—buttoned-up, and encased in his own world of calm and order: 'as an English country gentleman, he preferred out-door pastimes, and he did not make personal remarks because he was not particularly interested in persons, and in any case preferred silence to speech' (pp. 89–90). Laura's emotions and their domestic life are bothersome distractions from which he escapes behind his newspaper. Husbands, in a conversation between Laura and her sister, are seen as a different species from 'ordinary men', the latter noticing personal details, the former 'only unpleasant things. Anything wrong with the food, or anything one's forgotten' (p. 109). Laura herself is far from the modern type of competent, independent woman, she was born just too early for the sexual adventuring of the post-war generation: 'In Laura's day—that Grecian-nymph period that now appeared so remote—to let oneself be kissed was something that classed one' (p. 93).

Her querulous dissatisfactions are counterpointed to the glamorous metropolitan life led by her younger sister, Christine, who has succeeded by the end of the novel in marrying 'the richest commoner in England'. Where Laura battles with her repressed romantic instincts, Christine triumphs in the inter-war world because of her ultra-rationality and slight edge of cynicism. In writing to her sister of her forthcoming wedding, she summarizes her carefully measured feelings:

'I know you're dying to ask if I'm in love with him. Darling Laura, I've never been in the least romantic, and I'm not now, but I'm quite enough in love not to feel that I'm taking a mean advantage of having been the first decent woman he met after the *affaire* Bébée. I truly think we shall understand one another very well, and ought to be very happy.' (p. 251)

Despite its lack of emotional fireworks, Christine's approach to love is the one that seems to be ratified by the novel. It is Laura's romantic yearnings that lead her into dangerous emotional quicksands when she falls in love with another man, Duke Ayland, a musician she meets through her sister. Laura throws herself headlong into the romance of shared intimacy and secret meetings, but the novel itself is more circumspect. This is not romantic tragedy à la Madame Bovary: Ayland's main attraction for Laura, it is made clear, is simply the fact that he listens to her and takes her opinions seriously. Laura's swooning intensity of feeling is treated with gentle irony, and one is led to suspect that even Laura herself is aware of the essential unreality of her emotions:

> 'Now, I've got to think this out quite steadily', Laura said to herself as she lay down.
> Steadiness of thought, however, eluded her. She sought to induce it, and succeeded only in involving herself with a number of metaphors. She felt that she must steer between the rocks, swim against the current, stand by her guns, stay the course, and even—towards the dawn—follow the gleam. (p. 152)

Romance is so impossible in the modern climate, it is implied, that even the language associated with it is worn out and clichéd.

Laura ultimately decides that she cannot leave her husband for Ayland because it would mean losing her children in the ensuing divorce battle; her innate sense of propriety refuses to allow her to simply conduct a secret affair, much as she might desire to. She renounces Ayland not in the grand gestures of romantic tragedy, but in the knowledge that their love will not survive the lack of proximity. She returns to her domestic life, and in the final words of the novel its bleak assessment of the lot of the average woman is hammered home:

> In a flash of unavoidable clear-sightedness, that Laura would never repeat if she could avoid it, she admitted to herself that the average attributes only, of the average woman, were hers. . . .
> It dawned upon her dimly that only by envisaging and accepting her own limitations, could she endure the limitations of her surroundings. (p. 336)

Romance remains the stuff of fiction, irreconcilable with the stultifying duty demanded by 'the things of respectability' (p. 336), chief among which is her marriage vows. The average woman—both Laura and her imagined reader—is required to endure the inadequacies of the married state, but may gain some bleak satisfaction from a clear-sighted appraisal of the particular ways in which it fails her.

An alternative representation of contemporary attitudes to marriage is given by Margaret Kennedy's *Together and Apart* of 1936, written, according to the author's daughter, because 'at this period she and my father were puzzled and distressed by what amounted to an epidemic of divorce among their acquaintance'.[15] Betsy Canning, middle-aged mother of three, suddenly announces to her husband that she would like a divorce. She proposes that they conduct themselves in a civilized and rational manner, and explain things logically to their children, but her coolly rational plan is upset by the interference of her mother-in-law, who, in trying to save the marriage, manages to set the Cannings against each other, and prevents any chance of a reconciliation. They separate bitterly, Alec having allowed himself to be seduced by their naive teenage au pair, Joy. He sets up an unhappy establishment with Joy and their illegitimate baby, Betsy marries her very unattractive but wealthy and titled cousin, and their adolescent son descends into a maelstrom of sexual confusion as a result of witnessing the initial kiss between his father and Joy. What they have lost is revealed in a pivotal scene when the estranged couple pass each other, after many years, one going up and one coming down on an Underground escalator:

Each turned at the same moment, she to stare upwards and he to stare down. The slight movement broke the spell of their surprise. Expression came back into their faces. Alec smiled broadly, not a smile of greeting or of courtesy, but as if he could not help it. Their glance was intimate, unreserved; such a smile as they might have exchanged at any time during their married life, if something had happened that they both thought ridiculous.

'How like us to manage our first meeting like this!' ran the message in his eyes. 'And what are you doing, my girl, chuff-chuffing in the Underground?' And her eyes said:

'Don't laugh, Alec! This isn't funny.' (pp. 242–3)

It is this intimacy, established over a long marriage, that they have wilfully discarded, and the rest of the novel elegiacally confirms its loss, without offering them any way back. Despite its sense of the waste of divorce, the novel is briskly cynical about the state of modern marriage. Alec has for years been conducting an affair with a married woman, which Betsy has vaguely condoned. When she asks for the divorce, this affair is one weight thrown into the balance, but

[15] Introduction by Julia Birley to the Virago edition of Margaret Kennedy's *Together and Apart*, 1936 (London: Virago, 1981), p. viii.

it is made clear that neither has taken it very seriously, with Alec positively amazed that it should form part of his wife's complaints against him: 'He stared at her. What on earth . . . oh, good God! She meant Chris Adams. She was thinking of his adultery, a thing so irrelevant that he had forgotten all about it' (p. 38). A brittle open-eyed quality pervades all of the novel's pronouncements about marital realities, so one of the couple's friends writes to his wife about Betsy's incomprehensible attitude to her estranged husband:

'Every petty grievance is raked up, even to little things that must have been forgiven and forgotten years ago. In 1920 he pushed her so that she fell downstairs. Good heavens! One push is surely allowed in every marriage. I nearly told her that I once knocked you out with a hot water bottle.' (p. 154)

Adultery is a trivial factor in the breakdown of the marriage, much worse is Alec's moral laziness in allowing Betsy to call all the shots: her brisk competence—'busy bustle'—is simply a front she puts on for the world: 'he knew that she wanted to pause and that she needed someone who could make her drop it, stop it, be quiet. That he had never done so was his worst failure as a husband' (p. 35). Alec's easy-going somewhat bohemian attitudes (he is a successful popular librettist) align him with those other iconic post-war male protagonists already examined, just as Betsy's breezy practicality places her as a modern woman; this text, however, is deeply suspicious of these contemporary gender roles, seeing them as the root cause of a modern epidemic of divorce. It is because Alec has failed to 'rule' Betsy that she has become unhappy and they have fallen out of sympathy:

He had no doubt of his own superiority. He knew himself to be more reasonable, more equitable, to have a greater desire for integrity and a clearer mind. It was he, and not she, who should have directed their joint lives. But he doubted his power to assert all this. She was too nearly his equal, too civilized and sensitive. He could not rule her brutally, as though she had been an animal or a slave. And to direct her in any other way would exhaust the whole of his mind and spirit. Life was not long enough to attempt such a thing. (pp. 37–8)

Alec's thoughts on the failures of his marriage are given with scant textual irony: he is to blame not for his assumption of superiority, but for his lack of will; his avoidance of violence is presented as highly forbearing. Yet at the same time as espousing these retrogressive positions about gender roles within marriage, the text also idealizes the contemporarily fashionable notion of the companionate marriage. Alec's relationship with the youthful Joy founders on the lack of shared interests as the initial overwhelming physical attraction between them burns itself out almost immediately and they are left trapped in a marriage between near-strangers. Alec berates Joy particularly for her failure to read: sexual passion is seen as a false and ephemeral factor on which to base a relationship, while shared culture is of fundamental importance.

We find a similar advocacy of the marriages of intellectual equals and social companions in *Gaudy Night*, where the issue of the marital prospects of the educated woman is a marked preoccupation. The ideal is presented in the thumbnail portrait of the married life of one of Harriet's contemporaries:

Phoebe Tucker was a History student, who had married an archaeologist, and the combination seemed to work remarkably well. They dug up bones and stones and pottery in forgotten corners of the globe, and wrote pamphlets and lectured to learned societies. At odd moments they had produced a trio of cheerful youngsters, whom they dumped casually upon delighted grandparents before hastening back to the bones and stones. (p. 18)

Phoebe shares her husband's career, and her degree is accorded value by its usefulness in their joint endeavours: it is a clear vindication of the idea of women's higher education that her marriage and her intellectual interests can dovetail so neatly. Others are not so fortunate: another old college friend Harriet meets at the Gaudy reunion—Catherine Freemantle, 'the outstanding scholar of her year'—has married a farmer and endured a difficult life of physical labour and economic hardship. She looks ten years older than her contemporaries and is bitter about her lost expectations. She remains convinced, though, that she was right to sacrifice her own interests to her husband's—to toil alongside him rather than earn money by writing and pay someone else to work the land. The paradox of her existence is that it is the intellectual's adherence to the principles of a companionate partnership that has ironically separated her from her intellectual life. She and Harriet debate the notion of 'one's own job' and how to recognize it, with Catherine asserting that the husband's interests take primacy—' "one is rather apt to marry into somebody else's job" ' (p. 48), while Harriet maintains the need to follow one's own star. She does concede, though, that ' "marriage is the really important job" ' (p. 48). It is the inevitability of this logic that keeps Harriet single for so long, shying away from the sublimation of her own individuality and personal ambitions in a partnership that her culture considers a full-time focus for women's lives. That other intellectual women are similarly marriage-shy is indicated by the brief comic presence in the novel of yet another of Harriet's contemporaries, an American known formally as Miss Schuster-Slatt, who is a passionate advocate of eugenics, and runs a campaign devoted to 'the encouragement of matrimony among the intelligentsia' and its sinister concomitant 'sterilisation of the unfit' (p. 30). Harriet's response is to agree 'that intellectual women should marry and reproduce their kind; but she pointed out that the English husband had something to say in the matter and that, very often, he did not care for an intellectual wife' (p. 45). This dereliction on the part of men is viewed sardonically by Harriet, who muses later that

> the rule seemed to be that a great woman must either die unwed, to Miss Schuster-Slatt's distress, or find a still greater man to marry her. And that limited the great woman's choice considerably, since, though the world of course abounded in great men, it contained a very much larger number of middling and common-place men. The great man, on the other hand, could marry where he liked, not being restricted to great women; indeed, it was often found sweet and commendable in him to choose a woman of no sort of greatness at all. (pp. 52–3)

The women dons of Shrewsbury college debate the issue of eugenics when discussing crime and punishment; they consider the German take-up of the idea of enforced sterilization for those considered unfit, and condemn it, not purely on its own terms, but because it is associated with other aspects of Nazi ideology such as 'the relegation of woman to her proper place in the home'. It is this fate that the primitively domesticated Annie figures so alarmingly for Harriet, who can only finally accept the prospect of marriage to Peter when it is clear that he values her as an intellectual equal. It is of deep significance (though—presumably—unintentionally farcical) that his proposal and her acceptance are given in Latin, in the words of the conferment of Oxford degrees, as they stand both garbed in their academic gowns under the Warden's windows in the medieval setting of New College Lane. It is a fantasy—one imagines of deep attraction to the highly intellectual and sadly single Sayers—of a union of equals, of a great woman finding one of the few available great men to match her. It is quite clear that this marriage, at least, will not founder in silent resentments and regrets.

The ambivalence with which marriage is treated in much women's middlebrow fiction of the inter-war years is equalled by the representations of motherhood we find in this fiction. It is significant that Harriet responds duplicitously to Annie's enquiry of whether she is fond of children: ' "Oh, yes", said Harriet. Actually, she did not care much for children; but one can scarcely say so, bluntly, to those possessed of these blessings' (p. 115). The hysterically resentful Annie is one of the few mothers in *Gaudy Night*, and it is notable that the idealized marriage of working equals managed by Phoebe Tucker is dependent on her 'dumping' her three children on grandparents for much of the year. The subject of breeding for intellectual women is rendered risible and associated with Nazism through the importunings of Miss Schuster-Slatt: although it is accepted as an inevitable part of the package of marriage, motherhood for this novel is at best an inconvenience, at worst a contributory factor in criminal psychosis. In many middlebrow women's novels of this date, motherhood is bestowed on the most stupid and animalistic of women: typical examples are *Cold Comfort Farm*'s hired girl, Meriam, with her quartet of illegitimate children (who her practical mother plans to train up as a jazz-band), and the imbecilic maidservant Olive in E. Arnot Robertson's *Ordinary Families*, who drowns her baby although her liberal employers have made every provision for her to be able to bring it up. A similarly hostile portrait of young mothers as stupid, impractical, and neglectful of their usually illegitimate children is that of the naive seductress Joy in *Together and Apart*, who has to be shown how to settle her baby for breast-feeding by her teenage stepdaughter. Sexually obsessed with her husband, Joy is sullenly resentful of the baby produced by their pre-marital affair, threatening to kill it and herself when Alec rejects her emotionally. Earlier, cynical friends are amazed when Alec plans to marry his pregnant mistress— ' "the Joy-girl is going to have a baby, so Alec thinks he has got to marry her. This defeats comment, don't you think?" ' (p. 147)— and the general attitude of the novel towards her motherhood seems to be one of amused contempt.

Even more dismissive of motherhood is *Four Frightened People*, in which the doctor, Judy, expresses an extreme lack of interest in the fact that one of the native women has just given birth, aided by Mrs Mardick; ' "A confinement is of less novelty to me than a tiger drive", I explained, "though I shouldn't mind if I never saw either of them again" ' (p. 199). Her distaste for childbirth is both philosophical and aesthetic, with her medical experience providing a further logic within which her contempt for the bodily experiences of femininity can be legitimated:

[M]aternity is a totally ungracious thing, beneath the sentimentality heaped upon it. Only once have I seen it made beautiful for an instant, by a chance grouping of a woman's thick white thigh, statuesque in its rigidity, and the new-born child lying in the arch made by her raised knee, with its arm thrown back above its head, and the strangest expression of peace that I have ever seen on the face of a living child. The cord was not yet cut, stretching in an arc between them. For a second I was staggered by such unexpected loveliness as they showed together, and then I bent over them to help her, and the scene changed back instantly to a normal birth, which is generally uglier than death, only so much pleasanter to witness that one rarely realises it. (p. 200)

The event of childbirth is uniquely beautified by its momentary resemblance to something like a Henry Moore sculpture; the child is awe-inspiring, not in its first moments of independent life, but in its resemblance to death; the ugliness, rather than the creativity of the average birth is what preoccupies her. This account, representing a radical refusal of one of the defining elements of femininity, is unusual in its intensity, but nonetheless represents a clear tendency in the middlebrow women's fiction of this date. The novel's contempt for maternity is not confined to Judy: Arnold bitterly resents his wife for her preoccupation in their children:

'[T]he girl I married has become the mother of my children, and nothing more. Her choice, not mine. No, that's not fair; just her nature and certainly not mine. You must have met some of the young women—no particular brains, just average—who marry and have children and then—well, goodness knows what happens to every intelligent interest and opinion they ever had. Just swamped, apparently, in a rush of maternity to the head.—Women in comfortable circumstances, I mean, who have no need to be permanently immersed in little Johnnie's bath, and what he said in it, to the exclusion of everything they've ever had in common with a man.' (pp. 306–7)

By the end of the novel, Arnold is very happy to have discarded this maternally-obsessed woman in favour of the intellectually rigorous

Judy. His complaint of his wife's immersion in the children is one repeatedly expressed by husbands in women's middlebrow fiction, to the extent that Delafield's female characters view their desire to discuss their children with their husbands as a dreadful addiction, to be repressed until it breaks out uncontrollably. *The Way Things Are* opens with a virtually identical representation of husband and wife irredeemably separated by their attitudes towards the children (even the offending child's name is the same):

> 'Did I tell you what Johnnie said, after he'd had his reading-lesson to-day?'
> 'No.'
> Laura embarked upon her anecdote.
> She had not intended, nor even wished, to tell it. She knew very well that her husband did not wish to hear it.
> Nevertheless, she told it. And her secret sense of her own futility and weakness took all conviction from the manner of her telling, so that even a much more amusing story than that of a five-year-old's repartee would have been bereft of sense and all spirit.
> When the recital of his son's witticism had petered out, Alfred Temple said, 'H'm', compromising between a short, unamused laugh and a curt ejaculation, and then he and Laura were silent again. (p. 1)

Alfred's terminal coldness towards wife and sons casts a chilly pall over the whole novel—it is the note of genuine desperation produced by his attitude that Delafield removes in her later Provincial Lady novels, where the husband's uninterested approach to domestic affairs is presented as typically and endearingly masculine.

The cultural ideal of motherhood was shaped in these years by a new school of behaviourist infant-care, dominated by the ideas of Frederick Truby King and John B. Watson. Truby King's theory of 'Mothercraft' (based on his early experiments in the artificial feeding of calves) extolled breastfeeding as the most hygienic option, and succeeded in reversing the new fashion for 'scientific' formula feeding of babies with his (presumably) reassuringly detailed instructions, timetables, and prescriptions for the nursing mother. Curiously, from our own perspective, this recommendation of breastfeeding was accompanied by an emphasis on leaving infants alone for long stretches of time—preferably out of doors, even in midwinter. The 'Truby King Baby' was imaged as a prodigy of independence, rolling happily around the yard like an exuberant puppy, needing no toys but nature and its own fingers and toes.[16] Even more devoted to the ideal of the independent infant was ex-academic and advertising copywriter John Broedus Watson, whose *Psychological Care of the Infant and Child* sold over 100,000 copies. In the interests of achieving socially competent children, Watson advised mothers to refrain from kissing and caressing their babies, declaring that 'there are rocks ahead for the over-kissed child'. As Christina Hardyment has persuasively argued in *Dream Babies*, her study of the history of childcare advice, Watson and other infant-care advisers in the years between the wars were heavily influenced by the spectre of Freudian ideas about the infant psyche: 'a careful study of the manuals shows that writers began to recommend measures designed to forestall Freudian-style traumas, although they refused to recognize Freud openly.'[17] In a devastating misreading of Freud, Watson and others decided that the complexes of the 'Essay on Infant Sexuality' could be avoided if children were treated by their parents with a careful lack of emotion—if you showed your son no love, he would be in no danger of developing an Oedipus complex:

The sensible way to bring up children is to treat them as young adults. Dress them, bathe them with care and circumspection. Let your behaviour always be objective and kindly firm. Never hug and kiss them. Never let them sit in your lap. If you must, kiss them once on the forehead when you say goodnight. Shake hands with them in the morning. Give them a pat on the head if they have made an extremely good job of a difficult task. Try it out. In a week's time you will find how easy it is to be perfectly objective with your child and at the same time kindly. You will be ashamed of the mawkish, sentimental way you have been handling it.[18]

We find the legacy of such advice in much of the middlebrow fiction of the inter-war period: Mrs Miniver, as Alison Light notes, 'wouldn't dream of doting upon, or losing herself entirely in, her children. It is certainly not the centre of her femininity as it may have been for her mother or her daughters in the 1950s.'[19] In middlebrow

[16] See Christina Hardyment, *Dream Babies: Child Care from Locke to Spock* (London: Jonathan Cape, 1983), 165–79; Diane Richardson, *Women, Motherhood and Childrearing* (London: Macmillan, 1993), 35; George K. Behlmer, *Friends of the Family: The English Home and its Guardians, 1850–1940* (Stanford: Stanford University Press, 1998), 163.
[17] Hardyment, *Dream Babies*, 165–6.
[18] John B. Watson, *Psychological Care of the Infant and Child* (London: Allen & Unwin, 1928), quoted in Hardyment, *Dream Babies*, 174–5.
[19] Alison Light, *Forever England: Femininity, Literature and Conservatism Between the Wars* (London: Routledge, 1991), 124.

family novels such as E. Arnot Robertson's *Ordinary Families* (1933) and Nancy Mitford's *The Pursuit of Love* (1945), emotionally controlled and cheerily vague mothers are presented as an accepted norm. Scrupulously distanced, comradely mothers are found particularly in the children's books of the time: we need only think of the jolly parent-free adventuring enjoyed by Enid Blyton's Famous Five, or of the sensible mother of Arthur Ransome's Swallows, who allows them to spend a holiday sailing alone after receiving a telegram from her travelling husband tersely ruling ' "BETTER DROWNED THAN DUFFERS IF NOT DUFFERS WON'T DROWN" '.[20] The ideology does not come easily to all—some novels, notably Delafield's, depict mothers' adherence to the new model of maternity as a conscious struggle with their instincts for care—but it is notable that even the reluctant do conform. The Provincial Lady refers to Robin, her son, 'in a detached way as "the boy" ' so that others 'shan't think I am foolish about him', and receives compliments about her daughter 'in an off-hand manner, tinged with incredulity, in order to show that I am a modern mother and should scorn to be foolish about my children'.[21] Laura too tries constantly to overrule her strong feelings for her younger son, and present an emotionless front: ' "Never let the child see that he has been the centre of unusual excitement", said the little book read by Laura in her children's infancy' (p. 9); but *The Way Things Are* presents a graphic, if humorous, riposte to the dominant childcare ideology in its depiction of what children get up to when left alone. Distracted by the presence of Duke Ayland, Laura forgets that she has sent Johnnie to await a punishment in her bedroom:

For the first time in several years, Laura had suffered a temporary amnesia, and had ceased to be aware of her own motherhood. She was forcibly reminded of it as she entered her bedroom, where Johnnie, decked in the slender contents of his parent's jewel-case, disposed of at random on his fingers, on the front of his holland overall, and round his legs and arms, sat absorbed in a small volume of Dr Marie Stopes, that had been bestowed by Laura beneath a pile of her more intimate underwear at the back of her chest of drawers. (p. 99)

---

[20] Arthur Ransome, *Swallows and Amazons*, 1930 (London: Random House, 1993), 2.
[21] *Diary of a Provincial Lady*, 1930, collected with other novels in the series as *The Diary of a Provincial Lady* (London: Virago, 1991), 3; 24.

Rather than the manly independence supposed to be created in boys by benign maternal neglect, the exuberant Johnnie comically threatens a life of transvestism and unhealthy sexual curiosity.

The small volume of Dr Marie Stopes is probably her infamous *Married Love* (1918), which had sold half a million copies by the mid-1920s. Combining a startling openness about the sex act with a heightened poeticism, Stopes succeeded in freeing the discourse of sexuality from the previous alternatives of simple smut or the scientific analysis of abnormalities:

> Her achievement was to be explicit about sex while making it sound a beautiful experience within the grasp of hard-pressed, puzzled readers. No one had come near to doing this before.[22]

Writing about erections, the significance of the clitoris, mutual masturbation, and the desirability of nakedness, Stopes opened the eyes of the post-war generation to new sexual pleasures and possibilities. Her emphasis was on the attainment of sexual harmony within marriage and her work formed part of a significant discourse in the inter-war period on companionate marriage, which raised the expectations of women in particular, and may have contributed both to the growing divorce statistics and the middlebrow literature of marital dissatisfaction already considered.[23] The increased popular awareness of psychological theories, particularly those of Freud, in the years after the war also made openness about sexuality more acceptable, and homosexuality more visible.[24] In its fashionable aspect, the key point of Freudian ideas was their promise of sexual liberation:

---

[22] Paul Ferris, *Sex and the British: A Twentieth-Century History* (London: Mandarin, 1994), 109.

[23] See Jeffrey Weeks, *Sex, Politics and Society: The Regulation of Sexuality Since 1800, 1981* (London: Longman, 1989), 206, 210; Cate Haste, *Rules of Desire: Sex in Britain World War I to the Present*, 1992 (London: Pimlico, 1994), 58–9.

[24] Robert Graves and Alan Hodges note that 'the name of Sigmund Freud was first popularly heard about 1920, though his methods were in repute during the war. They were used by the psychologists confided with the task of treating shell-shocked patients in such special hospitals as Maghull near Liverpool and Craiglockhart near Edinburgh' (*The Long Week-end: A Social History of Great Britain 1918–1939*, 1940 (Harmondsworth: Penguin, 1971), 98). Nicola Beauman also dates the popular dissemination of Freudian ideas to about this year, naming Barbara Low's *Psychoanalysis: A Brief Account of the Freudian Theory* (1920) as one of the first books to explain Freud to a general readership. (*A Very Great Profession: The Woman's Novel 1914–39* (London: Virago, 1983), 148).

'The first requirement for mental health is an uninhibited sex-life. To be well and happy, one must obey one's sexual urge. As Oscar Wilde widely counselled: "Never resist temptation!" ' Such was the Freudian gospel as it filtered down into people's minds, through translations, interpretations, glosses, popularizations, and general loose discussion.[25]

With his finger on the pulse of middlebrow attitudes, E. F. Benson mocked the new craze in the form of Lucia, always the first in her quiet backwater to catch on to a fashionable idea, who in *Mapp and Lucia* (1935) declares that ' "Tranquillity comes with years, and that horrid thing which Freud calls sex is expunged. We must read some Freud, I think; I have read none at present" ' (p. 71). In much the same vein, Deirdre in *The Brontës Went to Woolworths* remarks that 'female servants always prefer the master of the house. I don't read Freud, but I suspect that he would explain why, in gross and in detail—particularly in the former' (p. 115). Such Freudianism without Freud informed a great deal of middlebrow women's fiction between the wars.[26] Often treated with comic irony, it nevertheless profoundly influenced attitudes to sexuality and gender roles and relations. We find a clear recognition of the powerful sway of watered-down Freudianism in *Gaudy Night*, for example, where characters drop psychological buzz-words routinely into general conversation—' "Reaction, I expect. Repressed emotional instincts and all that" ' (p. 27). As befits her much-touted intellect, Harriet may actually have read Freud, musing after an erotic dream as to its true interpretation:

'This won't do', said Harriet. 'This really will not do. My sub-conscious has a most treacherous imagination.' She groped for the switch of her bedside lamp. 'It's disquieting to reflect that one's dreams never symbolise one's real wishes, but always something Much Worse.' She turned the light on and sat up.

'If I really wanted to be passionately embraced by Peter, I should dream of something like dentists or gardening. I wonder what are the unthinkable depths of awfulness that can only be expressed by the polite symbol of Peter's embraces.' (p. 103)

[25] Graves and Hodges, *The Long Week-end*, 99. Jeffrey Weeks's assessment supports that of Graves and Hodges: 'It was indeed in a fairly bowdlerized form that Freudianism made its main penetration into Britain' (*Sex, Politics and Society*, 155).
[26] Katherine Mansfield remarked on the striking sudden influence of Freud on fiction in 1920: 'I am amazed at the sudden "mushroom growth" of cheap psycho-analysis everywhere. Five novels one after the other are based on it: it's in everything' (*Letters*, vol. ii, ed. John Middleton Murry (London: Constable, 1928), 13 Oct. 1920, 53).

Despite the humorous scepticism reflected here, it is Harriet's familiarity with Freudian ideas that actually distorts her understanding of the case she is investigating. Blinded by psychological assumptions, she takes it for granted that a repressed sexual animus lies behind the vicious letters and spiteful pranks bedeviling the women's college. It is for this reason that she suspects that one of the celibate female dons must be the culprit. Caught in this mental bind particularly because these fashionable ideas mesh with her own anxieties about her life as a single professional woman, she needs Lord Peter to cut through the obfuscating simplicities of psychology and point out that sexual frustration does not necessarily lead to insanity:

'Isn't it a fact that, having more or less made up your mind to a spot of celibacy you are eagerly peopling the cloister with bogies? If you want to do without personal relationships, then do without them. Don't stampede yourself into them by imagining that you've got to have them or qualify for a Freudian case-book.' (p. 283)

The novel actively works to discredit the Freudian mind-set, luring the reader into its assumptions, playing on the parallels between Freudian methods and those of the detective, only to ultimately dismiss the former, in the voice of Lord Peter, and in the logic of the denouement, as both obscurantist and simplistic:

'It's no use saying vaguely that sex is at the bottom of all these phenomena—that's about as helpful as saying that human nature is at the bottom of them. Sex isn't a separate thing functioning away all by itself. It's usually found attached to a person of some sort.... The biggest crime of these blasted psychologists is to have obscured the obvious. They're like a man packing for the week-end and turning everything out of his drawers and cupboards till he can't find his pyjamas and toothbrush.' (p. 283)

What Freudianism misses, according to this logic, is one of the key ideas animating Golden Age detective stories—the profound individuality of each crime and criminal, and hence the ingenious originality of each plot.

Another novel actively working through issues raised by the new psychology is Delafield's *The Way Things Are*, in which we are early informed that 'conflict, in the language of psycho-analysis, was the almost incessant companion of Laura's psychological existence' (p. 14). The degree of irony implicit in this statement is difficult to gauge, as the novel gains many of its effects by alternately taking seriously and dismissing the angst of its protagonist. Whatever the novel's underlying attitudes, the world Laura inhabits is one deeply informed by psychological ideas. When her more worldly-wise younger sister quizzes Laura on the state of her marriage, she flaunts an airy familiarity with the principles of psychoanalysis: ' "any decent analyst would tell you that you're doing yourself a great deal of harm by this constant pretence. It's bound to create the most frightful repressions. What sort of dreams do you have?" ' (p. 108). Even provincial Laura, though, realizes the implications of dream-analysis: 'Laura, even though she did live in the country, knew all about Herr Freud and his theories, and declined to commit herself in any way upon the subject of dreams' (pp. 109–10). The intense fashionableness of psychology in their milieu is underlined by the metropolitan dinner party where the guests thrill with the enjoyable shock of discussing sexual perversions:

> In a sudden pause, the voice of the medical student rang out:
> ' . . . and I said, "My dear girl, there's nothing to be *ashamed* of! You're abnormal, that's all—simply and naturally, abnormal." '
> In an instant, the conversation had not so much turned upon, as rushed upon, the subject of abnormality. It seemed to be taken for granted that the only abnormalities worth discussing were those concerned with sex, and that these could not be discussed exhaustively enough. . . .
> Words, hitherto met with by Laura only in the works of Havelock Ellis, hurtled enthusiastically through the room. (pp. 157–8)

In the course of the novel, this well-informed medical student—the comically-named Losh—becomes Laura's guide to theories of repression, libido and other pressing psychological concerns, advising her ' "to take out the whole subject of Sex and look at it" ' (p. 207). Laura's refusal to risk losing her children in divorce is in Losh's opinion simply a predictable aspect of her psychological make-up: ' "most Englishwomen have the maternal instinct much more strongly developed than the mating instinct" ' (p. 289). Psychology, for Laura, represents the chimerical lure of the world of passion and self-indulgence that she can never allow herself to have. With a notable textual irony, she ultimately realizes that the insights of psychoanalysis are one of the many things she will have wilfully to repress if she is to return to her unsatisfactory married life.

The work of Marie Stopes and the popularization of psychology created an environment in which the public discussion of sex began to be respectable. Middlebrow women's fiction flirts with this new licence, treading a risky tightrope between the outrightly pornographic and the overly coy, working to develop an original language for the articulation of the sexual for a 'respectable' female readership. Sex, as Robert Graves noted, was the hot new literary topic, virtually a required ingredient if a book was to be taken seriously:

The most compelling fiction of the day was sex-problem fiction. The philosophical promiscuity of Aldous Huxley's, the gallant degeneracy of Michael Arlen's, and the earnest mysticism of D. H. Lawrence's sex-ridden men and women were weighed and compared even in Suburbia. A new character was introduced into the English novel: the tragic female Don Juan with her fatal lust for boxers, bull-fighters and such.[27]

The sexualized female protagonist becomes an increasingly stock figure in the feminine middlebrow during this period: from Delafield's Laura teetering on the brink of an affair, to Sayers's Harriet Vane, and Arnot Robertson's Judy Corder, both with sexual affairs behind them, sexual experience outside marriage is newly presented as a commonplace part of women's lives.[28]

Trying on a succession of the sexual and emotional identities newly on offer in the post-war world, Rosamund Lehmann's Judith flirts seriously with lesbianism, in the shape of an intensely loving relationship with Jennifer, her beautiful college friend. Initially, this relationship is figured in terms that echo the legitimized passionate friendships of the Victorian era, seemingly less transgressive than dalliances with the mysterious opposite sex, but in the course of the book Jennifer's feelings are revealed in more and more clarity as incontrovertibly Sapphic. Judith fails to acknowledge the intensity of their relationship, sinking into it with relief after the betrayal by

[27] Graves and Hodges, *The Long Week-end*, 100.
[28] In this respect, the feminine middlebrow echoes the more radical contemporary discourses on sexuality, but perhaps not the lived reality: most historians of sexuality argue that although the relaxing of sexual morality allowed a degree of sexual freedom among the upper and middle classes in the inter-war years, it usually stopped short of full intercourse. Virginity was still a prized possession for women, and 'heavy petting' was the order of the day. See Haste, *Rules of Desire*, 70–2; Weeks, *Sex, Politics and Society*, 207. On the other hand, Paul Ferris in his *Sex and the British: A Twentieth-Century History*, cites a survey of the sexual histories of six thousand women carried out by a Harley Street doctor, Dr Eustace Chesser, in the 1950s, which showed that of 'women born between 1904 and 1914, who reached sexual maturity in the nineteen-thirties' one in three had slept with a man before marriage (p. 128). Perhaps all that is indicated is the impossibility of recovering an accurate history of people's sexual behaviour; all we can know is what they choose to tell us.

Roddy, reading Jennifer's declaration of jealous love in terms of friendship. It is only with the arrival on the scene of Geraldine Manners—an older woman with close-cropped hair and a sultry, masculine face—and Jennifer's transfer of her affections to the newcomer, that Judith appears to understand more of the nature of the other's feelings. Both disliking and attracted to Miss Manners, Judith withdraws into solitude, her comprehension of the sexual relationship between the other women expressed in terms of imagined scenes of Jennifer wrestling with Geraldine, 'vying with her... a match for her in all magnificent unfeminine physical ways' (p. 158). The first relatively clear statement the text gives of the sexual nature of this relationship comes in Judith's tortured refusal to imagine it: 'Now she would leave her with Geraldine and not trouble to ask herself what profound and secret intimacies would be restored by her withdrawal' (p. 162). Such evasions belong not just to Judith but to the novel itself, which succeeds spectacularly in combining a revolutionary daring in the representation of sexuality with nimble sidesteps of any area that might attract the censor's attention. This feat is the more remarkable if we consider that *Dusty Answer* was published the year before Radclyffe Hall's notorious and banned *Well of Loneliness*, whose most overt representation of lesbian sex acts lies in the words 'And that night they were not divided'. The reader of *Dusty Answer* is offered the choice of maintaining her technical innocence, or fully understanding the sexual subtext. When Jennifer despairingly hints at her feelings for Judith before dropping out of Cambridge to travel decadent Europe with Geraldine, she oscillates between images of Judith as all-knowing and utterly pure of mind:

She began to cry, and stopped herself. 'There are things in life that you've no idea about. I can't explain. You're such a baby really, aren't you? I always think of you as the most innocent thing in the world.'
    'Jennifer, you know you can tell me anything.'
    Yet she knew, while she pleaded, that she shrank from knowing.
    'Oh yes, it's true, you understand everything.' (pp. 179–80)

Just so the reader, who is able to simultaneously know and not know what the novel is telling her. Heterosexual sex is represented with an equally careful juggling of veiling and declarative language. In the pivotal scene of love-making between Judy and Roddy, it is genuinely impossible to tell exactly what had occurred:

He put his hand beneath her chin and turned her face up to his.
'Lovely Judy. Lovely dark eyes . . . Oh your mouth. I've wanted to kiss it for years.'
'You can kiss it whenever you want to. I love you to kiss me. All of me belongs to you.'
He muttered a brief 'Oh!' beneath his breath, and seized her, clasped her wildly. She could neither move nor breathe, her long hair broke from its last pins and fell down her back, and he lifted her up and carried her beneath the unstirring willow-trees. (pp. 222–3)

In the recriminations that follow the next day, Judy refers to what has taken place between them as ' "that sort of thing—kissing" ' (p. 228), but the later reference to 'the shame of her surrender' (p. 230) suggests something more.[29] In a subsequent conversation with Martin, in which he characterizes Roddy as ' "a bit of a sensation-hunter" ', Judith cynically realizes that she had played him wrongly:

That was it then: she had been a new sensation: one that had quickly palled, because she had been so swiftly, so entirely yielded up to him. She should have whetted his appetite by offering only a little at a time and then withdrawing it: so, he might still be desirous of her. Instead she had satiated him at the outset. (p. 246)

This seems unequivocal, and yet there is still the carefully maintained possibility that it is an emotional rather than a physical surrender that is being described.

The word 'sex' is used with seemingly conscious ambiguity in many women's novels between the wars. In a number of cases it undergoes a process of modulation throughout a text, so that an initial meaning of 'flirtation' or 'relationships between the sexes' changes to a starker connotation of 'sex act'. When Judy Corder talks of 'life and all the charming absurdities of sex' (p. 27) near the start of *Four Frightened People*, the context makes it clear that it is the sparrings of romantic flirtation that she refers to; in a conversation about repressions later in the novel, the terms 'sex-starved' and 'sex-shame' (pp. 156, 158) deal in much more bodily specific meanings. In *Gaudy Night* one of the dons, in the context of a discussion of whether detective fiction trivializes crime, enquires by analogy whether ' "anybody who had tragic experience of sex, for example,

---

[29] Gillian Tindall, in *Rosamund Lehmann: An Appreciation* (London: Chatto & Windus, 1985), 43, comments of this scene that 'in the conventions of the period [it] suggested that something more than a warm kiss was taking place'.

should never write an artificial drawing-room comedy" ' (p. 33), with 'sex' seeming to connote 'romantic love', but used as a more modern, scientific-sounding alternative. Actual sexual relationships, in this novel, are referred to in much more circumlocutory form, so an understanding and virginal woman don encapsulates Harriet's earlier affair in a tactful reference to ' "the more generous sins" ' (p. 97).

Lesbianism is treated with some tolerance in a number of middlebrow novels—E. F. Benson's tomboyish artist Quaint Irene with her man's dress and openly acknowledged 'schwärm' for Lucia is a notable example; portrayed as a gentle eccentric, her sexuality and her gender ambiguity is unthreatening, though represented in fairly stark terms:

> Outside in the garden Irene, dancing hornpipes, was surrounded by both sexes of the enraptured youth of Tilling, for the boys knew she was a girl, and the girls thought she looked so like a boy.[30]

Male homosexuality, in contrast, is viewed with some suspicion. Benson's camp Georgie is kept firmly emasculated, devoted to piano duets and his embroidery, but, in contrast to Irene, never seen in sexualized terms. His sexuality is so irrelevant that in one of the later books—*Lucia's Progress* (1935)—he is annexed in marriage to the commanding Lucia. This erasure of Georgie's evident homosexuality is the more remarkable given the homosexuality of Benson himself (and, indeed, many members of his family, including his mother).[31] Given Benson's virtuoso parodic emulation of the feminine middlebrow (see discussion in Chapter 2), one can perhaps conclude that he recognized a latent hostility towards male

---

[30] E. F. Benson, *Mapp and Lucia*, 1935 (Harmondsworth: Penguin, 1970), 132.

A number of critics and historians have noted that the lesbian becomes an increasingly visible figure in the inter-war period, following Havelock Ellis's identification of the 'invert' and the notoriety produced by Radclyffe Hall's *Well of Loneliness*. Deirdre Beddoes sees this increased prominence in negative terms: 'the toleration of passionate friendships between women as innocent attachments which had existed in the Victorian era, was replaced by homophobia and public anger against lesbians' (*Back to Home and Duty*, 28). Jeffrey Weeks, though, suggests that the greater visibility allowed for the development in the period of 'a much more coherent lesbian sense of self': 'the permanent paradox remained that authoritarian moral codes in acting out their logic... produce by an inevitable reflex, an enhanced sense of identity' (*Sex, Politics and Society*, 220–1).

[31] See John Tosh, 'Domesticity and Manliness in the Victorian Middle Class: The Family of Edward White Benson', in Michael Roper and John Tosh (eds.), *Manful Assertions: Masculinities in Britain since 1800*, (London: Routledge, 1991), 58–9.

homosexuality in the form. This is certainly the case with *Dusty Answer*, which despite its sensitive treatment of lesbianism represents male homosexuals in terms of near-caricature. The key figure is Roddy's great college friend, Tony Baring, who, on first meeting, is immediately understood by Judith as posing a threat to her hoped-for relationship with Roddy:

> He had a sensitive face, changing all the time, a wide mouth with beautiful sensuous lips, thick black hair and a broad white forehead with the eyebrows meeting above the nose, strongly marked and mobile. When he spoke he moved them, singly or together. His voice was soft and precious, and he had a slight lisp. He looked like a young poet. Suddenly she noticed his hands,—thin unmasculine hands,—queer hands—making nervous appealing ineffectual gestures that contradicted the nobility of his head. She heard him call Roddy 'my dear'; and once 'darling'; and had a passing shock. (pp. 95–6)

Sensual, effeminate, and emotionally possessive of Roddy—this description of Tony makes no bones about his homosexuality, nor his campness. We are never allowed to see beneath this surface: he is known to us simply as Judith's antagonist: 'She remembered that Tony had been suddenly hostile; his eyes, stony and watchful, had fastened on her when she came in from the verandah with Roddy' (p. 100). A key to the novel's resentment of Tony is his exclusivity and clubbishness—his ability to draw Roddy into a world from which Judith, as a woman, is permanently excluded: 'The voices came up to her again, like a reiterated warning. "Keep away. You are not wanted here. We are all friends, men content together. We want no female to trouble us" ' (p. 100). The novel draws a veil over Roddy's own sexuality, but hints strongly that he has a serious involvement with Tony: when Judith puts it to him that Tony loves him, he replies complacently "I think he does" ' (p. 150), but omits to respond when asked if the corollary is also true. Such feelings between men are by no means seen as unnatural by the novel, indeed male–female relationships are perceived, even by Judith, as more dangerous:

> 'It is so terrible to be hated. Tell him I won't do you any harm.'
> But perhaps that was not true. Perhaps she meant endless mischief. Supposing she were to take Roddy from Tony, from all his friends and lovers, from all his idle Parisian and English life, and attach him to herself, tie him and possess him: that would mean giving him cares, responsibilities, it might mean changing him from his free and secret self into something ordinary, domesticated, resentful. Perhaps his lovers and friends

would be well advised to gather round him jealously and guard him from the female. She saw herself for one moment as a creature of evil design, dangerous to him, and took her hand away from his that held it lightly. (p. 150)

Roddy's lovers—those who love him, or those with whom he has sexual relations?—are clearly male, part of a club formed perfectly respectably in the upper-middle-class world of same-sex educational establishments.

Robert Graves and Alan Hodges, writing two decades later, date a transition in the social status and visibility of male homosexuality to just this moment:

Homosexuality had been on the increase among the upper classes for a couple of generations, though almost unknown among working people. . . . In most cases the adolescent homosexual became sexually normal on leaving school; but a large minority of the more emotional young people could not shake off the fascination of perversity. In post-war university circles, where Oscar Wilde was considered both a great poet and a martyr to the spirit of intolerance, homosexuality no longer seemed a sign of continued adolescence. . . . So long as one acted consistently in accordance with one's personal hypothesis and was not ashamed of what one did, all was well. Thus homosexuals spent a great deal of their time preaching the aesthetic virtues of the habit, and made more and more converts.[32]

The attitudes rather contemptuously described in this passage perfectly encapsulate that curious mixture in *Dusty Answer* of on the one hand familiarity with same-sex sexuality as a comfortable extension of friendship, and on the other a sense of a dawning culture of homosexuality that specifically excludes outsiders from its hidden mysteries and fellowships.[33] It is Graves's 'fascination of

[32] Graves and Hodges, *The Long Week-end*, 97. Cate Haste's research supports this contention: 'At Oxford University after the war, it was claimed to be a positive fashion to be "queer" as part of the rebellion of the Bright Young Things against the moral order. John Betjeman exclaimed in a radio programme: "But everybody was queer at Oxford in those days!" Goronwy Rees, also up at the time, described how homosexuality was "among undergraduates and dons with pretensions to culture and a taste for the arts at once a fashion, a doctrine and a way of life." It was "very largely the particular form which the revolt of the young took at the universities at that time" ' (*Rules of Desire*, 87–8).

[33] 'In certain strata (the ancient universities, literature, the higher echelons of the state) there was possibly a greater openness than previously; and for many homosexuals, reflecting in old age, the 1930s may have seemed a golden age. . . . [Some] managed to develop relationships and integration into the (largely secretive) subcultures' (Weeks, *Sex, Politics and Society*, 220.) It is, of course, just this world that Charles Ryder is drawn

perversity' that afflicts the adolescent son, Kenneth, in Margaret Kennedy's *Together and Apart*: traumatized by the Freudian scene of witnessing his parent's sexuality (his father kissing Joy), his damaged sexual attitudes lead him into 'vicious' behaviour at school. He falls in with Beddoes—'a boy with so doubtful a reputation that most right-minded people thought it a scandal that he should be in the sixth at all' (p. 169)—and becomes evidently corrupted, to the extent that his young sister recognizes the change in him immediately: 'This Beddoes was horrid and he had made Kenneth horrid. To her it was as clear as daylight' (p. 179). Like *Dusty Answer*, the novel initially skirts around the precise details of the relationship between the two boys, but its sexual nature is made abundantly clear by a subsequent passage that functions as a sort of psychological case study. Kenneth's 'moral breakdown' is explained as the result of his confused feelings for his parents: 'he believed that his mother was entirely blameless . . . and would have died rather than distress her by any revelation of his own sensuality' but he is not only shocked but sexually excited by the evidence of his father's 'depravity'. He is saved from complete nervous collapse under the pressure of this emotional conflict by the maid in his mother's Paris flat, 'a good-natured wanton, who seduced and consoled him in a motherly way'. Sex with a woman cannot, however, provide an outlet for Kenneth's damaged psycho-sexual urges:

> Yvonne was kind, but she could not do much for his sick imagination and he was too young to appreciate her. He needed stimulus from somebody more like himself. He went back to school a ready prey for Beddoes, or anyone else a little older and a little more experienced. Yet he still, despite the confusion of his mind, desired to be worthy of his mother. . . . If, at any time, his association with Beddoes should threaten her peace of mind he believed himself capable of dropping the whole business easily. (pp. 203–4)

Homosexuality is a youthful perversion in which vulnerable boys are 'preyed' on by the vicious; a predilection in this direction is created by a warped idea of adult sexuality provided by the parents, and by an over-dependence on the mother: this 'case study' echoes the dominant ideas about the subject promulgated by psychologists and by sexologists such as Havelock Ellis. Kenneth does not enjoy

into as an undergraduate in the Oxford of the inter-war period in the 1945 *Brideshead Revisited*—a world of romantic male-to-male passions and heightened aesthetic sensibilities, presided over by the Wilde-like Anthony Blanche, European-sophisticate and intimate of Cocteau and Diaghilev.

his homosexual experience: 'At no time had he really liked Beddoes; but in the beginning there had been a queer excitement, a nervous obsession, which took the place of sympathy' (p. 264). The attraction is to consider himself as thoroughly bad, 'driven to the devil by a world which had ill-treated him'. For this novel, homosexuality reflects in an extreme form an over-sexualized modern world: Kenneth eventually 'recovers' when he is able to view his father's relationship with Joy as 'just a married couple' (p. 311), without excitement or mystery—when, in other words, he achieves a desexualized perspective.

The combination in this 1936 novel of a determined openness about sexuality with a strong sense of the sexual as a distorting and potentially damaging element in relationships points to a shift in attitudes about sexuality in the 1930s. Historian of sexuality Jeffrey Weeks comments that the relaxation of sexual taboos in the 1920s was followed by a decline in the various movements for sexual reform in the following decade:

> Amongst certain strata of the population the 1920s saw a relaxation of some sexual taboos: the new feminists spoke of sexual pleasure, birth control was more openly advocated, progressive intellectuals espoused sex reforms, while homosexuality caused a certain fashionable frisson. By the 1930s this was certainly changing. Dora Russell has recalled how a new authoritarianism entered into personal relationships in the 1930s. . . . Simultaneously the reform organisations went into decline, and hopes for radical changes faded as more immediate political and economic concerns dominated.[34]

Although, as Weeks insists, this decline in sexual radicalism in the 1930s was tempered by the growing discourse on sexual satisfaction within marriage initiated by the work of Marie Stopes, it does seem that the appetite for sexual licence was dwindling in this decade. This is certainly the sense we get from the women's middlebrow novel, where openness about sexuality becomes a subject for determined parody in the 1930s. Finding a scrap of newspaper amongst their belongings while in the jungle, three of Arnot Robertson's four

---

[34] Weeks, *Sex, Politics and Society*, 199–200. Weeks is, however, anxious to temper this acknowledgement of a shift in attitudes to sexuality with a recognition that there were, of course, significant continuities across the two decades. In particular, he rejects the over-schematizing model of earlier feminist historians (he singles out Kate Millett) who discovered a sexual revolution in the 1910s and 1920s, followed by a backlash in the more politically conservative 1930s. (Kate Millett, *Sexual Politics* (London: Rupert Hart-Davis, 1971.))

frightened people view with amused contempt the report of 'an international congress of biologists for the study of sexual problems, headed "Experts on Love" ': ' "Fair makes one yearn for the refinement of civilisation, doesn't it?" Stewart said mildly' (p. 136). The despised and suburban Mrs Mardick is condemned also for her 'modern' insistence on discussing sex:

> Mrs Mardick was one of the women who, when their own underproof physical ardours have waned, find their main sexual stimulant in forcing themselves to discuss sex freely with their children, to the embarrassment of the latter. This mild and perhaps harmless modern vice is on the increase, among conscientious elderly women whose innate Victorianism is balanced by a resolve not to lose touch with the day at any cost. (p. 152)

Taken deeply seriously by true moderns such as Judy, sex is trivialized by becoming so much a part of popular currency that the Mrs Mardicks of the world feel obliged to become experts.

The smart modernity of sexuality as a subject of conversation is repeatedly mocked by middlebrow women's fiction of this date: the sex-mad Mr Mybug in *Cold Comfort Farm* (1932) pesters Flora on their nature walks with forced sexual allusions, seeing birch stems as phallic symbols and buds as nipples and virgins. His lack of interest in anything but sex is seen as 'understandable, if deplorable':

> After all, many of our best minds have had the same weakness. The trouble about Mr Mybug was that ordinary subjects, which are not usually associated with sex even by our best minds, did suggest sex to Mr Mybug, and he pointed them out and made comparisons and asked Flora what she thought about it all. Flora found it difficult to reply because she was not interested. She was therefore obliged merely to be polite, and Mr Mybug mistook her lack of enthusiasm and thought it was due to inhibitions.[35]

True sophisticates, the feminine middlebrow begins to imply, find sexual discourse obvious and uninteresting; so in E. Arnot Robertson's first novel, *Cullum* (1928), a smart young man's cynical (if secondhand) aphorism about women and sex is greeted dismissively by his jaded friends:

> 'Who knows for certain what his female relatives are in these days of emancipation?' put in Raymond, seizing the loophole for the saying that was burning a hole in his brain, and running it off at great speed so that he should not be disappointed again. ' "Nowadays a virgin of twenty is an

---

[35] Stella Gibbons, *Cold Comfort Farm*, 1932 (Harmondsworth: Penguin, 1983), 121.

anachronism; of twenty-five, an improbability; of thirty, a tragedy. No woman can be said to be her own mistress until she has tried the obvious alternative." The man in my room in the office said that this morning. I think it's rather neat, don't you?'

'I'm sure we shall', Ropes told him kindly, 'towards the end of the week, when we're more used to it.'[36]

The fashionably sex-conscious are mocked as paradoxically gauche in Delafield's *The Way Things Are* in the person of Bébée, the flighty daughter of one of Laura's titled neighbours, who throws herself at a famous married writer, going as far as to move in with him and his wife, despite their feeble protestations. Declaring that ' "polygamy is a necessary concomitant of genius" ' (p. 208), she refuses to see that the object of her affections is not interested in leaving his wife for her. The text does not allow her even the dignity of tragedy, with Laura remarking trenchantly, in response to a friend's comment that Bébée's life is ruined, that ' "She is very foolish, of course—idiotic, and very badly behaved—but do you think that people's lives are easily ruined nowadays? It seems to me that they can do almost anything, especially girls" ' (p. 223). Bébée resembles in some respects the unfortunate Joy in Margaret Kennedy's *Together and Apart*, who naively offers to give herself to the married Alec to provide him with the evidence to secure a quick divorce, completely failing to understand the respectable convention whereby the man fakes adultery for this purpose. In a letter to Alec she sets her own value very low:

'You are the whole of life to me. Of course I know that you do not, and never can, love me like this. But, after what happened the other night, I don't feel that you would mind going away with me for a little while, and afterwards I should never bother you, or ask for anything, or ever expect to see you again. I should have had a little bit of happiness and that is more than many people have.' (pp. 95–6)

From an exuberant representation of youthful high spirits, Joy is transformed by her relationship with Alec into a catatonic lump of raw emotion. For both this book and Delafield's, the young mistress is a foolish, pathetic figure, letting the gospel of sexual liberation dupe her into selling herself cheap. It is significant that Joy presents her offer of herself to Alec as typical of the behaviour of her generation, announcing that an affair will not ruin her life because she is planning to leave her job and run a bookshop with a friend who

[36] E. Arnot Robertson, *Cullum*, 1928 (London: Virago, 1990), 259–60.

' "will not mind about my private life because she has done it too" ' (p. 96). The sympathies for the older married woman rather than the naively passionate young girl in Kennedy's novel represent a significant shift from those in her infamous *Constant Nymph* of 1924: by 1936, what had been a radical association of sexual with emotional freedom was clearly beginning to look decidedly overworked. The middlebrow women's fiction of the 1930s views the sexual emphasis of modern life with increasing disdain but, reluctant to concede its bohemian pose of utter unshockability, maintains a resolute openness about matters sexual. As with the determined outflankings that allow the feminine middlebrow to maintain a class authority in the face of constantly shifting social identities, so its mockeries of and reservations about contemporary sex-consciousness enable it to throw a cloak of superior sophistication over its growing conservatism.

Largely radical in its embracing of new gender roles and in its revised codes of romance, the feminine middlebrow of the inter-war years was increasingly conservative, though carefully, brightly, avant-garde, in its response to the accompanying sexual licence. A consideration of the treatment of these issues in the 1940s and early 1950s will test the assumption that still generally prevails that the culture of this period, following a brief flurry of sexual radicalism in the war-years, is marked by the reimposition of traditional codes of femininity. It was one of the guiding assumptions of the feminism of the 1970s that the years after the Second World War saw a concerted establishment attempt to push women back into the home.[37] Later historians have moderated and qualified this argument, but do concur that a concatenation of factors contributed to a post-war ideology of what Jeffrey Weeks has called 'maternalism', which strongly encouraged women to have more children, and placed an increased emphasis on the 'proper domestic environment' in which those children should be brought up.[38] Weeks points to the foundation of the

---

[37] A position largely predicated on Betty Friedan's identification in her 1963 *The Feminine Mystique* of what she called 'the problem that has no name'—the hegemonic effects of the pro-domestic ideology unceasingly directed at American women by the advertising industry and psychoanalytic establishment among others in the years after the Second World War.

[38] Historians are notably eager to distance themselves from the provocative generalizations of 1970s feminism, while often arguing themselves back round to a fairly similar position. Jeffrey Weeks insists that there is no evidence for a conscious government campaign to persuade women back to the home in the post-war years, but does find much evidence for an ideological barrage that had precisely the same effect (*Sex, Politics and*

Welfare State as a key factor in formalizing a long-standing concern with the falling national birthrate: its initiating document, the 1942 Beveridge Report, declared baldly that 'with its present rate of reproduction the British race cannot continue', and numerous other official and semi-official bodies voiced similar concerns. Although these concerns had been present in the inter-war years, 'what was new was the social and political context in which they were now expressed, for the creation in the 1940s and 1950s of a political consensus around the idea of a Welfare State did imply a more coherent interventionism in wide areas of social life than ever before.'[39] Diane Richardson, in her 1993 study of *Women, Motherhood and Childrearing*, supports the idea of the post-war period as one in which 'there emerged a particularly intense concentration on the mother'.[40] She suggests that a key influence was the new 'permissive', child-centred theories of childcare, particularly those of John Bowlby and Donald Winnicott.[41] In a direct reversal of the inter-war behaviourist model, they argued that the early attachments formed by an infant are crucial to its future mental and physical health, and placed particular emphasis on the bonding with the mother. Instead of the infant being trained to accommodate the needs of its parents, the new childcare doctrine required a mother willing to adapt herself to every need or desire of the child.

The intense social focus on motherhood was accompanied by an increased emphasis on marriage—in the Beveridge Report, according to Weeks

[T]here was a pervasive concern . . . to reinforce and encourage marriage; amounting to an ideological reconstruction of marriage as a vital occupation and career, so that 'Every woman on marriage will become a new person.'[42]

Society, 232–9). Both he and Diane Richardson reject the notion that the closure of state nurseries after the war was a deliberate move to push women out of the work force, but both conclude that it was a contributory factor in the decline of female employment in the late 1940s (*Women, Motherhood and Childrearing*, 46).

[39] Weeks, *Sex, Politics and Society*, 232–9; William Beveridge, *Social Insurance and Allied Services* (London: HMSO, 1942), 154. The report was that of an interdepartmental committee, of which Beveridge was the chairman.

[40] Richardson, *Women, Motherhood and Childrearing*, 43.

[41] John Bowlby's major work was *Child Care and the Growth of Love* (London: Penguin, 1953); Donald Winnicott, a paediatrician and psychoanalyst reached a large audience in the 1940s and 1950s when his ideas were popularized in women's magazines. In 1944 he made a series of BBC wartime broadcasts to mothers which formed the basis of his later book *The Child, the Family and the Outside World* (London: Penguin, 1964). (See Richardson, *Women, Motherhood and Childrearing*, 43–4.)

[42] *Sex, Politics and Society*, 235, quoting Beveridge, 135, 131.

Welfare benefits were withheld from women co-habiting with men to whom they were not married; the new discipline of social work developed with the explicit aim of shoring up the conventional family unit; and the marriage guidance movement underwent a massive expansion.[43] Liberals and conservatives, feminists and anti-feminists alike—all supported the institutions of marriage and family.[44] The new concern with marriage can be traced directly to the experiences of the war years, when huge numbers of both men and women found themselves for the first time in extra-marital relationships. After long years alone, many women took solace in affairs, with the result that nearly a third of illegitimate children in the last two years of the war were born to married women. The divorce rate, unsurprisingly, shot up, with petitions filed on the grounds of adultery increasing from 50 per cent in 1938 to 70 per cent in 1945.[45] Attempts to 'rescue' the institution of marriage after the war included an elaboration of the discourse on sexual satisfaction within marriage begun by Marie Stopes. An example is the first booklet of the Marriage Guidance Council (founded in 1938)— *How to Treat a Young Wife*—published soon after the war, which advised husbands on how to develop their wives' sexual potential.[46] A strong need to control pre-marital sexuality resulted in what Weeks has called 'a curious obsession with "petting" in the sex literature of the period', as an attempt to head the young off from full-blown intercourse. The same ideological drives can be discerned behind the strong public anxiety about, and increase in prosecutions for, both prostitution and (male) homosexual offences.[47]

Given its responsiveness to new social trends, we might well expect the middlebrow women's novel to echo some of these shifts in

---

[43] See Weeks, *Sex, Politics and Society*, 235–9; Haste, *Rules of Desire*, 143–7.

[44] Elizabeth Wilson, arguing that post-war feminists and radicals, by shifting the grounds of their belief to embrace the pro-family ideology were in part responsible for the retreat of women to the home remarks that 'the orchestration of consensus on the position of women in postwar Britain was the achievement of a deceptive harmony out of a variety of noisy voices; and perhaps that false harmony says something about what ideology might partly be' (*Only Half-Way to Paradise: Women in Post-War Britain 1945–1968* (London: Tavistock, 1980), 3–4).

[45] Haste, *Rules of Desire*, 109.

[46] Revised and reissued as *Sex in Marriage*, the booklet had sold more than half a million copies by the late 1960s. See Weeks, *Sex, Politics and Society*, 237.

[47] Jeffrey Weeks notes that prosecutions for homosexual offences increased five-fold in the period between 1938 and the mid-1950s, though the Wolfenden Committee found little evidence that the incidence of such offences was actually increasing. (*Sex, Politics and Society*, 239–40.)

attitudes to gender and sexuality, but in fact what we largely find in this fiction in the 1940s and early 1950s is a remarkable degree of continuity with the gender attitudes of the inter-war period. The novels of the war years do tend to take as their subject the social flux and sexual licence typical of that time, but the behaviour they depict does not differ noticeably from that found in the novels of the inter-war period. Julia's husband in Elizabeth Taylor's 1945 *At Mrs Lippincote's* has been conducting an affair while his military posting has separated them, but so too had Alec in Kennedy's *Together and Apart*, without the excuse of the separation. The war makes acceptable the sexual relationships outside marriage of the female protagonists in Elizabeth Bowen's *The Heat of the Day* (1949) and Nancy Mitford's *The Pursuit of Love* (1945), but *Gaudy Night*'s Harriet Vane and *Four Frightened People*'s Judy Corder are also sexually experienced single women. In fact, it is perhaps significant that both Bowen's Stella and Mitford's Linda are not young ingenues at the time of their affairs, but are both divorced matrons, whose sexual adventurings are arguably less shocking than those of women (like Harriet and Judy) who have never been married. Bowen's novel does tackle the vexed subject of war-babies conceived outside marriage, but it is notably the feckless lower-middle-class Louie, and not the heroine Stella who is left with an illegitimate child. Although the novel ends with the possibly optimistic image of Louie and her baby as representatives of the future, she in fact differs very little from all those other irresponsible lower-class unmarried mothers of the inter-war novels. In some cases, wartime novels suggest an environment of more sexual constraint than that which had prevailed before the war: in Delafield's *The Provincial Lady in Wartime* (1940), there is a not-altogether-convincing attempt to suggest that the upper-middle-class young during the war had actually adopted stricter sexual standards than those that had operated for the older generation between the wars. The Provincial Lady enquires if Serena, her youthful co-worker in the air-raid shelter canteen, plans to marry her boyfriend:

Serena doesn't know. Probably not.
Remind myself that standards have changed and that I must be modern-minded and enquire boldly whether Serena is considering having An Affair with J. L.
Serena looks unspeakably shocked and assures me that she isn't like that at all. She is very old-fashioned, and so are all her friends, and nowadays it is a wedding ring or nothing.

Am completely taken aback and realise that I have, once again, entirely failed to keep abreast of the times.

Apologise to Serena, who replies that of course it's all right and she knows that in post-last-war and pre-this-war days, people had some rather odd ideas, but they all went out with the nineteen-twenties.[48]

We find a similar, but more nuanced, statement about the shifts in sexual attitudes between the 1920s and the years around the Second World War in Mary Renault's *The Friendly Young Ladies* of 1944, which is set a year or so before the war, but clearly reflects many of the concerns of the years of conflict. The young and up-tight Elsie, the novel's ostensible protagonist but actual butt, leaves in shock a party at which a group of young doctors and nurses are singing obscene ditties. She is followed by Joe, a writer, who explains the songs as a healthy outlet for the stresses of the singers' daily lives:

'No one who does what these people do, and sees what they see, could go on taking the human body seriously all their spare time. If they did, they'd go loco.... The women particularly. On top of their own troubles, they've got several generations of hush-hush and brooding in corners, and then all that nervous frank-and-fearless stuff in the twenties, to get off their chests. Personally, it makes me feel good to see them. Healthy as your mother sweeping the house.'[49]

A straightforward apprehension of the body's place in a fully-lived life, rather than a nervous intrusion of the sexual into everything, is presented as the dominant characteristic of the moment (with the travails of the pre-war medics clearly standing-in for the more general tensions and realities of the wartime experience). Sexuality is considered in many wartime fictions in much the same way as escapist reading—as necessary release, but the actions depicted and the language employed are no more overt than in those inter-war novels which employ representations of the sexual with an air of experiment and daring.[50]

Just as we fail to find an abrupt transition in the feminine middlebrow's treatment of matters of gender and sexuality before and

---

[48] E. M. Delafield, *The Provincial Lady in Wartime*, 1940, collected with other novels in the series as *The Diary of a Provincial Lady* (London: Virago, 1991), 493.
[49] Mary Renault, *The Friendly Young Ladies*, 1944 (London: Virago, 1985), 127.
[50] As Jenny Hartley remarks: 'Female sexual pleasure is often a contentious issue, and it was particularly so at this time, when official policy firmly decreed fidelity but people's attitudes were apparently becoming more lenient. Sex seems to have been acceptable in fiction as long as it was not too enjoyable' (*Millions Like Us: British Women's Fiction of the Second World War* (London: Virago, 1997), 66).

during the Second World War, so too—and despite the many social and political changes of those years already outlined—we find far more continuities than we might expect in the wartime novels and those of the ten years that followed. The continuation into the middlebrow women's novel of the 1940s and early 1950s of the ambivalent gender identities of the inter-war fiction is clearly apparent. The sardonically attractive Wing Commander with whom protagonist Julia bonds in Elizabeth Taylor's *At Mrs Lippincote's* (1945) is first pictured leaning against the mantelpiece doing his wife's knitting, a point of characterization that tempers his cool authority and appears to be designed to make him more, rather than less appealing to the female reader.[51] The love object of the youthful governess Cassandra in Taylor's novel of the following year, *Palladian*, is her somewhat effeminate employer, Marion, who cuts an effetely aristocratic figure with 'his exaggeratedly long hands like the hands in an Elizabethan portrait, the greenish gold hair, his rather affected clothes'.[52] Mary Renault's *The Friendly Young Ladies* (1944) focuses on the boyish Leo, who writes cowboy yarns and lives on a houseboat on the Thames with her lesbian lover, while the detective plot of Josephine Tey's 1950 *To Love and Be Wise* hinges on the gender identity of a mysteriously beautiful young man. And yet if we don't find a turning away from such gender ambivalence in the middlebrow literature of the years during and after the war, we do find the subject treated with a degree of anxiety that perhaps reflects the social return to more firmly differentiated gender roles.

In *Palladian*, her rather cynical reworking of *Jane Eyre*, Taylor problematizes gender identities and relations without coming to any clear conclusion. The delicately sexless love of Cassandra and Marion is counterpointed to the self-loathing lust of the encounters between Marion's cousin Tom and the local pub landlady, but both relationships are treated with a cool authorial contempt. Cassandra has decided to fall in love with Marion before she even meets him, 'as if she were a governess in a book' (p. 182), and their courtship is

---

[51] Elizabeth Taylor, *At Mrs Lippincote's*, 1945 (London: Virago, 1995), 23.
[52] Elizabeth Taylor, *Palladian*, 1946 (London: Virago, 1985), 31.
Marion's effeminacy is prefigured by his name and the extreme reaction to it of the teacher who arranges the job of governess for Cassandra: ' "My cousin, Marion," Margaret wrote, "is looking for someone to teach his little girl." "*His!*" I thought, "*Marion! His!*" But I discovered that it was one of those names like Evelyn or Hilary or Lindsay that can be either. With an "o", you see. But "o" or not, I think it rather girlish for a grown man' (p. 13).

characterized by a 'cerebral intimacy' as he teaches her Greek, and gives her back the hand he has been holding 'as if it were something he had borrowed, that he was punctilious about returning' (p. 82). Tom, killing himself with drink in an attempt to forget Marion's dead wife, Violet, with whom he had conducted a long-term passionate affair, slakes his lust on the compliant Mrs Veal, whom he despises:

> [S]he was a tawdry thing, not worthy of any tenderness. She thought it was pent-up passion he released upon her. . . . She would not have understood that he wreaked vengeance upon her, used her brutally in his mind. (p. 59)

Tom's sexually-assertive masculinity is as poisonously destructive as the alcohol with which he obliterates his consciousness; indeed he imagines the drink in sexual terms, casting it in his own image, and himself in the role of abused female partner: 'a dreadful metaphor had occurred to him—that his conflict with alcohol was sexual and he like a starved and frantic woman striving by intense yet hopeless concentration to find peace from a casual and heedless lover' (p. 97). Sexuality is imaged as toxic, a force which destroys families and creates devastating secrets. After Marion's young daughter is killed in a meaningless accident, Tom reveals that she was actually his child. What appeared to be a *Jane Eyre* narrative is revealed as in fact *Wuthering Heights*, with the cuckolded Marion in the role of Edgar Linton. In terms reminiscent of the denouement of Daphne du Maurier's *Rebecca* (1938), the dead wife Violet is revealed by Tom as evil, because sexual: ' "you believed her to be good. I knew her to be bad and sometimes she hated me for knowing it" ' (p. 166). Yet Marion, and the novel, refuse these categories, and Tom's notion that Violet's death in childbirth was punishment for her sins is dismissed as gothic. The modern world is represented by Tom's sister, Margaret, a doctor, who is pregnant with her first child throughout the novel, and goes into labour at the end. Briskly rational, and refusing to be cowed even by the drama of Violet's hideous death from eclampsia, she treats her pregnancy as a matter of science, not melodrama, insisting, like *Four Frightened People*'s Judy Corder, on her own aloofness from the murk of feminine sensibility:

> 'Metabolism', she murmured to herself. The word was so Greek, so clear and sharp and so unlike the Anglo-Saxon language of the old wives. She did not care for female-talk, as she called it, unless it was very far removed from women gossiping over gates or over the four o'clock fire; unless it was clear, decisive, scientific. (pp. 111–12)

The novel views all its characters with a somewhat sardonic eye: Margaret and Marion, in their inter-war gender reversals, are understood as stereotypes (in the eyes of outsiders 'Margaret made everything right for Marion, her capability cancelled his effeminacy' (p. 185)), but naive virgin Cassandra and the aggressively masculine Tom are equally creatures of cliché. Although gender roles and sexuality are actively investigated by the novel there is little of the sense of optimistic experimentation with which the inter-war fictions approached these topics, which are instead envisaged as iron bands, against which the characters impotently strain.

The increasingly tense response to gender in the women's middlebrow fiction of this period is demonstrated also in Josephine Tey's *To Love and Be Wise* of 1950, in which gender ambiguity is represented as both fascinating and evil. The rather slight detective interest focuses on the appearance in and subsequent disappearance from an English village of a strikingly beautiful young man, Leslie Searle. Searle, who turns out to be a famous American photographer, charms the bohemian set who have colonized the picturesque Salcott St Mary, while also disconcerting them with his air of decadence—a middle-aged romantic novelist declares that Searle makes her feel abandoned: ' "I am sure he was something very wicked in Ancient Greece." '[53] Others see him as demonic, in an attempt to understand the fascinating air of wrongness he exudes. Tey's series detective Grant, responsible by a series of coincidences for introducing Searle into the hot-house environment of the artistic village, is thrown at their initial meeting when Searle laughs up at him as they are pressed together by the crush of bodies at a literary party. The implication of Searle's homosexuality is presented in only the most coded terms, with Grant and his Sergeant raising and dismissing the possibility purely through tone of voice:

> 'What was he like, sir?'
> 'A very good-looking young man indeed.'
> 'Oh,' Williams said, in a thoughtful way.
> 'No', said Grant.
> 'No?' (p. 75)

Much of the tension in the novel is over the question of whether Searle will manage to lure away the very nice Liz Garrowby from her self-satisfied radio-star fiancé Walter Whitmore. When Searle

[53] Josephine Tey, *To Love and Be Wise*, 1950 (Harmondsworth: Penguin, 1986), 28.

disappears, presumed drowned, on a canoe expedition, Walter, his companion, is the obvious suspect. But in the twist ending that is perhaps not so surprising for a modern readership more familiar with such ideas, Searle is revealed to be alive and well and in fact a woman. She has lived as a man for years for career purposes and has staged her/his own disappearance to implicate Walter (whom she blames for the suicide of Walter's first wife, Searle's cousin). Slight and unconvincing as a detective story, the novel is nonetheless interesting for its exploration of transvestism, and for the air of mingled fear and erotic tension with which it treats the subject.

Considerably more overt is Mary Renault's *The Friendly Young Ladies* (1944), very much a text of the mid-century, with its representation of lesbianism balanced between Havelock Ellis's inverts and the self-assertion of the gay rights movement to come. Its central character, Leo, has always been boyish, given to playing and fighting with the local lads. Shortly before running away from home she shocks to the core her conventional parents with her violent disavowal of her gender:

With her feet apart, and her fists pushed down into her shabby tweed pockets, she had said, unbelievably, 'If I were a man I wouldn't be here. And I bloody well wish I were.'[54]

Nevertheless, it is with one of her male friends that she 'elopes', and it is only after a disastrous first sexual experience with him, a lonely period in a bedsit in London, and a serious illness, that Leo begins a relationship with the ultra-feminine Helen. The novel treats their partnership with a dignified circumspection that is yet more overt than anything we have seen in the fiction of the inter-war period. When Leo's timid and repressed younger sister Elise also runs away from their constantly rowing parents, she joins Helen and Leo on their houseboat, but fails to spot the nature of their relationship. The clues are laid very carefully, so that the reader, more sophisticated by definition than the callow Elise, cannot fail to understand them. She is offered Helen's room to sleep in, and when she protests is told that they only *call* it Helen's room, because she keeps some of her things in it. Later she is struck by the profusion of Helen's feminine belongings scattered around Leo's ship-shape masculine room:

[54] Renault, *The Friendly Young Ladies*, 8.

So, Elsie thought, she had turned out with a vengeance, taking all her things, and camped with Leo. It was very good indeed of both of them to put up with it so cheerfully. She would have liked to say so, but felt, for some reason, too shy. (p. 77)

What Elsie dimly apprehends is glaringly apparent to the reader, but remains always encoded, both by the novel and by the characters themselves. When Peter, an ebullient young doctor who intrudes himself into their lives, attempts to psychoanalyse Leo, he suggests that she resents the obtuseness of other people who fail to understand the nature of her relationship with Helen. Her response is categorically negative:

'For one thing, stupidity about people like me is all to the good and makes life much more comfortable all round. . . . I don't feel separate from the herd, if by the herd you mean ordinary people and not public mobs . . . Why should they pamper oddities, anyway? It's they who are in charge of evolution. They think it's better not to be odd, as far as they bother to think at all, and they're quite right. There are shoals of women made up pretty much like me, but a lot haven't noticed and most of the rest prefer to look the other way, and it's probably very sensible of them.' (p. 178)

In her determined refusal to privilege her own sexuality, Leo speaks for Renault herself who declared in an Afterword to the 1984 Virago edition of the novel that 'congregated homosexuals waving banners are really not conducive to a goodnatured "Vive la différence!" ' (p. 283). The novel's reticence about lesbianism is presented as a matter of good taste and sexual privacy, but it also reflects a hesitancy about the whole issue. Peter, the self-conscious sexual modern, is mocked for his arrogant assumption that his charms will serve to 'adjust' the sexuality of both Helen and Leo, but the novel itself has adopted just such a logic by the end when Leo has fallen in love with her friend Joe after he has 'cured' her of her fear of sex with men. Although there is none of the self-loathing that we find in earlier depictions of lesbianism, there is a sense that what lesbians do in bed is not 'real' sex: both Helen and Leo conduct regular flirtations with men, and Leo at least has chosen the relationship as a retreat from heterosexual sex. The key to understanding the novel's contradictions seems to lie in its response to masculinity: like Leo, Renault privileges the masculine over the feminine, and as a writer has been particularly drawn to the male-centred, homoerotic culture of Ancient Greece and Asia Minor (for instance in *The King Must Die*

(1958) and *The Persian Boy* (1972)). It is not so much homosexuality about which she is ambivalent (heterosexual unions are presented as typically deceitful and emotionally abusive), as femininity. Pathetic little sister Elsie is characterized particularly by the hopeless, frilly clothes she wears, and by her taste for formula romance (though Leo's own masculine formula fiction is thoroughly approved of). In the culminating sex scene between Joe and Leo, it is not the betrayal of Helen that casts a pall, but the loss of Leo's masculine side, and the easy companionship it has made possible between her and Joe. When afterwards he writes asking her to come away with him, Joe describes her gender ambiguity baldly:

'There are two people in you. One of them I have known much longer than the other. I am missing him, already, as much as I ever missed a friend. I should like him back—sometimes. But you know, now, how much he counted for when he came between my woman and me. . . . I can't tell how much he means to you. Perhaps, ultimately, he is you, and has the immortal part of you in his keeping.' (pp. 274–5)

The sacrifice of Leo's masculinity is legitimated only by the superior attractions of the bohemian Joe—modest, kindly, practical, a world-famous writer with a ranch in Arizona: what girl could resist? In the face of this paragon of masculinity, Leo's ersatz variety crumbles. It is notable that Renault herself, looking back, condemned the ending for its silliness, remarking that 'one cannot contemplate without a shudder their domestic life' (p. 281).

Joe's brand of masculinity, with its combination of physical courage, intellectual strength, and emotional self-containment is very much a product of the war years. The development of this new masculine gender identity after the more passive model of the inter-war years is a concern for a number of novels set during the war. As discussed in Chapter 2, the Nazi spy Robert in Elizabeth Bowen's *The Heat of the Day* (1949) justifies his betrayal of his country in terms of a masculinist ideology that castigates the culture of the inter-war years as oppressively, damagingly female. Another version of a new, war-fostered masculinity is considered in Margery Allingham's *The Tiger in the Smoke* of 1952. In a novel much preoccupied with forms of manhood, Albert Campion's affable idiocy is considerably toned down, and contrasted with the more bluffly assertive manliness of his police companion, Chief Inspector Charlie Luke, and the various subjects of their investigation. Their initial focus is on the apparent sighting of an Army Major, supposed killed in the war, on the eve of his wife's remarriage. The dead Major Elginbrodde (in fact being impersonated by one of a gang of villains in order to gain access to a hidden treasure) and his wife's fiancé, Geoffrey Levett, emerge as strikingly similar characters, exemplars of courage, daring, and competence:

> Geoffrey Levett . . . had a strong-featured uncommunicative face and a solid, powerful body. His brown eyes were intelligent and determined but not expressive, and both his light hair and his sober clothes were well and conventionally cut. There was nothing in the look of him to show the courage of the man, or the passion, or the remarkable if untimely gift he had for making money.[55]

The two men are essentially interchangeable, a fact recognized by Elginbrodde before his death when, knowing his wife Meg would choose another man just like himself, he left the secret of his family treasure to be given to her next husband on their wedding day. The idea of trusting his wife herself with the information is clearly unthinkable—we are a long way from the adventurous camaraderie of Campion and Amanda in *Sweet Danger*.

The text is, in fact, somewhat suspicious of both Levett and Elginbrodde, largely on the grounds of their recklessness and unpredictability. They are creatures of the war and as such may be revealed as untrustworthy in the humdrum light of the years after. In fact, both are vindicated—Elginbrodde died a hero, and Levett shows great daring and presence of mind when imprisoned by the criminal gang at the centre of the investigation. The suspicion, though, indicates an anxiety about the new model of assertive masculinity that the two men represent. It is a model that finds its most extreme form in the person of Jack Havoc, the arch-criminal at the centre of the narrative. The tiger of the title, Havoc is a magnificent masculine animal:

> He took his time and let them look at him, well aware that he was worth seeing. He was just under six feet, with long bones and sloping shoulders, most of his phenomenal strength in his neck and thigh-muscles which moved visibly under his sleek pre-war clothes. His beauty, and he possessed a great deal, lay in his hands and face and in the narrow neatness of his feet. (p. 131)

---

[55] Margery Allingham, *The Tiger in the Smoke*, 1952 (London: The Hogarth Press, 1987), 9.

Utterly without morality, Havoc is a killing machine, a force released by the war, which has lain dormant in a prison cell ever since, and is now prowling London in the fog. If his brand of ultra-masculinity is feared by the novel, his opposite, the effeminate man, is despised. In this extremely paranoid novel, a curious group of lesser criminals form an interesting centrepiece: they are a motley street band claiming to be ex-Service men, selected for their disabilities and deformities. Alongside a dwarf, an albino, an 'innocent', and others, is Bill—an effeminate. Giggling and mincing, dressed in picturesque rags, he is a monstrous figure, and—in a curious twist on the prevailing theme of courage in action—he takes a masochistic pleasure in danger, finding fear a sexual 'excitant'. Any form of effeminacy in the novel is ruthlessly exposed: even the benign camp of the designer of Meg's wedding dress must be condemned by her doughty and trustworthy old journalist friend. In the light of this crackdown, it comes as no surprise that Campion himself seems much more sober and conventional, although we are assured that 'he was still the slight, elegantly unobtrusive figure exactly six feet tall, misleadingly vacant of face and gentle of manner, which he had been in the nineteen-twenties' (p. 14). Amanda—now his wife—seems genuinely unchanged, retaining her trademark impetuous courage, although her role is more minor than in previous novels. Femininity is not a dominant concern: what this novel is really interested in is masculinity, the degree to which it has been changed by the war, and the extent to which those changes are to be approved or feared. This emphasis is absolutely typical of the feminine middlebrow of this date: it is Leo's masculinity more than her lesbianism that is the central focus of *The Friendly Young Ladies*; Leslie Searle is demonically fascinating as a man, vaguely attractive as a woman; the tortured bond between Tom and Marion is the only relationship not to be treated as literary cliché in *Palladian*. Rather than the reconsideration of femininity that contemporaneous social changes might lead us to expect from the feminine middlebrow of the 1940s and 1950s, what we actually find is a deeply worried reassessment of masculinity.

What we also fail to find in this fiction is any significant representation of the new models of childcare and maternity. In *Palladian* motherhood is alternately the site of gruesome horror represented by Violet's death in childbirth (the scene given with none of the veiling sentimentality of its Victorian equivalents) and the later death of her daughter, or the brisk, unemotional fact insisted on by the rational Margaret:

> 'Forgive my mentioning my own private affairs', said Margaret casually, 'but I find, mother, that I am expecting a child.'
> The old woman started, her fork jagged across her plate.
> 'Why Margaret, what a way to say such a thing! What a way to tell your mother such a thing! In the middle of a meal.'
> 'It was the way I preferred', said Margaret cruelly. (p. 29)

Similarly in *At Mrs Lippincote's*, Julia discusses with absorbed fascination the 'greatly exhilarating' experience of the birth of her daughter, concluding in 'a shocking, light voice' that ' "the child was dead in no time" ' (p. 147). The lightness is clearly a disguise of emotion—Julia is virtually alone in the fiction of this date in being an unusually devoted mother—but it indicates an adherence to the inter-war codes of maternal emotional restraint rather than the later models of determined self-sacrifice. A recognition of a choice of possible maternal ideologies is given in *The Tiger in the Smoke* when Amanda sends her young son to the country to remove him from danger, while choosing herself to remain with her husband:

> [Campion] drew his mind away and reflected on Amanda. She had made up her mind to stay, whatever the boy had said. Now that Rupert had grown out of babyhood her prime allegiance had returned to himself and they were partners again. She would look after him and he must look after the three of them. It was not the only sort of marriage but it was their sort. (p. 169)

Such a transfer of allegiances away from the child is clearly deeply approved of: the spectre of the maternally-absorbed woman remains a horrible thing for this fiction. In *To Love and Be Wise*, one of the major suspects in Leslie Searle's disappearance is Emma Garrowby, the stepmother of Liz, whose devotion to her daughter is represented as 'ruthless maternalism' (p. 103), the more unnatural because it has no basis in a biological tie. Also figures of horror are the family of writer Silas Weekley—a rather monstrous cross between D. H. Lawrence and Mary Webb—whom he maintains in rural poverty despite his huge book royalties. Obsessed with fertility, Silas keeps his downtrodden wife 'suckling and suffering' (p. 112), surrounded by hordes of ill-disciplined children, while he locks himself in his studio and pretends to write. The description of Mrs Weekley, a minor character who has no role in the plot, serves as an emblem of what the feminine middlebrow appears to fear in the new maternal ideology:

> She must have been pretty once. Pretty and intelligent; and independent. Grant remembered hearing somewhere that Weekley had married an elementary schoolteacher. She was wearing a sacking apron over a print wrapper, and the kind of old shoes that a woman all too easily gets used to as good enough to do chores in.... Her unwaved hair was pulled back into a tight desperate knot. (p. 117)

That Mrs Weekley's subjugation to the maternal lot is ideological is of great significance: this is not a poor woman, but one who has lost caste, looks, and independence through motherhood. In the virtually gothic grotesquery of her domestic life we find the clearest sign of the feminine middlebrow's resistance to the new cult of the mother.

Very much a product of the inter-war years, the feminine middlebrow clings in the years during and after the Second World War to those radical representations of gender roles and sexuality that had established its textual codes. Yet we discern in the novels of the later years a profound anxiety about the changing social determinants of gender, which emerges in a re-examination of masculinity, and in a nervous shying away from the new ideology of maternalism which was increasingly dominating women's lives. These subtle negotiations with a changing ideology of gender echo those other complex adjustments whereby the feminine middlebrow proves itself uniquely responsive to the shifting tastes and identity of the expanding middle class from the 1920s to the 1950s. Adeptly incorporating the latest literary and cultural fashions while treating highbrow excesses with a jovial disdain; benefitting from the new reading institutions while continually reiterating a note of unease about such popularity: the woman's middlebrow novel establishes itself as both exclusive and accessible. With its ideal reader repeatedly constructed as a woman simultaneously discriminating and abandoned to the pleasure of the text, the feminine middlebrow is understood as both cultured and enjoyable—floating comfortably between the mire of the lowbrow and the lofty difficult peaks of highbrow. Unlike their male contemporaries in thrall to myths of aristocratic glamour, women middlebrow novelists annex aristocratic culture to establish new codes of middle-class identity, demonstrating a positively triumphalist assumption of social ascendance. The rise to social prominence of the lower middle class is greeted by the feminine middlebrow with fear and contempt but also with a recognition of the lower-middle-class identity of many of its readers. As being middle-class becomes increasingly a matter of contest, it manages to perform the paradoxical feat of affirming the cultural superiority of the upper middle class, while ensuring that its codes are available to all. The same ideological flexibility is apparent in the treatment of domesticity, where the repeated descriptions of house moving and home decoration indicate an anxiety about the changing conditions of domestic life in the period. As servants gradually but inexorably disappear from the middle-class home the feminine middlebrow palliates their loss by representing them with increased hostility. Responding ambivalently to the new ideology that offered domesticity to the middle-class woman as both stylish and fulfilling, this fiction both ironizes the new cult of the domestic and recasts it in aesthetic rather than technological terms, presenting the middle-class housewife to herself in the image of the bohemian creative artist as a fantasy to compensate her for the unaccustomed drudgery of her new life. So too, in the image of the eccentric family, it works to establish bohemian and asocial elements as an intrinsic part of an upper-middle-class cultural identity. The feminine middlebrow of these years deals in apparently highly conventional subjects, but makes them into something strange. Far from being the cosy, smug literature caricatured by its detractors, it is highly subtle and flexible, continually negotiating changing social structures and ideologies, balancing conservatisms and radicalisms in order to both consolidate and question the new class and gender identities of its readers.

Bibliography

FICTION 1918–1959

Given in order of publication, with date of first publication when the edition used is not the first edition. Only novels quoted in the text are included here; those mentioned in passing will be found in the index.

ALLINGHAM, MARGERY, *Sweet Danger*, 1933 (Harmondsworth: Penguin, 1987).
—— *More Work for the Undertaker*, 1949 (Harmondsworth: Penguin, 1954).
—— *The Tiger in the Smoke*, 1952 (London: The Hogarth Press, 1987).
BENSON, E. F., *Miss Mapp*, 1922 (London: Transworld, 1984).
—— *Mapp and Lucia*, 1935 (Harmondsworth: Penguin, 1970).
—— *Lucia's Progress*, 1935 (London: Transworld, 1984).
BOWEN, ELIZABETH, *The Last September*, 1929 (Harmondsworth: Penguin, 1987).
—— *The Death of the Heart*, 1938 (Harmondsworth: Penguin, 1962).
—— *The Heat of the Day*, 1949 (Harmondsworth: Penguin, 1962).
CHRISTIE, AGATHA, *Three-Act Tragedy*, 1935 (London: Pan Books, 1983).
—— *The Hollow*, 1946 (London: Fontana, 1973).
—— *Crooked House*, 1949 (London: Fontana, 1959).
COMPTON-BURNETT, IVY, *Parents and Children*, 1941, in *A First Omnibus* (Harmondsworth: Penguin, 1994).
COMYNS, BARBARA, *Our Spoons Came From Woolworths* (London: Eyre & Spottiswoode, 1950).
COOPER, LETTICE, *The New House*, 1936 (London: Virago, 1987).
COOK, E. THORNTON, *They Lived: A Brontë Novel* (London: John Murray, 1935).
DELAFIELD, E. M., *The Way Things Are*, 1927 (London: Virago, 1988).
—— *Diary of a Provincial Lady*, 1930 (London: Virago, 1991—collected with other novels in the sequence as *The Diary of a Provincial Lady*).
—— *The Provincial Lady Goes Further*, 1932 (London: Virago, 1991, details as above).
—— *The Provincial Lady in Wartime*, 1940 (London: Virago, 1991, details as above).
DENNY, NORMAN, *Sweet Confusion* (London: John Lane, 1947).
DICKENS, MONICA, *One Pair of Hands*, 1939 (London: Michael Joseph Ltd., 1952).

FARRELL, M. J., *Full House*, 1935 (London: Virago, 1988).
FERGUSON, RACHEL, *The Brontës Went to Woolworths*, 1931 (London: Virago, 1988).
GIBBONS, STELLA, *Cold Comfort Farm*, 1932 (Harmondsworth: Penguin, 1983).
—— *Conference at Cold Comfort Farm* (London: Longmans, Green & Co. Ltd., 1949).
HOLTBY, WINIFRED, *The Crowded Street*, 1924 (London: Virago, 1984).
KENNEDY, MARGARET, *The Constant Nymph*, 1924 (London: Virago, 1992).
—— *Together and Apart*, 1936 (London: Virago, 1981).
—— *The Feast* (London: Cassell & Company and The Book Society, 1950).
LEHMANN, ROSAMUND, *Dusty Answer*, 1927 (Harmondsworth: Penguin, 1986).
—— *The Echoing Grove*, 1953 (Harmondsworth: Penguin, 1983).
MACKAIL, DENIS, *Greenery Street*, 1925 (Harmondsworth: Penguin, 1937).
MACAULAY, ROSE, *Crewe Train* (London: E. Collins Sons & Co. Ltd., 1926).
MARSH, NGAIO, *A Surfeit of Lampreys*, 1941 (Harmondsworth: Penguin, 1959).
MITFORD, NANCY, *The Pursuit of Love*, 1945 (Harmondsworth: Penguin, 1970).
—— *Love in a Cold Climate*, 1949, in *The Nancy Mitford Omnibus* (Harmondsworth: Penguin, 1986).
RENAULT, MARY, *The Friendly Young Ladies*, 1944 (London: Virago, 1985).
ROBERTSON, E. ARNOT, *Cullum*, 1928 (London: Virago, 1990).
—— *Four Frightened People*, 1931 (London: Virago, 1982).
—— *Ordinary Families*, 1933 (London: Virago, 1986).
SAYERS, DOROTHY, *Gaudy Night*, 1935 (London: Hodder & Stoughton, 1987).
SMITH, DODIE, *I Capture the Castle*, 1949 (London: Reprint Society, 1950).
STRUTHER, JAN, *Mrs Miniver*, 1939 (London: Virago, 1989).
TAYLOR, ELIZABETH, *At Mrs Lippincote's*, 1945 (London: Virago, 1995).
—— *Palladian*, 1946 (London: Virago, 1985).
—— *A Game of Hide-and-Seek* (London: The Book Club, 1951).
—— *The Sleeping Beauty*, 1953 (London: Virago, 1982).
TEY, JOSEPHINE, *Brat Farrar*, 1949 (Harmondsworth: Penguin, 1987).
—— *To Love and Be Wise*, 1950 (Harmondsworth: Penguin, 1986).
THIRKELL, ANGELA, *Wild Strawberries*, 1934 (Harmondsworth: Penguin, 1954).
—— *Summer Half*, 1937 (Harmondsworth: Penguin, 1951).
—— *The Brandons*, 1939 (Harmondsworth: Penguin, 1950).
—— *Before Lunch*, 1939 (Harmondsworth: Penguin, 1951).
TRIGG, ROBERTA, *Haworth Idyll: A Fantasy* (Richmond, Virginia: Whittet & Shepperson, 1946).

BIBLIOGRAPHY 259

TUTTON, DIANE, *Guard Your Daughters*, 1953 (London: The Reprint Society, 1954).
WAUGH, EVELYN, *Brideshead Revisited*, 1944 (Harmondsworth: Penguin, 1980).
WEST, REBECCA, *The Return of the Soldier*, 1918 (London: Virago, 1980).
WILSON, ANGUS, *The Wrong Set*, 1949 (Harmondsworth: Penguin, 1959).
WOOLF, VIRGINIA, *To the Lighthouse*, 1927 (Oxford: Oxford University Press, 1992).
—— *Orlando*, 1928 (Oxford: Oxford University Press, 1992).

OTHER CONTEMPORARY SOURCES

Archives Consulted

The Tom Harrisson Mass-Observation Archive, University of Sussex.
The John Johnson Collection, Bodleian Library, Oxford.

Books

AMIS, KINGSLEY, *The Letters of Kingsley Amis*, ed. Zachary Leader (London: HarperCollins, 2000).
BAKER, JOHN, *Low Cost of Bookloving: An Account of the First Twenty-One Years of Readers Union* (London: Readers Union, 1958).
BEAUCHAMP, J., *Women Who Work* (London: Lawrence & Wishart, 1937).
BETJEMAN, JOHN, 'In Westminster Abbey', *Old Lights for New Chancels*, 1940, *Collected Poems* (London: John Murray, 1958).
BEVERIDGE, WILLIAM, *Social Insurance and Allied Services* (London: HMSO, 1942).
BOULESTIN, X. MARCEL, *Simple French Cooking for English Homes* (London: William Heinemann Ltd., 1923).
BOWLBY, JOHN, *Child Care and the Growth of Love* (London: Penguin, 1953).
CONNOLLY, CYRIL, *Enemies of Promise*, 1938 (Harmondsworth: Penguin, 1979).
DELAFIELD, E. M., *The Brontës, Their Lives Recorded by Their Contemporaries* (London: The Hogarth Press, 1935).
EYLES, M. L., *The Woman in the Little House* (London: Grant Richards Ltd., 1922).
GRAVES, ROBERT, and HODGES, ALAN, *The Long Week-end: A Social History of Great Britain 1918–1939*, 1940 (Harmondsworth: Penguin, 1971).
GRAY, PATIENCE, and BOYD, PRIMROSE, *Plates du Jour, or Foreign Food* (Harmondsworth: Penguin, 1957).

HEATH, AMBROSE, *Good Food: Month by Month Recipes* (London: Faber & Faber, 1932).
—— *Kitchen Front Recipes and Hints: Extracts From the First Seven Months' Early Morning Broadcasts by Ambrose Heath* (London: Adam & Charles Black, 1941).
JEKYLL, LADY, (AGNES), *Kitchen Essays with Recipes and their Occasions*, 1922 (London: Collins, 1969).
LANCASTER, OSBERT, *Here, of All Places: The Pocket Lamp of Architecture* (London: John Murray, 1959).
LANGLEY MOORE, JUNE, and LANGLEY MOORE, DORIS, *The Pleasure of Your Company: A Text-book of Hospitality* (London: Gerald Howe Ltd., 1933).
LEAVIS, Q. D., *Fiction and the Reading Public*, 1932 (London: Chatto & Windus, 1978).
LEWIS, ROY, and MAUDE, ANGUS, *The English Middle Classes* (London: Phoenix House, 1949).
LOWINSKY, RUTH, *Lovely Food* (London: Nonesuch Press, 1931).
MANSFIELD, KATHERINE, *Letters*, ed. John Middleton Murry, 2 vols. (London: Constable, 1928).
MAUGHAM, W. SOMERSET, *The Writer's Point of View* (London: Cambridge University Press, 1951), recording the text of the 9th Annual lecture of the National Book League, delivered at the Kingsway Hall on 24 October 1951.
MITFORD, NANCY, 'The English Aristocracy', *Noblesse Oblige*, ed. Nancy Mitford, 1956 (Harmondsworth: Penguin, 1968).
—— *The Letters of Nancy Mitford*, ed. Charlotte Mosley (London: Hodder & Stoughton, 1993).
MOWAT, CHARLES LOCH, *Britain Between the Wars 1918–1940*, 1955 (London: Methuen, 1964).
ORWELL, GEORGE, 'Bookshop Memories', 1936, *The Collected Essays, Journalism and Letters*, ed. Sonia Orwell and Ian Angus, i, *An Age Like This, 1920–1940* (London: Secker & Warburg, 1968).
—— 'In Defence of the Novel', 1936, *Collected Essays, Journalism and Letters*, vol. i.
—— *The Lion and the Unicorn: Socialism and the English Genius*, 1941, *Collected Essays, Journalism and Letters*, ii: *My Country Right or Left, 1940–1943* (London: Secker & Warburg, 1968).
—— 'Good Bad Books', 1945, *The Collected Essays, Journalism and Letters*, iv: *In Front of Your Nose, 1945–1950* (London: Secker & Warburg, 1968).
PRIESTLEY, J. B., *English Journey* (London: William Heinemann Ltd., 1934).
Punch, 3 Aug. 1938, vol. cxcv.
—— 2 Nov. 1938, vol. cxcv.

QUAGLINO, *The Complete Hostess*, ed. Charles Graves, 1935 (London: Hamish Hamilton, 1936).
SAYERS, DOROTHY, *The Letters of Dorothy L. Sayers: 1899–1936: The Making of a Detective Novelist*, ed. Barbara Reynolds (London: Sceptre, 1996).
SPRY, CONSTANCE, and HUME, ROSEMARY, *Hostess* (London: J. M. Dent & Sons, 1961).
STOPES, MARIE, *Married Love*, 1918 (London: G. P. Putnam's Sons, Ltd., 1922).
—— *Wise Parenthood: A Practical Handbook on Birth Control*, 1918 (London: Putnam, 1937).
TARRANT, MOLLIE, *Class* (unpublished manuscript for Mass Observation, undated but post 1949).
WATSON, JOHN B., *Psychological Care of the Infant and Child* (London: Allen & Unwin, 1928).
WAUGH, EVELYN, 'An Open Letter to the Honourable Mrs Peter Rodd (Nancy Mitford) on a very serious subject', *Noblesse Oblige*, ed. Nancy Mitford, 1956 (Harmondsworth: Penguin, 1968).
WHITE, HILDA, *Wild Decembers: A Biographical Portrait of the Brontës*, 1957 (New York: E. P. Dunton & Co., 1958).
WOOLF, VIRGINIA, 'Hours in a Library', 1916, *Granite and Rainbow* (London: The Hogarth Press, 1958).
—— 'Women and Fiction', 1929, *Granite and Rainbow* (London: The Hogarth Press, 1958).
—— 'Middlebrow', *The Death of the Moth and Other Essays* (London: The Hogarth Press, 1942).
—— *The Diary of Virginia Woolf*, ed. Anne Olivier Bell, 5 vols. (London: The Hogarth Press, 1977–84).
—— *The Letters of Virginia Woolf*, ed. N. Nicholson and J. Trautmann, 6 vols. (London: The Hogarth Press, 1975–80).

SELECTED CRITICAL AND HISTORICAL STUDIES POST 1959

ACTON, HAROLD, *Nancy Mitford: A Memoir* (London: Hamish Hamilton, 1975).
ARMSTRONG, NANCY, 'The Rise of the Domestic Woman', in Nancy Armstrong and Leonard Tennenhouse (eds.), *The Ideology of Conduct: Essays on Literature and the History of Sexuality* (New York and London: Methuen, 1987).
BATEMAN, H. M., *The Man Who . . . and Other Drawings*, ed. John Jensen (London: Methuen, 1975).
BEAUMAN, NICOLA, *A Very Great Profession: The Woman's Novel 1914–39* (London: Virago, 1983).

BEDDOES, DEIRDRE, *Back to Home and Duty: Women Between the Wars, 1918–1939* (London: Pandora, 1989).

BEHLMER, GEORGE K., *Friends of the Family: The English Home and its Guardians, 1850–1940* (Stanford: Stanford University Press, 1998).

BELL, QUENTIN, GARNETT, ANGELICA, GARNETT, HENRIETTA, and SHORE, RICHARD, *Charleston Past and Present*, 1987 (London: The Hogarth Press, 1993).

BENNETT, ANDREW, and ROYLE, NICHOLAS, *Elizabeth Bowen and the Dissolution of the Novel* (London: Macmillan, 1995).

BOURDIEU, PIERRE, *Distinction: A Social Critique of the Judgement of Taste*, 1979, translated by Richard Nice (London: Routledge & Kegan Paul, 1986).

BOXSHALL, JAN (compiler), *Every Home Should Have One: Seventy-Five Years of Change in the Home* (London: Ebury Press, 1997).

BRAITHWAITE, BRIAN, WALSH, NOËLLE, and DAVIS, GLYN (compilers), *Ragtime to Wartime: the Best of Good Housekeeping 1922–1939* (London: Ebury Press, 1986).

BROOKNER, ANITA, Introduction to Margaret Kennedy, *The Constant Nymph* (London: Virago, 1983; 1992).

CLARK, SUZANNE, *Sentimental Modernism: Women Writers and the Revolution of the Word* (Bloomington: Indiana University Press, 1991).

COCKBURN, CLAUD, *Bestseller: The Books That Everyone Read 1900–1939* (London: Sidgwick & Jackson, 1972).

CUNNINGHAM, VALENTINE, *British Writers of the 1930s* (Oxford: Oxford University Press, 1988).

CUTFORTH, RENÉ, *Later Than We Thought: A Portrait of the Thirties* (Newton Abbot: David & Charles, 1976).

DICK, KAY, *Ivy and Stevie* (London: Duckworth, 1971).

DRIVER, CHRISTOPHER, *The British at Table: 1940–1980* (London: Chatto & Windus; The Hogarth Press, 1983).

FERRIS, PAUL, *Sex and the British: A Twentieth-Century History* (London: Mandarin, 1994).

FOSTER, SHIRLEY, and SIMONS, JUDY, *What Katy Read: Feminist Re-Readings of 'Classic' Stories for Girls* (Iowa: University of Iowa Press, 1995).

FURBANK, P. N., *Unholy Pleasure or the Idea of Social Class* (Oxford: Oxford University Press, 1985).

GENTILE, KATHY JUSTICE, *Ivy Compton-Burnett* (London: Macmillan, 1991).

GREIG, CICELY, *Ivy Compton-Burnett: A Memoir* (London: Garnstone Press, 1972).

GROVE, VALERIE, *Dear Dodie: The Life of Dodie Smith* (London: Chatto & Windus, 1996).

HANSCOMBE, GILLIAN, and SMYERS, VIRGINIA L., *Writing for Their Lives: The Modernist Women 1910–1940* (London: Women's Press, 1987).
HASTE, CATE, *Rules of Desire: Sex in Britain World War I to the Present*, 1992 (London: Pimlico, 1994).
HARDYMENT, CHRISTINA, *Dream Babies: Child Care from Locke to Spock* (London: Jonathan Cape, 1983).
HARTLEY, JENNY, *Millions Like Us: British Women's Fiction of the Second World War* (London: Virago, 1997).
HORNER, AVRIL, and ZLOSNIK, SUE, *Daphne du Maurier: Writing, Identity and the Gothic Imagination* (London: Macmillan, 1998).
INGMAN, HEATHER, *Women's Fiction Between the Wars: Mothers, Daughters and Writing* (Edinburgh: Edinburgh University Press, 1998).
JACKSON, ALAN A., *The Middle Classes 1900–1950* (Nairn: David St John Thomas, 1991).
JEFFERY, TOM, 'A Place in the Nation: The Lower Middle Class in England', in Rudy Koshar (ed.), *Splintered Classes: Politics and the Lower Middle Classes in Interwar Europe* (New York: Holmes & Meier, 1990), 70–96.
JOANNOU, MAROULA, *'Ladies, Please Don't Smash These Windows': Women's Writing, Feminist Consciousness and Social Change 1918–38* (Oxford: Berg, 1995).
—— (ed.), *Women Writers of the 1930s: Gender, Politics and History* (Edinburgh: Edinburgh University Press, 1999).
KENNEDY, RICHARD, *A Boy at the Hogarth Press* (Harmondsworth: Penguin, 1972).
LASSNER, PHYLLIS, *Elizabeth Bowen* (London: Macmillan, 1990).
LEWIS, JANE (ed.), *Labour and Love: Women's Experience of Home and Family, 1850–1940* (Oxford: Basil Blackwell, 1986).
LIGHT, ALISON, *Forever England: Femininity, Literature and Conservatism Between the Wars* (London: Routledge, 1991).
LEE, HERMIONE, *Virginia Woolf*, 1996 (London: Vintage, 1997).
LONGMATE, NORMAN, *How We Lived Then: A History of Everyday Life During the Second World War*, 1971 (London: Arrow, 1973).
MCALEER, JOSEPH, *Popular Reading and Publishing in Britain 1914–1950* (Oxford: Clarendon Press, 1992).
BILLIE, MELMAN, *Women and the Popular Imagination in the Twenties: Flappers and Nymphs* (London: Macmillan, 1988).
MILLETT, KATE, *Sexual Politics* (London: Rupert Hart-Davis, 1971).
MITFORD, JESSICA, *Hons and Rebels*, 1960 (Harmondsworth: Penguin, 1962).
MOODY, NICKIANNE, 'The Boots Booklovers' Libraries', *Antiquarian Book Monthly* (Nov. 1996), 36–8.
OSBORNE, JOHN, *A Better Class of Person: An Autobiography 1929–1956*, 1981 (Harmondsworth: Penguin, 1982).

PASSTY, JEANETTE N., *Eros and Androgyny: The Legacy of Rose Macaulay* (London: Associated University Presses, 1988).

PLAIN, GILL, *Women's Fiction of the Second World War: Gender, Power and Resistance* (Edinburgh: Edinburgh University Press, 1996).

POWELL, VIOLET, *The Constant Novelist: A Study of Margaret Kennedy 1896–1967* (London: Heinemann, 1983).

—— *The Life of a Provincial Lady: A Study of E. M. Delafield and Her Works* (London: Heinemann, 1988).

RADWAY, JANICE, *A Feeling for Books: The Book-of-the-Month Club, Literary Taste and Middle-Class Desire* (Chapel Hill: University of North Carolina Press, 1997).

RICHARDS, J. M., *Castles on the Ground: The Anatomy of Suburbia* (London: John Murray, 1973).

RICHARDSON, DIANE, *Women, Motherhood and Childrearing* (London: Macmillan, 1993).

RYBCZYNSKI, WITOLD, *Home: A Short History of An Idea* (London: Heinemann, 1988).

SAMUEL, RAPHAEL, 'Middle Class Between the Wars', *New Socialist* Jan./Feb. (Part I); June/July (Part II) 1983.

SCOTT, BONNIE KIME (ed.), *The Gender of Modernism* (Bloomington: Indiana University Press, 1990).

SHOWALTER, ELAINE, *Sister's Choice: Tradition and Change in American Women's Writing* (Oxford: Clarendon Press, 1989).

—— *Hystories: Hysterical Epidemics and Modern Culture* (London: Picador, 1997).

STEVENSON, JOHN, *British Society 1914–45, 1984* (Harmondsworth: Penguin, 1990).

STEVENSON, RANDALL, *The British Novel Since the Thirties* (London: Batsford, 1986).

STONEMAN, PATSY, *Brontë Transformations: The Cultural Dissemination of Jane Eyre and Wuthering Heights* (Hemel Hempstead: Harvester-Wheatsheaf, 1996).

TAYLOR, A. J. P., *English History 1914–45* (Oxford: Clarendon Press, 1965).

TINDALL, GILLIAN, *Rosamund Lehmann: An Appreciation* (London: Chatto & Windus, 1985).

TOSH, JOHN, 'Domesticity and Manliness in the Victorian Middle Class: The Family of Edward White Benson', in Michael Roper and John Tosh (eds.), *Manful Assertions: Masculinities in Britain since 1800* (London: Routledge, 1991).

WEEKS, JEFFREY, *Sex, Politics and Society: The Regulation of Sexuality Since 1800* (London: Longman, 1981; rev. edn. 1989).

WHITE, CYNTHIA, *Women's Magazines 1693–1968* (London: Michael Joseph, 1970).

WILSON, ELIZABETH, *Only Half-Way to Paradise: Women in Post-War Britain 1945–1968* (London: Tavistock, 1980).
WINNICOTT, DONALD, *The Child, the Family and the Outside World* (London: Penguin, 1964).

Index

adolescent 'Bildungsroman 12
adultery 216–17, 218–19
Alcott, Louisa M. 7–8, 55, 172–6, 195
Allingham, Margery 197
  The Fashion in Shrouds 209–10
  More Work for the Undertaker 32 n., 183–5, 186
  Sweet Danger 150, 209–11, 252
  The Tiger in the Smoke 251–3, 254
America 86
anti-semitism 154–5
Appointment with Death 183
aristocracy 13, 86, 105, 189, 199, 209
  middle-class annexation of 60–72, 153, 185
Arlen, Michael 10
Armstrong, Nancy 108
artists 22, 152–3, 159–60, 161, 165
At Mrs Lippincote's 30, 48, 51–2, 112–14, 137–8, 141–3, 147, 176, 178, 182–3, 244, 246, 254
Austen, Jane 11, 47, 52, 178–80
avant-garde 11, 19, 24–6

Bagnold, Enid 26
BBC 86–7
Beauvoir, Simone de 173–4
Before Lunch 39, 50
Benson, E. F. 13, 14, 59–60, 62, 102, 145–6, 228, 234–5
  Lucia's Progress 234
bestsellers 13, 16, 18
Betjeman, John 37, 75
Beveridge Report 242
birth-control 150–1, 227
  see also Marie Stopes
Bloomsbury 30–1
Blyton, Enid 226
bohemianism 22, 34, 93–5, 100–1, 103, 112, 128, 130, 132–4, 136–48, 152–60, 165, 215, 219
book clubs 19, 36, 43–6
Boots' Booklovers Library 12, 36–9, 41–2
Boulestin, Marcel 139–40, 142
Bourdieu, Pierre 20

Bowen, Elizabeth 13, 15, 24
  The Death of the Heart 41–2, 78–81
  Encounters 15
  The Heat of the Day 89–90, 98–104, 244, 251
  The Last September 62–3
Bowlby, John 242
Boyd, Primrose 142
Brandons, The 34–5
Brat Farrar 151, 183, 188–91
Brideshead Revisited 62, 64, 76, 151
Brief Encounter 37
Brontës 11, 30, 53, 90, 97, 132–3, 173, 176–83, 195
  Branwell 179–80
  Charlotte 55, 142, 178–9, 246
  Emily 92
Brontës, Their Lives Recorded by Their Contemporaries, The 177
Brontës Went to Woolworths, The 89, 93–8, 132–3, 149, 150, 159, 160, 162–3, 172, 176, 180–2, 228
Browne, Karen 132
Browning, Robert 47
Buck, Pearl 45

Céline, Louis Ferdinand 7–8
Chesterton, G. K. 23
childhood reading 14
children 201–2, 217, 218, 223–7
children's literature 12, 14, 49, 52, 55
Christie, Agatha, 45, 53, 62, 72
  Appointment with Death 183
  Crooked House 183, 186–8
  The Hollow 21–2, 53
  The Murder of Roger Ackroyd 53
  Three-Act Tragedy 115–16
Clark, Suzanne 25
class 11, 15–16, 20, 22, 56, 57–107, 153, 191
  see also aristocracy; middle class; working class
Cockburn, Claud 26
Cold Comfort Farm 24, 30–1, 34, 55, 150, 151, 176, 179–80, 222, 239
comic novels 12

Complete Hostess, The 125
Compton-Burnett, Ivy 13, 26, 87, 151, 191–6
  Daughters and Sons 26
  Parents and Children 192–6
  Pastors and Masters 15
Comyns, Barbara 132–4
Conference at Cold Comfort Farm 31–2
Connolly, Cyril 12, 15
Constance Spry 137
Constant Nymph, The 10, 14, 136–7, 139, 143–5, 151, 152–60, 162–3, 172, 174, 241
Cook, E. Thornton 177
cookery books 109, 115, 124–7, 134–6, 139–43
  and literature 141–3
cooking 113, 125, 130, 138–43
Cooper, Lettice 111–12, 121–2, 127–8, 146, 150
country-house novels 12, 13, 62–4
Coward, Noel 72
creativity 149, 152–3, 159–60, 165, 174, 183
Crewe Train 30 n., 118–19, 128–30, 137, 144, 150, 159–60, 174
Crooked House 183, 186–8
crossword puzzles 21, 22, 87, 183–4
Crowded Street, The 89–93
Cullum 34, 50–1, 239–40
Cunningham, Valentine 14
Cutforth, René 58–9, 84

Daisy Chain, The 53
Daughters and Sons 26
David, Elizabeth 139
Death of the Heart, The 41–2, 78–81
Deeping, Warwick 55
decorating 130, 143–8
Delafield, E. M. 24, 72, 103, 178
  The Brontës, Their Lives Recorded by Their Contemporaries (compiler) 177
  Diary of a Provincial Lady 29–30, 35, 52, 53, 71, 119–20, 128–30, 176, 215, 226
  The Provincial Lady Goes Further 30, 35, 52, 53
  The Provincial Lady in Wartime 49–50, 52, 55, 173, 244
  The Way Things Are 40–1, 215–7, 224, 226–7, 229–30, 231, 240

Denny, Norman 7, 34, 49, 53, 55–6, 173
detective fiction 8, 12, 13, 22–3, 38, 53, 87, 104, 183–91
Diary of a Provincial Lady 29–30, 35, 52, 53, 71, 119–20, 128–30, 176, 215, 226
Dickens, Charles 11, 49, 55
Dickens, Monica:
  Flowers on the Grass 38
  One Pair of Hands 122–3, 139
divorce 218–20, 243, 244
domestic ideology 124–30, 147–8
domestic novels 12, 13
domesticity 11, 100–2, 108–48, 217
Driver, Christopher 115
du Maurier, Daphne 14
Dusty Answer 14, 15, 145, 150, 151, 158, 199, 202–3, 205, 212–13, 231–3, 235–6, 237

eccentricity 102–3, 104, 132, 138–9, 143, 149, 152, 158, 162, 166–72, 177, 182, 183–96
Ellis, Havelock 237
Enemies of Promise 15
entertaining 109–10, 134–9
eugenics 221
Eyles, Margaret 134

families 38, 149–95
  changes in size 150–1
  dysfunctional 156–7, 170–2
  identities of 149, 157, 159–60, 161–3, 174, 189–90
  see also fathers; mothers
Family Story 38
fantasy 150, 160, 180–3
Farrell, M. J. 62–4
Fashion in Shrouds, The 209–10
fathers 156–7, 163–4, 170–1, 174
Feast, The 33–5
femininity 102–3, 197–8, 202–9
feminism 206–7
Ferguson, Rachel 89, 93–8, 132–3, 149, 150, 159, 160, 162–3, 172, 176, 180–2, 228
Fiction and the Reading Public 12, 16–21, 22–3
First World War 11, 174, 197–202, 209, 213
foreign food 139–43
Forest, Antonia 151
Forster, E. M. 20

INDEX 269

Foster, Shirley 174
Fountain Overflows, The 151
Four Frightened People 199–200, 203, 205–6, 213–15, 222–4, 231, 233, 238–9, 244, 247
Frankau, Gilbert 38, 55
Friendly Young Ladies, The 245, 249–51, 253
Freud 163, 225, 227–30
Furbank, P. N. 83

Galsworthy, John 7–8, 19
Game of Hide-and-Seek, A 30, 55, 173
Gaskell, Elizabeth 181
Gaudy Night 65, 129, 199, 220–2, 228–9, 231, 233–4, 244
gender 197–256
gentry 62, 69–70, 90, 184–5, 188–90
Gibbons, Stella:
   Cold Comfort Farm 24, 30–1, 34, 47, 55, 150, 151, 176, 179–80, 222, 239
   Conference at Cold Comfort Farm 31–2
Girl From Woolworths, The 132
Good Food 140, 142
Good Housekeeping 109, 116, 124–6
Graves, Robert 12, 114, 131, 231, 236–7
Gray, Patience 142
Green Hat, The 10
Greenery Street 40
Guard Your Daughters 48, 53, 54, 55, 90, 104–6, 108–9, 123–4, 138–9, 146–7, 150, 151, 174–6

Hall, Radclyffe 55, 232
Hanscombe, Gillian 25
Haworth Idyll 177
Heat of the Day, The 89–90, 98–104, 244, 251
Heath, Ambrose 141, 142
Hemingway, Ernest 19
High Wind in Jamaica 45
highbrow 9–10, 12, 18, 20, 21, 25–35
Hodges, Alan 12, 114, 131, 231, 236–7
Hollow, The 21–2, 53
Holtby, Winifred 89–93
Hogarth Press, the 26
home:
   anxieties about 109–10
   imagining 108–11, 133, 147–8
   remaking 111–14
homosexuality 198, 227–8, 231–2, 234–8, 246, 248, 249–51

hostess manuals 109, 124
houses 100–2, 110–12
housework 115, 118, 123, 124–30
How to Treat a Young Wife 243
Hughes, Richard 45
Hull, Edith M. 156
Huxley, Aldous 72, 197

I Capture the Castle 32–3, 34, 44, 53–4, 150, 176, 178–9
insanity 175–6, 195
intellectuals 12, 13, 16, 21, 30, 165, 180, 220–1
Ireland 62–4
Ives, Catherine 125

James, Henry 11
Jeffery, Tom 58
Jekyll, Lady 126, 135–6
Joyce, James 11, 19, 32

Keane, Molly, *see* M. J. Farrell
Kennedy, Margaret:
   The Constant Nymph 10, 14, 136–7, 139, 143–5, 151, 152–60, 162–3, 172, 174, 241
   The Feast 33–5
   Together and Apart 218–20, 222, 237–8, 240–1, 244
Kipling, Rudyard 20
Kitchen Essays 126, 135–6
Kitchen Front Recipes and Hints 141

Lady Chatterley's Lover 55
Lancaster, Osbert 75
Langley Moore, June and Doris 117, 132, 135
language 85, 86–7, 93–4, 104–5
Last September, The 62–3
Lawrence, D. H. 19, 254
   Lady Chatterley's Lover 55
Leavis, Q. D. 12, 16–21, 22–3, 44–5, 53
Lehmann, Rosamund 14, 27, 145
   Dusty Answer 15, 150, 151, 158, 199, 202–3, 205, 212–13, 231–3, 235–6, 237
lending libraries 12, 36–43
   Boots' Booklovers Library 12, 36–9, 41–2
lesbianism *see* homosexuality
Lewis, Roy 85–6
Life of Charlotte Brontë 181

Light, Alison 71, 84, 87, 151, 186–7, 191–2, 225
Little Women 7–8, 55, 172–6, 195
Lonsdale, Freddie 72
Lorna Doone 52
Love in a Cold Climate 38, 67–8
Lovely Food 126
lowbrow 10, 12, 55
lower middle class *see* middle class
Lowinsky, Ruth 126

Macaulay, Rose 15, 24, 27
  Crewe Train 30 n., 118–19, 128–30, 137, 144, 150, 159–60, 174
  Told By An Idiot 151
Mackail, Denis 40
Mackenzie, Compton 7–8, 38
magazines 18, 47, 109, 115–17, 124–6
manners 11, 85, 87, 89
male novelists 34–6
male readers 8–9, 13, 18
Mansfield, Katherine 15, 27
'Mapp and Lucia' novels 59–60, 228, 234–5
market research 109
marriage 198, 207–8, 215–22, 242–3
Marsh, Ngaio 151, 158, 183, 185–6, 187
masculinity 197–204, 246–53, 255
Mass-Observation 57–9, 74, 82, 111, 130–1, 134
maternalism 241–2
Maude, Angus 85–6
Maugham, Somerset 7–8, 23
Maurier, Daphne du 247
middle class 10–11, 12, 13, 16, 20, 57–107, 168–9, 195–6, 199
  annexation of aristocracy 60–72, 153, 185
  culture 87–8, 102–3, 104–5
  divisions within 83–9
  and domestic labour 124–30
  lower 13, 41, 58 n., 74–82, 84–9, 90, 94–5, 99, 103–4, 106–7, 244
  'middle' 99–102
  poverty 72–4, 130–4
  and servants 114–24
  upper 76–7, 78, 80–1, 82, 84–90, 91–2, 94–5, 98, 99, 103, 104–7, 153, 157–8, 180
Mitford, Nancy 166–7, 185–6
  'The English Aristocracy' ('U' and non-'U') 86–7, 137

Love in a Cold Climate 38, 67–8
The Pursuit of Love 151, 158, 166–72, 226, 244
modernism 11, 15, 24–7, 108, 151–2
modernity 93, 143–8
More Work for the Undertaker 32 n., 183–5, 186
mothers 153, 163–5, 171, 174–6, 181, 192–4, 198, 201, 222–7, 241–2, 244, 247, 253–5
Mrs Miniver 71, 72, 103, 119, 225
Murder of Roger Ackroyd, The 53

National Velvet 26
Nazis 102, 166–7, 207, 221, 251
neurosis 149, 163, 170, 172, 180, 182, 183, 187, 188, 191, 199
New House, The 111–12, 121–2, 127–8, 146, 150

One Pair of Hands 122–3, 139
Orczy, Baroness 45
Ordinary Families 95–6, 150, 151, 160–6, 190, 222, 226
Orlando 113
Orwell, George 12, 50, 59, 62
  'Bookshop Memories' 14, 17–18, 24
  'Good Bad Books' 23–4
  The Lion and the Unicorn 74, 75–6, 81–2, 87
Osborne, John 76, 86
Our Spoons Came From Woolworths 132–4

Palladian 246–8, 253–4
para-modernism 25
Parents and Children 192–6
Pastors and Masters 15
Plats du Jour 142
Pleasure of Your Company, The 117, 132, 135
Porter, Jimmy 86
Priestley, J. B. 19, 82
  English Journey 75
  The Good Companions 43, 45
Priory, The 49–50
Prisoner of Zenda, The 54
Provincial Lady Goes Further, The 30, 35, 52, 53
Provincial Lady in Wartime, The 49–50, 52, 55, 173, 244
Punch 70–1

Pursuit of Love, The 151, 158, 166–72, 226, 244
Pym, Barbara 38

Quaglino 125

Radway, Janice 29
Ransome, Arthur 161, 226
readers 7–56
 men 8–9, 49, 51–3
 undiscriminating 50–1
 women 7–56, 178
 reading 46–56, 216
 for instruction 47–8
 for pleasure 22–4, 48
 in wartime 49–50
Rebecca 247
Renault, Mary 245, 249–51, 253
The Return of the Soldier 200–2, 211–2
Rich, Adrienne 173
Ricardson, Diane 242
Robertson, E. Arnot:
 Cullum 34, 50–1, 239–40
 Four Frightened People 199–200, 203, 205–6, 213–5, 222–4, 231, 233, 238–9, 244, 247
 Ordinary Families 95–6, 150, 151, 160–6, 190, 222, 226
romance 215–7
romantic reticence 198, 209–15
romantic novels 10, 11, 12, 14, 32, 38, 50
Ruck, Berta 55

Samuel, Raphael 65, 72, 83, 84, 88
Sayers, Dorothy 65, 77–8, 129, 197, 199, 203–4, 206–8, 220–2, 228–9, 231, 233–4, 244
Scott, Bonny Kime 25
Second World War 64, 86, 98–104, 112–14, 123, 126, 141, 198, 243–6
servants 60, 68–70, 112, 114–24, 135, 193–5, 215, 228, 237
sexuality 95–6, 100, 154–6, 169–70, 198, 202–4, 213–5, 218, 227–34, 238–41, 243–51
 see also homosexuality
Shakespeare, William 50, 54
Sheik, The 156
shell-shock 198–200
shocking novels 14
Showalter, Elaine 173–4, 198–9
Simon, Judy 174

Simple French Food For English Homes 139–40
Sitwell, Osbert 19
Sleeping Beauty, The 30, 51
Smith, Dodie:
 I Capture the Castle 32–3, 34, 44, 53–4, 150, 176, 178–9
Smyers, Virginia M. 25
snobbery 68, 82, 84–7, 97–8, 107
social climbing 91–2
speech 85, 86–7
Starr, Leonora 38
Stein, Gertrude 45, 173
Stevenson, John 61
Stopes, Marie 150, 227, 238, 243
Struther, Jan 71, 72, 103, 119, 225
suburbia 20, 101, 110
Summer Half 47–8, 50, 52, 66
Surfeit of Lampreys, A 151, 158, 183, 185–6, 187
Sweet Confusion 7, 34, 49, 53, 54, 55–6, 173
Sweet Danger 150, 209–11

Tarrant, Molly 57, 58, 74, 82
Taylor, A. J. P. 61
Taylor, Elizabeth:
 At Mrs Lippincote's 30, 48, 51–2, 54, 112–14, 137–8, 141–3, 147, 176, 178, 182–3, 244, 246, 254
 A Game of Hide-and-Seek 30, 55, 173
 Palladian 246–8, 253–4
 The Sleeping Beauty 30, 39, 51
Tey, Josephine:
 Brat Farrar 151, 183, 188–91
 To Love and Be Wise 246, 248–9, 254–5
Thackeray, William 54
They Lived: A Brontë Novel 177
Thirkell, Angela 47, 65–7, 72, 103, 185–6
 Before Lunch 39, 50,
 The Brandons 34–5
 Summer Half 47–8, 50, 52, 66
 Wild Strawberries 66–7
thriller 10, 11
Tiger in the Smoke, The 251–3, 254
To Love and Be Wise 246, 248–9, 254–5
To the Lighthouse 28, 30 n., 66–7, 78, 140, 142–3, 151
Together and Apart 218–20, 222, 237–8, 240–1, 244
Told By An Idiot 151

Trigg, Roberta 177
Truby King, Frederick 224–5
Tutton, Diana 48, 53, 54, 55, 90, 104–6, 108–9, 123–4, 138–9, 146–7, 150, 151, 174–6

'U' and 'non-U' 86–7, 93–4, 105, 137
upper middle class *see* middle class
Upward, Edward 59

Victorians 11, 24, 47–8, 53, 54–5, 89, 90, 93, 97, 109, 112–13, 114, 132–3, 150–1, 172–83, 253
Voyage au bout de la nuit 7–8

Walpole, Hugh 8
war 64
Watson, John Broedus 225
Waugh, Evelyn 14, 59, 72, 185, 197
  Brideshead Revisited 62, 64, 76, 151
  Decline and Fall 15
Way Things Are, The 40–1, 215–7, 224, 226–7, 229–30, 231, 240
Webb, Mary 254
Weeks, Jeffrey 238, 241, 242, 243,
Well of Loneliness, The 55, 232
West, Rebecca 19, 151
  The Return of the Soldier 200–2, 211–2
When the Cook is Away 125

Whipple, Dorothy 49–50
White, Antonia 24
White, Hilda 177
Wild December's 177
Wild Strawberries 66–7
Wilder, Thornton 19
Wilson, Angus 14, 102–3
Winnicott, Donald 242
Wodehouse, P. G. 13, 20, 38, 59, 72, 197
Woman in the Little House, The 134
Women's Leader 116
women readers 7–56, 178, 216
Woolworths 131–4
Woolf, Leonard 26, 160, 177
Woolf, Virginia 7–8, 11, 15, 19, 26–8, 120–1, 140, 160, 177
  Flush 45
  'Hours in a Library' 23
  Orlando 113
  To the Lighthouse 28, 30 n., 66–7, 78, 120, 142–3, 151
  'Women and Fiction' 27
  The Years 26
working class 16, 18, 95–6, 98, 114–24, 134

Yates, Dornford 38, 72
Yonge, Charlotte M. 11, 53, 55